MEDIA _
_ CROSSROADS

MEDIA _

INTERSECTIONS OF SPACE AND IDENTITY
IN SCREEN CULTURES

_ CROSSROADS

Edited by

Paula J. Massood, Angel Daniel Matos,

and Pamela Robertson Wojcik

DUKE UNIVERSITY PRESS | DURHAM AND LONDON | 2021

Library of Congress Cataloging-in-Publication Data
Names: Massood, Paula J., [date] editor. | Matos, Angel Daniel,
editor. | Wojcik, Pamela Robertson, [date] editor.
Title: Media crossroads : intersections of space and identity in
screen cultures / edited by Paula J. Massood, Angel Daniel Matos,
and Pamela Robertson Wojcik.
Description: Durham : Duke University Press, 2021. | Includes
bibliographical references and index.
Identifiers: LCCN 2020027532 (print) | LCCN 2020027533 (ebook)
ISBN 9781478010616 (hardcover)
ISBN 9781478011743 (paperback)
ISBN 9781478021308 (ebook)
Subjects: LCSH: Space and time in mass media. | Mass media. |
Gender identity in mass media. | Space perception. | Identity
(Psychology) and mass media. | Women's studies.
Classification: LCC P96.S7 M435 2021 (print) | LCC P96.S7 (ebook) |
DDC 302.23—dc23
LC record available at https://lccn.loc.gov/2020027532
LC ebook record available at https://lccn.loc.gov/2020027533

DUKE UNIVERSITY PRESS GRATEFULLY ACKNOWLEDGES THE
INSTITUTE FOR SCHOLARSHIP IN THE LIBERAL ARTS, COLLEGE
OF ARTS AND LETTERS, UNIVERSITY OF NOTRE DAME, WHICH
PROVIDED FUNDS TOWARD THE PUBLICATION OF THIS BOOK.

CONTENTS

III _ URBANISM AND GENTRIFICATION

IV _ RACE, PLACE, AND SPACE

V _ STYLE AND/AS INTERSECTIONALITY

Paula J. Massood, Angel Daniel Matos,
and Pamela Robertson Wojcik

INTRODUCTION

Intersections and/in Space

In *The Practice of Everyday Life*, Michel de Certeau suggests that the city can be seen from different perspectives: from above, as looking at a map or panorama, or from the ground, through the experience of walking. While the view from above produces a legible picture for a voyeur—what de Certeau calls theoretical space—the view from below is social and immersive, lived and experienced, rather than viewed from a distance. The possible paths taken by a walker are myriad and dependent on factors such as race, ethnicity, class, ability, age, and gender. Walkers, for de Certeau, "create networks of . . . moving, intersecting writings [that] compose a manifold story that has neither author nor spectator, shaped out of fragments of trajectories and alterations of spaces."[1] Indeed, a city can provide "a way of conceiving and constructing space on the basis of a finite number of stable, isolatable, and interconnected properties" that intersect and connect and yet differ depending on the space, the representation, the group, or the individual.[2] Along these same lines, critics such as Henri Lefebvre have further noted that "any space implies, contains, and dissimulates social relationships—and this despite the fact that a space is not a thing but rather a set of relations between things (objects and products)."[3] Spaces not only shape the connections and relationships that manifest in their confines, but the spaces themselves are simultaneously inflected by the very social interactions and intersections staged within them.

Consider three seminal and differing cinematic views of urban space, each mapping a distinct experience of New York City. First, Woody Allen's *Manhattan* (1979) consciously glorifies the city.[4] In an opening voice-over,

Allen's character, Isaac, dictates, "Chapter One. He adored New York City. He idolized it all out of proportion. No. Make that, He romanticized it all out of proportion. To him, no matter what the season was, this was still a town that existed in black and white and pulsated to the great tunes of George Gershwin." Isaac continues, revising this to consider New York "a metaphor of the decay of contemporary culture." However, viewers are already immersed in the idealized/romanticized view offered by the opening audiovisual montage. We see a series of black-and-white images of the skyline, a neon sign reading Manhattan, the Empire Diner, various quaint street corners, snow-covered streets, lovers on a rooftop, and a crescendo of fireworks, all scored to the soaring notes of Ira Gershwin's "Rhapsody in Blue." This self-referential opening does not so much ironize Allen's relationship to the city as provide a précis or guide to what follows, as the remainder of the film is black and white, uses instrumental Gershwin songs at key romantic moments, and presents an idealized view of New York.

Rather than the decay of modern culture, Allen's New York revolves around the preservation, circulation, and production of culture as central to the city. The characters in Manhattan are all artists. Isaac writes for television and is working on a novel; his best friend Yale (Michael Murphy) publishes a magazine; his girlfriend Mary (Diane Keaton) is a journalist who writes about Brecht and other cultural topics; his ex-wife Jill (Meryl Streep) writes a tell-all book; her girlfriend Connie (Karen Ludwig) is a visual artist. Even Tracy, the high school girl Isaac dates (Mariel Hemingway), wins a theater scholarship that will take her to another iconic city, London. Apartments in the film overflow with books and works of fine art. Moreover, Allen situates his characters amid numerous cultural institutions: the Hayden Planetarium, the American Museum of Natural History, the Metropolitan Museum of Art, the Museum of Modern Art, the Whitney Museum of American Art, the Solomon R. Guggenheim Museum, Lincoln Center, galleries, and movie theaters specializing in auteurist film and art cinema. The characters do not just pass by these institutions. They engage with them, comment on the art, and argue about Sol Lewitt, Ingmar Bergman, and more. This is a very specific city, in which intersections and connections are highly determined by class, ethnicity, and gender.

In contrast to Allen's *Manhattan*, William Friedkin shows a gritty, economically precarious, and multiracial side of the city in *The French Connection* (1971). The film triangulates New York in an international crime network extending from Marseilles, France, to Washington, DC. Friedkin's city avoids the landmarks and neighborhoods of Allen's film. Instead, *The French Con-*

nection is situated in the working-class ethnic neighborhoods of Brooklyn and Manhattan's Little Italy. This New York is filled with rubbish-strewn streets, empty lots with burning fires, graffiti, junkies, and dingy bars. Where Allen's film highlighted high art and intellectual pursuits, Friedkin's features a nightclub where the African American female R&B group the Three Degrees perform a raucous version of "Everybody Gets to Go the Moon." In Allen's film, characters have the privilege of taking leisurely walks through beautiful neighborhoods and in parks, and on a few occasions they drive to the country, exercising a freedom of movement that transcends urban, suburban, and rural borders. In Friedkin's film, movement is much more proscribed; characters drive purposefully from one place to the next, or run and chase one another, or take the subway pressed into crowded filthy cars. Allen's city emphasized soaring height through shots of the skyline and bridges. *The French Connection* focuses less on expansive long shots of the cityscape and, instead, frames characters in low-rise areas, beneath overpasses, or in subway stations, showing space as oppressive and enclosed. This is a city of class difference and division: the white American Popeye Doyle (Gene Hackman) eats takeout pizza and drinks coffee standing on a cold sidewalk while white French mobsters idle over a multicourse meal in a posh restaurant and a homeless man sleeps in the doorway.

Whereas *Manhattan* and *The French Connection* appear to traverse broad swaths of the city, Spike Lee's *Do the Right Thing* (1989) purposely narrows our view to a single block in Brooklyn. In his representation of the Bedford-Stuyvesant neighborhood, Lee presents what Paula J. Massood has described in relation to Lee's *She's Gotta Have It* (1986) as a "heteroglot collection of characters [that] suggests that the urbanscape is home to a highly complex and variegated community," one where a variety of races, ethnicities, classes, genders, and abilities intersect.[5] Depicting twenty-four hours in the life of a single neighborhood block on the hottest day of the year, *Do the Right Thing* shows the tensions and eruptions that occur among and amid its diverse population—what Massood refers to as a "heteroglossia (racial, economic, generational, and gendered)."[6] The film details the interactions among African American, Korean, white, and Latinx characters of different classes, ages, abilities, and genders. The young African American pizza delivery man Mookie (Lee) works for the white Italian American Sal (Danny Aiello) alongside Sal's sons Vito (Richard Edson) and Pino (John Turturro), and much of the film takes place in Sal's pizza parlor. Rather than monumental spaces, Lee focuses on the local—neighborhood spots such as a convenience store, a pizza parlor, a storefront radio station, the stoops and sidewalks in front of brownstones, all filled with characters who walk, sit, bike, and drive through the streets, intersecting each other's paths for good and bad.

Manhattan, The French Connection, and Do the Right Thing are all shot on location, but they slice and segment the city in radically opposing ways. While Allen strives to still see the romantic ideal city despite the "decay," Friedkin focuses on what Siegfried Kracauer refers to as "blind spots of the mind," the "things normally unseen" because "habit and prejudice prevent us from noticing them," such as refuse, dirt, waste, and garbage, or objects and scenes so familiar and ordinary that we do not notice them.[7] Lee, as well, shows unromantic aspects of the city in depicting racism, police brutality, and violence, but he photographs Bed-Stuy in a rich color palette that provides it with a self-conscious beauty distinct from Allen's black-and-white glamor. Where Allen's film presents a touristic monumental view of Manhattan and Friedkin offers something like the underbelly with clashes between diverse characters who pass through the city, Lee submits a more intimate and situated view of a specific neighborhood and everyday life.

We begin with these films to suggest the ways in which a consideration of intersectionality and/in space might deepen our understanding of various screen cultures. Each film offers a view of the city that is selective and ideological. Where Manhattan delimits its view to focus exclusively on an ideal of a privileged white Manhattan, The French Connection focuses on diversity, and Do the Right Thing shows the city as an intersectional space. Each film, as well, benefits from an intersectional analysis. Thinking about intersectionality and space together aids us in seeing the whiteness of Manhattan as much as it helps analyze the use of race as signifier of the underworld in The French Connection—so that the performance of the Three Degrees signifies as more than a musical amuse-bouche in the middle of a crime narrative—or to probe the racial conflicts in Do the Right Thing. We can see how each text frames its view of the city according to a particular conception of its inhabitants, its conflicts, and its systems of privilege and oppression. Thinking about intersectionality, moreover, allows us to see not only how Do the Right Thing positions conflicts between and among races, but how characters are defined simultaneously through race, gender, class, and age, and how neighborhood shapes their identities and interactions. Intersectionality as a theoretical concept also allows us to see the limitations of the racial imagination in Manhattan, which suppresses difference, and in The French Connection, which renders difference largely ornamental.

The decision to begin *Media Crossroads: Intersections of Space and Identity in Screen Cultures* with a focus on a selection of films set in what is arguably American cinema's most iconic urban space and directed by a trio of male auteurs is purposeful; it illustrates that much of the work on space and media can be more aptly described as cinema and the city. And yet there is an ever-growing body of work that looks to how different media screen different spaces. How does a television series such as HBO's *Big Little Lies* (2017–19) or Showtime's *Weeds* (2005–12), for example, offer reassessments of the myth of an American suburban utopia through attention to a cross-section of female narratives. Each show focuses on privileged suburban women as a means of reimagining the aesthetics of the melodrama or, more precisely, the woman's film. *Big Little Lies* is particularly resonant here as part domestic thriller and part film noir that, through its exploration of the hermeneutics of suspicion surrounding a murder, provides intersecting storylines of complicated characters. Each woman brings her own history of trauma to the narrative—a history that is informed by the intersecting forces of class, race, and gender and enabled by the show's suburban setting.

These cinematic and televisual explorations of space have been enriched by contemporary digital media, including web streaming and gaming, which have provided a productive field for exploring the intersections of space and media. Take, for example, Issa Rae's *Insecure* (2016–present), a comedy series on HBO that features Rae as a young African American woman in Los Angeles maneuvering through career, relationships, and life. The show is based on Rae's web series, *Awkward Black Girl* (2011–13), which streamed on YouTube for two years. The show, identified as a "precarious girl" comedy by Rebecca Wanzo, focuses on a "young African American woman struggling with two aspects of her identity that may seem incongruous—being both black and awkward." Such attention to these areas provides a nuanced approach to intersectionality that considers "the nexus of identification and alienated shame."[8] Moreover, *Insecure* complicates understandings of space and intersectionality more fully than some of our earlier cinematic examples: it not only details the experiences of an educated, middle-class Black woman in the city, but its distribution history suggests the possibility of media spaces to further intersect and adapt in the twenty-first century.

Other media, such as video games, invite different questions about identity and space, especially since they typically demand a higher degree of interaction and involvement between player and the digital space represented on the screen. As Laurie Taylor has argued, video game spaces are composed of more than just programming code. They are "experiential

spaces generated through code and the player's interaction with the execu-
tion of that code through the medium of the screen."[9] Players thus develop
an intimate relationship with both the spaces and the characters represented on-screen through their inputs and interactions, and the player has
a varying degree of control over the structure and navigation of game space.
Game designers, through their coding and programming, ultimately enjoy
a high modicum of control not only in terms of how players perceive the
space of a gameworld, but, even more so, regarding how varying representations and intersections of identity affect how players navigate these spaces.

Consider, for instance, *The Elder Scrolls*, an immensely popular series of
fantasy role-playing video games developed by Bethesda Game Studios that
has been around since the mid-1990s. In earlier iterations of the series,
players were mostly limited to customizing their characters by selecting
a "class" or "vocation," which had a direct effect on how the game was
played. In the original game in the series, *The Elder Scrolls: Arena* (1994),
players could modify their character by selecting their avatar's name, gender, race, a predetermined selection of character faces, and a variation of
three overarching professions or classes: warriors, mages, and thieves.[10]
While the various character subclasses in *The Elder Scrolls: Arena* provided
different options for digital embodiment, navigating its gameworld, and
interacting with other characters and enemies, selecting a class ultimately
limited what players could or could not do with their selected character. A
later game in the series, *The Elder Scrolls V: Skyrim* (2011), not only increased
character-customization options—thus allowing players to customize the
race, gender, skin tone, weight, facial complexion and structure, hair, and
overall appearance of their character—but also eliminated the use of a
rigid class system, granting players more flexibility to develop a character's
strengths, weaknesses, and abilities through gameplay.[11] Thus, the avatar's
skills, abilities, and identities are consistently shaped and altered according
to how the player interacts with the spaces and characters in *Skyrim*'s gameworld. Unlike film and television texts, which often become static after
they are produced and distributed, the interactivity and customization
granted by a video game ultimately presents different affordances and hindrances when it comes to the interdependent relationship between player,
avatar, and spatiality.

While video games open up possibilities for intersectionality that are
unique to their interactive components and, thus, potentially level the
playing field, intersectional analyses of space must also be mindful of the
fact that there are various other elements, especially in terms of production

and audience, that complicate the more utopic potentialities of interactive cultural works. For instance, it has been widely acknowledged that sexism and misogyny have been rampant in both the video game community and industry, a reality that gained widespread attention through the activism of Anita Sarkeesian, whose critiques of sexism in video games made her the recipient of harassment, ridicule, and violent threats. Furthermore, considerations of the relationship between identity and screen cultures must address how this intersectionality manifests in cultural production itself, and how it is complicated by the identities of the people who craft the texts. In video games, for instance, there is not only a lack of gender, racial, and sexual diversity within the titles but a dire absence of diversity among the people who create them, especially high-budget "Triple-A" games. Similarly, the film industry has been critiqued for its lack of diversity among directors and the limited roles accorded nonwhite and female actors, as seen in movements such as #OscarsSoWhite, which drew attention to the lack of racial diversity in Hollywood, and the documentary *This Changes Everything* (Tom Donahue, dir., 2018), which examines gender disparity in American cinema. While most of the essays in *Media Crossroads* examine intersectional spaces by focusing on the content, structure, and form of various texts, the collection also includes essays that attend to matters of production, distribution, and reception.

Underlying this collection is the editors' belief that all spaces are intersectional. Insofar as people inhabit and use spaces, those spaces are available to be inhabited by intersectional identities; to show intersections among and between people; and to address issues of privilege, oppressions, and resistance. *Media Crossroads: Intersections of Space and Identity in Screen Cultures* takes this approach to space and extends it across a variety of media. It is intended as a course reader and major research tool for undergraduate and graduate students and faculty in cinema and media studies, gender studies, and other interdisciplinary fields. The volume aims to consider space and place in cinema and other media via critical intersectional lenses and multiple interpretive strategies. Work on gender and space has been productive and rich across numerous disciplines, and we seek to place such studies in conversation with research on sexuality, race, ethnicity, age, class, ability, and other domains of identity as they relate to space. Individual essays take up one or more of these categories in relation to examinations of various spaces in cinematic and media representations. The spaces considered range from the small and intimate, such as dressings rooms or bathrooms, to the large and social, such as cities, suburbs, regions, nations. They include spaces such as the cinema and amusement park; representations of real spaces, such as Portland or New York; and animated and digital fantasy spaces. Across these various spaces, authors consider intersectionality not only in terms of the intersecting identities that define individuals (old and Jewish; young, transgender, and Latinx; and so on) but also in the way identities intersect in spaces (in conflicts or connections between young and old, Black and white, rich and poor, and so on) and in the way screens produce intersections between and among various identities through spectatorship, play, and social media. Given the volume's focus on intersectional approaches, many of its chapters also emphasize how representations of space in film and media address matters of oppression, discrimination, privilege, and inequity.

Certainly, the notion of intersectionality is under some pressure. As Jennifer Nash detailed in a recent review essay, feminists and scholars in American Studies, especially, have been contentiously debating the concept—its origins, methodologies, efficacy, relationship to identity politics, relationship to Black feminism, and more. At base is a fear that the institutionalization of intersectionality has "allowed [it] to become 'ornamental' or, worse, a synonym for diversity."[12] In addition, part of this backlash is due to the concept's depoliticization and association with neoliberal frameworks, thus leading to the rise of revisions of intersectional thought that "aim to erase the ideas and actions of Black women, Latinas, the working poor and underemployed, LGBTQ people and similarly subordinated groups from intersectionality's legitimate narrative."[13] With these challenges in mind, we consider intersectionality, along with Vivian May in *Pursuing Intersectionality, Unsettling Dominant Imaginaries*, a useful rubric to understand "privilege and oppression as concurrent and relational."[14] As Patricia Hill Collins and Sirma Bilge also suggest, intersectionality is a form of critical inquiry marked by an investment in social inequality, power, and social justice. Thus, we seek to use the concept as an interpretive lens and method to consider various spaces in various screen cultures, and how these spaces reflect, reinforce, or dismantle intersecting forms of resistance and domination.

Building on such formulations of the concept, we believe that intersectionality is defined by and through space and that such understandings of relationality, overlap, and potential friction must inform any analysis of mediated identity. In what is largely hailed as the essay that coined the term "intersectionality," "Demarginalizing the Intersection of Race and Sex: A Black Feminist Critique of Antidiscrimination Doctrine, Feminist Theory and Antiracist Politics," Kimberlé Crenshaw adopts two spatial metaphors to explain intersectionality. The first, "an analogy to traffic in an intersection, coming and going in all four directions," maps intersectionality as a spatially defined experience. She writes, "Discrimination, like traffic through an intersection, may flow in one direction, and it may flow in another. If an accident happens at an intersection, it can be caused by cars traveling from any number of directions and, sometimes, from all of them." Crenshaw suggests that, rather than thinking of one form of discrimination at a time, we consider the "combined effects of practices which discriminate on the basis of race, and on the basis of sex" that may impact the Black female pedestrian in the intersection.[15] Thus, metaphorically, the impact can come from multiple directions, making it impossible to sort out or discern which did more damage; the harm is caused by the combination of forces working in concert.

Of course, even two forms of discrimination can be compounded, and Crenshaw's second spatial metaphor suggests that individual bodies can carry multiple disadvantages and suffer multiple simultaneous intersecting forms of discrimination. In countering the legal analysis that limits discrimination to a "but for," meaning that a person would not be discriminated against "but for" their race *or* "but for" their sex—an analysis that imagines discrimination as singular and as targeting, deliberately or implicitly, a class of people, one class at a time—Crenshaw suggests that the legal standard privileges whiteness and patriarchal power, which are not treated as explicit categories. Such a model denies that Black women, for example, might be disadvantaged or discriminated against because of both race and sex in ways that cannot easily sort out a "but for" of discrimination. "Imagine a basement," she writes, "which contains all people who are disadvantaged on the basis of race, sex, class, sexual preference, age and/or physical disability."[16] In Crenshaw's spatial metaphor—which subtly references the infamous diagrams of slave ships—the bodies in the basement are stacked on top of one another, with those who have only one disadvantage on top and those who have the most at the bottom. The ceiling of the basement is the floor where those who are not disadvantaged reside. A hatch in the ceiling allows those with one disadvantage to climb out to the floor above. But those below, whose identities are impacted by some combination of race and sex and sexual orientation and age and class and physical disability (or, at the bottom, by *all* of those)—and, we could add, by religion, nationality, and other prejudicial identities—cannot get out of the basement because the inequalities they face are not singular.

It is no accident that Crenshaw uses spatial metaphors to characterize intersectionality. Not only do they allow us to imagine intersectionality in visual terms—as a convergence of forms of discrimination or as the deep burden and difficult climb of oppression—but they also suggest the ways in which space is lived and meaningful, equally defined through and de-limiting human activity. Space is produced through interconnected webs of power; it is relational and contingent; it is experienced and yet under-stood differently by different people. Space and place can be contested, lost, changed (through forces of globalization, immigration, white flight, gen-trification, and more), and those frictions often occur within and between intersectional identities.

Despite Crenshaw's use of spatial metaphors to characterize intersec-tionality, most of the discourse on the subject has tended to focus on the body—and especially the figure of the Black woman—as emblematic of in-tersectionality.[17] Certainly, Crenshaw's metaphors suggest ways in which discrimination impacts the body, whether through the visceral quality of imagining multiple simultaneous accidents affecting the pedestrian or the weight of multiple bodies standing on one's shoulders in the basement. However, her images of intersectionality also conjure the idea that inter-sectional identities exist in, and experience discrimination in and through, specific spaces. In this sense, it matters where that body is placed: whether it is walking in a crowded urban traffic intersection, among other walkers, or locked away in a basement, in a hierarchical structure. Thus, we argue that intersectionality—and its various aesthetic, cultural, and political determinants—must be considered in and through space.

Thus far, in film and media studies, spaces have not been discussed much in terms of intersectionality. Indeed, much writing on space in film and media studies has not been attendant to identity, let alone intersec-tionality. Many books on the city, for example, focus on archaeological views of the city, seeking to uncover the material artifacts of a city through their cinematic representation. Studies of the city might consider theo-ries of urbanism; modernity and postmodernity; early cinematic render-ings of the city; postwar cinema's exploration of peripheral, disintegrating urban space; growth and transformation in cities; cinematic forms and genres related to the city such as city symphonies, documentary, musicals, government-sponsored films, or film noir; film production and location shooting in cities; and other topics that illuminate the city but may not deal explicitly with the city's inhabitants or consider the mutually imbri-cating factors of space and identity.[18]

Certainly, many excellent books deal with questions of space and identity. Sabine Haenni discusses ethnic immigrant cultures as subject and spectator of early cinema. Jacqueline Majuma Stewart considers the relationship between African American urban culture and early cinema. Paula J. Massood considers African American film and urban life, with an emphasis on African American filmmaking. Merrill Schleier examines ideological and gendered meanings, and especially constructions of masculinity, ascribed to skyscrapers in American films from the 1930s to the 1950s. And Pamela Robertson Wojcik considers children as mobile participants in urban life.[19] Beyond studies focused on the city, Amy Corbin considers such diverse spaces as Indian Country, the white South, and the suburbs in her examination of multicultural spectatorship, and Natalie Fullwood examines representations of gender in the everyday spaces of beaches, nightclubs, offices, cars, and kitchens in *Cinema, Gender, and Everyday Space: Comedy, Italian Style.*[20] While the list is not exhaustive, each example has sought to broaden and make complex normative understandings of space as white, male, and privileged. The examples also remind readers of the rich variety of spaces we inhabit and represent.

While these books draw attention to the ways in which space and identity are mutually configured, they tend to focus on one kind of difference at a time—to consider gender, for example, or race, but not usually concurrently. The editors themselves have been guilty of this in some of their previous work. In both *The Apartment Plot* and *Fantasies of Neglect*, Wojcik devoted a chapter to African American representation, segregating the discussion of Black characters and issues from the other chapters. Thus, when Wojcik discussed bachelors in *The Apartment Plot* or girls in *Fantasies of Neglect*, those categories were assumed to be white, and all African American characters, whether male or female, were considered one. Likewise, in *Black City Cinema: African American Urban Experiences in Film*, Massood's primary focus was on urban spaces defined by and through African American men. Moreover, discussions of spaces, such as the Watts neighborhood, overlooked the area's history as a suburb of the city of Los Angeles. Finally, Matos's previous explorations of the kitchen as a site of gay domesticity in American television focused on representations of middle- to upper-class white gay men, thus foreclosing opportunities to examine how the space of the kitchen inflects the representation of queer women and people of color.[21] As these examples suggest, in considering one difference at a time—one gender, race, ethnicity, sexuality, class, age, and so on—the opportunity to consider the ways in which those identities are shared in individual bodies and the way in which those identities intersect in spaces is lost. The editors have thus envisioned this volume as a way to counteract such compartmentalized and limited approaches to identity that are commonplace in the field.

This volume considers space and bodily identities together to examine the multiple intersections that occur within spaces—between and among identities, within identities, and between and among various imaginings of spaces. We consider spaces in progress through gentrification, revanchism, mobility, and migration and spaces contested among and between various identities—queer and straight, white and Black, local and global, young and old. We consider spaces as sites of turf wars and displacements and reflect on who gets pushed to the side and who comes out on top. These disputations are viewed not as singular battles but as part of a complex web of intersections within and among various groups and individuals. We consider how genre, field, and mode—whether the selfie, the musical, the heritage film, the avant-garde film, the video game, animation, or TV crime show—shape our understanding of space and intersectional identities. We analyze, moreover, different media and how varying screen spaces produce disparate intersections, whether through hailing one or more ideal spectators, resistant or against-the-grain spectatorship, interactive game playing, or social media interactions.

Part I, "Digital Intersections," considers how digital texts and new media can stage alternative ways of thinking through the relationship between space and identity. The media explored in this section are not only interactive but also blur the distinction between the space of the text and the space of the viewer/user/spectator. The essays reveal the fragility of boundaries and binaries such as public and private, child and adult, text and decoder, human and nonhuman, and also demonstrate the political viability of using digital texts and media to disrupt normative understandings of identity, spatial navigation, and activism. Moreover, the essays explore how social media and video games allow users to adopt an experiential approach to space in that they invite people to witness and move through (virtual) worlds from an intersectional perspective, thus expanding and complicating real-world understandings of what it means to exist and dwell in a space and of how spaces reinforce and disrupt hegemonic and oppressive ideological frameworks.

Nicole Erin Morse's essay on transgender activism and bathroom selfies, for instance, discusses how activist art pressures transphobic public policy through its interrogation of the space of the public bathroom. The essays by Angel Daniel Matos and Matthew Thomas Payne and John Vanderhoef focus on similar radical and political potentialities through the analysis of video game space. Matos examines Nintendo's *The Legend of Zelda* series to show how video game spaces can be structured in queer ways, in that they disrupt binary and hierarchical thinking and encourage players to consider multiple and intersectional ways of engaging with real and digital worlds. In a similar vein, Payne and Vanderhoef examine the figure of the intersectional digital flâneuse in a series of "walking simulator" video games and discuss how this figure offers players opportunities to situate themselves within marginalized and politicized subjectivities. The essays invite readers to consider how digital spaces provide new and unprecedented ways to stage interactive considerations of lived and virtual experience and how queer, transgender, racial, and political thinking can inflect our understanding of that experience.

Part II, "Cinematic Urban Intersections," explores similar dynamics of disruption and inflection, focusing on films situated in cities and urban spaces. The essays trace how various media map a series of artistic, urban, and cultural connections and intersections while also disrupting divides such as fiction and nonfiction, mobility and immobility, and integration and separatism. In the spirit of disrupting these divides, the media examined in this part offer representations of urban life and experience that complicate binaries of race, gender, class, and age and consider the relationship that exists between specific locations and people's access to sociocultural, economic, and political power. In addition to examining the intersectional and spatial dimensions of urban space, the essays are invested in exploring matters of urban temporality, in that they consider the ways in which urban spaces provide distinct models for approaching matters such as futurity, presentism, development, growth, and the merger of temporal constructs such as the past and present.

Paula J. Massood's examination of the experimental filmmaker Shirley Clarke's short films and her debut feature, *The Connection*, explores how these texts use hybrid forms to tell marginalized stories and how they implement New York City as a site of intersecting political, aesthetic, and sociocultural forces and collaborations. Jacqueline Sheean's essay analyzes the dynamics of cruising in Madrid's urban peripheries as represented in Eloy de la Iglesia's *La semana del asesino* (1972) and suggests that cruising and mobility offer a means for mapping intersections of various identities in urban space. Amy Corbin explores comparable instances of urban intersectionality in her examination of place making and homesteading practices in Ramin Bahrani's American dream trilogy and considers how the urban spaces in these films are fashioned and molded by the interactions that they stage among diverse characters. Finally, Pamela Robertson Wojcik examines a cycle of youth films that she categorizes as "slow death cinema" and interrogates how systems of privilege and inequity simultaneously generate and demarcate youthful characters' social and spatial mobility.

Further expanding these ideas, Part III, "Urbanism and Gentrification," focuses on the economic, political, and administrative tensions that arise through the movements and displacements put into practice through gentrification. The essays emphasize the emancipatory potentialities and limits of the texts and media that they examine and highlight the ways in which films and television shows subvert or delegitimize tropes centered on urban life and neoliberal development. The essays also highlight how various media productions refuse to acknowledge the dynamics of oppression, color-blindness, and white supremacy that are upheld through gentrification and how they (perhaps inadvertently) perpetuate the narratives and fantasies of neoliberal thought.

Joshua Glick's essay on Gray Power activism as reflected in Barbara Myerhoff and Lynne Littman's documentary *Number Our Days* (1976), for instance, explores the political viability of documentary practice and its potential to shed light on the issues of gentrification experienced by elderly residents in Venice, California. Noelle Griffis's examination of the television show *Nashville* and its unique production details demonstrates how the show simultaneously redefined the conservative, heteronormative local music industry and led to the urban revitalization in the city of Nashville, Tennessee—while also problematically contributing to a growing sense of inequality and minority displacement in that city. Elizabeth Patton examines analogous issues in her examination of *Portlandia*'s (2011–18) implementation of intersectional erasure in its representation of Portland, Oregon, in that it uses neoliberal practices to replace overt and tangible forms of racism, discrimination, and oppression. Erica Stein considers the figure of the gangster and its relationship to notions of real estate and upward mobility in select films and television shows and demonstrates how these gangster narratives highlight the criminality of the American dream, in that they are reliant on the mistreatment and oppression of class and racial difference.

The essays in Part IV, "Race, Place, and Space," consider the intersections of race, gender, and other domains of identity in a range of spaces, including small, personal, and private spaces, such as the dressing room, and large, public spaces, such as the theme park. In broad terms, they explore the points of convergence between the regulation and control of spaces and the ways in which bodies and racial discourse are controlled. They also emphasize the emancipatory potentialities and restrictions made available through these spaces and how various characters of color must find ways to negotiate their identities in places that reinforce and perpetuate hegemonic, supremacist values.

Desirée J. Garcia, for instance, examines the role and function of the Black maid within the space of the dressing room, as represented in classical backstage musicals produced in Hollywood, and makes a case for how these films paradoxically enable and inhibit women's achievement. Sarah Louise Smyth examines the ubiquity of whiteness and the absence of people of color in British heritage cinema, focusing particularly on the spatiality of the country house and its capacity to challenge the ideals of patriarchal whiteness that it upholds and perpetuates. Merrill Schleier, in her examination of queerness, race, and class in midcentury film, explores similar logics of the white spatial imaginary as conveyed through suburban space. In particular, she examines how Gerd Oswald's film *Crime of Passion* (1956) implements prescriptive gender and sexual ideologies and racialized suburban structures/practices as a way to confine its protagonist's queerness and difference. Finally, Peter Kunze examines how Black media culture uses theme parks as a narrative setting and, in turn, interrogates how this space simultaneously engages with and destabilizes neoliberal ideological frameworks. The four essays in this part thus create a broad narrative that explores the tensions and complications that arise when considering race vis-à-vis various lived and fictional experiences, and they reflect on how considerations of race and space complicate and further nuance our understanding of notions such as class, labor, and entertainment as represented in film and television.

Part V, "Style and/as Intersectionality," takes an in-depth look at how style and aesthetics can be used to either mobilize or foreclose intersectional thinking and explores the ways in which formal, material, and structural elements are used (often self-consciously) to construct an intersectional space. This part stresses both generative and unproductive ways of using form to convey a politics of intersectionality. While some essays explore how a text's aesthetics and formalistic features demonstrate an underlying investment in intersectional frameworks even as its surface features indicate otherwise, others demonstrate how intersectionality is used in a tokenistic fashion, offering viewers a text that seems politically viable and radical on a surface level but proves, on closer inspection, to be conservative and assimilationist in its purview.

Ina Rae Hark, for example, points out how all of the events that occur in the police procedural *Happy Valley* (2014) reduce the show's political potentialities by focusing on the protagonist's psyche as a site of intersectionality, thus making the show's intersectional connections a diegetic product of the protagonist's mind that simply serve as metaphors for her consciousness. Kirsten Moana Thompson points out how Disney's *Moana* (2016) focuses significantly on the aestheticization of material surfaces and how these surfaces espouse traits such as liminality and hybridity, ultimately suggesting an underlying politics of (self-reflexive) intersectionality. Conversely, Malini Guha examines how the formal features of Bertrand Bonello's *Nocturama* (2016) initially gesture toward an intersectional politics but are proved to be flat on closer inspection. In spite of *Nocturama*'s implementation of a seemingly intersectional style, Guha makes a case for how it ultimately implements intersectionality in an "ornamental" fashion. All in all, the essays in this part invite us to explore how formalistic and aesthetic features can push viewers to think about the need for and importance of structural change and, furthermore, the extent to which these features augment (or foreclose) the antihegemonic bent and emancipatory potential of intersectional thought.

It is our hope that the essays in this volume establish innovative and unexpected possibilities for examining and interpreting spaces as represented in film, television shows, video games, and new media. We anticipate that these possibilities will open up new avenues for approaching spatial inquiry as an invitation for political action or for complicating our understandings of the relationship between spaces represented onscreen and the bodies that inhabit them. The chapters serve as an index to the worlds, spaces, and people represented in (new) media and how these representations make claims about different possibilities and difficulties for being, moving, dwelling, and coexisting with others. *Media Crossroads* offers a variety of case studies that explore both the potentialities and the limits of intersectional approaches to space and gender, drawing assistance from other fields of criticism and inquiry that include, but are not limited to, critical race theory, queer theory, new media studies, economics, and cultural studies. Readers are encouraged to explore generative commonalities and tensions among the essays found in the entire collection. We hope readers will develop a nuanced understanding of how different genres and media provide distinct and fresh ways to think through the connections among space, gender, identity, and oppression and how these connections can be effectively examined via cultural productions created for the screen. We envision these chapters as starting points in important conversations in the study of gender, space, identity, and screen cultures, and we are certain that the readers of this book will expand, modify, and draw from this volume to suit their intellectual, political, pedagogical, and critical needs.

I _ DIGITAL INTERSECTIONS

"WHERE DO ALIENS PEE?"

Bathroom Selfies, Trans Activism,

and Reimagining Spaces

A selfie posted on Facebook shows a slight, blonde white woman standing at a bathroom mirror with a row of urinals behind her. A portrait shared on Instagram depicts a visibly gender-nonconforming brown person in the middle of a public bathroom, posed between the urinals and the stalls. And in a YouTube video, two people—a young brown man and a middle-aged white woman—sit conversing in the cramped quarters of a bathroom stall that is festooned with holiday lights. As distinct as these media are, all three are different attempts to intervene in debates about the right of trans people to use public bathrooms. The stakes are high: as people of color and people with disabilities have also found, being able to safely access public bathroom facilities is fundamental to being able to participate in the public sphere. All efforts—legal and social—that restrict trans people's ability to use public bathrooms are ultimately attempts to legislate and harass trans people out of existence. In the face of this existential threat, trans media creators and their cis allies have responded by using social media platforms to re-present, reenvision, and even reimagine both the fight for trans rights and the space of the public bathroom.

Legal battles over public bathroom access attempt to make impossible trans resistance and existence, but trans activism in turn holds the promise of new possibilities that would make our current organization of space impossible.[1] In response, "bathroom bills" require people to use gendered bathrooms based on the sex that they were assigned at birth.[2] Such legislation is premised on the assumption that pubic bathrooms—and in practice, particularly women's bathrooms—must be preserved as spaces of privacy and refuge.[3] While men's bathrooms are understood to be sexually charged social spaces, extensive gender policing attempts to ensure that women's bathrooms protect cis women and girls from sexuality (consensual and nonconsensual), objectification, and "the public."[4]

In this chapter I discuss how activist art challenges transphobic public policy by compelling us to question our assumptions about the *space* of the public bathroom. Far from being limited to gender alone, these assumptions are classed, raced, and connected to ability. As a result, the questions posed by this activist art propel a collective reimagining of what public bathrooms could be. First, I examine a set of bathroom selfies from the #Occupotty social media campaign and show how bathroom selfies document (and contribute to) the fragility of the boundary between public and private in public bathrooms. I also explore how the #Occupotty selfies problematically emphasize *disjunction* between bodies and spaces rather than deeper, structural problems of exclusionary spaces. Next, I show how a portrait of the trans activist Alok Vaid-Menon makes evident that public bathrooms are always already spaces of sexuality. Finally, I explore how Dylan Marron's Seriously.TV YouTube series *Sitting in Bathrooms with Trans People* (2016) uses art, play, and digital technology to transform public bathrooms. I contend that the intersectional collaborations within Marron's series pave a new, necessary direction for media activism around trans people's access to public spaces.

Following Marron's series—and the insight from crip theory that it is spaces that disable people rather than people who are disabled—activist media must refocus the viewer's attention away from transitioning bodies and toward transforming spaces.[5] As Sheila Cavanaugh puts it, "The project of the twenty-first century is to build a fluid and less exacting plumb line, one that does not mirror an essential connection between sex and gender, body and identity, but makes room for new and unexpected configurations of gender and sexed embodiment in space."[6]

Following Wendy Brown's account of effective solidarity, in which alliances are built not on the experience of a wounded identity but on a shared desire for a new world, the task of reimagining public bathrooms is not only about gender identity but has implications for all those whose access to public spaces is currently limited by bathroom design.[7] While my first two case studies explore and contest assumptions about public bathrooms without offering an alternative to these anxieties and disavowals, *Sitting in Bathrooms with Trans People* offers a new way of experiencing these public spaces as sites of community building, connection, and joy.

Of course, the stakes of this issue extend far beyond the representational field. I am writing in 2018 about media created in 2015 and 2016, when trans rights seemed to be expanding.[8] Now, trans-affirming public accommodations laws are at the center of the Trump administration's attacks on LGBTQ people as well as the target of anti-trans activism in the United Kingdom.[9] At this historical moment, as government bodies in the United States attempt to deny the existence of trans people altogether, trans peoples' ability to participate in the public sphere feels even more tenuous than before. Although this issue is not about representation alone, media are critical tools through which we can imagine—and then create—alternative possibilities.

#Occupotty

Bathroom selfies make use of the bathroom mirror to capture the reflection of both selfie creators and their camera phones. In addition, instead of the constricted framing produced by a front-facing smartphone camera held at arms' length, bathroom selfies place the viewer at a greater distance from the photographer and generally include more of the surrounding space. As a result, bathroom selfies can convey a message that is not only about identity, but also about place. Bathroom selfies don't just say "here I am"; rather, they say, "*here* I am."[10] Using the affordances of bathroom selfies, a Canadian trans woman named Brae Carnes began using social media in February 2015 to criticize efforts to undo trans civil rights legislation.[11] Posting selfies she had taken in men's bathrooms, Carnes captured image after image of herself reflected in bathroom mirrors, her slender, blonde, feminine form flanked by urinals.

Over time, other trans people joined Carnes, both in Canada and in the United States, taking bathroom selfies and posting them on social media with the hashtags #Occupotty and #WeJustNeedToPee. By posting selfies taken in the bathrooms that match the sexes they were assigned at birth, trans people demonstrated that bathroom bills do not in fact preserve the sex-segregated privacy that they are purported to produce. Instead, the selfies organized around these hashtags assert that bathroom bills would generate gendered chaos in public bathrooms, for they would force slender blond trans women to touch up their makeup beside urinals while burly bearded trans men would be required to use women's bathrooms. In her posts, Carnes emphasizes the juxtaposition between her body and the space

that surrounds her through her poses, captions, hashtags, and other strategies. As Carnes stands in front of urinals, her selfies ask the viewer to compare her gender presentation with the space that surrounds her on all sides.
Soon surpassing the attention paid to Carnes, the Twitter user Michael C.
Hughes—a tall, burly trans man whose selfies depict him looming over cis
women who were his collaborators—became one of the most visible participants in the viral selfie campaign.[12] Although visually compelling, Hughes's
selfies reinforce the transmisogynistic premise of the legislation they op-
pose: there is something wrong when someone who looks like a man is in
a space designated for women.[13] Rhetorically, #Occupotty selfies juxtapose
bodies and spaces, and by highlighting such visible disjunctions between
bodies and spaces, #Occupotty calls for us to rethink who is allowed in each
gendered bathroom while leaving the spaces of public bathrooms—from
quotidian aspects of their design to the very premise of binary gendered
spaces—uninterrogated.

However, the form of the bathroom selfie opens other interpretive possibilities, revealing more complicated truths about public bathrooms. By
capturing the reflection of the camera alongside the selfie creator and the
surrounding space, a bathroom selfie highlights not just the image of the
selfie creator but also the means of its own production. Through this reflexive gesture, bathroom selfies make apparent that in contemporary culture
public bathrooms are, in fact, even more public than the name might imply.
The ability to take and then circulate selfies even from within the bathroom can be read as an extension of surveillance culture into a space that
might appear to be protected from surveillance. Yet, as Cavanagh details,
public bathrooms are panoptic in design; the mirror and other reflective
surfaces ensure that "we see how we are being seen, and the triangulation
of the panoptic eye is multiplied by the number and kind of mirrors in
the room."[14] Rather than being private spaces, as those supporting anti-
trans legislation often assert, public bathrooms are designed to be spaces
of observation, performance, and surveillance. Bathroom selfies show that
public bathrooms are spaces in which the boundary between public and
private is not firm but constantly negotiated, with self-performance and
self-documentation the grounds on which this unfixed boundary is continuously mediated.

Selfies are accused of cultivating the panoptic impulse to engage in
self-surveillance, but bathroom selfies by trans people take control of
the surveillant gaze.[15] In this case, the choice to broadcast one's image
works with and against the omnipresent regime of visibility to which

trans people are subjected. The specific work that bathroom selfies can do becomes particularly obvious when Carnes's selfies are compared with a 2015 photoshoot she did with the photographer Chad Hipolito for the Canadian Press.[16] Unlike Carnes's selfies, which depict her body as well as the space surrounding her equally in focus, Hipolito's photographs dramatically deemphasize the bathroom through tightly controlled focus, showing a fashionably dressed Carnes posing before blurry backgrounds that are only barely recognizable as rows of urinals. Some of the portraits from the photoshoot show Carnes in the act of taking a selfie, while others represent her pouting with a pink cell phone in hand.[17] Here, the professionally produced images no longer capture her act of self-representation. Instead, they capture the profoundly feminized act of gazing at her own image. While Carnes's selfies show her to be clearly aware of the camera and of her own agency in representing herself, her pose in Hipolito's photographs implies ignorance of his camera's presence, transforming the scene into a conventional representation of a beautiful woman unaware that she is being observed. While admittedly Carnes's selfies ask the viewer to compare her body with the space that surrounds her, and thus paradoxically solicit the kind of scrutiny that trans people routinely face in public bathrooms, Hipolito's photographs take this process of objectification and gender policing further. In them the camera is no longer in Carnes's control, and her body is separated from the background. Rather than asking the viewer to compare bodies and spaces, as in the #Occupotty selfies, the professional portraits simply display Carnes's body. They ask us to assess whether she looks like a woman, and assert (correctly) that she *is* a woman—because she is successfully incorporated into traditional tropes of female representation.[18]

By making Carnes the *object* of the male gaze, these images refute the transmisogynistic belief that trans women are masculine subjects who subject cis women to this gaze within the gender-segregated seclusion of the women's bathroom. Rhetorically, however, the images maintain that women must be protected from the male gaze by gender-segregated facilities—they simply assert that anyone who looks as feminine as Carnes should also be so protected. The very premise of transphobic public policies is preserved, alongside the traditional belief that women must be protected from men. While the #Occupotty selfies position trans women as agents of the look who engage in self-representation, they fail to imagine alternatives to gender-segregated public bathrooms. Nonetheless, through their reflexive gesture, bathroom selfies put pressure on the assumption that public bathrooms are spaces of sequestered privacy. Indeed, it was Carnes's bathroom selfies that produced the conditions that made the idea of a glamorous professional photoshoot within a public bathroom even thinkable.

Where Do Aliens Pee?

While #Occupotty draws attention to the gendered spaces of public bathrooms without problematizing their gender segregation, a full-length portrait of the trans artist Alok Vaid-Menon directly questions this aspect of public bathroom design. Originally posted on Instagram, the portrait shows Vaid-Menon standing in a men's bathroom, lunging forward slightly, between a row of urinals and a row of stalls. With one hand on their hip and one hand over their crotch, Vaid-Menon poses, trapped between the two available options (figure 1.1). The caption directs the viewer to interpret the stalls and urinals as oppositionally gendered, for it asks, "umm where r aliens supposed 2 pee??? #nonbinary." Some other option, it asserts, exists beyond the gender binary. But "nonbinary" is not only the answer provided in the caption; instead, it is a theme that the portrait reiterates visually. In addition to occupying the literal space between the urinals and the stalls, Vaid-Menon's pose combines feminine- and masculine-coded gestures. A hand on a popped hip has feminine connotations, while a hand over a crotch invokes both masculine-coded crotch grabbing and feminine-coded modesty. The portrait suggests that gender-neutral public bathrooms are the necessary answer to the question in the caption.

Yet proposals for gender-neutral bathrooms have long encountered fierce opposition that is founded on a set of intertwined anxieties and disavowals. Even though gendered bathrooms do not in fact protect against the fears they are supposed to quell, the idea of gender-neutral bathrooms is so threatening that it has been used to undermine other efforts toward civil rights, perhaps, most notably, Phyllis Schlafly's successful argument that passage of the Equal Rights Amendment would mandate gender-neutral bathrooms and threaten the safety of cis women and girls.[19] Advocating for bathroom access has long been restricted by the "specter of unisex bathrooms."[20] Yet in calling for public bathrooms beyond the gender binary, Vaid-Menon's portrait does not simply make this demand. Instead, Vaid-Menon's pose points to one of the deepest anxieties underlying resistance to gender-neutral bathrooms: the false belief that trans women are

1.1 Alok Vaid-Menon stands between stalls and urinals in a selfie posted on Instagram under the handle @darkmatterpoetry. Digital image, used with permission.

sexual predators. As Cáel Keegan notes, there is a "total lack of evidence" for the argument that trans women pose a threat to cis women; moreover, the idea that penises (rather than rapists) are the source of sexual violence denies the reality that gender-segregated bathrooms have never effectively prevented sexual violence and that cis women can in fact be perpetrators of sexual violence.[21] Still, the transmisogynistic belief persists that trans women introduce sexual violence into a space that otherwise protects cis women from *all* forms of sexuality.

There is a deep disavowal at work in the current design of public bathrooms. Based on raced and classed norms regarding privacy and heterosexual sex, public bathrooms have been designed to deny the reality that sexuality and elimination are inextricably linked.[22] From the work of the Marquis de Sade and psychoanalytic theories of childhood development to the intertwined regulation of sewers and sex work, elimination and sexuality are conjoined experiences through which the solidity of the subject is undone, both haunted by abjection.[23] Yet public spaces have been designed to discipline bodies and to control these unruly tendencies.[24] In response to the undeniable existence of queer sexuality, some public bathrooms are being designed with fewer and shorter doors.[25] These design modifications aim to surveil and prevent queer public sex, but they also undermine the purported value of privacy that mandates gender-segregated public bathrooms in the first place. Noting that "the disciplining of sex in toilets is not only about the regulation of gender" but also about a classed "identification with white patriarchal succession," Cavanagh writes that "the spectacle of sex in bathrooms brings to light the disavowals upon which [white] heteronormative and typically cissexual gender identifications are forged."[26] Paradoxically, then, gender-segregated public bathrooms attempt to preserve sexuality for the white hetero- and cis-sexual marital bed by producing homosocial spaces that make queer, public sex possible. Despite this dizzying vortex of illogic, the belief that gender segregation protects cis women from sexual violence—and sexuality—is deep-seated.

In their pose, Vaid-Menon's hand substitutes for their genitals, and spread wide, their fingers are particularly emphasized, invoking a queer phallicism that is lesbian-coded. This gesture simultaneously highlights the role that genitals play in the conflict over trans women's access to women's bathrooms and troubles the assumption that women's bathrooms are spaces free from sexuality until they are opened up to transfeminine people with penises. By highlighting Vaid-Menon's hand, the portrait reminds us that hands are gender-neutral sex organs. As both sex organs and banal appendages used in countless other everyday activities, hands continually cross the very boundary between public and private that gender-segregated bathrooms are intended to preserve. Welcome in any bathroom, hands are capable of penetrating and being penetrated, undoing both the binary between masculine and feminine and the binary between public and private. Thus, the portrait not only asks "where r aliens supposed 2 pee?" but also undermines the hetero- and cis-sexist presumption that sexuality can be excluded from public bathrooms through gender segregation. In the #Occupotty selfies and in this portrait, several realities of public bathrooms are revealed: contrary to popular assumptions, public bathrooms exist at an intersection between public and private; they are spaces of performance; and they are not, and have never been, spaces free of sexuality.

Sitting in—and Transforming—Bathrooms
with Trans People

While it is critical to deconstruct myths about public bathrooms, it is not enough to merely show that anti-trans legislation and transphobic social oppression are based on false assumptions. Instead, it is necessary to imagine new possibilities—as Cavanagh puts it, "a more inclusive and luxurious bathroom" for all.[27] Doing so requires an intersectional analysis that considers the myriad ways that current bathroom design restricts access to the public sphere. One key example of such coalitional politics can be found in the tactics of People in Search of Safe and Accessible Restrooms (PISSAR), a direct-action group of transgender and disability activists united by the conviction that "people with all sorts of bodies and all sorts of genders should be free to pee, free to shit, free to bleed, free to share a stall with an attendant or change a baby's diaper."[28] In patrolling, assessing, and occupying public bathrooms, PISSAR worked toward accessibility from the premise that their members' bodies were not the central barrier to access; instead, they asserted that people are disabled by the built environment.[29] Therefore, it is spaces rather than bodies that must be transformed. Following this insight, I examine how *Sitting in Bathrooms with Trans People* reconstructs the space of the public bathroom by drawing on the skills and knowledge of trans people, interracial solidarity, digital technology, humor, improvisation, and play. Although arguably unrealistic and impractical, the bathrooms that the series envisions demand that we imagine possibilities far beyond our current reality, drawing on camp aesthetics to denaturalize and challenge otherwise unexamined norms.

In the first episode of the series, the camera tilts up rapidly from a white tile floor to capture two slight young men of different races standing in front of two urinals, their backs to the camera and their hands hidden from view. Marron, on the right, asks, "So this is like what trans people do in bathrooms?" Jackson Bird, on the left, answers Marron affirmatively and turns around to face the camera, revealing that he is calmly eating waffles. Together, Marron and Bird continue eating their waffles in front of the urinals, playfully subverting transphobic fears about what trans people might do in public bathrooms—as well as the counterassertion that trans people just want to quietly use the bathroom like anyone else. Refusing the dictates of respectability politics—which would demand that trans people assimilate into society as it already exists—the six episodes of *Sitting in Bathrooms with Trans People* use camp to reimagine the space of the public bathroom. As many scholars have noted, camp cannot be limited to a homosexual male aesthetic.[30] Instead, camp might be best understood as a broader "queer discourse" that seeks to challenge cultural norms.[31] As it parodies the naturalized status of gender, camp is the perfect tool to deconstruct the naturalized status of binary gendered bathrooms—as well as other assumptions about the natural and appropriate uses of these public spaces.[32] Each episode features a different trans guest, and the space is continually transformed to accommodate their needs, interests, and passions. In every case, the space is reimagined but never reconfigured, for each episode works with the original layout of an unremarkable, multiuser public bathroom. The series transforms the long, narrow row of sinks into a tattoo parlor and a vaudeville stage while the doors of the bathroom stalls become the set for both a sitcom opening and a perfectly synchronized burlesque entrance. Through props, set design, and digital modification a public bathroom becomes a space for trans people to dance, celebrate, and play, rather than a space of danger, threat, and social and legal oppression. Transforming the space this way—and drawing out the time spent in the bathroom by dwelling within it—*Sitting in Bathrooms with Trans People* makes us experience the space of the bathroom anew.

Within the series, the long row of sinks becomes far more than a utilitarian feature. In reimagining the sinks, the series dreams beyond their function as a site of corporate networking and emphasizes their role as a space for social bonding, self-presentation, and performance.[33] Episode 1 features a "boozy vocab lesson," as Bird and Marron lean against the sinks drinking beer and Bird explains the term "cisgender." During an interview with the activist Lea Rios, the long, narrow space between the stall doors and the sinks becomes a dramatic stage for a *West Side Story* homage, as Marron and Rios advance toward the camera, snapping their fingers in sync. Later in the episode, this space that appeared so restrictive from one camera angle is opened up, as Rios and Marron use the counter and the mirror behind the sinks as a barre for a ballet lesson. The trans model Amira Gray also uses the space between the stalls and the sinks as a stage, but as she struts toward the camera, a wider framing is paired with digital effects that overexpose the white walls, evoking flash photography and the glamor of the runway. In a closer framing, Marron and Gray use the sinks as an altar where they worship Beyoncé.

The series works with the stall doors in a similar way, reimagining them while moving back and forth between close framings that emphasize the

1.2 Kate Bornstein and Dylan Marron stand outside a bathroom stall in Seriously .TV's YouTube series *Sitting in Bathrooms with Trans People.*

narrowness of the public bathroom and moments in which the space seems to expand. In episode 4, the author and activist Kate Bornstein gives Marron a "Doctor Who 101" that begins with the pair standing, backs to the camera, in front of a stall door that is decorated to look like the Tardis, the blue police call box from the popular British television show (figure 1.2). The tight framing shows Bornstein and Marron from the shoulders up, both close to each other and very close to the stall door. As Bornstein says, "A word of warning, it's . . . bigger on the inside," the camera first cuts to a wider side angle. Then, through a match-on-action cut, we see the pair walking into an enormous digitally created Tardis interior that they admire in wonder. Across the series, the rhythmic alteration between tight and open framings continues. In episode 1, Bird and Marron explode out of the bathroom stalls waving strips of toilet paper above their heads in what a title card describes as a "ribbon dance." As they dance with these improvised ribbons, the mobile camera moves with them, a startling contrast to the tight, stable framings that immediately preceded this moment. During the runway sequence in episode 3, the wide shot along the row of sinks abruptly gives way to a tight profile two-shot of Marron and Gray facing each other. The series continues alternating between open and claustrophobic framings, and in episode 5's interview with the trans gamer Oliver Chinyere, the row of sinks is transformed and expanded using scale. With Chinyere and Marron digitally shrunk and turned into digital avatars, the

1.3 Kate Bornstein and Dylan Marron walk through the bathroom stall door and into a Tardis in Seriously.TV's YouTube series *Sitting in Bathrooms with Trans People*.

1.4 The bathroom transforms into a racing video game during Dylan Marron's interview with Oliver Chinyere for Seriously.TV's YouTube series *Sitting in Bathrooms with Trans People*.

bathroom counter becomes the track for a pixelated racing game, with the sinks creating a kind of obstacle course (figures 1.3 and 1.4).

This rhythmic movement is central to how the series balances its informational interviews and expansive imaginative sequences, producing a viewing experience in which the confines of the bathroom as it is and the experiences the interviewees relate break open into celebration and joy. Challenging the demand that trans people adapt to spaces that have been designed by and for cis people, the series shows Marron, the cisgender host, following the lead of his trans interlocutors and learning from them about how to inhabit each transformed bathroom space. Of course, the campy exuberance of *Sitting in Bathrooms with Trans People* cannot provide a practical blueprint for "a more inclusive and luxurious bathroom," and there is a risk that, for some viewers, the camp aesthetic jars their own assessment of the seriousness of this issue. Perhaps this is one reason that the series has failed to achieve the kind of viral popularity that #Occupotty briefly enjoyed. However, against the earnest assimilationism of #Occupotty, *Sitting in Bathrooms with Trans People* gives viewers the opportunity to *feel* what it might be like if the spaces of public bathrooms were unconstrained by the histories and anxieties that have shaped their design. While #Occupotty continues practices of bathroom surveillance and gender policing, and Vaid-Menon answers the question "where r aliens supposed 2 pee?" with the important yet minimal solution of gender-neutral bathrooms, *Sitting in Bathrooms with Trans People* invites viewers to dwell within the bathroom and experience it through trans people's stories, skills, expertise, playfulness—and creativity. Only with such unbridled imagination will we be able to transform these everyday spaces *and* the societal beliefs that create our current conditions.

THE QUEERNESS OF SPACE AND THE BODY
IN NINTENDO'S *THE LEGEND OF ZELDA* SERIES

One of the most influential and enduring video game series of all time, Nintendo's *The Legend of Zelda* has consistently elevated the art of game design and spatial representation. Space is central to how these games are played and how their stories are told, and most of the iterations of this series are set in vast, breathtaking, immersive gameworlds that encourage discovery and exploration.[1] *Zelda* games are consistently recognized by critics for how they push players to think deeply about how spaces are designed, how they can be navigated, and how they assist players in fulfilling a game's objectives.[2] Although all of the games' narratives are loosely and chronologically connected to one another, virtually every installment in the franchise can be considered a standalone game that draws elements and imagery from high fantasy, mythological tropes, and science fiction narratives to offer a distinct take on the hero's journey.[3] These journeys focus on different manifestations of a sword-wielding hero named Link and his efforts to save the fictional land of Hyrule and the eponymous Princess Zelda from an ancient, perpetually reincarnating evil—typically with the assistance of various creatures, deities, and an arsenal of magical tools and weapons.

Although games in the series are known for their innovative puzzles and combat systems, it is their integration of spatial design and gameplay that truly sets them apart. This interdependent relationship between spatial design and gameplay was underscored in the first game in the series, *The Legend of Zelda*, released in 1986 for the Family Computer Disk System.[4] It is notable for implementing an open-world format that gave players little to no navigational guidance: most areas in the gameworld are accessible from the start of the game, and there is no exact order in terms of how goals should be completed. This first game in the series was revolutionary in the gaming field. Not only was it the first home-console video game to include a battery-backed save function, which allowed players to save their in-game progress and engage with the game's adventure for an extended period of time, but it also allowed players to experience an unprecedented amount of freedom, choice, and agency due to its combination of open spatiality and exploration. This first game and subsequent *Zelda* titles are not only critically acclaimed and frequently placed on lists for the best video game of all time, but they have also become massive best sellers that push the bar in terms of gameplay and spatial reasoning. For instance, one of the latest games in the series, *The Legend of Zelda: Breath of the Wild*, not only was the top award-winning game of 2017, but had sold more than 17.41 million copies for the Nintendo Switch as of March 31, 2020.[5] Needless to say, almost anyone who has had experience with video games has probably heard of the *Zelda* series, and even players who do not play or enjoy this franchise cannot deny the impact it has had in the field of gaming.

Although the first game's open-world format and excruciating lack of player guidance was one of its original trademark features, the series' eventual transition from a 2D to a 3D format presented technical obstacles that pushed developers to create games that favored progressive structures over emergent structures and that included an exorbitant amount of player assistance and hand-holding.[6] Frequently approached as linear and cloying, recent games in this series became more invested in linear storytelling and presented players with little autonomy in terms of determining the order in which tasks should be completed. While many of these games retained quintessential elements that define a *Zelda* playing experience, such as puzzle solving, combat, and an array of imaginative weapons and artifacts, they nonetheless quashed the sense of exploration, disorientation, freedom, autonomy, and discovery that was instrumental to the founding game of the series.

In addition to the franchise's increasing embrace of linearity and lack of player freedom, the series has gained notoriety from a narrative perspective. Nintendo's *The Legend of Zelda* series seems not only linear and straightforward, but also potentially conservative in its treatment of elements such as gender, sexuality, and identity performance. Tison Pugh, for instance, has demonstrated how the series partakes in a tradition of sexist and gender-regressive video games, since its titles frequently "adhere to the trite formula of a male protagonist rescuing a female victim," thus suggesting that they are designed with a normative, heterocentric audience in mind.[7] Pugh urges critics, however, to uncover the series' queer potentialities as observed "from portrayals in various games' margins and from resistant players interpreting against the grain."[8] Pugh argues that earlier *Zelda* games pressured suspicious interpretations of their gender and sexual frameworks through queer-coded characters and narratological elements, thus highlighting an underlying queer impulse present in the games. Other critics, such as Bonnie Ruberg, have pointed out that *all* video games emanate a sense of queer potentiality, regardless of whether this queerness is explicit or implicit. Ruberg suggests that queerness and video games share mutual ambitions in that they both rely on "the longing to imagine alternative ways of being and to make space within structures of power for resistance through play."[9] Ruberg further highlights other resonances between queer frameworks and games, covering everything from "their emphasis on world-building, to their denaturalization of the normative body, to their invitation to rethink the mechanisms of desire."[10]

Focusing on gameworld space and design, the denaturalization of the normative body, and the mechanisms of kinship and desire, this discussion further parses out the non-normative potentialities embedded in the *Zelda* series. I examine how a selection of its games can be approached as queer through their spatial design and core gaming mechanics. Here, rather than using queer as a concept exclusively to describe interactions among people who engage in non-normative forms of sexuality and gender expression, I draw from the frameworks developed by Mel Chen to approach queerness as "an array of subjectivities, intimacies, beings, and spaces located outside of the heteronormative" and as a framework that is "immanent to animate transgressions, violating proper intimacies."[11] I also approach queerness in video games similarly to Ruberg, who characterizes it as a resistance to "the hegemonic logics that dictate when it means to be an acceptable, valued, heteronormative (or homonormative) subject."[12] Through a queer perspective, I argue that the *Zelda* series uses its spaces and structures to challenge universalizing approaches toward being and to disrupt monolithic narratives on growth, identity, and the body. An examination of space using queer and intersectional approaches to identity and embodiment shows how a queer impulse saturates these games, further demonstrating how the *Zelda* series is not as conservative or regressive as it may seem on the surface.

A recurring mechanic found in many *Zelda* games, along with puzzle solving and exploration, is the ability to reiteratively transform the avatar's body. Through the use of magical artifacts or rituals, Link can change his shape, size, species, or identity performance to facilitate his exploration of spaces that otherwise would be inaccessible to his default form. The element of transformation has been a central convention in nearly half of the core *Zelda* games published since the 1980s, and through these alterations the games exhibit the potential to disrupt both monolithic and normative understandings of being, relating, and dwelling. In *The Legend of Zelda: Twilight Princess*, for example, Link possesses the power to shift between a humanoid and wolf form, which grants players a varied array of possibilities in terms of navigation, mobility, and ability.[13] In his wolf form, Link could detect scent trails and ghostly figures that are invisible to human eyes and leap toward ledges that otherwise would be impossible to reach. In other games, such as *The Legend of Zelda: A Link between Worlds*, Link can transform his body into an animated painting, granting him the power to transpose himself over and travel through wall surfaces, collapsing the boundaries between 2D and 3D space and gameplay.[14]

The element of bodily alteration works in conjunction with spatial frameworks to unsettle the progressive structures of many *Zelda* games. More specifically, the transformational processes often represented in the *Zelda* series mirror theoretical approaches to transmogrification—an oftentimes magical, unexpected, technological, or speculative transformation, "a process of (un)becoming strange and/or grotesque, of (un)becoming other."[15] Although the progressively structured games in the series arguably favor straightforward gameplay and have a lack of overt queer discourse, the spaces present in them disrupt normative conceptions of identity, growth, and the body. Navigation of these linear and structured environments require Link's body to become a site of constant transmogrification in that he must persistently (un)become strange and other to explore different areas of a gameworld. More specifically, practices of transmogrification in these highly regulated and closed gameworlds stage queer potentialities that dispute adulthood as a teleological developmental period, denaturalize the normative body, blur the divide that exists between kinds or species, and undo temporal boundaries such as the past and the future. The series' implementation of transmogrification tropes thus offers players opportunities to "acknowledge important similarities, overlaps, resonances, and intersections between a range of modified bodies."[16] Although the series currently spans nineteen official games, an examination of *The Legend of Zelda: Ocarina of Time* and its direct sequel, *The Legend of Zelda: Majora's Mask*, sheds light on the interplay of space, transmogrification, and queerness present in many progressively structured *Zelda* games.[17] Afterward, the discussion addresses how this interplay unfolds in one of the latest games in the franchise, *The Legend of Zelda: Breath of the Wild.*

Although immersing oneself in a gameworld is a form of entertainment, effective navigation of video game space requires familiarity with a game's rules. There is always potential for people to play these games perversely or against their intended design, especially with the rise of game modifications (commonly known as "mods"), in which players and fans alter or reconfigure a game to change its appearance or gameplay features.[18] Engagement with a video game's intended design demands an understanding of its underlying logics, mechanics, and gameplay possibilities—and how they respond to or differ from the conventions of the player's world. Ian Bogost argues that video games are "models of real and imagined systems" that encourage gamers to "explore the possibility space of a set of rules— we learn to understand and evaluate a game's meaning" and, furthermore, understand how they present an argument about "how social or cultural systems work in the world—or how they could work, or don't work."[19]

Focusing on such rules of gameplay, Mia Consalvo has described how the uncanny relationship that exists between players and video game avatars can promote queer forms of engagement. She approaches the player-avatar relationship as queer in that players are "masked" through the identity of the character they control. Consalvo further frames this relationship through spatial and temporal frameworks, characterizing gameplay as a period of liminality "where the player is between her 'real' life and the life of the character on screen. As the rules of real life are temporarily lifted, so are social expectations, at least for some players."[20] Given their speculative setting, *Zelda* games frequently provide players with opportunities to control an avatar that disrupts physical and cultural rules that players often take for granted in the real world through processes such as transmogrification, thus highlighting queer ways of understanding bodies and the spaces they traverse.

Ocarina of Time (OOT), the fifth main installment of the *Zelda* series, implements spatial and temporal logics that dismantle real-world understandings of identity, especially in regard to representations of growth and development. In a central plotline in the game, Princess Zelda asks a child Link to assist her in stopping the threat imposed by Ganondorf (the game's main villain) by accessing the Sacred Realm, an ethereal, otherworldly space where the Triforce resides. A recurring motif in the series, the Triforce is a divine relic that possesses the power to grant the wish of any being who places their hands on it. Throughout his journey, Link discovers the resting place of the Master Sword, a legendary, Arthurianesque blade capable of repelling evil and the final key needed to access the entrance to the Sacred Realm. Unknown to Link, a child does not possess the physical strength or prowess needed to wield the blade; thus, when he pulls the weapon out of its pedestal, one of the game's most drastic bodily transformations occurs. Link reawakens in the Sacred Realm after losing consciousness, only to realize that he now inhabits the body of a young adult (see figures 2.1 and 2.2). As explained to him by the spiritual guardian of the realm, "Only one worthy of the title of 'Hero of Time' can pull [the Master Sword] from the Pedestal of Time. . . . However, you were too young to be the Hero of Time. . . . Therefore, your spirit was sealed here for seven years."[21]

Here it is worth thinking through how the Master Sword serves as a symbol of growth, adulthood, and liability. Children are framed as incapable of wielding the power inherent in the Master Sword, thus prompting a temporal leap to a moment in which Link's body and mind are deemed capable of commanding the blade. The phallocentric readings of this sword are quite palpable here. The first *Zelda* game for the Family Computer Disk System represents swords as symbols of male power that are passed down from older generations, and they are "depicted as part of normative rituals in which male power is dispersed by other male authorities and recognized as such by foes and romantic interests alike."[22] Although *OOT*'s Master Sword is not passed down to Link by another male authority figure, it still retains its status as a phallic symbol contingent on hegemonic male and adult power, especially since Link's status as a child prevents him from achieving immediate mastery of the weapon. Link's subsequent transformation into a young adult body reifies a normative division between childhood and adulthood in which adults are portrayed as capable and physically proficient while children are framed as the opposite. While *OOT* initially upholds this normative split through the implementation of phallocentric and hegemonic ideals, it takes an unexpected turn once it is revealed that Link possesses the ability to travel back and forth through time by using the very blade that he pulled out of the pedestal: "If you want to return to your original time, return the Master Sword to the Pedestal of Time. By doing this, you will travel back in time seven years."[23] The introduction of this time-traveling ability subverts the linear development of the game, especially since players have complete freedom to return to Link's child state after this possibility is disclosed. Furthermore, Link's body is not permanently transformed through this process. Rather, it becomes a site in which he is free to continuously (un)become either a child or an adult.

2.1 AND 2.2 Link's transformation from child to young adult in *Ocarina of Time 3D*. In the image on the top, a child Link draws the Master Sword from the Pedestal of Time. In the image on the bottom, Link transforms into a young adult after being sealed in the Sacred Realm for seven years.

By introducing a mechanic in which Link can to return to his child body with all of the knowledge that he has obtained as a young adult, the game disrupts the phallic, teleological frameworks that it initially implements with the seven-year leap into the future: "Past, present, future. . . . The Master Sword is a ship with which you can sail upstream and downstream through time's river."[24] After this point in the game, altering Link's body is an ability needed to ensure successful completion of OOT's quests. Link, for instance, must travel to the past to collect key items that no longer exist in the future and to take advantage of the spatial implications that come along with possessing the stature and frame of a child's body. Seth Giddings has pointed that games facilitate the traversal through previously restricted areas by introducing new game mechanics or items that grant different abilities: "These powers are carefully designed to allow access to new sections of the gameworld, as much a playful and temporally determined set of keys or codes as either a cursor or a character."[25] While this convention is common in video games with progressive structures, even open-world games with emergent structures such as Breath of the Wild contain geographies that are inaccessible until Link obtains a special set of protective clothing or brews a protective elixir. Once Link can inhabit the body of a child and young adult in OOT, the spaces encountered in the gameworld present obstacles that require time travel to be surmounted, disrupting linear, normative conceptions of the game's chronotope. Although structured in a rigid format, the element of time travel in OOT upsets the inflexibility of the game's structure and pushes players to think about space, time, and Link's body as elements that are subject to change and transformation.

A notable example of OOT's gameworld necessitating a dual embodiment of identity can be found in the Spirit Temple, one of the game's major dungeons. In the Zelda series, dungeons are typically self-contained areas that are labyrinthine in their structure, commonly housed underground or within large, looming buildings. An obstacle course of sorts, they are primarily designed to test the player's in-game knowledge and skills. Players must take advantage of experience accumulated during gameplay, and adapt to new challenges, to overcome a series of obstacles that lead to a location where a key item or upgrade is located.[26] The Spirit Temple stands out in OOT because Link is required to embody the positionality of a child and a young adult to successfully complete it. One-half of the dungeon's entrance hall, for instance, can be accessed only by crawling through a small hole in a wall through which the body of a larger person cannot fit. The other half of this area is blocked by a massive stone block that is too heavy for any person to move independently. To overcome these obstacles, the player must inhabit the body of child Link, who is small enough to crawl through the hole in the wall. In this section of the dungeon, the player obtains a pair of magical adult-size gauntlets that enhance the strength of any person who wears them. Link must then travel to the future, where he is now large enough to wear the gauntlets, and move the large stone block that obstructs access to the rest of the dungeon. Even though these tasks must be completed in a set order, the dungeon is designed so that the player must embody different developmental stages to overcome certain obstacles, thus disrupting some of the constrained and normative expectations that are implemented through linear gameplay.

Consalvo suggests that video games allow players to bypass the rules of real life, which in turn provides the means to disrupt sociocultural expectations and normative approaches toward identity.[27] Not only does OOT support temporal frameworks that allow players to bend the conventions of linear chronology and development, but, furthermore, its spatial design demands that the player continually transmogrify Link's body to complete the game. Players oscillate between the positionality of a child and a young adult to access unexplored spaces, and this ability highlights just how queer the game's spatial conventions can be. Furthermore, by controlling an avatar that can alter his age and body, players could develop a queer understanding of development and growth. Kathryn Bond Stockton has critiqued the notion of "growing up," a normative and teleological phenomenon that prioritizes concepts such as linearity, verticality, knowledge, and stature. When donning a normative perspective toward human development, one questionably approaches adulthood as the pinnacle of knowledge and experience, which in turn casts childhood as a period of lack. The gameworld of OOT disrupts these perspectives, providing players with a speculative instance of sideways growth, which suggests that "the width of a person's experience or ideas, their motives or motions, may pertain at any age, bringing 'adults' and 'children' into lateral contact."[28] By including spatial obstacles that demand different forms of embodiment, OOT partakes in a queer project of lateralization in that it stresses the cultural and spatial advantages of being both a child *and* an adult, pressuring the tendency to categorize these developmental categories as either good or bad, desirable or undesirable.

Other games in the *Zelda* series, such as *Majora's Mask* (MM), also challenge normative frameworks through the mechanic of transmogrification. *Majora's Mask* is temporally structured in a three-day cycle that culminates with the apocalyptic crashing of the moon on the gameworld's surface. A child Link must reiteratively time travel to the beginning of this three-day cycle until he obtains the tools and knowledge necessary to prevent this apocalypse from unfolding. As explained by Lee Sherlock, the repeating structure of MM demands that players "gain affordances in the game through items and materials, and at the same time, create a historical account defined in context of the items taken."[29] In addition to this temporal logic, MM introduces a mechanic that raises the stakes in terms of the relationship between space and identity: Link must use magical masks to transmogrify his body into that of another being.[30] By inhabiting the body of another being, he can not only access previously unreachable areas, but also forge both positive and antagonistic relationships with different people and creatures.

These masks, vessels that contain the spirits of characters who have died, allow Link to inhabit the physical bodies of those characters. The masks allow Link to transcend the limitations of a human body by granting him abilities such as breathing and walking underwater, heat resistance, flight, and enhanced strength. Once players gain access to the transformation masks, they must decide which embodiment is needed to traverse the game's spaces and obstacles. (For a detailed description of the transformation masks, see figure 2.3.) Similar to OOT, various spaces in MM require Link to consistently transmogrify his body to complete quests and puzzles. For example, the Stone Tower Temple, one of the final dungeons of the game, requires players to apply all of their knowledge about transformation acquired in previous areas of the game. Link must use the abilities of his Deku scrub form to access areas that are out of reach. At other times, he must traverse spaces that are inaccessible to his human body, such as underwater basins or pools of lava, thus necessitating the use of a Goron or Zora mask. Link must also revert back to his human form to use tools such as bows and swords. Completion of the dungeons in MM requires players to develop an understanding of how to navigate gameworld spaces using different versions or transformations of the self, leading to an understanding of the body as a nonmonolithic, nonstatic, denaturalized site of being.

The queer potentialities of transmogrification in *Majora's Mask* become salient when considering how these processes present privileges and hindrances to players as they navigate the gameworld. Different embodiments either enable or disrupt prospects for kinship, collectivity, or task completion. Consider, for instance, the treasure chest minigame present in MM's central town, Termina, in which the player is given a limited amount of

2.3 Primary transformations in *Majora's Mask 3D:* Deku scrub Link, Goron Link, and Zora Link (from left to right). One of the game's distinctive features is the ability to use magical masks to transmogrify Link into different beings, which grants him the ability to access previously unreachable areas and use specific abilities such as gliding in the air, walking on hot surfaces, or swimming underwater.

time to navigate a maze and find a prize hidden in the area. The cost of playing this game and the prize in the chest will change according to the body that Link dwells in when talking to the shop worker. When embodying child Link, the clerk charges 20 rupees (the game's currency) to play the minigame. When wearing the Zora mask, the shop owner charges Link only 5 rupees to play, and she makes remarks and gestures that denote her attraction to the avatar. Upon laying eyes on Zora Link, she coos flirtatiously and exclaims, "Well, hello there, handsome! Wanna play?"[31] On one hand, embodying different identities grants players advantages in terms of spatial navigation and interactions with other, nonplayable characters. On the other hand, the game demonstrates how being and dwelling in certain bodies can lead to potential disadvantages, discriminatory practices, and biases.

These biases and disadvantages are perhaps most notable when Link, in his Deku scrub form, attempts to complete a series of tasks to become part of a gang of children known as the Bomber Kids, a group that regulates access to the Astral Observatory (a key area that Link needs to enter). Even though Deku Link completes the tasks, the children do not allow him to join. When the leader considers letting Link join the group and consults with the other members, they say, "No way! No scrubs!" Afterward, the leader explains, "Once, we let some kid who wasn't human join our gang, and, boy, did we ever regret it! Sorry!"[32] MM is structured so that players experience discrimination and prejudice on the basis of the being that the avatar embodies at a given time. Interactions such as these push players to virtually experience the implementation of unfair and corrupt ideological systems, and these encounters can potentially prompt contemplation on how these in-game forms of oppression mirror those present in the real world.

Link's ability to transmogrify his body can be framed both as a source of opportunity and as a source of anxiety. Sherlock approaches Link's transmogrification as a narrative of loss, focusing on the apprehensions that Link's initial alteration causes him. When Link is first transformed into a Deku scrub against his will, his initial reaction is one of horror, as evidenced by the shriek that he emits when gazing at his reflection post-transformation. Indeed, when Link first transforms into a Deku scrub, there is a crisis in terms of time and identity: "his anxiety over his new form is addressed through the idea of returning, of going *back*, to a self of the past."[33] While Sherlock is right in pointing out this anxiety, this reading does perpetuate a dichotomous perspective in which Link's human form is framed as "normal," whereas his embodiment as a Deku scrub is cast as "strange" or "other." *Majora's Mask* pressures this dichotomous perspective through spatial means. Since different spaces and in-game events constantly demand different processes of transmogrification, it becomes increasingly difficult for players to distinguish which embodiment is strange, which embodiment is different, and which embodiment is "monstrous" or "natural." Although Link develops the ability to once again embody a human form and obtains the ability to oscillate between his child self and the forms of other beings, a full return to a past self is impossible. As Link traverses MM's gameworld embodying different positionalities, he experiences how other beings dwell through space and interact with other people, and, as Sullivan would put it, he acknowledges "important similarities, overlaps, resonances, and intersections" between himself and these other beings through this reiterative process of bodily alteration.[34]

Disrupting the avatar's identity and body is not an option in this game. Rather, it is a core component of the game's rules and its approach toward spatial design and navigation. These rules and mechanics are queer in that the player must consistently view bodies as multifaceted, pluralistic, and potentially ever transforming rather than approaching them as static and singular. As T. Garner would put it, transmogrification in the *Zelda* series "repudiates an individualized conception of the body and the self; there is no 'us versus them,' always 'us and them (and them . . .),' to the extent that none of these terms is intelligible without the others." Furthermore, it "undermines the concepts of bodily integrity and wholeness as it necessitates a consideration of the 'intra-active' character of materiality."[35] In a sense, Link's body becomes a vessel for multiple narratives and materializations of being—a conduit for different possibilities of dwelling, navigating, and existing in a given space. In addition, players must experiment with the multiple outcomes that different embodiments generate in the gameworld. A resistance to transmogrification, and a resistance to partake in different ways of being and thinking in MM, would allow the narrative's looming apocalypse to transpire. It is important to recall that these elements of transmogrification and spatial navigation are very much in sync with how these games were *designed* to be played, thus highlighting how queer frameworks can be extracted from the narrative and ludological components present in the actual games. In turn, this pressures the heterocentric and conservative narrative elements of the series and the notion of these games as entirely linear or restrictive.

Both OOT and MM are installments of the *Legend of Zelda* series created before the boom in popularity of contemporary open-world-style games— games such as the most recent one in this franchise, *Breath of the Wild* (BOTW), which grant players the ability to approach tasks and objectives freely and resist linear gameplay. BOTW was envisioned by developers as a return to the game's nonlinear origins and a departure from the series' current conventions in that it is a colossal open-world game that provides players with multiple options in terms of storyline and gameplay. The game is so lax in its structure and narrative, for instance, that a skilled player could ostensibly venture into the final boss's lair shortly after the tutorial section, without ever having to become familiar with the game's lore, challenges, or major storylines.[36] With the reimplementation of an open-world format, the introduction of gameplay mechanics such as the ability to climb practically any vertical surface, and the development of a highly interactive physics engine, players seldom encounter restrictions when navigating BOTW's gameworld and can partake in a gaming experience that suits diverse playing styles. Zach Hines has noted that space is central in BOTW's design and that the game can be approached more as a "walking simulator" that forgoes the colonialist narrative fostered by other open-world games and replaces it with "an expansive, hand-crafted landscape there to be observed and discovered rather than conquered."[37] This sense of unprecedented liberty has led other critics to praise BOTW for expanding the possibilities of open-world gameplay:

What elevates *Breath of the Wild* above its open-world contemporaries is its sheer freedom, both in its non-linear questing structure and in your ability to climb almost any surface and travel in any direction once you leave the starting area. . . . Like many open-world games it delivers on the implied promise that if you can see it out in the distance, chances are you can eventually reach it—but here, figuring out how to get there is more often than not a satisfying puzzle in itself, and one that never gets old.[38]

Breath of the Wild provides countless affordances to players through its landscape and its spatial design. Successful navigation of this vast and rich landscape, similar to that of other *Legend of Zelda* games, demands that the player adapt Link's identity performance to the particularities of the distinct geographies and locations encountered in the gameworld. At the most basic level, Link has to alter his armor and clothing to comply with rises and falls in temperature that take place when venturing into ecologically diverse regions such as deserts and mountaintops. In a significant section of the game, the player must find a way to purchase an outfit consisting of a veil, top, and pants that disguise Link and assist him in infiltrating the premises of Gerudo Town, a matriarchal settlement that men are forbidden from entering (see figure 2.4).

Breath of the Wild grants players an unequalled degree of control and freedom compared with previous games in the *Zelda* series, which for the most part demand that players come up with particular solutions to puzzles and combat scenarios and require that tasks be completed in a rigid order. Nonetheless, there is much value to be found in these older games, which are structured around linear, progressive gameplay. The limited, self-contained areas and landscapes present in the older games, in conjunction with the gameplay mechanic of transmogrification, provides players with opportunities to think deeply about the avatar's body as a site of perpetually changing and shifting identities, thus putting space *and* the avatar's identity and body in the forefront of the game's goals and gameplay possibilities. *Breath of the Wild* does put players in scenarios in which identity performance must be altered through clothing to access other areas. However, not only are these moments of alteration *optional*, but the stakes of these alterations are diminished in comparison with those of previous games, which coerce players to think through and experience how (un)becoming "strange" and "other" highlights the different forms of privilege and oppression experienced by different beings. While BOTW is remarkably open in its structure and spatial design, it inadvertently forecloses the

2.4 Situational costumes and attire in *Breath of the Wild*. Link has to adapt his attire according to geography, climate, and culture present in certain gameworld regions. The images show, from left to right, the Snowquill set, which grants resistance to cold temperatures; the Gerudo set, which grants resistance to heat and allows Link to enter the matriarchal Gerudo Town; the Flamebreaker set, which grants the ability to explore volcanic regions; and the Zora set, which increases swimming speed and grants Link the ability to swim up waterfalls.

queer potentialities highlighted through the ontological and performative possibilities of transmogrification found in many of the series' progressively structured games.

While many older *Zelda* games are fairly closed and straightforward, their spatial designs and gameplay mechanics allow one to better appreciate their queerness and their intersectional approach to identity and oppression. All video games, despite the apparent freedoms and liberties that they bestow on players, are still systems of code that are bound to particular rules and conventions developed by game designers. As Steven Jones argues, "The delineated space of any game is necessarily a social convention. . . . Players come together and agree to stay inside of the circle, as it were, in so far as they remain players, abiding by the rules and working toward the objectives of the game."[39] Given the interconnected relationship between the gameworld and the realm of the player, there is much to be said about a series of superficially heteronormative games that invite players to engage in spatial narratives and forms of play that resist monolithic and teleological thought, and that push us to denaturalize our normative understandings of the body.

Even though Nintendo games have a propensity to create "spaces of narrative queerness" through the presence of potentially non-normative objectives and characters, Pugh has suggested that these elements "must be created in turn by the player accessing its moments of disruptive pleasure."[40] As Ruberg has noted, however, queer play and engagement can manifest not only through how we interpret a game, but also through the game itself: "A game's queerness may lay in its mechanics, or in its imagery, or in its control schema, or in how it creates a platform for emergent and transgressive forms of play."[41] My analysis argues, similar to Ruberg, that spaces of narrative queerness do not always need to be generated on behalf of players when playing *Zelda* games, for they are integral to the games' spatial design and gameplay conventions. The element of transmogrification present in the *Zelda* franchise emphasizes the relationship that exists between identity and space and the privileges, affordances, and hindrances that come along with different ways of being and dwelling in fictional and real worlds.

Further amplifying the queer impulses identified in previous examinations of the series, I suggest that, despite the heterocentric narratives and logics of the *Zelda* series, its spatial and bodily dimensions present players with a playground of queer potentiality. The spatial frameworks present in many of its games can conceivably push players to engage in queer play and thought and to immerse themselves in gameworlds where transmogrification is a generative process that is central to being, moving, and dwelling; where the hierarchy between childhood and adulthood is pressured; and where players are encouraged to consider multiple, intersectional, and alternative ways of exploring and existing in video game space. We can only begin to imagine the queer potentialities that will develop when and if open-world, nonlinear *Zelda* games fully embrace the element of transmogrification that has been so central in the legendary adventures of Link through the fictional spaces of Hyrule, Termina, and beyond.

THE DIGITAL FLÂNEUSE

Exploring Intersectional Identities and Spaces
through Walking Simulators

Around 2010 a design trend in independent game development emerged
built around exploring a game's virtual spaces through the first-person perspective at a walking pace. In the discourse of gaming culture, critics and
players quickly gave this genre the pejorative label "walking simulator."
Games in this genre include *The Stanley Parable, Dear Esther, Gone Home,
Sunset, Firewatch, Virginia,* and *What Remains of Edith Finch.*[1] Yet unlike other
first-person genres, such as shooters, racing games, or survival horror titles,
walking simulators eschew a focus on complex game mechanics and masculinized conceptions of competitiveness, player skill, and twitch reflexes
in favor of highlighting the relationship among subjectivity, space, stories,
and memory. The discourse surrounding these games thus intersects with
ongoing debates concerning the policing of "real" and "fake" games, or
games and nongames, a demarcation with profoundly gendered roots and
one that has manifested previously in regard to casual mobile and down-
loadable games.[2]

This chapter engages with walking simulators through the lens of intersectional game studies and what has been called the spatial turn in media
studies, which explores the co-constitutive nature of and relationship between media and space/place and brings together fields such as media and
cultural studies, geography, cartography, and communication studies.[3] The
chapter first traces the brief history of walking simulators in popular discourse before recontextualizing the genre through a discussion of intersectional game studies and theories of media and space. With an intersectional
game studies approach, we analyze the interlocking systems of oppression

and privilege across categories such as race, gender, sexuality, and class in walking sims. We use this theoretical foundation to examine the games *Sunset* and *Virginia*. The emphasis these two games place on walking female protagonists produces a digital flâneuse, characters who wander, explore, and excavate spaces that evoke crises of narrative, politics, and identity. *Sunset* explores race, privilege, domestic labor, and revolutionary politics all within the space of a high-rise apartment, detached from but deeply imbricated with the civil strife occurring in the streets below. Similarly, in *Virginia* players take on the role of a special agent of the Federal Bureau of Investigation (FBI) and woman of color who has traveled to a small Virginian town to investigate the disappearance of a young boy. Ultimately, this chapter argues that, while it is a culturally feminized and maligned genre in video game culture, the walking simulator engenders a unique protagonist: the intersectional digital flâneuse. This player subject position highlights the complexity of living in the world as intersectional beings, and it reminds us of the ways our lived identities bleed out into the world, shaping places, spaces, and the people who pass through them.

The Politics of Walking Sims

The term "walking simulator" might strike one as entirely mundane. How did such an innocuous sounding genre become so controversial? Although the recent proliferation of walking simulators is likely due to their ease of development, thanks to engines such as Unity, opportunities in digital game distribution, and the critical success of games such as *Dear Esther* and *Gone Home*, the genre itself (or, at least, its underlying gameplay) has been with us for some time. Nicole Clark suggests one such antecedent to current walking sims is Mary Flanagan's 2003 art piece "[domestic]," which allows players to explore the psychic space resulting from a house fire.[4] Even earlier progenitors include *The Forest* and *Explorer*, produced for the ZX Spectrum in 1983 and 1986, respectively.[5] These experimental titles were best known for their technical achievements, such as their massive procedurally generated worlds and underwhelming gameplay design.[6] One review of *Explorer*, which appeared in the Commodore 64 magazine *Zzap64!*, called it "unbelievably tedious, monotonous, pointless, fruitless and rubbish. If you really want to do some exploring, why not buy a rail or bus ticket?"[7]

So if the genre isn't new, and accusations of rudderless design aren't new, what explains the denigration of recent walking sims? The discourse that reemerged alongside the genre circa 2013 suggests the cultural backlash against them is a defense of hegemonic, masculinist play practices by a hegemonic, masculinist play community that sees its veritable heart of hearts (or genre of genres) under threat—namely, the first-person shooter (FPS).

Game designer-scholars Janine Fron, Tracy Fullerton, Jacquelyn Ford Morie, and Celia Pearce argue that we need to pursue and champion inclusive design principles to push back against "the hegemony of play." One component of their larger call to action is the need to craft "androgynous spaces" that are hospitable to men and women, boys and girls. This has not traditionally been the case for the FPS. They note, "These [FPS] games conceive of moving through space in a distinctly masculine fashion, in terms of both its role in the game experience, and the narrative milieu in which they take place. They epitomize what Judith Butler would call 'disciplinary regimes' that through repetitive performance construct both gender and gendered space. Their game mechanics value particular skills: mastery of quick reflexes and an ability to solve complex spatial rotation problems in real time."[8]

By eliminating the shooting aspects from first-person games, walking sims appropriate a well-known 3D spatial logic while opening up that space to new gameplay and storytelling possibilities. Consider, for instance, the husband escaping his wife's Alzheimer's by working as a forest ranger in *Firewatch*, or the mother and father dealing with their child's terminal disease in *That Dragon, Cancer*.[9] Although instantly recognizable in terms of perspective and navigation, thanks to their ties to the first-person shooter genre, walking sims divert from simulated violence in the service of more intimate and personal storytelling.

In addition to introducing new narrative expressions into a familiar interface, walking sims have drawn ire from a certain contingent of players for how they subvert the FPS's suturing of player subjectivity to a power fantasy of action and agency. According to Alexander Galloway, whereas the first-person perspective in film has been marginalized in cinematic language and confined to communicating alienation or "predatory vision," the same perspective in digital games has been successfully deployed to intuit for players a "sense of affective motion," speed, and readable action.[10] Put more simply, as Galloway explains, "Where film uses the subjective shot to represent a problem with identification, games use the subjective shot to *create* identification."[11] Ultimately, the condemnation of walking sims by a contingent of threatened players is less about the walking sim's lack of a certain something—not having a fail state or a skills-based design—than it is a radical reimagining of the central vantage point most associated with the first-person shooter and, more important, who it is that sees from that perspective. In this respect, as Nicole Clark notes, "The reification of the label 'walking simulator' does a better job of describing the kinds of people who create such labels than it does the games it purports to define."[12] This once again highlights the definitional influence of the discourse surrounding walking sims, as well as the underlying patriarchal power that fuels it.

Melissa Kagen argues that the debate about the design and artistic merits of walking sims highlights the tensions between the toxic masculinity of "hardcore gamers" and a changing gaming culture that reflects diversity, artistry, and mainstream accessibility.[13] Kagen links the backlash against walking sims to the reactionary politics of the 2014 #gamergate movement, which lashed out at progressive industry professionals, journalists, and academics. As critics have observed, #gamergate was driven by masculinist anxieties of shifting game designs, narratives, and player demographics.[14]

Kagen contextualizes walking sims within literary studies and a history of "wandering texts and digressive literature," which highlight how exploration itself is perceived as either appropriate and masculinized (goal-oriented) or transgressive and feminized ("aimless").[15] Kagen contends the accusation that walking sims are "boring" is profoundly gendered. Boredom has historically been feminized and linked to the escapist daydreaming of literary female characters who find themselves captives of patriarchal societies and customs.

Walking sims critique the reigning hegemony of play by curtailing the interactive affordances most associated with the FPS. These games shift the focus from skills-based technical mastery measured by one's kill-death ratio, spatial acrobatics, and completion speed to emphasizing types of identity exploration often ignored in games. As expressed more concretely in the next section, they also afford the production of a digital flâneuse—a strolling, feminized spectator position through which players experience virtual worlds as intimate, intersectional spaces of narrative, identity, and politics.

Theorizing the Digital Flâneuse in Video Games

In her discussion of walking sims, Kagen rehearses the development of Baudelaire's flâneur, a nineteenth-century literary character embodied by the figure of the gentleman writer who strolls through the emergent industrialized city as a detached observer, often admiring women and the beauty of everyday life.[16] Walter Benjamin evokes and advances the consideration of the wandering flâneur in his famously incomplete *The Arcade's Project* to describe the relationship among modernism, city dwelling, and the human psyche.[17] Taking Benjamin's formulations and radicalizing them, Guy Debord and the French situationists replace the passivity of the aimless flâneur with the active nature of the *dérive*, a kind of active drifting, an engagement with and domination of what Debord calls the psychogeographical features of a city environment.[18] Benjamin concentrated on the way the flâneur responded to stimuli from a cacophonous, modernist cityscape, but the situationists were interested in the ways engagement with city spaces could be directed toward political ends. Participants in a situationist dérive strive to shape the world around them and stimulate people through shock performance, which, Debord suggests, is a far more radical political act.

Feminist literary and media scholars such as Rachel Bowlby and Giuliana Bruno have revisited the flâneur to discuss the "impossibility" of its feminized opposite, the flâneuse, a woman free to equally wander cityscapes, spend without care, ogle men, and revel in the random encounters of a bustling modernist metropolis. Scholars have instead imagined analogous figures in media. For instance, Bowlby explores the flâneuse in the writings of Virginia Woolf as a figure that sutures the aimless walking of women to the process of writing, particularly in the story "Street Haunting," in which the sexless narrator stops in three separate stores to purchase shoes, books, and a pencil—the tools of wandering, contemplating, and writing.[19] Adapting the concept to media spectatorship, Bruno argues that watching a film is "an embodied and kinetic affair" similar to streetwalking. Yet unlike literal streetwalking, which offers a litany of dangers, Bruno suggests, transportive film watching is open to women, creating "a relative of the railway passenger and the urban stroller, the female spectator—a flâneuse."[20] With Bruno's emphasis on media spectatorship as a form of travel and movement, urban and otherwise, she frees the flâneuse from the material confines of streetwalking and opens up a critical subjectivity defined by feminized spectatorship based not on consumption or domination but, instead, on witnessing.

Introducing the developing concept of the flâneuse into the walking simulator videogame genre further changes the theoretical implications of the subject position associated with it. In walking simulators, the digital flâneuse is freed from city streets and from the subject position's assumed whiteness, able-bodiedness, and femininity. Protagonists in walking sims include divorced middle-aged men, female FBI agents of color, and even

blind women in the case of *Perception*.[21] Although the predominantly female protagonists of walking sims do wander, sometimes aimlessly, they
tend not to do so in city streets, no doubt because populated cities are too
demanding for many indie developers (who almost exclusively have shep-
herded the genre) to render digitally. Of course, according to Bruno, not
all spectatorship (or witnessing) is similar to the resistant practices of the
flâneuse. By returning to the domestic space as the central location of play
and denying players the opportunity to traverse multiple spaces outside
the home, many walking sims arguably diminish the radical potential of
the digital flâneuse. Walking sims that choose the home as their setting do
not foreclose the possibility of a digital flâneuse but, instead, interrogate
the limitations of radical witnessing and movement when it is limited to
the domestic sphere.

The multiplatform success of *Gone Home* offered a critical flashpoint
for gaming culture to reengage basic definitional questions concerning the
ontology of video games in general, and the artistic merit of walking sims
in particular. In *Gone Home*, players adopt the role of Kate, a college student who has just returned home after spending time abroad, only to find
her family absent. In a game ostensibly about exploring a vacant house,
Gone Home deconstructs the ideology of the nuclear family while illustrating how the residue of our everyday lives can tell profound stories about
us, including a young woman coming out as queer to herself and to her
family. Much of the recuperative scholarship about *Gone Home* comes in
the wake of Ian Bogost's 2013 complimentary dismissal of it as a narrative
failure compared with literature and "serious television" and as a game that
impresses players only insofar as the expectations for game narrative are already abysmally low.[22] Bogost is critical of the kinds of stories that walking
sims tell, as he similarly questioned why the critically praised walking sim
What Remains of Edith Finch was better suited as a game than, for instance, a
collection of short stories.[23] In reducing *Gone Home*'s Kate to merely a cursor that players move to experience the story, Bogost neglects to explore
the alternative subjectivity and questions around movement and agency
that walking simulators engender.

This chapter decenters the narrative discussion of walking simulators
and embraces instead subjectivity, space, and traversal. It contends that
walking simulators produce intersectional subject positions whose principal
interaction with the virtual worlds they inhabit is wandering, detached contemplation and a witnessing of everyday ephemera. Like *Gone Home*, *Sunset*
and *Virginia* invite players to embody the digital flâneuse, intersectional

female characters that wander through and witness virtual environments structured by literal and discursive frameworks of power. *Sunset* explores the constraints of this subject position when confined to a single high-rise apartment, while *Virginia* embraces a more agentive, radical interpretation of the digital flâneuse, highlighting player movement through multiple spaces and subjectivities.

Sunset and *Virginia*

Outside of a few standout titles such as *Gone Home* and *What Remains of Edith Finch*, the walking simulator genre is not typically associated with critical praise and commercial success. As of October 2017, *Gone Home* had sold more than 700,000 copies across several platforms and received a metacritic score of 86/100 on the PC.[24] *Edith Finch* was equally well received, earning a metacritic score of 89/100 on the PC. Instead of focusing on the most successful examples of the genre, however, this chapter examines two marginal titles that have not been well received by audiences. *Sunset* and *Virginia* received metacritic scores of only 66/100 and 77/100, respectively. *Sunset* reportedly only sold four thousand copies in its launch window, a dismal number for a commercial game that contributed to the closing of its developer.[25] Despite their lukewarm reception, attributed at least partially to the genre's reputation for being "boring," *Sunset* and *Virginia* provide key case studies from which to examine how walking simulators produce the digital flâneuse. Indeed, it is their deployment of marginalized, intersectional subjectivities and the way these characters move through space and interact with personal objects that provide these games with value beyond critical praise.

In *Sunset*, developed by the Belgian duo Michaël Samyn and Auriea Harvey, herself a woman of color, we play as Angela Burnes, a young Black woman and university-trained engineer from Baltimore, who works as a housekeeper in a high-rise penthouse in the fictional Republic of Anchuria. Having left the United States for South America because of the "stupidity" and "hate" occurring in the early 1970s, Angela finds herself working a job she dislikes in a "country going to shit." The name Anchuria comes from the O. Henry book *Cabbages and Kings* (1904), in which the term "banana republic" was coined. Stuck now in a virtual banana republic, Angela bears witness to a civil war between the repressive U.S.-backed regime of President Ricardo Miraflores and a group of revolutionaries, which includes her brother David. *Sunset* begins with Angela helping a wealthy and politically connected socialite and art dealer, Gabriel Ortega, move into a high-rise apartment and continues as Angela learns more about her employer and Anchuria's slide toward civil war. The game communicates the political strife through Angela's voice-over, her journal entries, the apartment's changing decor, and the transforming cityscape and audioscape outside its windows. While first-person shooters are known for their bombastic action, *Sunset* quarantines the player in a lifeless apartment while the "real" action happens off-screen. The game attempts to use the apartment as a locus through which to tell a larger story about political revolution, privilege, and identity.

Lacking overt action, *Sunset* produces a digital flâneuse through the player-character of Angela. The game explores the limitations of this subject position by forcing players to experience a social revolution only through a bird's-eye view from an apartment balcony, far removed from the fighting in the streets. Angela does brave the streets of the city, but these encounters happen off-screen, lost in the diegetic ellipses between playable game levels. Rather than enacting a fully realized digital flâneuse and challenging players to stroll through neighborhoods defined by civil strife and social upheaval, *Sunset* challenges the player with spatial confinement and highlights the tension between on-the-ground experiences of war and the detached form of witnessing afforded by wealth and privilege.

Sunset explores rather than challenges those systemic forces that often make public spaces such as city streets inhospitable to women or delimit women to support roles during political revolutions. The game does this by foregrounding Angela's complex relationship to her work as a domestic laborer. As a housekeeper, players are compelled to do menial labor while a political revolution erupts in the streets below. These tasks—ranging from vacuuming and dusting to washing dishes—make up the majority of the goals players must perform every time they reenter the apartment during their weekly cleaning appointments. The game deliberately juxtaposes the mundanity of these objectives with the growing political unrest outside, and with Angela's evolving relationship with Gabriel—an intimacy that is conveyed over time through handwritten notes (figure 3.1).

Sunset limits player interaction to walking slowly around the game's sole location, Ortega's large, modernist apartment, and to performing forgettable housekeeping chores and examining items. The reward for completing these tasks, other than crossing them off a list, is the commentary Angela provides, which elucidates the narrative, provides characterization,

3.1 Players in *Sunset* review their housekeeping duties as they ride the elevator to the penthouse.

and establishes the larger, diegetic world. *Sunset* highlights the inequitable class politics of Anchuria through Angela's cynical commentary and marginalized perspective as a Black housekeeper in a classist and racist South American country. Angela decries Ortega's fancy belongings, often calling them ugly and noting with derision how the sale of just one valuable could feed an entire family. At one point she opines, "The only thing that gives him any joy are the books and the little artifacts he rescues. In the Republic of Anchuria everyone suffers an affliction of the soul, rich and poor alike. For some it's meat on the table. For others, it's watching canvas burn." Cultural items scattered about Ortega's apartment reveal more insights about the owner's personality and the game's themes. Players earn achievements for discovering works of fiction, such as Aldous Huxley's *Brave New World* and Kurt Vonnegut's *Slaughterhouse-Five*, and nonfiction, including Brooks Adams's *Law of Civilization and Decay* and Raymond Williams's *Culture and Society*. Over the course of the game, Angela remotely constructs Gabriel Ortega's identity by making sense of his material belongings. According to the game's designers, depictions of the "ideal bachelor pad" featured in 1970s issues of *Playboy* influenced the design of Ortega's apartment. From his modernist and minimalist sensibilities to his taste in art, Ortega is presented in the game as an individual, cultured man of refined tastes, his bachelor pad similar to the one *Playboy* constructed against the perceived feminized suburbanization and conformity in the United States in the 1960s.[26] *Sunset* highlights Ortega's privilege and mobility through his perpetual absence, including his ability to momentarily seek refuge from the political strife abroad, while reminding players of their fixed place as a housekeeper within the walls of the apartment who must tend to his material belongings.

The player-character is caught between privilege and persecution, revolution and domestic labor, mobility and confinement—a contradictory status that further accentuates Angela's intersectionality. For example, Angela is limited to her role as a housekeeper in a high-rise apartment in *Sunset* but nevertheless plays a part in the country's revolution, channeling government secrets from Ortega to her brother and his rebel comrades. It is through this complex subjectivity—Angela's practicing of double-consciousness, as servant and revolutionary—that *Sunset* enacts many of its social and cultural critiques. Angela lambastes the excesses and contradictions of the wealthy, steals drinks on the job, and criticizes military bravado and hegemonic masculinity. At one point, while listening to the streets below, Angela comments, "The military parade is about to end. Oh, men and their desire to flex their muscles for each other." Players initiate this social and political commentary by traversing the apartment, bearing witness to its contents, noting the distant explosions and gunshots in the streets below, and continually confronting themselves as Angela in reflective surfaces.

Unlike many first-person games that do not render player bodies, *Sunset* spotlights Angela's physical form, using reflective surfaces such as elevator doors and windows to remind players who they are controlling. When the player is barred from certain rooms in the apartment, it is by glass doors that reflect Angela's face, dark skin, and Afro. Even when players take a break from work and relax on the master bed, the glossy ceiling reflects Angela's lounging body. Angela's natural hair and curvy form are integral to the game's subjectivity. Angela's Afro, in particular, reads well even in the player's shadow, which is cast across the apartment's surfaces. Rather than merely a reflection of Angela's fashion sense, however, highlighting her visage and Afro functions in *Sunset* to reclaim a lost history of political repression, revolutionary politics, and Black women's empowerment.[27] Through her vital reconnaissance, *Sunset*'s Angela arguably reconnects the Afro hairstyle to a revolutionary subjectivity, albeit one enacted through constrained wandering and witnessing.

The walking simulator genre, and its mechanical restraints, allows for the production of a subjectivity defined by spatial exploration, intersectionality, and an inherent critique of the hegemony of masculinity and violence in video games. *Sunset* enacts this subject position through a literal revolutionary character. Yet despite Angela's voice-over narration assuring us that she navigates the city's streets and checkpoints, players never move beyond the opulent apartment. As a game developed in Belgium, structured by individual days of domestic work, and concerned with the mundanity of everyday chores juxtaposed against questions of power, *Sunset* evokes the Belgian film *Jeanne Dielman, 23, quai du Commerce, 1080 Bruxelles* (1975). This "apartment plot" film explores the life of a woman and mother, confined to her house, over the course of three days as she routinely performs domestic duties while earning money as a sex worker by entertaining men in the evenings.[28] *Jeanne Dielman* ultimately concludes with its main character murdering her client, revealing the repressive conditions of her daily existence—both spatially, as she is confined to her house, and ideologically, as her choices are limited by a society structured and routinized under patriarchal rule. *Sunset* shares *Jeanne Dielman*'s interest in critiquing dominant gender roles. However, while both stories are restricted to domestic spaces, *Sunset* continually evokes the city beyond and below the player's view. *Sunset* edges toward a liberated digital flâneuse while exploring power as it relates to class, gender, race, and mobility, but ultimately the game never escapes the domestic prison at the center of its diegesis.

While *Sunset* explores the limitations of the digital flâneuse through a revolutionary domestic laborer, another walking simulator, *Virginia*, produces its contemplative and critical virtual stroller using a wholly different character type: an agent of the state. Yet even as *Virginia* produces a subjectivity imbricated with state power—a female FBI agent—the game equally explores the way that power shapes the gameworld and those characters who have the privilege of moving through it. Likewise, *Virginia* extends the detective work of *Sunset*'s Angela by making it central to the identity of its main character. As noted by scholars such as James Werner, the flâneur has shared many qualities with the classic detective character, as each makes a habit of blending into crowds, navigating the chaos of modernist cityscapes, and carefully observing details that others miss. As a newly minted FBI special agent, *Virginia*'s Anne Tarver continues the tradition of connecting mobility and observation to the work of detectives but subverts the classic trope by placing players in the body of a woman of color.

Even more than *Sunset*, *Virginia* strips away much of the interactivity expected of games and embraces a minimalist aesthetic to convey a tonally complex, dialogue-free, *Twin Peaks*–esque story. As Agent Tarver, players are sent to Kingdom, Virginia, to investigate the disappearance of a teenage boy while also investigating Anne's Latina partner, Maria Halperin.

3.2 Players inspect their appearance before an FBI graduation ceremony in *Virginia*.

Despite its narrative red herring concerning the missing boy, *Virginia* is deeply concerned with the solidarity of its leading female characters as they inhabit, investigate, and traverse the small Virginian town and find themselves subjected to systematic racism and exploitation.

As a silent game that relies on its orchestral soundtrack to convey its emotions and tones, *Virginia* reduces the player's point of view to a voiceless subjectivity. Because *Virginia* lacks the spoken commentary of *Sunset*, it deploys an archive of visual evidence to convey its story. Journal entries, photographs, microfiche, documents, and clothing: much of the game is spent examining these objects, highlighting the central conceit of detective work but, more important, the way our belongings provide biographical traces in our absence.

Virginia, like *Sunset*, foregrounds the main character's appearance by beginning the game with the player inspecting their reflection in a bathroom mirror (figure 3.2). Players see themselves as a woman of color who, after applying lipstick nervously, steps out onto a stage to graduate as an FBI agent. *Virginia* routinely places the player in front of mirrors, not only to illustrate the daily ritual of self-maintenance and the passing of time, but also to emphasize identification with this particular body. Agent Anne Tarver's distinct shadow can also be seen cast against floors and walls in many of the game's stylistically lit scenes. In Tarver's dream sequences, which contribute to the game's surreal experience, players have out-of-body experiences and can watch themselves sleeping on a bed or taking part in a cultish ritual.

While an agent of the state, Anne Tarver is nonetheless cast as other, particularly in the lily-white town of Kingdom, Virginia. Anne and her FBI partner, Maria, are among the only people of color in the town during their investigation. The enmity the town might hold for Anne emerges during a scene early in the game when players stop at a gas station to refuel. As players wait in the car for Maria to return, a blue convertible with three white teenagers pulls up. One of them knocks on Anne's window and flips her off before speeding away. This same privileged teenager, discovered to be a local acid dealer, later assaults Anne and Maria before being arrested.

Virginia's secondary storyline—Anne's internal affairs assignment to investigate her partner—conveys how systems of racial power run through society and serve to alienate people from one another. Anne must report on Maria's behavior to her white superiors. Near the end of the game, Anne imagines a future where she investigates a number of FBI agents. In this flash-forward sequence, players capitulate to dominant power structures and betray the trust of colleagues and subordinates in service to the corrupt, white FBI director. Anne is rewarded during this feverish montage with a series of promotions after investigating fellow agents, almost all of whom are also people of color. Intercut within this sequence are brief moments of Anne inspecting her reflection in mirrors, visibly tracking the physical toll that guilt takes on her for betraying personal trusts and acting as an agent of white authority. In this possible future, the game rewards Anne for her work by making her the new FBI director.

White identities are, in fact, linked to all stations of power in *Virginia*, including the FBI director, the local priest and police force, the city mayor, and army officers. The game alludes to the tacit collusion of white supremacy through fantasy sequences that place all of these disparate men together. For instance, in a dreamlike scene after Maria discovers that Anne is investigating her, Anne imagines the aforementioned men standing across a desk from her and reading approvingly the file that she has compiled on her partner. Later in the game, Anne discovers that Maria was investigating the FBI director, explaining why she is under scrutiny. Anne chooses not to betray her partner, and both women are jailed. The same group of men stare at the two women behind bars, representing a confluence of governmental, religious, and racial power that these two marginalized women cannot hope to overthrow.

Yet while *Virginia* highlights systems of power, it also never forgets that the avatars of such power are intersectional beings in their own right. Late in the game, players ingest a hit of LSD acquired from the violent drug dealer. In this bizarre final sequence, *Virginia* produces an almost transcendental intersectional subjectivity, where players briefly occupy the perspectives of key characters of power. As the police chief, players construct model boats.

As the mayor, players have an emotional breakdown in a photo booth. As the military officer, players pour whiskey into their morning coffee. As the corrupt FBI director, players eat a lonely dinner with their secretary; as the secretary, players comfort the FBI director, who is curled up into the fetal position on their lap. As the priest, players caress the wife of the game's missing child, Lucas, while she sits at their feet. *Virginia*'s rapid alteration in its final moments reminds us of the inescapable intersectionality of all subject positions. This humanizes but, importantly, does not fully redeem the men who collectively represent the matrix of domination in the game. Yet moving from one perspective to another signals that the digital flâneuse, beyond being an embodied (virtual) subjectivity in walking simulators, also provides the possibility to stroll among characters and subject positions through a contemplative, empathic engagement.

Conclusion

Game scholar Adrienne Shaw stresses that intersectional game studies needs to recognize that intersectionality encompasses more than siloed analyses of the matrix of domination and the marginalized identities that must navigate it. As Shaw suggests, "White, cisgender male, middle-class gamers/developers/characters are intersectional identities as much as Latinx, transgender women, working-class gamers/developers/characters are."[29] Treating all characters as intersectional beings involves recognizing "that people have different sides to their identity but also unpacks the implications those sides have in understanding the way their body moves through the world."[30] During its transcendental LSD sequence, *Virginia* suggests that even those figures representative of white authority have multiple intersecting identities and hidden aspects of their lives. While primarily grounding the player in Anne Tarver's body and experience, *Virginia* also stresses the multiple subjectivities of its nonplayer characters, a design decision few other games embrace. The walking simulator genre affords this subjectivity hopping, grounded as it is in the acts of witnessing and moving through spaces of power. The intersectional subjectivity that many walking simulators produce also becomes paradoxical positions between detached witnesses and identities that often stand out in otherwise homogenized communities. Angela's identity as an educated Black American woman uneasily coexists with her South American environment and position as a working-class housemaid. Likewise, Anne Tarver's identity as a woman of color matters in the mostly white Kingdom community, as does her identity as an FBI agent assigned to investigate other agents of color.

This chapter has theorized the digital flâneuse as an intersectional subject position engendered by walking simulator video games. *Sunset* and *Virginia* situate players within marginalized subjectivities that wander as detached but exposed witnesses through their gameworlds, which are rived with power dynamics. The digital flâneuse is an invitation for reflection; it is not some ready-made social panacea. This figure is neither a vehicle for what Lisa Nakamura has called identity tourism, or the appropriation of "racial identity without any of the risks associated with being a racial minority in real life,"[31] nor is it some spiritual guide for building empathy.[32] The agency afforded to players as digital flâneuses is limited; rather than consumption or domination, this subjectivity invites players to act as mobile witnesses to see and to move through virtual worlds from intersectional perspectives—whether they are divorced, working-class white men; young middle-class, college-educated white women; or professional women of color pulled between professional service and political solidarity.

II _ CINEMATIC URBAN INTERSECTIONS

BLURRING BOUNDARIES, EXPLORING INTERSECTIONS

Form, Genre, and Space in Shirley Clarke's *The Connection*

Shirley Clarke's career spanned decades and media and included dance films, fiction-nonfiction hybrids, and videotaped performance art and theater. Her work illustrates a deep understanding of cinematic form, often blurring the lines between experimental fiction and nonfiction conventions; diegetic and nondiegetic cinematic performance modes; and different, seemingly unconnected genres (e.g., the dance film and the city symphony). From *Bridges-Go-Round* (1958), her audiovisual symphony of New York City's bridges, through her later video experiments shot on the roof of the Chelsea Hotel, Clarke used the city as an active participant in the action, reminding audiences not only of New York's built environment but also of the diversity of experiences and individuals existing within the urbanscape. The city functions as more than locations for Clarke's filmmaking, however; it was, in essence, the site of intersecting aesthetic and political forces that laid the groundwork for her multimedia explorations of form and genre. It also provided the palette for her complex understanding of gender, race, and representation.

In her groundbreaking work on intersectionality, Kimberlé Crenshaw uses spatial metaphors—traffic intersections, basements, bodies—to describe the complex web of discrimination Black women experience daily.[1] Embedded in Crenshaw's work, and this essay more broadly, is an understanding of space, metaphorical and literal, as a crucial construct in the determination of identity. Individuals move through and inhabit different—sometimes overlapping, sometimes contrasting—spaces determined by geography, class, race, ethnicity, gender, and body ability. Urban space in particular intensifies such experiences, especially in a location such as New York, where millions of individuals live in close proximity, intersecting and colliding daily. The following discussion, therefore, understands New York City as more than mere background for Clarke's filmmaking. Instead, it posits the city as the site of crisscrossing aesthetic, social, economic, and political forces that enabled a young, wealthy dancer and daughter of Jewish immigrants to come into contact with a host of artists, performers, and scholars spanning the spectrum of race, ethnicity, gender, sexuality, and class. The result of such intersections and collaborations is films that make connections through difference and tell marginalized stories through hybrid forms.

The following begins with a brief consideration of Clarke's first shorts before moving on to a discussion of her debut feature, *The Connection* (1961). These early films evidence the formal and narrative hybridity that fascinated the filmmaker throughout her career and act as retrospective palimpsests of the aesthetic sensibilities and social consciousness of her later feature films. It is widely known that Clarke trained as a dancer before moving into film in the early 1950s, after studying filmmaking with the experimental filmmaker Hans Richter at City College. Clarke's first films, including *Dance in the Sun* (1953) and *Bullfight* (1955), illustrate her continuing interest in dance, along with her desire to create a cinematic choreography through camera movement and editing, one on full display in *The Connection*. *Bullfight*, for example, features Anna Sokolov, choreographer and founding member of the Actors Studio. The film eschews static long shots and instead cuts to close-ups and medium shots of Sokolov's face and upper body in the midst of movement. Moments of dance are intercut with footage from a bullfight, with the dancer's actions sometimes complementing, sometimes contradicting the death dance between the bull and the matador. As the contest between animal and human intensifies, Clarke adds blurred crowd shots and increasingly rapid editing to build tension. Overall, camera and editing engage in choreography of movement among dancer, bull, and matador that produces more than a recording of either a dance performance or a bullfight. *Bullfight* is itself a performance of cinematic choreography.

Clarke's ability to transcend genre by making a dance film that was itself a performance piece was also influenced by her kinesthetic understanding of movement and gesture, which contributed to her talent as a film editor. After making *Dance in the Sun*, for example, Clarke reminisced that she had discovered the "choreography of editing."[2] Her intuitive under-

4.1 Still image from *Melting Pot*.

standing of cinematic movement via editing was honed a few years later when she began working with the documentarians Willard Van Dyke, D. A. Pennebaker, and Richard Leacock on a series of short silent films commissioned for the United States Pavilion at the 1958 Brussels World Fair.[3] While Clarke's main task was to edit footage shot by others, she also filmed (with her husband Bert Clarke) and edited three shorts of her own. One of these loops, *Melting Pot* (figure 4.1), demonstrates the filmmaker's developing skill with editing and her growing interest in stretching the boundaries of the documentary form through montage aesthetics.

Melting Pot is intended to showcase the nation's diversity through footage of a variety of Americans going about their day. The film is organized around arrangements of people interacting with one another: men with men, women with women, men with women, women with children, men with children, children with children, and so on. The subjects, ranging in age, gender, race, and ethnicity, are tightly framed, with little surrounding area shown. People often intersect in the frame to create a sense of intimacy and community. They converse, laugh, argue, touch, and kiss one another in a world made even more vibrant by saturated colors that highlight different spaces, clothing, and skin tones. Rather than maintaining strict borders, the montage structure moves across racial and ethnic boundaries, ending, almost like a haiku, with a shot of a small white child waving an

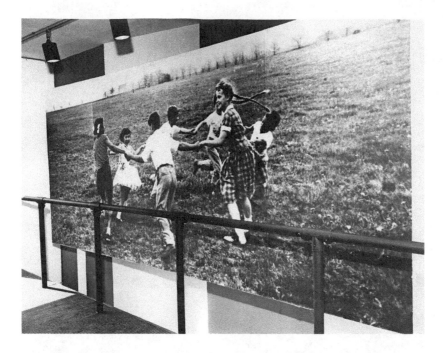

4.2 Photograph from Brussels exhibition, "Unfinished Business." © 1958 by Leo Lionni. Used with the permission of the Lionni family.

American flag. Besides projecting a unified nation, such aesthetics suggest how intersectional frameworks can be revealed with subtlety and beauty through form.

Melting Pot's message of American unity and collaboration across lines of difference was ironic, given that the American pavilion also was the focus of controversy surrounding an exhibition, "Unfinished Business," that explored in part the nation's ongoing struggle with segregation. One particularly contested piece was an enlarged photograph of children of different races, arranged in a circle and holding hands (figure 4.2), while another was of a mixed-race dance featuring an African American man and a white woman—similar visual matter as that projected in *Melting Pot* and Clarke's other shorts.[4] The aim of the exhibition's organizers was to acknowledge the nation's ills at a time when footage of civil rights protests in places such as Little Rock, Arkansas, was being broadcast globally. After pressure from southern politicians and other interest groups, the designers were forced to close the exhibition; remove most of materials on racial inequality in the United States; and reopen the exhibition with a different, less controversial focus. After the redesign of the exhibition, the loop films contained some of the only images of racial diversity in the American pavilion, and even these were shown on small screens embedded in different displays.[5] That Clarke's loops were allowed to stay, however, suggests their subtle ability to cross representational boundaries.

The Brussels loops reveal Clarke's understanding of cinema as a place where different genres, aesthetics, and art forms could intersect. The loops were silent, for example, and yet music was an important structural influence. According to Clarke, "We were told there would be no sound, and the one thing we couldn't do was jazz. So I made them all jazz."[6] This was not simply an editing strategy. Jazz was most commonly linked with urban African American artistic practices, and Clarke's inclusion of it in even such a subtle form worked, like her montage linkages as a whole, as a (in)visible political statement. Such links were more fully developed in *Bridges*, which began as another of Clarke's Brussels loops.[7] Like the other Brussels films, *Bridges* was shot in color and conveyed a dynamic sense of American life through its connective infrastructure and rhythmic editing. While the loops aimed to showcase "a colorful Americana, and to minimize that which is commonplace," the piece's connections proved to be too conceptual for the government bureaucrats who had commissioned it.[8] In the end, it was excluded from the American pavilion for its abstraction of material reality, an irony given that the Brussels Experimental Film Festival ran at the same time as the fair, and Clarke's other loops included more incendiary messages.

Freed from the restrictions of the U.S. State Department, Clarke reworked what became known as *Bridges-Go-Round* into a city symphony, a rhythmic exploration of New York's built environment that stressed the connective tissues yoking disparate parts of the metropolis and, by relation, the state and the nation together. Aesthetic freedom also meant that Clarke could add a musical accompaniment to the film's visual symphony and finally complete the first of her many jazz films. Two soundtracks were added: an electronic piece composed by Louis and Bebe Barron and a jazz and vocal arrangement by Teo Macero, commissioned when the director could not initially secure rights to the original Barron piece.[9] The film's experimental nature—in which "bridges become plastic materials for a highly abstract subjective study in structures and movements"[10]—was not a surprise, since the director had been playing with form all along. Such experimentation was also a reflection of her New York surroundings, which included documentarians and many independent filmmakers associated with what would soon be known as the New American Cinema Group. Like many of her filmmaking colleagues, Clarke was interested in experimental documentary-fiction hybrids, and *Bridges-Go-Round* was one of many experiments leading to her more extended and self-conscious efforts with *The Connection*.

Focused on breaking down formal boundaries, playing with genre, and self-consciously exploring performance, *The Connection* also develops Clarke's nascent exploration of American race relations first seen in the Brussels loops and *A Scary Time* (1961), a short film she made for the United Nations Children's Fund (UNICEF). *A Scary Time* film combines fiction and nonfiction modes in a public service announcement outlining UNICEF's global role in stemming childhood hunger and disease. First-person voice-overs of different American children talking about Halloween are intercut with footage of youth suffering from malnutrition and sickness in various African and Asian countries served by UNICEF, an editing structure that links American plenty with global good works. *A Scary Time*, like *Melting Pot*, creates a shared racial and ethnic space through a seemingly natural mixture of people, and both films echo Helen Levitt's *In the Street* (1948), especially their scenes of children at play.[11] While Clarke's early films exhibit elements of an intersectionality of subject and form, *The Connection* serves as a vital entry point into understanding her career-long interest in cinematic hybridity.

The Connection is an adaptation of an infamous experimental play of the same name by Jack Gelber that was staged by New York's Living Theater Company in 1959. The play tells the story of a mixed-race group of junkies and musicians who are gathered together in a downtown New York apartment waiting for their "connection," a dealer named Cowboy, to arrive with drugs. The production was staged as a play within a play, with the fictional play's producer and writer explaining to the audience that they are trying to stage a performance focusing on actual drug addicts. Other characters address the crowd, as well, and mingle with audience members during intermission (sometimes asking for drug money). The actual audience was also the audience for the play within the play, with the result that the "conventional invisible fourth wall between the stage and the audience appears and disappears."[12]

Clarke was not new to adaptation, given her work in dance film, which in its simplest terms translates choreography to the screen. Yet the Gelber piece was different; already a self-conscious act of political theater that "broke through the proscenium," asking theatergoers to participate in the experiences of drug addicts and assorted lowlifes, the play challenged

Clarke to create a similar reflexivity and intersectionality in film form.[13] Gelber initiated the work by transforming the play within a play's producer and writer figures into, respectively, a documentary director and his cinematographer.[14] The play within a play became a film within a film, with characters acknowledging the cinematic audience through direct address. Clarke's experience as a dancer, an editor, an experimental filmmaker, and a documentarian helped turn the play into a feature-length exploration of filmmaking practice and postwar American disillusionment that, like her earlier films, picked at borders, connections, and intersections.

Clarke's adaptation turns on a number of intersections within and between the stage and the screen. In his essay on the film, Angelos Koutsourakis argues that *The Connection* offers a "post-Brechtian version of Gelber's 'post-Brechtian' play," where the latter includes a "performing style that downplays the reproduction of a text and shifts emphasis from the text to the performance." As a result, "The text becomes a material for performative exploration."[15] In other words, each staging of the play, including its intentional slippage between character and actor, and between performance and "reality," depended on context-specific factors. For example, the play includes references to baseball teams that changed according to time and place. Clarke, therefore, was already faced with a highly self-conscious text, one grounded in the instantaneity and originality of its live performance. How, then, to capture these elements in the fixed spatiotemporal experience of the cinema, where once something is recorded it acquires permanence? The adaptation continues in the vein of the play through Clarke's employment of a moving camera that makes a performance out of the filmmaking process. In this self-consciousness, *The Connection* exhibits characteristics of what Ted Barron has called "performative realist cinema," where "the actions of an individual are staged for presentation to an audience" and "performance [is] a central concern . . . [in] filmic representation."[16] The camera therefore adds an element of immediacy to the viewing experience because spectators infer the three-dimensionality of the space even more than a static theater audience might. While they cannot match the variability of each individual staging of the play, such aesthetics contribute to a sense of being "in the text" as it happens.

The Connection exhibits a shift in Clarke's filmmaking style—a move that was partially influenced by its source text but that may have been affected just as much by people either directly or indirectly involved in the production. Despite the fact that she made kinetic dance films and experimental shorts, the "movement" in these earlier titles—including her collaboration with Willard Van Dyke on *Skyscraper* in 1959—was based primarily on her skills as an editor, which itself was influenced by her background in dance. As Clarke herself said of the early pieces, "I became a good director by becoming an excellent film editor to cover up the fact of my really rotten camera work."[17] Clarke did not film *The Connection*. It was shot by Arthur J. Ornitz, a seasoned cameraperson with film and television credits dating back to 1940. Ornitz was well versed in nonfiction and fiction modes. For example, his first project, *Power and the Land* (Joris Ivens, dir., 1940), co-shot with Floyd Crosby, combined relatively conventional documentary voice-over with scripted re-creations by the featured subjects. By the time he joined the production, Ornitz had alternated between television shows and low-budget B films shot in New York City.[18] There is no doubt that the combination of his cinematography and Clarke's editing contributed to *The Connection*'s cinematic fluidity.

The Connection opens with a written disclaimer and voice-over by J. J. Burden (Roscoe Lee Browne), the film within a film's African American cinematographer, explaining that he edited the footage together "as honestly as possible" after the white director, Jim Dunn (William Redfield), left the project. The next twelve minutes of the film involve the apartment's main resident, a white junkie named Leach, introducing the other characters, a mixed-race group of musicians and junkies. Each character speaks directly to the camera, either adding to Leach's introduction or rambling nonsense, before Dunn appears on-screen and directs his subjects to "just act naturally." As he interacts with the eight assorted African American and white (one who is coded as Jewish through his name and two who might be gay) musicians and addicts in the apartment, we learn that he is "not interested in making a Hollywood picture." Instead, he is just trying to make "an honest, human document" of the experiences of a group of drug addicts. While he mentions Sergei Eisenstein and Robert Flaherty, revealing his cinephile tendencies, the film within a film's reflexivity suggests a more interactive form of filmmaking than either the references to Soviet montage or early documentary suggest.

Based on this scene and others in which Dunn and Burden can be either heard or seen through what effectively registers as the camera's point of view, it is no surprise that the film is often connected to cinema verité. In many ways, *The Connection*'s film within a film follows the model of *Chronique d'un été* (1961), Jean Rouch and Edgar Morin's self-conscious study of a group of Parisians of different classes, races, genders, and ethnicities that acknowledged the directors as the film's catalysts and included its subjects in the production. As its moniker suggests, cinema verité was believed to be, in the words of Dunn, a more "honest" documentation that lifted the veil, or broke the fourth wall, on nonfiction subject matter. And yet even in this opening scene, *The Connection* disabuses the audience of the assumption of unmediated documentary truth. Such self-conscious rendering of the documentarian reveals Clarke's questioning of more traditional documentary form, an attitude honed through her collaborations—as one of the only women involved—with Van Dyke, Pennebaker, and Leacock on the Brussels loops; on *Skyscraper*; and through Filmmakers, Inc., a cooperative formed by the group and Albert Maysles in 1958.

The Connection's self-conscious approach to documentary is more complex, however, than Clarke's relationship with Filmmakers, Inc., first suggests. First, while Pennebaker, Leacock, and Maysles were producing a novel form of documentary film, it was not strictly what is now understood as "cinema verité." The year before *The Connection* was made, for example, Pennebaker, Leacock, and Maysles worked on Robert Drew's *Primary*, one of the first films associated with the Direct Cinema movement. The film, about the Wisconsin primary race in 1960 between John F. Kennedy and Hubert Humphrey, was groundbreaking. Using handheld cameras and portable sound equipment, the crew followed the candidates and provided an intimate look at public figures, one that had not been seen before. Footage was cut together without voice-over commentary or other nondiegetic sound, resulting in a documentary that seemingly allowed audiences to construct their own meaning from the film. According to Leacock, such a style allowed for the discovery of "some important aspect of our society by watching our society, by watching how things really happen as opposed to the social image that people hold about the ways things are supposed to happen."[19] The lack of commentary, the moving camera, and the prevalence of long takes formally suggested an absence of a director's mediating presence, one with the potential to shift marginalized subjectivities into the center.

Unlike many of her peers, who believed in the objective possibilities of this form of documentary, Clarke "contested the idea that cinema verité was a reliable replacement for traditional documentary filmmaking. She questioned the possibility of clinical objectivity when subjects are interacting with the camera and the filmmaker is shaping the final product through editing" (this, perhaps, because she was a skilled and sensitive editor herself).[20] The film's opening disclaimer is just one indication that *The Connection* was not going to fully adhere to either cinema verité or

Direct Cinema dogma because it neither allows Dunn the role of catalyst nor overlooks his presence in the text. Indeed, Dunn is utterly unreliable: he not only reveals the manipulation of his subjects (via direction and supplying cash for drugs), but also becomes enmeshed in the events by shooting up heroin, thereby becoming a twisted version of a Flaherty-like director who embeds with his subjects. By the film's conclusion (or even its beginning, if we remember the opening text identifying Burden as responsible for the final film), Dunn becomes a, if not *the*, subject of the film, leaving Burden with the added responsibilities (burden) of director and editor.

The documentary inflections of the film extend beyond its relationship to cinema verité and Direct Cinema. For example, Clarke's productive collaborations with Van Dyke provide other insights into *The Connection*'s fiction-nonfiction hybridity. Van Dyke was a photographer, cinematographer, and documentarian who began making films in the 1930s and was associated with a number of left-leaning film cooperatives, including NYKINO, Frontier Film Group, and American Documentary Films. Two of his earliest films, *The River* (1938) and *The City* (1939), for which he served, respectively, as cinematographer and codirector, are prime examples of the collaborative nature of American documentary filmmaking during the Roosevelt administration. *The River*, for example, brought Van Dyke together with the documentarian Pare Lorentz, the cinematographer Floyd Crosby, and the composer Virgil Thompson; commissioned for the 1939 World's Fair, the film was codirected by Ralph Steiner and featured a screenplay by Louis Mumford and Pare Lorentz and a score by the composer Aaron Copland. There is no doubt that Van Dyke's collaborative and transmedial approach to filmmaking influenced Clarke, along with other New York–based filmmakers, in the 1950s and '60s. As Ted Barron argues, for example, the roots of the "performative realism" associated with American Independent Cinema from this time stretch back to the 1930s and '40s, not only in person, but also in spirit and style.[21]

Another of Clarke's influences was the New American Cinema Group, of which she was a founding member and, like her other collaborations, one of very few women involved. The group was established in late September 1960 when the filmmaker and critic Jonas Mekas and the producer Lewis Allen invited twenty-one independent filmmakers in New York to pool their interests. In 1961 the group published its first "statement" in *Film Culture*, critiquing the "product [Hollywood] film" as "morally corrupt, aesthetically obsolete, thematically superficial, temperamentally boring."[22]

The signatories proposed, instead, a low-budget cinema of personal expression that was free of censorship and used alternative forms of financing and distribution. Clarke's *The Connection* was a prime example of this new form of cinema. Produced by Allen, who employed a profit-sharing approach to attract backers, the film was, as Mekas described elsewhere, "an attempt to put across on the commercial screen the new content, the new reality" of the cinema.[23]

The New American Cinema Group produced a wide variety of films, from documentaries to experimental shorts and features that, like Clarke's films, often blurred the lines between fiction and nonfiction. Preceding Clarke in feature-length fiction-nonfiction hybrids was her fellow group member Lionel Rogosin, whose *On the Bowery* (1956) and *Come Back, Africa* (1959) combined cinematic realism and social consciousness through such a blend. *On the Bowery*, for example, is Rogosin's examination of New York City's skid row area as presented through the stories of three residents. Marketed as a documentary, the film combines nonfiction footage of the Bowery's people and places with loosely scripted scenes taken from the life stories of subjects who often tell their own stories on-screen. What made the film *new* was that it borrowed from documentary conventions—like Flaherty, Rogosin spent time on the Bowery studying his subjects—but presented its subject matter through contemporary fiction and nonfiction aesthetics that, for example, allowed their experiences to be conveyed in their own voices—in effect, looking like Direct Cinema while almost its opposite. The result is a sympathetic portrayal of formerly ordinary Americans struggling with addiction.[24]

In an essay published in *Commentary* in 1962, Harris Dienstfrey argued: "For all the generally liberal or radical orientation of The New American Cinema, few pictures concern themselves with politics directly." Instead, "Society hovers like some malevolent ghost that must be exorcised. It is the object of the bitterest concern."[25] Like Rogosin's *On the Bowery*, *The Connection* makes no explicit connection to politics. It nevertheless takes a complex approach to its subject, particularly around issues of authorship and race, and in this way, like *Melting Pot*, it is more political than it first appears. First, its choice of subject matter—addiction, beat culture, jazz music—is wholly homegrown rather than "foreign." Second, it treats its subjects as matter of fact rather than as exoticized others (despite Dunn's efforts to do otherwise). In doing so, it questions the aesthetic, political, class, gendered, and racial bias inherent in any director's assumption of either personal or aesthetic objectivity.

Dunn's embodied presence in the frame reminds viewers of the (het-ero)norm behind the camera—one that is white, male, and privileged and entirely different from the nondiegetic Clarke and the diegetic Burden. The text repeatedly reminds us of the Burden's authorial role in the pro-duction, first through the opening disclaimer, which explicitly names him as its author, and via off-screen sound and camera movement—we hear his voice, and his point of view controls the image (he holds the camera for the majority of the film). Most of Burden's dialogue is a re-sponse to Dunn's directions and he rarely interacts with the characters in the apartment. One moment of interaction, however, is telling. Early in the film, while the characters criticize and tease Dunn for his artistic pomposity and outsider status, Jackie, one of the musicians, approaches the camera and challenges Burden over his involvement: "You sure have changed since Harlem. . . . Is your name going to be on this film?" Burden's response, "You've changed, too," is more than a rejoinder to a perceived slight; it also suggests a closer relationship between filmmaker and subject than that enjoyed by Dunn. Later it is revealed that Dunn has access to the group only through Jackie and Burden's previous his-tory, thereby suggesting, as well, Burden's enabling role in the project. If anybody is a catalyst, it is Burden.

For most of *The Connection*, Burden remains silent and off-screen (though never fully invisible because of the camera). During these times, especially when Dunn is incapacitated by heroin, the film comes the closest to resembling the unmediated effect of Direct Cinema. The camera is fluid, following characters around what becomes a three-dimensional space and suggesting Burden's privileged access to the story: he blends in with the subjects. Yet *The Connection* ultimately disallows viewers the voyeuristic pleasure enabled by this seemingly unfettered gaze: not only do characters play to the camera, but at times we are reminded of the filmmaker's bodily presence. One such example is crucial in understanding how *The Connec-tion* troubles the assumptions of objectivity embedded in the documentary project. Near the end of the film, after the drugs have arrived, Leach presses Cowboy for another hit. As he shoots up—the first instance of the action shown on-screen—there is an abrupt cut to a closer shot with Burden's reflection appearing in the window behind Leach (figure 4.3). The three-dimensionality of the image, with Leach in the foreground and Burden simultaneously off-screen and in the background, results in an effect that places the cameraman both in and yet removed from the diegesis. As Leach begins to overdose, Burden keeps the camera running, self-consciously re-

4.3 Burden reflected in the window.

minding the viewers that what is on-screen is, in the end, controlled by the one holding the camera.

The Connection's self-conscious aesthetics and liberal politics circulated both within and outside the text. The film was, for example, loosely connected to a certain type of downtown New York "hipsterdom" in its relationship to beat culture—via Gelber most directly, but also through Clarke's connections to other downtown figures, including Alan Ginsberg and Andy Warhol—and jazz music, which are used as a structuring component of the film's aesthetics.[26] The film's focus on social misfits, its beat temperament, and its inclusion of jazz and recognizable jazz musicians are direct borrowings from Gelber's play, which has been described as "a play within a play within a jazz concert."[27] But Clarke was no stranger to jazz musicians or jazz films, as is suggested by her work with the Barons and Teo Macero on *Bridges-Go-Round* and other films, and *The Connection* elicits a continuation of her interest in the choreography of image and music, one now featuring African American musicians, including Jackie McLean and Freddie Reed. Ornitz's camera glides in and around characters, keeping in "verité" character while also providing the music and musicians a rhythmic visual platform that matches the music's energy. Clarke's editing, always sensitive to rhythm and movement, contributes to the fluidity of the camerawork and soundtrack through the film's multiple musical interludes, where, like a backstage musical, the music is fully integrated into the narrative. Just as it is a self-conscious documentary, *The Connection* is a self-conscious jazz film, one of the first of its kind. Unlike the Brussels films, which disallowed music and, in the broader exhibition, racial mixing, *The Connection*'s aesthetic hybridity, diegetic and nondiegetic, is a political statement in and of itself.

Deconstructing the film's embedded politics becomes even more interesting if we take into account its surrounding cultural and industrial context. As discussed earlier, at this time the United States was experiencing increasingly violent protests over desegregation, with the battle of the "Unfinished Business" exhibition in Brussels a reminder of the threat that even seemingly benign photographs of different children at play could present to American spectators.[28] During the same time, however, Hollywood was making some attempts to integrate the film industry—after pressure from civil rights groups such as the National Association for the Advancement of Colored People. These efforts resulted in a number of low-budget "message movies" focusing on American racism through narratives of noble Black characters seeking equality in all-white worlds. Handcuffed by the Production Code, the films seldom provided real solutions to racism, infrequently presented diverse casts on equal footing, and were never directed by African American filmmakers. We therefore cannot underestimate the subtle or not-so-subtle threat presented by *The Connection*: made by a white woman romantically involved with the film's African American costar, Carl Lee, and featuring an African American director and a mixed-race cast and crew—many of them recognizable jazz musicians, some (McLean) with widely publicized arrests for drug possession— the film broke down multiple barriers while also building bridges across different constituencies.[29]

The Connection serves as a fascinating example of New York independent filmmaking in the late 1950s and early 1960s. At once enmeshed in a documentary tradition stretching over three decades, and as many years of experimental filmmaking history, the film is about more than a group of musicians and junkies waiting for a fix. Collaborative in spirit and in practice, the film's narrative maps a variety of artistic and urban connections and intersections: uptown and downtown, Black and white, observer and participant. Such linkages and border crossings extend to genre and form, with dance, theater, and novelistic devices adapted to film, the blurring of the boundaries between fiction and nonfiction, and an overall self-consciousness of storytelling techniques rooted in Clarke's early experimental and nonfiction shorts and developed through her relationships with filmmakers associated with documentary, with the New American Cinema Group, and with other artists connected to the city's downtown art and performance scenes. Indeed, Clarke's films are a product of an intersecting network of people, aesthetics, and industrial practices located in New York during the mid-twentieth century. They are more than multimedia; they are intersectional in construction, content, form, and message.

CHAPTER FIVE

Jacqueline Sheean

INTERSECTIONS IN MADRID'S PERIPHERY

Cinematic Cruising in Eloy de la Iglesia's
La semana del asesino (1972)

> Nowhere, unless perhaps in dreams, can the phenomenon of the
> boundary be experienced in a more originary way than in cities.
> **Walter Benjamin**, *The Arcades Project*

The credit sequence of Eloy de la Iglesia's *La semana del asesino* (1972) begins with a high-angle establishing shot.[1] The camera pans over a few old plaster buildings surrounded by unpaved roads and empty dirt lots, while brand-new high-rise apartments loom in the background. This nearly 180-degree panning survey of a Madrid suburb provides the lay of the land and contains what Giuliana Bruno has called a "cartographic transference," a mapping impulse that "establishes spatial parameters" and situates the viewer in space.[2] The cartographic panning stops over one house that seems particularly isolated, and we see children playing soccer in the empty lot nearby (figure 5.1). Then, with a zoom, de la Iglesia takes us through a skylight and into the living room of the dilapidated house to introduce us to our protagonist, Marcos (Vicente Parra), who reclines on a couch. The camera movement— from the totalizing overview of the neighborhood to the micro-cartography of the living room—illustrates the way that the gaze of neighbors can traverse private space. In this case, the seemingly self-contained private dwelling is actually "porous and permeable."[3] Until here, the editing seems to function according to the cartographic impulse described by Bruno. However, the film soon subverts the totalizing conventions of the cartographic establishing shot. A jarring reverse shot up to the fourteenth-floor balcony exposes Néstor (Eusebio Poncela), a voyeuristic neighbor, as he surveys the neighborhood below through a set of binoculars (figure 5.2). The shot thus links Néstor's panoptic gaze with the film's cartographic establishing shot.

The opposing high and low positions presented in this opening sequence stand in for the pronounced social incongruities of late-Francoist Madrid, calling particular attention to the stark divide between the bourgeois and the working classes. The camera maps these socioeconomic disparities onto the urban geography, both horizontal and vertical. If we zoom out again to the panning shot, we are able to visualize Madrid's divided geography, in which the geographic limits of streets and parks serve as partitions of socioeconomic status. The zones of new urban development contrast sharply with the run-down buildings and dirt lots of the shantytown. To echo Walter Benjamin's reflections, geographical and figurative boundaries come together in a striking manner in cities. Indeed, the explicit physical boundaries formed by streets, railroad crossings, or rivers often mirror the social borders of class, race, or identity. Boundaries serve to contain, to enclose, and to exclude. Yet they also imply the possibility of an intersection, as the demarcation of borders posits a space of meeting between groups. Similarly, while La semana del asesino traces a visual geography of the socioeconomic boundaries of Madrid in the 1970s, it also reveals intersections. The film shows how boundaries may be permeated and contested through the tactic of walking, such as during the late-night strolls taken by Néstor and Marcos or the camera movement that allows the spectator themselves to "walk" the city. Both narratively and phenomenally, the film is a form of urban journey, a mode of experiencing the very fabric of the city and of crossing its borders.

Set in 1972 in one of the radial housing developments of late-Francoist Madrid as Spain teeters on the precipice of its transition to global postmodernity, the film takes place on the periphery—historically, geographically, and socially.[4] A periphery is not simply an edge or an outer limit but a space conditioned by social, political, and cultural marginalization. To this end, the writers of Diccionario de las periferias argue that a series of factors constitute a peripheral space, including lack of resources, institutional abandonment, systematic exclusion, fear or suspicion regarding inhabitants, and inequality both within the periphery and in relation to the center.[5] Peripheries thus form both spatial and metaphorical boundaries; they mark zones of exclusion. As Benjamin observes, such boundaries are experienced in an originary way in cities and in dreams. To this I would add that film, too, allows for a primary experience of the boundary. This chapter then examines how La semana del asesino maps the lived space of Madrid's periphery both as a set of boundaries and as a set of intersections.

5.1 A cartographic shot that maps the socioeconomic disparities of Madrid's periphery. The new high-rise development contrasts sharply with Marcos's dilapidated home.

The film was marketed sensationally as a horror movie. When it was first shown at the Berlin Film Festival in 1972, the distributors reportedly provided the audience with sick bags.[6] Yet *La semana del asesino* mixes elements of gruesome horror with trenchant social criticism. The narrative draws attention to the alienation generated by peripheral urban developments and social marginalization. De la Iglesia would continue to expose the issues of marginalized urban populations over the course of his career. The Basque director became one of the most notable exponents of the understudied Spanish film cycle known as *cine quinqui*, a cinema largely characterized by the portrayal of urban delinquency, drug use, and prostitution.[7] In addition, *La semana del asesino* is the first of de la Iglesia's films to deal with homosexuality, another theme that would recur throughout his oeuvre. While a gay relationship is only implied in *La semana del asesino*, later films such as *The Deputy* (1978) and *Hidden Pleasures* (1977) feature explicitly gay characters and relationships.[8] As Paul Julian Smith notes, de la Iglesia's cinema contains complex interplay between Marxist politics and homosexual desire.[9] *La semana del asesino* in particular shows how sexuality is inflected by class and politics.

While de la Iglesia's formal and aesthetic decisions—particularly, the use of montage, eye-line matches, and high- and low-angle shots—map the socioeconomic disparities of the periphery, the director's emphasis on movement offers another lens through which to explore these divisions. The two opposing viewpoints represented by the high-rise and shantytown mirror

5.2 A reverse shot exposes the voyeuristic Néstor (Eusebio Poncela) on his fourteenth-floor balcony.

Michel de Certeau's conceptual pair of the voyeur and the walker. The film demonstrates how cruising, a model of homoerotic desire and a queered form of de Certeau's walking, can offer an opposing perspective to the voyeur. In presenting a mobile cinematics of homoerotic desire, de la Iglesia's film develops a form of cinematic cruising and imagines a perspective that is different from the voyeur's totalizing panopticism. The film traces an alternative geography beyond Madrid's circumscribed boundaries to reveal the city's intersections. Following Kimberlé Crenshaw's original coinage of the term, I consider intersectionality both literally, as a spatial configuration, and metaphorically, as a way of understanding the way in which subjects face varied forms of marginalization.[10] Cruising thus presents a mechanism for mapping the complex, and often clandestine, mingling of identities in urban space—namely, class, sexuality, and political identities.

Conceived Space

To understand the periphery of Madrid, one must return to the post–Spanish Civil War history of urban planning and social housing.[11] As the historian Julius Ruiz has shown, the Franco dictatorship harbored antipathy toward Spain's urban areas, as they had presented the greatest challenges to the nationalist uprising during the civil war. As the nation's capital both before and after the war, the city of Madrid in particular reflected a tension between liberalism and conservatism, industry and tradition. Drawn by employment opportunities, nearly two million Spaniards migrated to Madrid from the countryside in the 1950s and '60s, doubling its population.[12] While the dictatorship had anticipated substantial urban growth, the city still lacked available housing and was not prepared to absorb such large numbers of migrants.[13] The resulting housing shortage became a significant problem and set the backdrop for popular comedies such as *The Tenant* (José Antonio Nieves Conde, dir., 1958) and *The Executioner* (Luis García Berlanga, dir., 1963), which exposed the precarity city dwellers faced.[14] Influenced by such films, de la Iglesia set out to make his first explicitly ideological, "almost militant" film with *La semana del asesino*.[15]

While for Nieves Conde and Berlanga urban problems were the source of dark comedy, for de la Iglesia the socioeconomic inequality and the housing crisis in Madrid provide the context for a horror film. Indeed, the housing problem would get worse before it got better, and by 1975 an estimated 47 percent of the population lived in inadequate or substandard living conditions and at least 35,000 "infra-dwellings" like those shown in the film existed.[16] Yet this was also the period of Spain's so-called economic miracle, a boom in economic growth and industrialization from 1959 to 1974 in which the country's gross national product grew at one of the highest rates in the world. *La semana del asesino* reveals the underside of the much-lauded economic miracle by presenting the violent contrasts of Madrid's uneven urban development and focusing on those left behind by the country's newfound prosperity. The film's juxtaposition of substandard housing and the modern high-rises illustrates "how the socially abject can filter through the cosmetic façade of bourgeois modernity."[17] For de la Iglesia, the uncanny proximity between the socially abject infra-dwellings and the glossy bourgeois high-rises creates the perfect horror setting.

De la Iglesia was not alone in merging social critique with horror. Indeed, many Spanish directors of the period saw the horror genre as an opportunity to question and critique the dominant values of Francoism, as exemplified by films such as *The Blood Splattered Bride* (Vicente Aranda, dir., 1972) and *The Legend of Blood Castle* (Jorge Grau, dir., 1973).[18] Most Spanish horror films during this period were transnational productions, as the global genre was cheap to make and easy to export, consumable by audiences both at home and abroad.[19] *La semana del asesino*, for example, was filmed in both English and Spanish with an international cast and later redubbed in both languages. However, unlike Aranda's and Grau's films,

La semana del asesino does not present a generic setting. Instead, the film unfolds in what is recognizably the city of Madrid, although the particular suburb is not named. The Francoist censors resisted the overtly negative depictions of the suburb, and the film suffered massive cuts, leading to two very distinct versions—one for foreign and one for domestic audiences.[20] The censors objected not just to the film's graphic violence and homosexual innuendo, but also to its ideological content, which subverted both the values of National Catholicism and the dictatorship's more capitalistic *aperturista* (diplomatic and economic *apertura*, "opening") aspirations.[21] According to de la Iglesia, the censors feared the resurgence of the Spanish Black Legend—the idea that Spain had been unfairly characterized as uniquely backward and barbaric in European historiography.[22]

The suburbs in particular had long been a thorn in the dictatorship's side as they exposed the social failures of the regime's urban paradigm. Many of those who did not find housing within the city built shantytowns on the outskirts of Madrid, especially south and east of the city. The presence of such shantytowns was seen by the regime as a threat to civil order and governability. For example, postwar newspaper articles on "Red Madrid" cast the periphery of the city as a direct threat to the dictatorship using metaphors of disease and contagion.[23] While these shantytowns may indeed have posed public health risks due to a lack of basic sanitation infrastructure, this kind of immunological rhetoric also was commonly used by the dictatorship to describe potentially dangerous ideologies. The language of contagion was prevalent in Franco's political speeches and in Falangist literature, in which the ideas of communism and liberal republicanism were construed as a spreading sickness to be forcibly separated from the body politic. These beliefs aligned with broader twentieth-century intellectual currents influenced by Darwinism that regarded society as a social organism and applied biological laws to it. As the historian Helen Graham argues, "The issue was no longer the body politic, but the biological body of the 'nation' and the total control thereof. This was the crux of Franco's strategy both during and after the military conflict of 1936–39: the internal colonization of the metropolis, in order to destroy the 'alien' Republic nation/culture therein."[24] Here, the regime's use of an immunology analogy makes explicit the biopolitical aims that undergirded urban planning and economic policy.

In an effort to control the potentially rebellious populations of the shantytowns, the dictatorship launched urbanization initiatives such as the National Housing Plan of 1955. This plan involved the construction of housing developments to replace many of the slums and provide housing for those living in them. The five thousand new apartments constructed that year inaugurated eight *poblados de absorción* (absorption settlements) in radial areas such as Valverde, Entrevías, and Carabanchel Bajo that continued to grow in the coming decades. The poblados de absorción represented largely low-income and working-class neighborhoods and effectively partitioned the city along class lines. Yet the plan was intended to do more than just solve the housing crisis. Francoist urban development was a deliberate and concerted biopolitical effort that sought to exert control over the circulation of potentially unruly subjects in the city. José Luis Arrese, the first minister of housing during the dictatorship, "explicitly recognised the need to control 'all bodies that move within space'. If these movements manage to 'escape authority' then 'society would soon find itself wandering in the realms of the unknown . . . [toward] anarchy.'"[25] In this context, urban planning becomes a mechanism of biopolitics, or a mode of administering and regulating populations and subjects.

Peripheral Borders

La semana del asesino is set in the barren, banal landscape of an unnamed peripheral neighborhood in Madrid. The landscape is characterized by the typical large concrete and brick buildings of the period, while infrastructure such as paved roads and street lighting is conspicuously absent. As indicated by the title, the story takes place over the course of a week. The story starts on a Sunday, when Marcos, a factory worker, accidently kills a taxi driver in an altercation. Marcos refuses to involve the police because of his social class. "Police won't believe the poor," he says. He kills his girlfriend, Paula (Emma Cohen), on Monday when she insists he turn himself in to the police. Marcos then subsequently kills someone else each day for the rest of the week, as friends, family members, and neighbors begin to discover the corpses. The murders progress with a certain detached fatalism. It is as if the murder spree does not so much represent a temporary loss of control as it calls attention to the fact that Marcos lacks any sort of autonomy. Marcos's actions are simply reactions; he acts out of necessity.

As the English-language trailer for the film decried: "The Cannibal Man, living in today's jungle, kills for his freedom." Certainly, the sensationalist promotional materials for the film were meant to appeal to horror fans and played up the film's violent elements at the expense of its social critique. However, the reference to the jungle explicitly ties the urban and the natural together, evoking the idea of the city as a concrete jungle, a phrase often used to connote the violent nature of the city. The sensational translation of the film's title in English, *The Cannibal Man*, corresponds with this idea of the barbaric nature of urban life, but it also references Marcos's method for getting rid of his victims' bodies. After the bodies begin to accumulate in the house over the course of several days, Marcos realizes he must find a way to dispose of them. His gruesome solution is to dismember the corpses and carry them to work in pieces, where he slips them into a meat-processing machine and turns the bodies into broth. The method of disposal explicitly ties the murders to Marcos's labor at the industrialized slaughterhouse.

The factory itself highlights the tensions between the popular customs of the countryside and the alienation produced by the modern city. The first scene of the film's foreign release opens with a disturbing sequence of cows being slaughtered with mechanized precision and numbing repetition. Far removed from the ritualistic slaughter of animals in the village, as exemplified by popular Spanish *matanza* celebrations, the Flory meat-processing facility is the emblem of an industrialized mode of killing.[26] In the factory, the labor of slaughter is divided in Fordist fashion so that the cows are killed and processed by a number of workers who each carries out a specific repetitive task. This scene and others at the factory clearly present Marcos as an alienated worker. His life consists of little else than work and the repetitive journey to and from the factory every day. Working alone at the meat-processing machine, he is alienated not only from the other workers but from the product of his labor.

Even with the help of the efficient machine Marcos is not able to dispose of the bodies quickly enough, and the growing stench draws swarming flies and neighborhood dogs—including his neighbor Néstor's bulldog. The rotting bodies are literally skeletons in the closet, and Marcos must endeavor to conceal the smell in the sweltering heat of Madrid's summer. The pervasive heat, indexed by the beads of sweat on his forehead, also serves to build the psychological pressure within the film. Intensifying the sensation of impending psychosis, the sound of buzzing flies seems to follow Marcos outside the house. Adding to this tension, de la Iglesia's layered soundscape draws the maddening sounds of urbanity into the mix: jet planes and trains punctuate the diegesis, and the clock ticks ominously on Marcos's wall. The murder spree, just like every other event of his life, seems predetermined, the logical result of the film's building tensions.

Significantly, the murders originate from tensions between Marcos and his girlfriend—a relationship Marcos participates in with the same level of emotional detachment with which he performs his job. Marcos first (inadvertently) kills a taxi driver who physically assaults Paula for engaging in what the driver deems an obscene public display of affection with Marcos. In this altercation Marcos, compelled to fulfill his role as male protector, defends Paula by hitting the driver with a stone, leading to the driver's death. The next day, Marcos and Paula have intercourse for the first time, but then he strangles her when she threatens to turn him in to the police as they embrace in his bed. Marcos hides Paula's body underneath the bed as if to conceal the trace of both the murders and the intercourse. Every subsequent murder covers up these initial murders: Marcos reluctantly kills his brother, his brother's fiancée, her father, and a waitress at the neighborhood bar who attempts to seduce him. In an uncanny perversion of the consummation of the heterosexual relationship and the symbolism of the familiar matrimonial bed, Marcos arranges the bloodied corpses of his brother and his fiancée on the bed, effectively transforming it into a gruesome death bed.

For Carlos Gómez, the murders represent "a rejection of socializing mechanisms" and a perversion of modern labor and social conventions.[27] But as Andrew Willis and others have argued, Marcos is also trapped by the strict Franco-era laws and social conventions regarding sexuality and masculinity, or what he terms the "socializing process of Spanish machismo."[28] The film does not present Marcos as "a conventionally 'evil' character," Willis writes. Instead, "Heterosexuality and the desire for sex with women are shown as restrictions that entrap him."[29] During the dictatorship, homosexuality was a crime, punishable by up to five years imprisonment under the notorious Ley Sobre la Peligrosidad y Reformación Social (Law Regarding Social Dangerousness and Reformation).[30] The film shows how sexuality is necessarily conditioned by the laws it appears to transgress. That is, as Smith rightly notes, "Discipline both *polices* and *produces* the territories of homosexual affect."[31] It follows that when homosexuality is criminalized, sexual identity and desire must be expressed clandestinely.

Unknown to Marcos, the murders and his desperate cover-up are being watched through binoculars by his neighbor Néstor. The voyeuristic Néstor resides in a nearby high-rise and is both a dyadic foil and a potential romantic partner for Marcos. Although they represent different ends of the socioeconomic spectrum, both are victims of oppression, alienation, and marginalization. As Carlos Losilla has argued, "Parra [Marcos] is the product of defective social structures that have condemned him to a life that is unacceptable to him: loneliness, monotony of labor, romantic isolation. . . . But Poncela [Néstor], the storied poor rich boy, also lives at the margin of 'normality': voyeurism, repressed desire, indefinable angst. . . . Both in the end, although under different guises, are the result of the same situation."[32] Yet Marcos and Néstor experience oppression differently due to the pronounced differences in their social class.

Once we are allowed an interior view of Néstor's apartment, we become aware that it is the opposite of Marcos's claustrophobic, dilapidated house. Aside from the expansive panoptic views, Néstor's home is furnished with objects that signify good taste and high class. In the living room, modern art and stylish furniture mix with the traditional trappings of wealth, such as silver platters, fine crystal, and old family portraits. The wall décor in Marcos's home, by contrast, consists of a loudly ticking clock (which recalls the clock at the factory), a set of hanging metal tools (to emphasize that Marcos performs physical labor; the tools also double as murder weapons), and pinup posters (to show Marcos's poor taste and retrograde masculinity). Far from the middle-class bachelor pad studied by Pamela Robertson Wojcik, "in which the average male can see his idealized self reflected," Marcos's house is shabby and dated. Néstor's apartment, on the other hand, presents an idealized and masculine aesthetic of order.[33] In every way, Néstor inhabits the space of high culture, and Marcos that of the low, their spatial stratification mirroring their social class.[34]

With his privileged view from above, Néstor inhabits the position of the voyeur. Indeed, he takes pleasure in what he sees and begins to stage encounters with Marcos. But voyeurism is more than just a manifestation of scopic desire. In de Certeau's formulation, the voyeur obtains a whole and totalizing view of the city from an elevated, godlike position that transforms the world into "a text that lies before one's eyes." For de Certeau, this position is "an exaltation of a scopic and gnostic drive."[35] In other words, the voyeur practices a totalizing visualization that allows him to seize information and order it into knowledge, for it is only when one possesses the *legend* that the city becomes *legible*. While one might intuit the boundaries at ground level, the view from above allows one to grasp the way in which boundaries structure and divide the city. The voyeur's view contains a cartographic impulse that both visualizes and inscribes the boundaries of the city, and in doing so it inscribes urban subjects within a particular space.

In opposition to the voyeur, de Certeau posits the walker, an "ordinary practitioner" that lives "down below."[36] These dyadic positions represent

the division of perspective and power that define the subject's experience
of the city. However, the power of the voyeur lies not with the individual
but in a discursive structure that classifies, separates, and aestheticizes.[37]
Therefore, the godlike or totalizing perspective of the voyeur is only an illusion of power, as it is only a matter of relative position that transforms a
pedestrian into a visionary.[38] In the film, the view from above and the view
from below slip into each other when the perspectives are reversed through
the extreme zoom of a telephoto lens.[39]

Walking, Cruising, and Mapmaking

As de Certeau suggests, the subjects in the city below also have a part
to play in structuring the city. Walking is an enunciative, poetic practice
that participates *with* and *within* the established panoptic language of city
planning. The practice of walking eludes the voyeur's totalizing structure
without being outside of it. Through their wandering trajectories, the
walkers write the text without being able to read it, reinscribing boundaries but also crossing them. As de Certeau writes, "The long poem of
walking manipulates spatial organizations, no matter how panoptic they
may be: it is neither foreign to them (it can take place only within them)
nor in conformity with them (it does not receive its identity from them)."[40]
Walking is also a mode of looking that destabilizes the totalizing nature of
voyeurism or panopticism. Although it is not necessarily deliberate, walking is creative and productive, slipping the poetics of the everyday onto
the urban map.

In *La semana del asesino*, the urban map develops through cruising as
a sort of furtive and uncertain poem of desire and phantasy. Marcos and
Néstor meet in the undeveloped area between the slum and the high-rises,
where their walks trace the intersection of their respective neighborhoods.
In many ways, both Marcos and Néstor face a form of discrimination. Certainly, their identity and sexuality is conditioned by the repressive laws and
social mores of late Francoism. Their cruising is an illicit act, and it necessarily takes place in marginalized parts of the city and at night. In the absence of a safe meeting place during the dictatorship, queer meeting space
was not necessarily a physical space. Instead, it was an *ambiente*, or atmosphere, structured through coded social intercourse.[41] Cruising implies a
pleasure-seeking drift through these spaces and an interested willingness to
pick up the coded language of desire. In the film, Marcos and Néstor wan-

der through the marginalized space of the periphery. A long traveling shot films them walking toward the camera and captures a deep conversation regarding work and social expectations. Marcos's and Néstor's positions seem momentarily interchangeable in this sequence, as the pair is backlit and their faces are obscured by shadows and cigarette smoke. In the logic of cruising, Marcos's and Néstor's stratified positions are, in fact, fluid.

In an illustration of the uneven nature of discrimination, Néstor enjoys a freedom of movement denied to Marcos. He owns a sports car and moves freely throughout the city, even traveling to the beach when he desires. His movements are not policed, whereas Marcos is always under surveillance. Subject to the structures of containment and control that condition the space of the periphery, Marcos must show his identification to the Francoist authorities who take note of his movements. Néstor, however, identifies himself to the authorities as a resident of the high-rises (and hence a member of the mobile middle class) and is not required to produce identification documents. While his sexuality may expose him to discrimination and violence, his social class affords him the privilege of movement. As Crenshaw argues, discrimination is not perpetuated along a "single-axis framework" but is felt to varying degrees based on a subject's relative identity position.[42]

Like de Certeau, Benjamin also famously developed a critical practice of wandering, as exemplified by his figure of the flâneur. The flâneur experiences the modern city as an observant pedestrian, driven by unconscious desire and heedless of prescribed paths. Marcos and Néstor's walks are unhurried and undisciplined, usually with no explicit destination. However, Benjamin's flâneur is necessarily a bourgeois man, with the relative freedom and luxury of leisure time. Marcos experiences such freedom of movement fleetingly and only when in the company of Néstor. For example, Néstor takes him for a nighttime swim at the country club, where Marcos likely would not be admitted during daytime hours. Driven by desire, the flâneur also often crosses borders, a process that Benjamin describes as surprising or shocking.[43] The walker is caught off-balance, disoriented, out of sorts— like Marcos stepping off the high dive at the country club pool. Through their late-night wanderings, Néstor and Marcos cruise and cross the geographic boundaries of their neighborhoods and the social boundaries of economic class, and they push against the strict sexual and moral boundaries of the repressive dictatorship and National Catholicism.

Unlike more totalizing cartographic perspectives of the voyeur, the walker's perspective can expose the tangled webs of intersecting identities.

Yet Benjamin's flâneur is aloof and observes the city in a detached manner; he walks with the privilege of bourgeois leisure. Thus, Dianne Chisholm elaborates Benjamin's figure to propose a "cruising flâneur" that, much like the classical flâneur, strolls with a "desire that the city itself has induced with its intoxicating promenade of commodities."[44] Yet, as Chisholm continues, "Unlike the classical flaneur for whom there is no object, the cruising flaneur is on the outlook for love."[45] Cruising is driven by both desire and abandon, a yield to the amorous encounter. Yet cruising is also generative, providing a mode of signification through movement and affect. Similarly, the language of cinema is a language of motion and emotion.[46] The tracking shots in La semana del asesino allow the viewer to sense the urban environment as they visually "travel" through it. The film, in essence, constructs an affective map by overlaying subjective experience on the urban grid. Driven by fantasy and desire, the queer gaze of de la Iglesia's camera cruises and crosses the borders of the periphery and exposes points of intersection.

This cinematic cruising demonstrates that cinema's cartographic tendencies "need not always be colored by the impulse to conquer or by the language of power."[47] Instead, the daily (or nightly) movement of the cruising pedestrian provides a way to reterritorialize urban space. Cruising creates maps that are attuned to the city's microhistories of despair and desire; it can create queer spaces of intersectional contact across grids of power structured by race, class, or identity. In this context, cruising rewrites the urban geography to posit a non-concrete queer space, an ambiente that exists as a potentiality. For José Muñoz cruising is "not only or even primarily 'cruising for sex.'" Instead, it functions as a "necessary [mode] of stepping out of this place and time to something fuller, vaster, more sensual, and brighter."[48] In this context, cruising becomes a utopian practice that insists on the possibility for another world. The film's construction of queer space therefore has a utopian dimension in that it projects a space beyond the film's rigid present. While the film is far from idealistic, it conforms with Muñoz's Blochian formulation of utopia as "an insistence on something else, something better, something dawning."[49]

According to Muñoz, utopia has both a positive and a future-oriented valence and contains the negative function of critique.[50] La semana del asesino's queer aesthetic is indeed imbued with such utopian potentiality. In tracing an intersectional map through Madrid's periphery, the film posits a space beyond the overdetermined boundaries of its present while presenting a critique of the limits and barriers of Francoist modernity. Ultimately, the film's utopian projection is foreclosed when Marcos turns himself in to the police and exposes himself to the death penalty. This ending, which de la Iglesia describes as "stupid," was imposed by the Francoist censor.[51] In this sense, utopia is always only an abstraction, negated by the current reality. Yet the film also hints at openings in censorship and a queer cinema to come. As Muñoz observes, "Queer world-making . . . hinges on the possibility to map a world where one is allowed to cast such pictures of utopia and to include such pictures in any map of the social."[52] Cinema provides a tool to imagine such a map where borders erode, to imagine a map that includes utopia.[53]

ENCOUNTERS AND EMBEDDEDNESS

The Urban Cinema of Ramin Bahrani

Ramin Bahrani's first three films, sometimes called his "American dream trilogy," offer character and landscape portraits centered on urban workers in a service or postindustrial economy: *Man Push Cart* (2005), *Chop Shop* (2007), and *Goodbye Solo* (2008). Reviewers and scholars have primarily discussed the resemblance among Bahrani's films, Italian neorealism, and Iranian film (particularly the films of Abbas Kiarostami), as well as his contribution to American independent filmmaking as a practice.[1] While Bahrani's use of neorealism and quasi-ethnographic methods of immersing the production into real locations are important to comprehending his distinctive vision of the contemporary U.S. city, his cinematic sense of place and its implications for understanding intersectional identities deserve further investigation.

On the most literal level, Bahrani's multiracial casts of characters, both domestic and immigrant, continue to move American urban cinema beyond the lingering racial binary of Black versus white, illustrating the ways in which race, gender, nationality, class, age, and linguistic fluency all combine to shape distinct life experiences. In turn, the places they inhabit become "intersections" as these diverse individuals encounter one another. Bahrani's films give visibility to complex geographical theorizations of place formation, unraveling, and re-formation. The dramatization of these complex notions of place give a visual and narrative expression to some of the implications of intersectionality: that lived experiences shift depending on different aspects of one's identity experienced in a particular location and in relation to other positions of more or less power. In this essay I delineate three ways in which Bahrani's films use cinematic geography: depicting places as the intersections of diverse individual trajectories, showing how places are created and in flux due to different mobilities and immobilities, and revealing alternative modes of domesticity. Combining theories of intersectionality and dynamic place formation reveals the ways in which Bahrani depicts a constant tension between the structural constraints imposed on low-wage city dwellers and those residents' innovative acts of place making and homesteading.

Diverse Itineraries and "Ghetto Cosmopolitanism"

Recounting the narrative trajectories of each film and the variety of national and racial backgrounds from which the characters come is the first step toward understanding Bahrani's nuanced depictions of working-class urban American lives. The films are understated in tone and plotting, emphasizing repetitive routines of work that are punctuated by small but meaningful encounters. Bahrani's films depict the contemporary American city as a meeting ground for people "Othered" by mainstream American society, who can, at times, see past their differences to form—often fleeting—moments of solidarity. They also document the economies of the postindustrial city through a focus on the protagonists' employment in service jobs or living off the waste of industry. They make visible an urban experience that is neither the hypersegregated, parochial ghetto nor the transnational playground of the middle and upper class.

Man Push Cart tells the story of Ahmad (Ahmad Razvi), a Pakistani immigrant who makes a living selling coffee and bagels out of a cart on the streets of Manhattan. The film emphasizes the repetition of his daily life, starting with the predawn routine of pushing the cart through the streets on foot and continuing with brief interactions with a set of regular customers, most of whom are white professionals. This monotony is broken up by a friendship and quasi-romance with Noemi (Leticia Dolera), a young woman from Barcelona who works at a nearby newsstand, and by a complex relationship with Mohammed (Charles Daniel Sandoval), an upwardly mobile Pakistani man who recognizes Ahmad as a famous rock musician from Pakistan. These human bonds initially suggest Ahmad will transcend his malaise, if not his economic circumstances. But the film reveals that these relationships are only temporary, as Noemi decides to return to Spain and Ahmad starts to feel exploited by Mohammed. Ahmad's food cart is stolen just as he finishes paying off his loan, and the film ends on a bleak note as he fills in for another vendor, mechanically selling coffee and bagels on a different block to different customers. There is no sense of what he will do when the cart's owner returns.

Chop Shop finds a young boy, Alejandro (Alejandro Polanco), working amid day laborers and then in an automobile repair and scrap district, the so-called Iron Triangle of the Willets Point neighborhood in Queens.[2] Ale, an orphan, starts to work and live in a repair shop, and soon his teenage sister Izzy (Isamar Gonzales) joins him. Both siblings scramble to earn money for daily life while saving up to buy their own food truck. The adults around them include a white garage owner, a Pakistani chop shop owner, and a Latina food vendor. These individuals assist the children to varying degrees but also treat them as business associates, each remaining focused on his or her own economic self-interest. Ale and Izzy's entrepreneurial hopes are dashed when they are informed that the truck they have purchased requires brand new cooking equipment and $10,000 in renovations to make it legal to operate, and in one of the film's last scenes, they silently disassemble the truck for parts. The film ends on the most sparing note of optimism as the siblings playfully feed a group of pigeons outside the shop.

Goodbye Solo completes the trilogy through the story of Solo (Souleymane Sy Savane), a Senegalese taxicab driver who is married to a Mexican woman, Quiera (Carmen Leyva), and spends his time with African American, African, and white cab drivers in Winston-Salem, North Carolina. William (Red West), an elderly white man, asks Solo for a ride in two weeks to a cliff overlooking a canyon outside the city, with the mysterious request for no return drive. It becomes clear to Solo that William is planning suicide, and Solo embarks on a mission to convince William not to take his own life. Simultaneously, Solo studies for a flight attendant's exam, fights with Quiera over his unhappiness with his taxi job, and acts as a loving stepfather to Quiera's daughter, Alex (Diana Franco Galindo). Solo's stubborn cheerfulness is punctured when he fails the flight attendant's exam that he had been so confident of passing. He also comes to terms with the certainty that he cannot change William's mind about his suicide and reluctantly agrees to be his driver until the end, companionship being the only thing he can offer. Alex rides with Solo, and after they drop William off in the mountains, Alex resumes quizzing Solo from his flight attendant manual as they drive home. The ending feels slightly less bleak than those of the first two films, since both familial bonds and finances seem more secure. However, there is no indication that Solo will realize his ambitions to fly.

As can be seen from these plot summaries, Bahrani's films take the multiracial demographics of the working poor as a given and explore the tensions between human connections and economic or social constraints. There is a complex humanism that expresses the way shared conditions can link between people of different backgrounds, without asserting that everyone is the same underneath superficial differences in race and culture. This approach closely mirrors Vivian May's definition of intersectionality as a concept that insists "we are the *same and different* . . . intersectional models do not discard differences for some underlying essence, or focus solely on our similarities, in terms of our oppression."[3] So, for instance, an intersectional reading of *Man Push Cart* allows us to recognize the very real sense of connection that Ahmad and Noemi feel through their shared experiences as immigrants and sidewalk vendors. Yet Noemi is a white woman from a European country who has the means to make the return journey to her place of birth, while Ahmad's personal economic situation and that of his home country make a return journey implausible. The "matrix" thinking established by intersectionality theory also invites us to consider how two men of the same nationality and religion may also differ in their level of oppression. Meeting Mohammed initially gives Ahmad both financial support and a sense of solidarity with someone from his home country who knows about his life prior to emigration. Both Mohammed and Ahmad live with the potential of being marked as racial and religious Others in post-9/11 America. But within the context of their relationship to each other, Mohammed's class status and entrepreneurial ambitions exempt him from the economic disempowerment Ahmad experiences and lead to his exploitation of Ahmad's labor.

May notes that the origins of intersectionality in African American feminist thinking are sometimes mistakenly used to limit the concept's applicability to other groups. It is part of intersectionality's project to attend to the specific forms of oppression and domination that come with different identity categories; thus, using intersectionality as a lens to understand other experiences ensures, first, that everyone "has" a race and a gender, and second, that single identity markers always intersect with one another.[4] Studying male migrants *as men*, for example, prevents the migrant experience from being considered "male" by default. It also allows us to see how male privilege is distributed unevenly and how certain masculinities are expressed when influenced by race, religion, and migration.[5]

Bahrani's films not only illustrate this nuanced implementation of intersectional identities; they also represent the role of geography and situated experiences in understanding intersectionality.

In thinking through the relationship among masculinity, intersectionality, and place, Peter Hopkins and Greg Noble argue for studying the way that various masculinities are strategically employed or performed in different contexts to achieve specific aims. Geography can make these shifts visible through their located-ness: "Indeed, it is the peculiar domain of geography to explore not simply how masculinities are played out in different spaces, but how those spaces shape the very nature of the experience of masculinity, and how it articulates with other key dimensions of social relations. It is arguably the case that geography is the discipline best able to realise the significance of the plurality and complexities of masculinities."[6]

In *Goodbye Solo*, Bahrani illustrates the way that Solo performs various forms of masculinity and how these performances are affected by his other identities and locations. At home with Quiera and Alex, for example, he participates in family life while struggling between his career ambitions and Quiera's insistence that he maintain a stable, local job. His house thus hosts his vacillation between successful performance of father/provider and a fraught relationship that represents the frustration immigrant men often feel when their ability to provide financially and make decisions about employment is questioned by both host countries and their wives.[7] We see a third performance of masculinity in the ways Solo tries to connect with William: he repeatedly refers to Williams as "big dog," they shoot pool together, and Solo gets excited about taking him to a bar that has "girls with big booties." Here, a lens of intersectional geography helps us see how Solo uses a common understanding of heterosexual masculinity to bond with William, despite their differences in race, class, and nationality. This shuffling of identities is enabled by the space of the taxicab, separate from the domestic sphere, but it is also a location that signifies the inevitably transitory nature of their connection (figure 6.1).

While Hopkins and Noble's discussion of intersectionality and space is focused on masculinity, their point about the unique potential geographical thinking has within intersectionality studies applies more broadly. Two important aspects of intersectionality—that various identities fluctuate in prominence, depending on the situation, and that individuals' combinations of identities are linked to fluctuating levels of power—are made more visible via a cinematic narrative of dynamic places. When place is seen as a practice, as something that is constructed each time humans inter-

6.1 Solo (Souleymane Sy Savane) with William (Red West) in *Goodbye Solo*.

act, then we can understand that as intersectional because expressions of identity—of both the individuals and the location—are constantly shifting, depending on where the individuals are and what relations are permitted in what locations. Intersectionality's emphasis on power relations, however, reminds us that while we want to avoid the simplistic idea that places are inhabited in singular ways, we must also avoid spatial relativism—that while every location may have multiple identities, some uses of location do dominate or erase others.[8]

Bahrani starts with the assumption that U.S. cities are intersections in the literal sense—that is, transnational meeting grounds. The neighborhoods in his films are "extroverted places," the geographer Doreen Massey's terms for places that are shaped and constantly reshaped by global flows, rather than unchanging places of "heritage."[9] This is most evident in *Man Push Cart* and *Goodbye Solo*, whose main characters are immigrants from different places who encounter each other through work or family ties. In *Goodbye Solo*, a local multiethnic bar appears to be the place where the Senegalese Solo met the Mexican Quiera, and Solo's cab brings him into contact with William, who appears to be a white North Carolinian, and several African American passengers. Different passengers cause Solo to change the music playing from his car stereo, so the soundtrack evokes the African diaspora through rap and reggae, American country music, and Chicano pop. The "extroverted" condition of the film's settings is also vividly evoked through language: English is the common tongue among native speakers of Spanish, French, and Wolof, and Quiera's daughter, Alex, is at ease in this multilingual environment.

There is tension between the global flows that brought the characters to their locations and their current conditions of relative immobility, due to economics and social status, a tension that is captured in the phrase "ghetto cosmopolitanism," coined by Rami Nashashibi.[10] Ghetto cosmopolitanism provides an important corrective to some theorizations about the conquering of space through unlimited transnational movements or flows of culture. While global travel and the digital age have meant the conquest of space for a certain class of people, travel is obviously completely different for the one-way migrant. For low-income migrants, one transborder journey might take them to a new nation, but after that their income level, inability to speak the language of their new country, or limited personal network often causes them to stay in one place. While their neighborhoods may be cosmopolitan, this is not an elite cosmopolitanism characterized by the collapsing of spatial distinctions. Yet even as they are geographically immobile, they may live psychologically in multiple worlds.[11]

Looking back to an earlier era of migration to American cities, Nashashibi quotes the Chicago School sociologist Harvey Warren Zorbaugh, who described a 1920s slum as one of "the most cosmopolitan areas in a distinctively cosmopolitan city." Nashashibi then writes, "The postindustrial ghetto or slum is commonly described as a hyperisolated and an intensely parochial space, but I am inclined to hypothesize that Zorbaugh's observations about a slum- or ghetto-based cosmopolitanism have reemerged in a form associated with globalization and the transnational flow of culture, capital, and people in the contemporary era."[12] Nashashibi then argues for the theorization of a "global ghetto" to complicate some descriptions of cosmopolitanism that associate this experience with elite urban dwellers.

One can see in Bahrani's films an everyday, unrehearsed cosmopolitanism born out of shared economic struggle and shared urban spaces. Instead of living in a world in which cosmopolitanism appears mostly as either visual signs of culture or transitory experiences, Bahrani's characters are firmly embedded in cosmopolitan interactions.[13] Places are shared not out of a desire for multiculturalism, but out of necessity and as a consequence of global migrations. Thus, place-based experience becomes equally important, and in some cases overrides identity factors such as race, religion, and national origin.[14] Several scenes from *Chop Shop* show

African American, Latino, and Arab residents of the neighborhood mingling during barbecues, game nights, and drunken fights. In much of Ale's everyday life, his identification with this neighborhood and his economic status align him closely with the adults of different races with whom he works, even though, to an observer outside the neighborhood, Ale's race, gender, and youth might more typically be seen as his defining identities. In other settings, the identities that dominate Ale's experience shift, as when he and his friend Carlos (Carlos Zapata) sell candy on the subway. The shots of the boys' faces from the point of view of the subway riders listening to their sales pitch remind us of the gap between how these strangers might perceive Ale—classifying him based on visual signifiers of identity—and the complex life we know he lives in Willets Point. On the subway, Ale's sales pitch involves strategically using his youth to evoke sympathy from the subway riders, while in Willets Point, Ale's economic success depends on his ability to act as "adult" as possible. In this way, Ale strategically changes his behavior to emphasize different aspects of his identity, while location also offers different possibilities for crossing paths with individuals whose own, matrixed identities overlap with Ale's in different ways.

Mobility and Making Places

This investigation of how individuals' itineraries bring them into contact with others, whose identities are formed by different intersections of identities, in cosmopolitan ghettos then leads to a consideration of how one location can "host" diverse and shifting experiences of place. In each film, there is a tension between mobility and embeddedness—on the abstract levels of economics and psychology—that is literalized through the films' motifs of walking and motorized transportation. Streets and vehicles dominate the mise-en-scène, and the protagonists all have occupations that associate them with mobility. Ahmad pushes his wheeled coffee cart slowly along the street (figure 6.2), not having a truck with which to haul it.

Ahmad also walks the streets selling bootleg DVDs. Ale works on cars and spends much time directing the traffic within the cul-de-sac of auto repair shops, in addition to selling candy on the subway and pulling hubcaps off cars in parking lots. Solo, of course, spends much of his time driving, but he is restless in the repetitive circles of his taxicab route and dreams of working in an airplane.

6.2 Ahmad (Ahmad Razvi) at work in *Man Push Cart*.

The protagonists' mobilities are provisional and limited; they can move within certain spheres but not "upward." This quality of life in low-income neighborhoods is captured in the connotations of the word "ghetto": "While 'the ghetto' can refer to specific, concrete places, it has come to refer more broadly to a condition of urban immobility. Ghettos are the original no-go areas: outsiders and even the police are scared to go in, while insiders are unable to get out."[15] An early sequence in *Goodbye Solo* provides the most poignant depiction of this: following several shots of Solo driving passengers around at night, a full frontal close-up of Solo looking straight into the camera at night cuts to a shot of an airplane taking off at dawn, edited to appear as it is a direct point-of-view shot, though the time of day does not match up. Against a dusky rose-tinted sky, the plane's flight is accompanied by just a few subtle notes of nondiegetic music that blend into the sound of the airplane's engine so that a casual viewer would not detect them but might subconsciously link a feeling of uplift to the next shot, of Solo watching the plane from inside his cab. The implication is, of course, that this airplane represents Solo's dreams, but the material presence of the windshield, made obvious through the smears of dried wiper fluid, emphasizes the barrier between Solo and his ambitions. The sequence is a paradigmatic example of the metaphors that structure all three protagonists' experience of labor: by doing jobs related to physical mobility, economic mobility remains elusive.

When Ahmad's food cart is stolen, several minutes of screen time are spent watching him running through the streets in a futile attempt to find the single piece of equipment that is essential to his making a living. His frantic physical movement is contrasted to his inability to control his circumstances. The last scene, in which Ahmad is filling in for another cart vendor, features close-ups of Ahmad almost entirely swallowed by the predawn darkness and long shots in which he is literally unlocatable in the street. This is the culmination of a visual pattern throughout the film in which Ahmad is barely visible due either to darkness or to his placement in the far back of a busy street shot, where crowds and vehicles seem to swallow him up.

Despite the characters' embeddedness in their locations, they experience meaningful senses of place on the street and its related locations—alleys, garages, and Solo's taxi—zones through which many people pass without much thought. Through characters' encounters in these locations, Bahrani's films demonstrate the geographical concept of places as repeatedly "made" in different configurations rather than as existing static physical locations. So, for example, Massey argues for the reclamation of the notion of "place" from what was seen as a conservative construct: an unchanging location, the boundaries of which are policed by those in power. Massey writes, "What gives a place its specificity is not some long internalized history but the fact that it is constructed out of a particular constellation of social relations, meeting and weaving together at a particular locus. If one moves in from the satellite towards the globe, holding all those networks of social relations and movements and communications in one's head, then each 'place' can be seen as a particular, unique point of their intersection. It is, indeed, a *meeting* place."[16]

So places are created each time people meet and interact; places are "becoming"—not "finished," as Allan Pred demonstrated by mapping daily paths of individuals and assembling them into a complex "time-geography" of a city that depicted "the interplay between individual behavior and experience, the everyday and place-specific workings of society, and particular forms of social and spatial transformation."[17]

In *Man Push Cart*, Ahmad's conversations with Noemi on the sidewalk where they both work punctuate the drudgery of his daily routine. Their growing relationship means that this particular sidewalk *becomes* a place, in the sense of a location made uniquely meaningful for two people and for a short period of time. In contrast, the same location would be experienced differently by Ahmad's customers and the hundreds of others who walk along it to get somewhere else. Each individual, with his or her own constellation of identities, would be experiencing the location distinctly, and for some it might register more as a "nonplace." In Marc Augé's theorization, "nonplaces" are spaces "devoid of human" meaningful interaction, often devoted to commercial transactions.[18] While some of Ahmad's customers have superficial and transactional conversations with him, most do not register as true interactions. Some customers do not even meet his eye as they wait for him to fill their orders. But while customers come and go, the viewer stays with Ahmad, experiencing both the repetition of these commercial transactions and the greater depth of his friendship with Noemi. So *Man Push Cart* invites viewers to understand its Manhattan sidewalks as physical sites for human interactions, each interaction creating a new place or nonplace.

Goodbye Solo offers a different possibility by creating a sense of place in a taxicab, which to many might feel like a "nonplace," simply a means to get somewhere else. Instead, Solo's cab is the primary location in which Solo and William's prickly relationship develops, as Solo talks about his family and his ambitions and asks William questions; William answers curtly; and extended silences follow. Anonymous passengers, as well as a few recurring characters such as Solo's friends and stepdaughter, Alex, enter and exit Solo's cab while the viewer remains with him, experiencing his solitude. At times, William and another passenger overlap, further extending the idea of the cab as a meeting place between individuals whose dominant identity markers might usually keep them apart. Finally, the choice to end the film with Alex quizzing Solo from his flight attendant manual yet again presents the car as an extension of the family home. For a moment, Solo and Alex transform a space of commerce into a supportive place, including inverting the conventional arrangement of an adult helping a child with homework.

Loss of Home and "Homesteading"

As immigrants, Ahmad and Solo have permanently left their original homes, so their attempts to form relationships in places of transit are attempts to repair their severed sense of home, both in the domestic familial sense and in the national cultural sense. Bahrani's focus on male domesticity answers calls from both feminist and migration scholars to decouple the automatic association of men with work and women with home. *Man*

Push Cart derives much of its pathos from Ahmad's lack of a home or family in New York: it is not by choice that he works and avoids domesticity. His apartment is barely glimpsed in a film that follows him constantly walking or riding the subway, earning extra money in the evenings after working his coffee cart. He is mourning his wife's death and, for reasons left unclear, her family blames him for it and has taken his son away. A scene representing Ahmad's futile attempt to get his son back is set in the parking lot of a Toys R Us store; the combination of the American corporation and the conversation set in a car signify his inability to maintain family ties in this country of material goods. Ahmad's attempts at "making places" in lieu of home and family circle around the idea of domesticity (fixing up Mohammed's apartment, traveling to a vacation cottage with Mohammed and Noemi) but are never lasting.

Goodbye Solo initially depicts Solo's domestic life with Quiera and Alex as much more successful and settled. Yet Solo's ambition to be a flight attendant leads to a fight with Quiera; he then spends the middle portion of the film sleeping on a couch in a motel room with William, who has moved out of his home in preparation for his suicide. The two displaced men are frequently joined by Alex. These scenes epitomize homemaking by men not related by blood and are striking for their emphasis on masculine homemaking. When Solo tries to tidy up the room and do William's laundry, William rebuffs him in his usual manner. Yet in a later scene, William makes sandwiches for the three of them: instructing Alex to get napkins in one breath while in the next helping Solo with English vocabulary from his flight attendant manual. Alex and William then settle in to watch a football game while Solo continues to study. William is engaging in the type of multitasking of domestic and caretaking activities that traditionally would be associated with female characters. In this unusual scene, we see two very different men caring for each other and a child to whom neither is related by blood. Similar arrangements, of cohabitation and nurturing between unrelated people, have been described as "queer domesticity," where "queer" signals not only sexual relations but also living arrangements that challenge the norms of middle-class, heterosexual marriage.[19] The film contrasts the queer domesticity of the men in the motel with William's estrangement from his family of origin. This aspect of his backstory is undeveloped, but it is hinted that this is the reason for his suicide, and Solo repeatedly drives William to a movie theater where his grandson works. William buys tickets from this young man, who has no idea they are related. William's "stalking" of his grandson in place of real family relations can be compared to the *Man Push Cart* scene in which Ahmad watches his son through an apartment window. Yet in *Goodbye Solo*, William and Solo's queer domesticity is presented not as deviant or emotionally empty but, rather, as a creative act of occupying a location that is usually temporary and endowing it with the significance found in caretaking.

This incarnation of place making can be connected to what Edward Casey calls "homesteading," in opposition to "homecoming": journeying to a new place to make a home instead of returning to a former home.[20] Any story of migration is one of homesteading, which, to be successful, demands that one be able to integrate qualities of one's old homeplace into the new home place, as well as adapt to the distinct qualities of the new environment. The scenes from *Goodbye Solo* in which Solo acts as a stepfather to Alex and establishes a marginally familial relationship with William add another layer of homesteading to the original migration story of Solo.

In *Chop Shop*, Ale and Izzy engage in a more sustained act of homesteading when they take up residence inside Rob's auto shop, extending the idea of forming relationships in places of transit to actually living in an industrial space devoted to repairing vehicles. The film starts at the moment Ale has located his sister from an unknown recent past. He asks her whether she has been staying in a safe house, and she says no but will not say where she has been. When we later see her working as a prostitute, we can speculate about her journey until this point. Walking from the subway, the siblings enter the empty industrial neighborhood. Ale leads Izzy to the room he has settled into on the second floor of the repair shop, showing her around as proudly as a wealthy homeowner. When Izzy voices skepticism that they can live there, Ale responds, "Look, there's a bed, a microwave *and* a fridge. Look [opening the fridge to demonstrate that he's stocked it with grape soda], look: country club!" Bahrani said that his creative team designed the second floor of the shop to feel "like a kid's tree house."[21] Several times, scenes of Rob leaving for his home at the end of the day are followed by Ale and Izzy locking up the garage from the inside. In this way, Bahrani contrasts Rob's "normal" routine of working in one location and then going home with Ale's determination to make an industrial space into a familial home—and a safe space for his sister.

Ale's hopeful act of homesteading may remind us also of Michel Foucault's concept of heterotopia, specifically in the sense of a countersite that is both the opposite of the American home and its mirror. Foucault initially defines heterotopias as "counter-sites, a kind of effectively enacted utopia in which the real sites, all the other real sites that can be found within the culture, are simultaneously represented, contested, and inverted."[22] In this scene, home is *represented* via Ale's confident assertion that the room has everything that is essential to a home: refrigerator stocked with grape soda and a bathroom, as well as, of course, a bed. Home is *inverted* in that Ale transforms a space of commerce into a domestic space. This domestic space is hidden to the outside world; no one would ever suspect children would be living there. Finally, we could see this scene as one that *contests* the American notion of home. It unsettles the boundary that was erected in the nineteenth century between work and home—once fewer people were farmers or craftspeople who lived above their workspace. That distinction between workspace and home space was essential to notions of the good, middle-class life: home was meant to be an oasis of family and relaxation— of course, an ideal that was based on the point of view of a man working outside the home. The consensus around the physical qualities that made a good home is thus also a socially constructed consensus on what a home should be. This is to say not that *Chop Shop* is suggesting that society should endorse children living in such a location, but that, given the circumstances, Ale is empowering himself through a creative act of homesteading. He carves out a safe place for two vulnerable young people and resurrects their sibling family. Throughout the film, Ale remains fiercely protective of their home, yelling at Izzy for having friends over who will "mess up" the place and jeopardize their extralegal housing agreement.

Thus, homesteading transforms a dehumanized industrial *space* into a domestic *place*. From this point on, the film is laced through with familial moments between the two, having tickle fights, chasing each other in the streets, and buying items to care for each other. The film's ending, with Ale and Izzy opening the garage door in the morning to feed the pigeons, is a heterotopic twist on the standard imagery of a suburban family opening their door to let the dog out or get the newspaper. Two children emerge from their created home space to enjoy the "view" from their front door, which to many outside observers would instead read as a ramshackle industrial space.

The place making and homesteading that marks all three of these films forms a unique cinematic representation of the dynamic nature of "place." Rather than a static physical location, Bahrani's narratives allow us to see the way that locations are shaped by interactions among diverse individuals, as well as the way that different locations call different aspects of those individuals' identities to the forefront at any given moment. To see characters make meaningful places—or even homes—in spaces of commerce or transit is to understand the shifting nature of identities and of relationships. Yet Bahrani never lets viewers forget that places are also governed by economic and social forces, and so considering intersectional identities also means considering which identities are suppressed as the individuals who possess them move from place to place. In this way, Bahrani's trilogy is a compelling demonstration of intersectionality in storytelling. The films depict the complexity of human identities and places with what could also be considered a "complex humanism," in that connections are made across difference for reasons both emotional and strategic, and these connections form moving stories. The tension between these encounters and the structural positions in which Bahrani's characters are embedded ensure the films do not succumb to a simplistic utopianism or relativism in which anything is possible. Instead, the films' beauty is in their clear-eyed evocation of places and identities in all their dimensions.

PERPETUAL MOTION

Mobility, Precarity, and Slow Death Cinema

One strong tendency of teen films has been to orient teens toward a normative and hopeful conception of adulthood that links geographic mobility to social mobility—the idea of moving away from one's childhood home and up the social ladder. In recent years, however, as the certainty of moving up has diminished, a spate of films has revealed the normative orientation itself—the assumptions about social mobility and the ability to successfully enter adulthood—as having been bent, distorted, or derailed. As mobility has been refigured as and through precarity, instead of social mobility, these films have shown youthful characters in a kind of hypermobility or perpetual motion in place. This essay, then, considers how precarity produces a sense of placelessness and underscores how social and spatial mobility are both produced and delimited by systems of privilege and inequity.

The films under consideration are not a genre but a cycle, "a series of films associated with each other through shared images, characters, settings, plots or themes."[1] They are auteurist and independent: *The Last Black Man in San Francisco* (Joe Talbot, dir., 2019), *The Florida Project* (Sean Baker, dir., 2017), *Lean on Pete* (Andrew Haigh, dir., 2017), *Good Time* (Josh and Benny Safdie, dirs., 2017), *American Honey* (Andrea Arnold, dir., 2016), *Tramps* (Adam Leon, dir., 2016), *Tangerine* (Sean Baker, dir., 2015), *Heaven Knows What* (Josh and Benny Safdie, dirs., 2014), *Gimme the Loot* (Adam Leon, 2012), and, an early harbinger of the cycle, *Wendy and Lucy* (Kelly Reichardt, dir., 2008). This essay focuses on films set in the United States, but the trend is certainly more global than that. These are films of what has come to be called the precariat, an intersectional class of people who lack labor security and have unstable sources of income, people who have "no ladders of mobility to climb," people who live with anxiety.[2] The precariat consists of factions that may or may not interconnect and may or may not feel a class affinity, including those from the traditional working or lower middle class, migrants and ethnic minorities, and youth.[3] The world's youth, the largest youth cohort in history, make up the core of the precariat as "a generation of young people struggling to secure livelihoods in the most dismal labor market since The Great Depression."[4] The films encompass but are not limited to youth, yet the films about older characters—*The Last Black Man in San Francisco, Tangerine, Good Time, Wendy and Lucy*—emphasize an ongoing sense of difficulty that marks the characters as not fully inhabiting stereotypical expectations of adulthood such as jobs, child-rearing, homeownership, or other markers of having transitioned out of adolescence. This is in keeping with Guy Standing's claim that one feature of precariousness is a prolonged adolescence.[5] However, for purposes of length, I restrict my comments mostly to films about youth.

I characterize these films as slow death cinema. I take the term "slow death" from Lauren Berlant, who describes it as "the physical wearing out of a population and the deterioration of people in a population that is very nearly a defining condition of their experience and historical existence . . . the phenomenon of mass physical attenuation under global/national regimes of capitalist structural subordination and governmentality," a way to characterize experience that "is simultaneously at an extreme and in a zone of ordinariness, where life building and the attrition of human life are indistinguishable, and where it is hard to distinguish modes of incoherence, distractedness and habituation from deliberate and deliberative activity, as they are all involved in the reproduction of predictable life."[6] Berlant's notion of slow death captures an ongoing experience of difficulty; feelings of exhaustion; and the lack of futurity, "where life building and the attrition of human life are indistinguishable." Slow death ironically gets at the sense of hypermobility and perpetual motion—"distractedness and habituation" as opposed to "deliberative activity"—that describes both the actions of characters in these films and the aesthetic of the films themselves.[7]

Slow death differs from the focus on death in some teen cinema, such as *The Fault in Our Stars* (Josh Boone, dir., 2014) and *Me and Earl and the Dying Girl* (Alfonso Gomez-Rejon, dir., 2015), because where those films mark death as a tragedy in which an individual is denied the future, slow death cinema lacks faith in the future and represents what characters in *Spring Awakening* describe as the more draining "bitch of living" rather than the melodrama of mortality. Slow death cinema is also distinguished from slow cinema; it is, in many ways, its opposite, as the films generally have relatively fast-paced editing and elliptical action rather than extended long takes, slow death signified here ironically through hypermobility as opposed to stasis.[8]

Youth Films and Fantasies of Mobility

To understand slow death cinema, it is necessary to contrast it to more optimistic representations of youth and mobility, such as *American Graffiti* (George Lucas, dir., 1973). The film situates white middle-class adolescence in relation to a kind of mobility in place, the often overlooked "everyday mobility on the streets and public spaces of neighborhoods," as teenagers cruise the streets of Modesto, California, and drag race, less with an idea of getting somewhere than simply moving—to flirt, connect, and party.[9] This mobility exists in opposition to an idea of fixity, associated with adulthood, insofar as the teenagers are never shown at home. Instead, along with frequent shots of the characters driving aimlessly around Modesto, they are seen in parking lots, at Mel's diner, at a dance at the school gym, at an airport, and in other transitory spaces. They project ideas of mobility onto the super-cool DJ Wolfman Jack, who is rumored to play records from "Mexico someplace" or a "plane that just flies around in circles," resistant to the more mundane reality that he broadcasts from a small station outside the town.

Of course, the film also positions this mobility as a liminal and ideally temporary state. The film is set on the final night of summer before two characters, Steve (Ron Howard) and Curt (Richard Dreyfuss), are supposed to leave for college. At the end of the film, however, Steve opts to stay in Modesto so as not to leave his girlfriend, Laurie (Cindy Williams). John Milner (Paul LeMat), the twenty-something drag racer who still hangs with high schoolers, and Terry, or Toad (Charles Martin Smith), the loser, are also left behind. Curt leaves on an airplane to go to college. We discover in the end titles that Steve never leaves but becomes an insurance salesman, marrying Laurie and presumably never going to college, while Milner dies in a car crash and Toad disappears in Vietnam. Only Curt escapes and survives, a writer in Canada.[10] The film suggests that for its middle-class characters, mobility in place is fine as long as one does not get stuck spinning one's wheels, like John. It posits forced mobility, like that of the military, as deadly, and it suggests that staying, opting for the safety of fixity—the girl, the job—is its own kind of death. Curt, the artist who escapes Modesto and Vietnam both, is the success story. Thus, the film suggests that growing up and being socially mobile entails voluntary geographic mobility.

American Graffiti's positioning of mobility is typical of many teen films. *Dazed and Confused* (Richard Linklater, dir., 1993) similarly shows white middle-class teens engaged in a kind of mobility in place, driving around the small Texas town, and partying, on a similar night of transition: the last day of school as juniors cycle up to being seniors in high school, and eighth-graders are ritually hazed and eventually accepted into high-school social circles. As in *American Graffiti*, those in *Dazed and Confused* who linger too long and fail to exit the teen world are viewed as failures. For example, Ben Affleck's O'Bannion fails to graduate and thus overin-vests in his second year of participating in the ritual hazing of new fresh-man, and Matthew McConaughey's Wooderson still hangs with teens in his early twenties and dates teen girls, stating, "I get older, they stay the same age."

We can think of the fixation on cars and other forms of mobility in youth films as linked to an idea of restlessness and nervous energy, a tem-porary state of crisis and movement prior to the real transition to adult-hood, a moment frequently marked by leaving. A condition for the teen film, according to Catherine Driscoll, is "a modern idea of adolescence as personal and social crisis" and a narrative centered on "difficulty."[11] Mobil-ity in place is not the only way this feeling of crisis is expressed. Some films, such as *Paper Towns* (Jake Schreier, dir., 2015) and *The Fault in Our Stars*, show white middle-class teens on road trips or traveling; some are situated more in the domestic or school setting, such as the John Hughes films that define the 1980s teen genre. But those films, too, often suggest that the successful transition to adulthood and social mobility will be tied to some form of leaving—for example, films that end with a lower-class character heading to college, such as *Lady Bird* (Greta Gerwig, dir., 2017), *Boyhood* (Richard Linklater, dir., 2014), and *Real Women Have Curves* (Patricia Car-doso, dir., 2002) or, presumably, successful college application, as in *Dope* (Rick Fumuyiwa, dir., 2015) or *Me and Earl and the Dying Girl*. In films such as *American Graffiti* and *Dazed and Confused*, those characters who do not ori-ent themselves toward the future via geographic and social mobility can be seen as deviant, resistant, failures, or exceptional in some way. This model rules even many films that show the attainment of that dream as difficult, as with *Real Women Have Curves*, *Boyhood*, and *Lady Bird*.

My reading of *American Graffiti* takes for granted that we, as spectators, will view Curt's trajectory as better than Steve's; that we understand that being a writer who flees from the draft is better than being a married insurance salesman in Modesto. And I think that has been the agreed-on view of the film for decades. However, the last time I taught this film, in the class Film and Popular Music in 2018, it soon became apparent that my assumptions about success were not shared by my students. As we discussed the film, it became clear that my students felt that Steve's trajectory was the success story. I assumed that perhaps they objected to Curt's politics and did not value draft dodging in the same way that someone who grew up in the Vietnam era might. But it was less that they did not approve of Curt than that they felt that Steve's having a job as an insurance salesman, and having the security of that job, was good. To them, Curt, as a man without a home or clear steady job, represented precarity, and Steve represented stability. They saw the same things I did—mobility and autonomy, on the one hand, and stability and fixity, on the other—but they attached the opposite values to them than I did.

As Tim Creswell suggests, mobility is a pliant term, "a kind of blank space that stands as an alternative to place, boundedness, foundations and stability."[12] The meanings of mobility can vary dramatically, depending on how place, stability, and fixity are defined. Creswell writes: "Mobility as progress, as freedom, as opportunity, and as modernity, sit side by side with mobility as shiftlessness, as deviance, and as resistance."[13] Forms of mobility usually associated with freedom includes tropes of modernity, such as the flâneur's aimless strolling, or train travel, as well as tourism, voluntary migration, and geographic mobility for jobs, better housing, and other forms of social mobility. For these models, in Creswell's account, mobility is viewed as "unremittingly positive . . . fluid, dynamic . . . , progressive, exciting and contemporary."[14] These models of mobility are opposed to things viewed as rooted, static, and bounded, which are seen to be reactionary and dull. Under the more negatively viewed modes of mobility—homelessness, nomads, gypsies, refugees, exile—fixity becomes an ideal, not reactionary or dull but grounding. Mobility, in this sense, looks like rootlessness.

Of course, neither the freedom to be mobile nor the ability to be rooted is ever accorded equally. We can think of mobility as defined not only in terms of freedom versus rootlessness but via privilege and precarity. As Timothy Shortell and Evrick Brown note, "For the powerful, mobility is a lifestyle choice. . . . [F]or the powerless, mobility is often forced—by the state, by the threat of violence, or impoverishment. And for some, mobility is denied entirely—by imprisonment or segregation."[15] Thus, ideas of mobility vary not only according to which kind of mobility one discusses—travel versus migration, for example, voluntary migration versus involuntary, the figure of the flâneur versus homelessness, and so on—but also in relation to which community, at which historical moment in time.

Slow Death Cinema

Slow death cinema registers the present-day precarity of youth, as well as a sea change in conceptions of mobility. Considered as a cycle, *The Florida Project*, *Lean on Pete*, *Good Time*, *American Honey*, *Tramps*, *Tangerine*, *Heaven Knows What*, *Gimme the Loot*, and *Wendy and Lucy* all have hallmarks of a certain mode of realism. The films feature characters marginalized by some combination of youth, class, race, ethnicity, and sexuality who operate on the fringes of society as sex workers, gamblers, graffiti artists, hustlers, drug dealers, and itinerant workers. They are shot on location in sections of the city associated with poor, ethnic, underclass communities, including laundromats, cheap diners, streets, buses, and subways or in landscapes riddled with cheap motels, fast-food restaurants, racetracks, and strip malls. They are often shot using handheld digital cameras or even an iPhone 5 for *Tangerine* (though *The Florida Project* is shot on film). *American Honey*, *The Florida Project*, *Heaven Knows What*, and *Tangerine* all employ nonactors, and the rest use mainly unknown actors, not stars. When present, stars are subsumed into character roles or play against type. The narratives tend to be compressed—one night and day for *Tangerine*, *Good Time*, *Gimme the Loot*, and *Tramps*; days or weeks for the remainder. The narratives are loosely organized, elliptical, and episodic, picaresque in structure but neither first person nor comedic.[16]

Each film has different degrees and kinds of mobility. *The Florida Project* is about a poor young white mother raising her daughter by hustling money however she can, including selling stolen goods and prostitution. It takes place entirely within a small circuit of trashy motels and abandoned homes adjacent to the Disney theme park in Orlando. Consisting largely of single mothers and their children, the motels' populations live hand to mouth in crowded rooms, the children playing in empty lots, parking lots, and motel walkways. The characters live rootless, unstable lives in the space of the motel. They are forced to move regularly from one room to the next to avoid claiming residence.

While mobility in *The Florida Project* is mainly a lack of stability, in other films characters are more explicitly on the move. In *Lean on Pete*, the teenage Charley (Charlie Plummer) moves to Portland with his dad and gets a part-time job at a racetrack, where he becomes attached to a horse named Lean on Pete. Before the boxes are even unpacked in their new home, his dad is badly beaten and sent to the hospital, so Charley secretly moves to the racetrack. When the horse is going to be sent to the glue factory, Charley steals a truck and the horse and leaves, first in the truck, and then walking from Portland to Laramie, Wyoming, to seek his estranged aunt. Charley is shown on long runs in Portland, then extended sequences when he first drives, then walks the horse across deserted landscapes. In a variant of the road movie, *American Honey* crisscrosses the Midwest on the premise that a racially diverse group of teens has been hired to sell magazine subscriptions door to door, not only in suburban developments but also at oil rigs and truck stops—a near-perfect caricature of low-paying, outmoded, and itinerant work. They travel in a van, getting drunk and high, and stay at a series of motels, never stopping for more than a night.

Some films show urban peregrinations. In *Heaven Knows What*, a group of junkies negotiate New York, moving among temporary shelters and squats; sidewalks where they beg for money; parks and benches where they get high; and such public spaces as the library, diners, and drugstores. In *Gimme the Loot*, a teen boy and girl, Malcolm (Ty Hickson) and Sophia (Tashiana Washington), are seeking cash to bribe their way in to graffiti bomb Met Stadium and thus traverse the city by subway, bicycle, and on foot, visiting parks, playgrounds, fast-food joints, trailers, and squats, only briefly touching down in a home at the end (figure 7.1). In *Tramps*, the characters move among various neighborhoods in New York and the suburbs of Connecticut as they initially engage in a mysterious briefcase exchange that goes wrong, then try to find the right case to deliver it and get paid.

The films all emphasize mobility by showing extended tracking shots or sequences of characters walking, as well as shots on trains, buses, and vans. While some are shot with languorous long tracking shots, most have very short shots, with frequent discontinuous edits. These scenes dominate the narratives—in a very real sense, mobility is the plot—and emphasize the characters' restlessness and rootlessness.

Unlike in suburban teen narratives, cars are rarely driven in these films. In *The Florida Project*, most of the characters, despite living in a motel, do not have cars. Only the boss, Krystal (Riley Keough), travels by car in *American Honey*, letting her favorite employee, Jake (Shia LaBeouf), ride along.

7.1 Malcolm (Ty Hickson) and Sophia (Tashiana Washington) navigate the city in *Gimme the Loot*.

In *Gimme the Loot*, the characters spend the night in a friend's car staking out an apartment, but we never see the car move and they treat it as a home, setting up a TV inside. In *Tramps*, Ellie (Grace van Patten) drives a borrowed car for the drop only. Otherwise, she walks or takes trains. Most often, characters walk or use public transportation, and the films have frequent shots especially on trains and buses.

The narratives range in tone from relatively light, quasi-romantic comedies (*Tramps* and *Gimme the Loot*) to very dark and bleak in the rest. The bleakest films (*Heaven Knows What* and *The Florida Project*) are not moralistic or seeking pathos: both they and the lighter films are observational, almost like cinema verité, embedded in the world of the characters but distant from it. However, unlike verité the films employ a variety of techniques, including long takes, but more often rapid editing, dramatic changes in scale, and particularly sound, especially electronic music, to capture the instability and anxiety of the characters' lives. In the relatively light film *Tramps*, for example, Danny (Callum Turner), enlisted by his brother to make a handoff to a woman with a green purse, realizes he has taken the wrong briefcase from the wrong woman. We see his reaction as we crosscut to Ellie, his partner in the crime. Underscored with the tropical punk of "El Tigeraso" by Maluca, the frantic sounds of the nondiegetic score work with discontinuous editing, performance, and cinematography to focalize the character's tension and produce a similar anxiety in the film spectator.

While *Tramps* adheres to scoring conventions by dropping dialogue to maintain the integrity of the song, other films use sound in less conventional and more discordant ways. For example, in *Heaven Knows What,* the junkie Harley (Arielle Holmes) discovers that her boyfriend Ilya (Caleb Landry Jones) has ditched her on an interstate bus as we hear "Phaedra" by the electronic band Tangerine Dream in a complex layered sound mix that submerses but does not block the dialogue. Harley paces the bus, screaming at the driver and passengers demanding to be let out, trying to smash windows and doors. This scene, excruciating in its intensity and duration, typifies the feelings of intensity and instability typical of slow death cinema. That feeling is heightened when you know that the actress Arielle Holmes is playing herself in a film based on her own memoir of being a junkie.

The quotidian mobility of the characters in these films is explicitly opposed to travel or tourism. *The Florida Project* makes the contrast between everyday mobility and tourism evident in housing the characters on the outskirts of the Disney tourist attraction, a site they have never visited. In *Heaven Knows What,* Harley and Ilya hatch some sort of plan to leave New York, but both force the bus to make unplanned stops and both return to the city. In *Tramps,* Danny has never traveled farther than Providence, Rhode Island. Ellie has traveled to Italy, but only with her criminal boyfriend. Indicating her inability to escape her situation through travel, she says, "Italy has a lot of shady people once you get past all the tourist stuff." In *Gimme the Loot,* the African American characters' relatively limited sphere of travel is contrasted with that of a rich white girl Malcolm meets when dealing drugs. The white girl, Ginnie (Zoë Lescaze), blithely lists her travels—"India, Costa Rica, Mexico, Paris, Italy . . . , three times in Italy, Spain, elsewhere in France"—and does not seem to recognize her own privilege or understand that Malcolm's limited travel to Florida only is not a question of taste, as she avers, "I'm sure you'd like it."

Mobility is also contrasted to the fixity of home. In *The Florida Project,* the transitory space of a motel substitutes for home. The children play in abandoned condos, the closest to a real home they ever see (figure 7.2). Projecting themselves into these imagined homes, the children picture typical children's rooms, imagining where beds, books, and toys would go, but ultimately view the homes through their own distorted sense of normal as they chant "Party with beer!"

Lean on Pete shows Charley with an unstable home life, then homeless, and temporarily in a trailer. When he stops briefly at one house of military veterans, he has to remind himself and the horse, "We just gotta keep going.

7.2 The kids in *The Florida Project* play in an abandoned home.

7.3 Starr's (Sasha Lane) gaze marks the suburban home as uncanny in *American Honey*.

This isn't our home." In *Heaven Knows What*, Harley spends time in a psychiatric institution, then has to move her things out of a shelter and stays in shooting galleries and an empty apartment that is being renovated. Her boyfriend Ilya dies in a fire when he stays in an abandoned building. *Gimme the Loot* shows Malcolm returning to a home he shares with his mother only in the last seconds of the film; otherwise, he and Sophia never are shown in or reference home. The first time Malcolm visits Ginnie in her clean and spare apartment, she is friendly and flirtatious. The second time, with her friends present, she treats him as a member of the underclass. Referring to him only as "the drug dealer," her friend tells Malcolm to remove his socks so as not to "bring the street inside" with him. *American Honey* shows Starr (Sasha Lane) fleeing an abusive home where her foster dad sexually abuses her. When the teens visit suburban homes to sell magazine subscriptions, the teens' presence is marked as odd and unwelcome in those homes (figure 7.3).

In *Tramps*, Ellie is in New York to escape her Pittsburgh boyfriend; Danny shares an apartment with his Polish mother and brother, but it is used as an illegal off-track betting site. When they go to the suburbs looking for the lost briefcase, they are viewed suspiciously as intruders, and a neighbor threatens to call the police. Once in the home, they view it as strange and distant, a place where the "living situation" is ideal, unlike either of theirs. In each case, the characters' encounter with home marks their distance from ever being able to inhabit such a space. Through the gaze of the characters, these homes seem *unheimlich*—unhomelike, strange, uncanny.

Ultimately, these films show the characters' mobility to be without terminus, or interminable. Their mobility becomes a kind of dwelling, "through intricate repeated, and habitual movements of people performing 'place-ballets.'"[17] Rather than move from point A to point B, they move in circles or toward dead ends, with narratives that resist happy endings and closure. Many of the films simply stop rather than conclude. In *Lean on Pete*, what should be a happy ending—the orphaned Charley reunited with his loving single aunt—is troubled by nightmares. He has lost both his father and the horse he tried to rescue in separate violent episodes. At the film's end, Charley is shown running in an extended tracking shot from behind; he then stops and looks at the viewer in a shot that echoes the famous end of *The 400 Blows*. However, where Antoine's gaze in *The 400 Blows* seems defiant, Charley seems lost and weary. At the end of *American Honey*, as the teens party at a lake, Star walks into the water, dunks, disappears, and then emerges in a kind of rebirth, seeming resilient but not renewed. *Heaven Knows What* ends with

7.4 *Heaven Knows What* resists closure.

Harley returning from the bus, entering a Dunkin Donuts, and joining her junkie friends, who note neither her absence nor her return. The credits roll while the action continues, refusing closure (figure 7.4).

Only *Tramps* allows its characters the possibility of escape as Ellie and Danny leave New York together to go to Providence. But neither has a job or purpose there, and the narrative resists the romantic closure it teases by having Ellie refuse Danny's kiss. In *Gimme the Loot*, Malcolm and Sophia never get the money, and their connection at the stadium never shows up. This film also teases, then thwarts, a romantic ending. *The Florida Project* devolves into the imaginary as the child Moonee (Brooklynn Prince), being taken away from her mother by child services, fantasizes that she escapes into Disneyland with her best friend, Jancey (Valeria Cotto), in the film's only digital sequence. We see the girls running through the Disney gates, past crowds of tourists, through the park. Even here, rather arriving and achieving their dream of escape, the characters disappear into the crowd, still running, and the scene stops as they disappear from view.

Tramps and the Mobility

Of course, mobility has been associated with precarity before. We might consider doomed youth road films—*They Live by Night* (Nicholas Ray, dir., 1948), *Gun Crazy* (Joseph H. Lewis, dir., 1950), *Bonnie and Clyde* (Arthur

Penn, dir., 1967), *Badlands* (Terrence Malick, dir., 1973), or *True Romance* (Tony Scott, dir., 1993)—which are about criminality, outsider status, a romantic notion of fate. The mobility of these characters exists in opposition to an idea of security and stability, as a form of deviance or resistance. Another genre of youth and mobility would be child-soldier films such as *War Witch* (Kim Nguyen, dir., 2012) and *Beasts of No Nation* (Cary Joji Fukonaga, dir., 2015) that show the violent unhoming and involuntary mobility of children forced into war. Closest to the films I am discussing would be tramp films of the late 1920s and Depression era such as *Beggars of Life* (William A. Wellman, dir., 1928), *Modern Times* (Charles Chaplin, dir., 1936), *Sullivan's Travels* (Preston Sturges, dir., 1941), and the youth film *Wild Boys of the Road* (William A. Wellman, dir., 1933).[18] These films emerge out of the "tramp scare" of the early twentieth century that posited mobility as "deviance, shiftlessness, amoral" and as "suspect 'other' to the warm glow of place."[19] Tramp films vary on whether they depict the tramp as seeking social mobility—a job, a better life—or as merely moving, with no plan to work. But both the tramp scare and tramp films underscore both meanings of mobility as, on the one hand, movement or change of place, and, on the other, a population viewed as unruly and dangerous—mobility, in its historical sense, as the mob, the rabble, the common people, the populace.

Slow death cinema relates to the tramp films as "organic reminders of the country's unforgiving attitude toward placelessness."[20] Both slow death cinema and earlier tramp films portray forms of mobility that do not have hope of social mobility, wherein mobility stems from insecurity and does not have an end point. These films show characters as unhomed and disoriented toward the future, and taken together they point to a suddenly large and mobile populace whose stories underscore the limits of social mobility. Slow death cinema differs from the tramp films, however, in that these films are less about a temporary crisis than a new reality. As Alexander Means argues, the stagnation of social mobility "is, in fact, *the normal state* of mature capitalist economies" as capitalism has reached an "overripe state in which workers are suffering slow-motion but inexorable obsolescence."[21]

Lauren Berlant suggests that crisis rhetoric belies the point that slow death is neither exceptional nor banal but, rather, "a domain of revelation where an upsetting scene of living that has been muffled in ordinary consciousness is revealed to be interwoven with ordinary life after all, like ants scurrying under a thoughtlessly lifted rock."[22] Rather than a temporary crisis, these recent films capture features of "slow death" described by Berlant: "the long term conditions of privation" that are not "traumatic events" but "discrete time-framed phenomena"—that is, "episodes . . . that make experience while not changing much of anything."[23] More than simply describe the populations represented, slow death captures the films' aesthetics as episodic, resistant to closure, and filled with drama, but not raised to the status of tragedy or exceptionality.

Slow death cinema points to a population that is simultaneously marginalized and representative of an underacknowledged dominant. In this sense, the characters in these films might be the ants Berlant describes, who signify the upsetting scene of living that we have so far avoided seeing. With a future of "increasing precariousness defined by a vulgar race to the bottom for ever more scarce resources and degraded livelihoods for the majority of workers," where "those who make very little money in their first jobs will probably still be making very little decades later," youth today have no clear means to imagine "the promise of flourishing" that previous generations did, and they have lost faith in "a fantasy world to which generations have become accustomed."[24]

As Creswell writes in relation to the figure of the tramp: "The story of mobility in American needs to include less central stories, often untold: tales of marginality and exclusion, which cast a different light on the grand narratives of nationhood, of progress, of democracy, and of modernity."[25] What is required now is to flip the narrative and recognize that those stories are not marginal at all. If we link slow death cinema to tramp films, we can see that there have been genres of precarity all along. Confident, future-oriented narratives such as *American Graffiti* may be the exception rather than the rule (and, indeed, *that* narrative was always already nostalgic for a lost moment of innocence).

In a world in which, as a recent *Atlantic* article put it, "Poor at 20" means "Poor for Life"; in which 1 percent of the global population holds 82 percent of the wealth; and in which economic inequality "reflects and exacerbates deeply rooted and expanding class and race inequalities across societies" and "young people are facing a future of great uncertainty," we need to consider what fantasies we are selling ourselves about youth and the arc of futurity.[26] If instead of leaving on a jet plane youth are stuck spinning their wheels, can we any longer hold on to a fantasy of some magic kingdom that promises "happily ever after"? The question now is how we escape slow death and convert mobility to mobilization to turn those spinning wheels into a revolution.

III _ URBANISM AND GENTRIFICATION

SENIOR CITIZENS UNDER SIEGE

Number Our Days (1976) and Gray Power

Activism in Venice

The anthropologist Barbara Myerhoff and the filmmaker Lynne Littman's documentary *Number Our Days* (1976) was a work of Gray Power activism at a time when rising gentrification in Venice, California, threatened to displace the area's elderly residents. *Number Our Days* has received only passing mention in histories of American documentary, which tend to focus on filmmakers based in the nonfiction centers of Boston, New York, and San Francisco. Cinema and media studies scholars have often written about Venice, but primarily as a backdrop for slapstick comedies in the 1910s (frequently doubling for Coney Island), film noir thrillers in the postwar period, and counterculture dramas in the era of New Hollywood.[1] However, *Number Our Days* played an important role in helping to advance the "reflexive turn" in visual anthropology and advocating for some of the city's most vulnerable residents. The film captured the senior citizens' deep ties to Venice and challenged the boosterist notion that new urban development needed to radically revamp the neighborhood's existing social infrastructure.

The elderly had for decades lived as part of a working-class cluster of communities. While the decline of the local amusement industry, environmental mismanagement, and municipal neglect all hurt Venice's economic base during the 1940s–50s, these forces also resulted in affordable rent and eclectic, more nonconformist styles of living. These communities, as the historian Andrew Deener notes, constituted "public cultures" in which individuals' lives took on social meaning within distinct locations. Public cultures denote the sets of codes and practices that characterize particular enclaves, as well as how they exist in complementary and contentious relation to others around them.[2] Living near Ocean Front Walk, Jewish senior citizens were part of a broader social geography that included African Americans and Latinx in Oakwood, white bohemian artists and activists near the canals and Abbot Kinney Boulevard, and the homeless on Rose Avenue. Rising gentrification began to exert an uneven force on this social landscape in the 1970s as the influx of white, affluent homeowners, along with tourists and entrepreneurs, threatened to displace local stakeholders and long-standing residents.

Number Our Days situates its subjects along multiple identificatory axes, including age, ethnic heritage, and class status, showing how each of these factors influenced their daily lives. The film also demonstrates how the shifting landscape of the region informed their community and illustrates the social frictions with which they had to contend. As the geographer Gill Valentine writes, "space and identity" are "co-implicated." Venice was at once a shared terrain and an intersectional site where tensions arose between wealthy and working class, old and young, religious and secular. But just as Venice during this period, following the psychologist Patrick R. Grzanka's reflections on the politics of place, was "the terrain on which systems of oppression are elaborated, produced, and reinforced," it was also a site of resistance. *Number Our Days* made the elderly community visible to itself and raised awareness among Angelenos as to the challenges they faced. Significantly, the documentary both had tangible benefits for the lives of its subjects and served as a catalyst for future forms of creative activism.[3]

Contentious Transformations

Myerhoff and Littman traveled in different professional circles, but their interests in feminism, art, and local politics brought them together for *Number Our Days*. During her time as a doctoral student in anthropology at the University of California, Los Angeles (UCLA), in the late 1950s, Myerhoff volunteered in a variety of home-management capacities with elderly Angelenos. As a professor at the University of Southern California (USC) and an affiliate of the university's Andrus Gerontology Center, she became increasingly engaged with the city's aging population and began fieldwork on the Jewish émigrés living in Ocean Park. Myerhoff saw her "Social Contexts of Aging" project as a form of embedded social work and felt a personal connection to her subjects. She herself was a daughter of Eastern European Jewish immigrants. Myerhoff saw the community as culturally vibrant yet suffering from "severe invisibility."[4] Her aim was to help the residents to better understand one another and to bring them much-needed resources. Myerhoff employed what the scholars Patricia Hill Collins and Sirma Bilge describe as a "praxis" approach to community-engaged work that brings scholarly theories and analytical methods into productive dialogue with real-life settings and problems.[5]

Having grown up in the shtetls of Romania, Lithuania, and Poland, the elderly Venetians had fled to the United States in the early to mid-twentieth century to escape religious persecution and pursue socioeconomic opportunity. As the historian Amy Hill Shevitz writes, many had lived their adult lives in northeastern or midwestern cities before moving to Los Angeles, where they settled in Venice as pensioners. They came for the warm climate, cheap rents, and pleasures of collective living.[6] It was here that they could sustain their *Yiddishkeit*, a vernacular Jewish culture that had been all but decimated during years of pogroms, legal restrictions, day-to-day anti-Semitism, and, most recently, the Holocaust. The senior citizens could practice their religion and speak in their *mama-loschen* (mother tongue). They spent their days chatting with friends and frequenting the ocean-side synagogue, delicatessen, bakery, cheap hotels, associational clubs, and Israel Levin Senior Adult Center.

While more than ten thousand Jews lived in Venice in the mid-twentieth century, urban redevelopment initiatives and rising gentrification had begun to displace them. Organizations such as the Community Redevelopment Agency and the Los Angeles Department of City Planning, in collaboration with business and real estate interests, saw the distressed infrastructure of the region as an opportunity for sweeping reinvention. They designated Venice a "slum" and moved aggressively to raze rather than rehabilitate existing domestic and commercial buildings and create afresh a more affluent coastal community. Venice began to be viewed as a potentially profitable vacation spot for out-of-town travelers, a beachfront residence for young professionals, or a weekend shopping destination for Angelenos. The development of wealthy Malibu and Santa Monica to the north and Marina del Rey to the south also drove rents up throughout the 1970s. This move to revamp Venice was connected to broader shifts taking place in the metropolis. Urban theorists of the Los Angeles School, such as Edward Soja and Mike Davis, describe this period as one of intense

economic restructuring in which the high-tech, media, real estate, and service industries expanded, particularly within the west side of the city and
outlying suburbs. Contemporary with this growth was the effort by city
authorities, in partnership with the wealthy elite, to brand Los Angeles a
"world city" in which international entrepreneurs and tourists would find
a welcome environment.[7] Residents lamented that they had once been able
to find a studio or one-bedroom apartment for well under $100 a month,
but rents were rising fast by $50–$100 or more.[8] The journalist Milton
Takei wrote in the *Free Venice Beachhead* that Urbatec's plans to renovate the
Ocean View Hotel involved raising rents beyond what inhabitants would
be able to afford. The journalist Susan Squire wrote in *Los Angeles Magazine*,
"The rapidly moving rehabilitation of Venice's commercial district promises to take the best of the old, artsy-funky, free-for-all and down-and-out
Venice and combine it with the best of the new money and the high tastes
filtering into the area." Around the new commercial enclave of Washington Street, per capita income had increased by 31 percent since 1968, and
property values went up 20 percent in 1973. The artist Horst Schmidt-
Brummer's elegant photo book *Venice California: An Urban Fantasy* (1973)
revealed how the capitalist "auctioning off" of Venice was an attack on
its vernacular culture of eclectic signs, public spaces, and distinct institutions. While gazing out from the top floor of a new condo, the developer
J. Allen Radford told *Los Angeles Magazine*, "There are some poor people
down there now, but they won't get to remain by the water. The property
is too valuable. . . . In a pure capitalist society, what causes value is the ratio
of supply to demand. There's only so much land near the water." The *Los
Angeles Times* writer Dial Torgerson despairingly commented, "The poor
shall not inherit the shoreline."[9]

Myerhoff participated in antigrowth, pro–affordable housing marches,
rent strikes, and petitions, at times joining forces with the Legal Aid Foundation of Los Angeles and the Peace and Freedom Party. At the Israel Levin
Center, Myerhoff organized "Living History Classes" in which the elderly
would share stories about their ambivalent relationship to Europe, the joy
of the communities they made for themselves in the United States, and
their anxieties concerning neighborhood development in the present.
These classes served as therapy for the senior citizens and empowered them
to take ownership over their lives. Myerhoff also saw how the experiences
of center women, many of whom had outlived their partners, were particularly marginalized. Too often within traditional Judaism and secular social
contexts, women's domestic labor, as well as their professional endeavors

outside the home, were minimized or completely ignored. Myerhoff envisioned her journaling sessions, consciousness-raising circles, and art classes as aligned with the aims and cultural practices of the feminist movement. These dialogic and collaborative methods of documentation and disclosure provided an oppositional alternative to the (male-dominated) systems of cultural production in the academy, entertainment industry, and art world that embraced hierarchical learning structures and promoted the cult of the "genius."[10]

Myerhoff met the filmmaker Lynne Littman while giving a presentation of her Venice project at the Woman's Building. Located downtown at Grandview Avenue near MacArthur Park, the Woman's Building hosted the Feminist Studio Workshop, along with the cooperative gallery Womanspace, the local chapter of the National Organization for Women, and the Sisterhood Bookstore. Littman had been making feminist films for the local PBS station KCET since the early 1970s. She began her career as an associate producer for the filmmaker Bill Greaves's pioneering *Black Journal* (1968), the first nationally syndicated Black public affairs series. She also crewed on award-winning WNET investigative documentaries, including *What Harvest for the Reaper* (1968), about the exploitation of migrant agricultural laborers on Long Island, and *Diary of a Student Revolution* (1969), about students at the University of Connecticut protesting the school's close ties to the Vietnam War. The filmmaker Agnès Varda recruited Littman to Los Angeles to make *Lions Love* (1969), a satirical portrait of Hollywood glamor featuring a group of performers living in a small compound above the Sunset Strip.

Littman stayed in the city to pursue a nonfiction career. She found a position in KCET's visionary Human Affairs Department, where she, along with her colleagues Jesús Salvador Treviño, Sue Booker, and Taylor Hackford, focused on local social justice issues. Littman made a stirring portrait of five widowed women, age twenty-eight to seventy-four (*Till Death Do Us Part*), a film about the separation of a child from his parents (*In the Matter of Kenneth*), and an investigative piece about a playgroup being displaced from its facility in Pasadena (*Power to the Playgroup*). Her most prominent film of the early 1970s was *Womanhouse Is Not a Home*, which captured the ephemeral Womanhouse exhibition. Helmed by the artists Judy Chicago and Sheila de Bretteville, it was one of the first large-scale exhibitions of feminist art in the country. Students from the Feminist Art Program at Fresno State transformed each room in a large Hollywood mansion at 533 North Mariposa Avenue into a thematic installation. Rooms focused on topics such as domestic labor and the female body and held staged theatrical performances by artists. Littman also led advocacy efforts for women to gain a greater foothold in the film and television industry and apprenticeship programs at the American Film Institute. Myerhoff and Littman bonded over these shared interests and decided to make a documentary based on Myerhoff's work in Venice; KCET provided a $30,000 budget and a venue for its eventual broadcast.[11]

Rituals of Resistance

Myerhoff and Littman challenged conventional ethnographic filmmaking's emphasis on creating an authoritative record of a "primitive," "isolated," and "foreign" culture. So, too, did they avoid the early 1960s' Direct Cinema technique of detached, noninterventionist observation of social phenomena.[12] They took a more interactive approach and structured their film around the elderly residents' daily rituals and routines. Myerhoff herself often appeared on-screen during interviews (both asking and answering questions) and offered periodic voice-over commentary. The two filmmakers wanted to foreground the idea that the documentary constituted a process in which authority was shared and each party communicated their investments and vulnerabilities. The elderly had the opportunity to ask questions and serve as the interpreters of their own experience. This method drew on Myerhoff and Littman's connection to feminist art making and teaching and, at the same time, contributed to what they saw as a "reflexive" turn in anthropology. Myerhoff viewed this turn as stemming from a number of factors, including ethnographers' personal involvement with their subjects, a greater diversity of people going into the discipline, Indigenous communities asserting more agency and independence within ethnographic studies, and the influence of left-leaning subdisciplines on the larger field of anthropology. Their approach resonated with the call from the filmmaker David MacDougall, following the anthropologist-filmmaker Jean Rouch, to push beyond the common tropes of "observational cinema" and conceptualize visual anthropology as a dynamic encounter between filmmaker and subject. However, there was a clear limit to the elderly Venetians' participation. While they helped guide Myerhoff and Littman's attention, leading the filmmakers to record those actions and events that they deemed important, they did not have editorial control, let alone the final cut. It was thus not the kind of coauthored project that MacDougall pointed toward as a new horizon of possibility for social documentary, where the film's construction involved collective screenings, allowing for the "corrections, additions, and illuminations that only their response to the material can elicit."[13]

The first scene in *Number Our Days* presents an alternative Venice from the one that so often surfaced in glossy magazines and real estate advertisements. After a brief long shot of beach, palm trees, and the Pacific Ocean, a whip pan shifts attention to the Israel Levin Center. Voice-over by klezmer musicians on the bandstand in the interior of the center invite the filmmakers and viewer inside: "You've got your camera ready? The Hora." The folk song "Hava Nagila" plays against a montage of elderly residents shuffling toward the center's entrance. Once inside, the viewer takes on the first-person perspective of the mobile, verité-style camera, as if she were a participant in the fast-paced dance. Members lock arms and spin, sway, hold hands, or tap their feet as they sit on the outer edge of the dance floor. The swirling 16 mm cinematography seems to echo Rouch's appeal for a balletic camera in ethnographic films, one that is not simply fixed to a tripod but is "just as much alive as the people it is filming. . . . Instead of using the zoom, the cameraman-filmmaker can really get into his subject, can precede or follow a dancer, a priest, or a craftsman."[14] The performance of center members is at once a confident assertion of their presence in Venice and a joyous expression of their solidarity.

The scenes that follow expand on this event, revealing the little actions and encounters that give meaning to the senior citizens' lives. The social weight placed on pedestrian activities also points to the significance of the film's title. "Number Our Days" comes from a psalm traditionally read by a rabbi at a Jewish burial: "Man is like a breath / His days are as a fleeting shadow / In the morning he flourishes and grows up like grass / In the evening he is cut down and withers / So teach us to number our days / That we may get us a heart of wisdom." The passage conveys both the fragility of life and the imperative to live deliberately and intentionally, to infuse each moment with meaning.

Number Our Days depicts the Israel Levin Center as a place where residents are able to connect with their past while also cultivating relationships in the present. Religious and secular rituals that take place on-site function as a form of collective affirmation and community building. The center helps construct a kind of found *mishpucha* (family) for seniors while also helping them work through feelings of loneliness and anxiety about old age. Myerhoff and Littman intimately position the viewer alongside members during birthday celebrations, Shabbat prayers, High Holy Day meals, New Year's festivities, guest lectures, and musical performances. As Myerhoff would later write, these events involve a process of "re-membering" in which individuals recall disparate people and experiences from the past and enfold them within their life stories.[15] Senior citizens speak of these daily practices as acts of cultural survival: if they do not do them, the culture will be lost forever. At the same time, the embodied performance of these rituals gives the seniors a sense of purpose. In essence, it sustains them.[16]

Myerhoff and Littman speak with many members of the center as they go about their daily routines. They interact with Bertha, who spends her mornings taking a long stroll along Ocean Front Walk, generously feeding flocks of pigeons and sharing "personal stories with messages about courage, dignity, and autonomy" with friends and strangers alike. Bertha speaks with Myerhoff about how sad she is to have outlived both her husband and her children (figure 8.1). She says that she has found solace and companionship with center members, however. In another encounter, Myerhoff speaks with Pauline inside her apartment. Pauline explains she never had the opportunity to pursue a career outside the home and sacrificed a great deal for her family. Still, she says, she takes tremendous pride in having taught herself to sew at an early age. She became an expert craftswoman, transforming *schmattas* into elegant outfits for her family and friends. Old photographs, heirlooms, and the sewing machine itself enable her to share her story in a highly expressive manner. Pauline proudly states that she still puts these skills to use making hats and dresses for center functions.

Number Our Days consciously works to film the community in an egalitarian manner, focusing equally on event organizers and audience members. It features Myerhoff not only as a director but also as a spectator and participant. The center's director, Morrie Rosen, is often present on camera in a variety of roles. He is described in the film as "sometimes [a son], sometimes a father, always an advocate and protector of the old people. He is with them every day, scolding, worrying, teasing . . . and fighting with the outside world for their survival." Walking along Ocean Front Walk, Rosen emphasizes the stakes of urban development. Gesturing toward swaths of cleared land and new commercial restaurants, he scolds the "profiteers" who not only have moved into Venice, but are displacing the elderly by razing buildings and demanding steep rents.

Myerhoff and Littman's film takes aim not only at the advertising industry's attempt to recast Venice as a glittery seaside resort, but also at liberal visions of urban transformation. In his popular BBC documentary *Reyner*

8.1 Myerhoff with Bertha. *Number Our Days* (1976), 16 mm. Originally broadcast on KCET, accessed through the Internet Archive.

Banham Loves Los Angeles (1972), the urban theorist Reyner Banham offers several barbed quips concerning the onslaught of gentrification in Venice; however, he highlights the white male "fine arts squad" and "muscle artists" as the people who are becoming increasingly marginalized.[17] Banham's depiction ultimately romanticizes the contrast between youthful, free-spirited bohemians and the forces of sanitized capitalism. *Number Our Days* highlights a demographic in Venice that received little public attention and was also more vulnerable to the changes sweeping the area. Still, *Number Our Days* misses the opportunity to broaden the discussion of displacement to consider how a cross-section of Venetians are threatened. Rosen fails to mention how the hypercapitalization of the area, combined with the prevalence of ageism, racism, and classism that accompanied such development, was affecting working-class African Americans, Latinxs, bohemians, and the homeless.[18]

The film concludes with two Yiddish musical performances. The first features a klezmer band playing "Bei Mir Bistu Shein." The second is "Kinderjohren," sung by the actress Naomi Pollack. Together, the two performances speak to mutually constitutive aspects of the residents' lives. The former song is an expression of playful romantic desire, all about enjoying the present and relishing the possibilities of a future relationship. "Kinder-johren," by contrast, is a solemn ballad about nostalgia for youth and the acknowledgment that old age brings isolation and eventually death. In the context of the film, the song evokes both the ending of life and possible displacement. Together, these performances speak to the elderly's resilience in the face of these forces.

The Shout of Recognition

Number Our Days enjoyed a warm reception following its broadcast on KCET on the evening of October 4, 1976. Journalists for mainstream publications wrote enthusiastic reviews; however, many of them saw the film as a sentimental portrait of old age and ignored the contentious issues surrounding economic restructuring in Venice. The *Los Angeles Times* journalist Lee Margulies called the film "a poignant portrait of old age—the peacefulness and the loneliness, the dignity and the disregard, the pride and the pain." *Number Our Days* went on to win the Oscar in the documentary short subject category, which led PBS to broadcast it at flagship stations such as WNET (New York), WTTW (Chicago), and WETA (Washington, DC). It also won an Emmy and a duPont award. The *New York Times* critic John J. O'Connor described the film as a "moving portrait of loneliness, pride, humor, [and] bitterness," and periodicals ranging from *Variety* to the *Washington Star* responded in similar fashion. Intellectuals and community organizations in Los Angeles took a more nuanced and socially engaged view. Commenting on the plight of the elderly, Anne Geyer wrote in USC's *Daily Trojan* that "their modest pensions and meager Social Security benefits have been no match for rising inflation, the continual encroachment of high-priced development and a growing influx of youth into the area. Many of these retirees have been forced into a life of bare subsistence."[19]

The prestigious awards and nationwide broadcasts nonetheless made many of the elderly Venetians feel like movie stars. When Myerhoff and Littman received the Oscar, one member exclaimed coyly: "You are surprised? We knew we'd get it!" Watching the film at the Israel Levin Center gave the members a sense of recognition. They often talked at the screen and to one another, clapping, laughing, and crying as the documentary played. A close-up in the film focused on a photograph of a young woman. With that close-up, Mr. Stoller, a community member, told Myerhoff, "You gave me back my wife. . . . After all this time, she comes back to me."[20] Not everybody was pleased with the documentary, however. Those who did not make it into the final cut or were not consulted in the first place took their absence as a personal slight and expressed their severe displeasure to the filmmakers.

The high visibility of *Number Our Days* resulted in material benefits for residents. More than $25,000 in donations streamed into the center. The checks came mainly from Jewish liberal organizations within and beyond Los Angeles, but they also came from secular social work agencies, legal aid organizations, and educational institutions. The money was used to improve the center's infrastructure; to fund programming; and to subsidize members' day-to-day needs for food, rent, and clothing. Letters to Myerhoff and Littman also spoke to the documentary's many uses. Faculty in the Anthropology Departments at the University of Missouri and University of Oregon wrote that they were inspired by the interactive style of the film and were determined to incorporate it into how they taught visual anthropology. Synagogues, churches, and other faith organizations expressed interest in screening the film, believing it could help their congregations think more meaningfully about the connection among religion, social outreach, and local politics. Hospitals and medical facilities wrote that they were using the film to teach students and employees how to interact ethically and compassionately with geriatric populations. Center affiliation also greatly increased following the film, rising from about one hundred to more than 450. *Number Our Days* contributed to a climate of pressure to increase affordable housing options and resources for underserved citizens in Venice. As part of this effort, the documentary engendered a culture of politically resistant media making at the center.[21]

From Documentary Film to Community Media

Littman went on to have an illustrious career; however, she found it difficult to work with KCET. Public television, following trends in commercial media, moved away from hard-hitting investigative reporting and social documentary and toward ratings-friendly "docudrama" and entertainment programming. Increasingly, both commercial and noncommercial outlets felt less need to cover marginalized communities as the government cracked down on radical politics and minority liberation movements began to splinter and suffer from in-fighting. There was also less public funding for public media. According to Littman, PBS had become "broke" and "baroque." By 1980, she had left KCET to work as an independent producer for network television and occasionally intersected with studio Hollywood. As a core member of the women's committee of the Directors Guild of America, she also passionately advocated for more women behind the camera, as well as in film schools and grant-funded programs.[22]

Myerhoff continued to work with center members in Venice. Most immediately, she wrote a long-form literary ethnography that expanded on the observations, conversations, and testimony of the documentary. Also titled *Number Our Days* (1978), the book offered a deeper dive into the life histories and daily routines of center members. Another outcome of the film was the "Life not Death in Venice" march (figure 8.2). A reckless teenage bicyclist had recently struck down and killed eighty-six-year-old Ann Gerber. When asked about the encounter, the bicyclist said, "I didn't see her." What amplified the danger of the event was the fact that Hollywood had just projected a majestic image of Venice as one giant skate park. The recently released teen film *Roller Boogie* (Mark L. Lester, dir., 1979) depicted Venice as a mecca for the young, athletic, and beautiful to indulge in high-speed skating and biking along the cement paths and boardwalk. Center members were determined to make the neighborhood aware of the consequences of such reckless leisure activities and draw attention to their presence in that public space. The march quickly took on the allure of performance art. Myerhoff and senior citizens wheeled a painted cardboard coffin from the center to the Bay City Synagogue.

Participants in the symbolic funeral procession carried signs that read "S.O.S: Save Our Seniors," "Let Our People Stay," and "Life not Death in Venice." The march, as Myerhoff would later write, was "their rejection of the assigned position of helpless victim." The event prompted Councilman Pat Russell to restrict skating and biking on Ocean Front Walk.[23]

The "Life not Death in Venice" art exhibition and cultural festival at the Davidson Conference Center at USC included a screening of *Number Our Days*, readings of works by Isaac Bashevis Singer, the theatrical presentation "Not as Sleepwalkers," and musical performances by Joseph Segal and Maggie Kuhn of the Gray Panthers.[24] Within the center, members painted a giant mural on one of the central interior walls. The expansive artwork constituted a form of social history—an extensive narration of their life journeys from the shtetls of Eastern Europe to the great cities of the American Northeast and Midwest, where they had participated in trade unions

8.2 Protest march. Photograph, "Life Not Death in Venice," box 169/275, folder 21; Barbara Myerhoff Papers, in Special Collections, Doheny Memorial Library, University of Southern California, Los Angeles, photograph courtesy of USC Special Collections.

and the fight for women's equality, and, finally, to their most recent experiences in Venice.

Number Our Days and the projects that followed it claimed significant victories, including heightened visibility and economic sustainability of the center within Venice. Elderly residents were also able to take ownership of how they represented themselves to one another, the broader region, and the outside world. They constructed what the cultural studies scholar Vivian M. May calls "resistant imaginaries." Giving creative expression to their life journey and daily experiences served not as "exercises in nostalgia" but, rather, a form of "countermemory" and vernacular wisdom. Their representations created a more inclusive understanding of Venice and critiqued dominant representations of the area.[25] In this way, *Number Our Days* anticipated the more recent transmedia endeavors that focus on contested cultural geographies. *Living Los Sures* (Christopher Allen/ UnionDocs, dir., 2014), *Hollow* (Elaine McMillion, dir., 2013), and *Highrise*

(Katerina Cizek, dir., 2015) feature collaborations among residents, artists, academics, technologists, and filmmakers to create new forms of public history. These projects synthesize different kinds of documentary practice, bridging online engagement and on-the-ground social organizing. In turn, they provide a way for residents to lay claim to their communities. In the present moment, characterized by the hypercapitalization of metropolitan areas and the aggressive corporate branding of "the local," documentarian-community collaborations from the 1970s provide precedents from which filmmakers might draw inspiration for ever more innovative and polemical projects.

MUSIC CITY MAKEOVER

The Televisual Tourism of *Nashville*

The official Gray Line bus for the television show *Nashville* takes fans of the series, which ran on ABC from 2012 to 2016 and CMT from 2016 to 2018, on a four-hour real estate tour of the Music City, visiting a wide range of locations that appear in the musical melodrama.[1] On the way to visit several residential sites, the tour guide explains that producers researched neighborhood demographics to choose houses and neighborhoods suited to each character's status and personality profile. The show's young alt-country up-and-comers share a shabby chic rental house in up-and-coming East Nashville. The country legend Rayna Jaymes (Connie Britton) and the twenty-something crossover sensation Juliette Barnes (Hayden Panettiere) both live in the old-money enclave of Belle Meade; however, Juliette's sleek modernist home stands in stark contrast to the traditional brick manor occupied by the elder Rayna, emphasizing the generational and stylistic divide among country performers that provides one of the show's central conflicts. The tour bus follows a similarly upwardly mobile trajectory, heading over the Cumberland River into gentrifying East Nashville before traveling through the revitalized downtown areas of The Gulch and 12 South on the way to Belle Meade, where the homes of fictional stars neighbor the estates of real-life country music royalty. The guided tour makes clear that the series' inclusion of homes, venues, and shops throughout metropolitan Nashville goes beyond the establishment of verisimilitude. *Nashville* actively constructs a televisual presence for a city known for country-western sounds but lacking urban iconicity.

As the geography of television production has expanded in tandem with production tax incentives, both official and unofficial locations tours for shows such as *Sex in the City* (1998) and, more recently, *The Walking Dead* (2010) have emerged to capitalize on the touristic potential of critically and commercially successful series with an established, loyal fan base. However, the immediate rollout of an official *Nashville* TV tour during the show's first season suggests a more direct approach: developing a television drama as a vehicle for tourism and urban branding.[2] Created by the Academy Award–winning screenwriter Callie Khouri, *Nashville* became the first multiseason narrative series set and filmed in the titular city, receiving more than $45 million in production expense rebates from Nashville Metro and the Tennessee Department of Economic and Community Development (TDECD).[3] Set in the unapologetically white world of country music, *Nashville* offered endless cross-promotional opportunities for local businesses, venues, and performers. Real-life Nashville-based musicians, including Luke Bryan and Kacey Musgraves, appear as themselves, as do Nashville's premiere music venues, from the tiny songwriter's haven the Bluebird Cafe ("the Bluebird") to the twenty-thousand-capacity Bridgestone Arena. The Nashville record label Big Machine released soundtracks for each season, and Steve Buchanan, president and chief executive of Opry Entertainment (until he retired in February 2018), served as the show's executive producer. Throughout the series, characters vie to play at Opry Auditorium and the Opry's Ryman Auditorium, emphasizing the significance of each location through expository comments. Buchanan, considered a master media strategist, realized one of his most ambitious ideas in *Nashville*: "to make a show that could raise awareness of Nashville's 'Grand Ole Opry,' and in turn, the city's greater music community."[4]

While *Nashville* may have been a network disappointment—ABC canceled the series after its fourth season due to steadily declining ratings—it succeeded wildly as an international urban-branding strategy, airing in approximately eighty countries, according to state officials. In the words of one TDECD spokesperson, "You're not only getting the 20-plus episodes per season, every advertisement and preview for the TV show is essentially advertising Nashville."[5] After the initial ABC cancellation, Nashville's Mayor, Megan Barry, issued a statement to express disappointment on behalf of the city, calling the show "an enormously successful promotional tool for our city." Implying that funds had already been earmarked for *Nashville's* continuation, likely a factor in the CMT deal that followed, Barry noted that "the state of Tennessee and Metro Nashville were prepared to support production for a fifth season to be filmed here."[6]

Advocates of film and television tax credits and tax-funded rebates claim that they are a worthy investment that reaps returns through job creation, production expenditure revenue, and the inestimable cultural prestige garnered from hosting a Hollywood film, network drama, or prestige cable series. On the other hand, critics cite the precarity of the production gig economy, the unequal distribution of state funds, and the questionable ethics of providing tax breaks to multibillion-dollar corporations.[7] While these debates remain essential, a singular focus on the political economy of production development leaves other, equally vital issues critically underexamined. Here I am centrally concerned with the use of film and television funding to aid in urban rebranding efforts through the commodification of cultures and communities for television consumption. In the case of *Nashville*, the television scholar Paola Brembilla explains, "the city is indeed a filming location and an essential part of the show, but it is also an investor, a stakeholder, and a rhetorical tool that, throughout five seasons, has created and shaped meanings."[8] The city's role as "stakeholder" in a series that claims, in its very title, to represent the totality of Nashville thus raises important questions about the ethics of production funding in relation to the politics of place and spatial representation.

The television scholar Myles McNutt has proposed the concept of "spatial capital," which he defines "as the value attached to space and place through a series' production, distribution, and reception," as a tool for evaluating the significance of location in a television series.[9] McNutt argues that shows that employ "place as narrative engine" (e.g., *The Wire*'s Baltimore, *Burn Notice*'s Miami) possess greater spatial capital, which he describes as having "inherent intersectionality," since shows that fall into this category typically explore cross-sections of society to motivate storylines.[10] *Nashville*, however, complicates a clean division between place as character and place as catalyst in ways that both limit and expand its intersectional potential. Rather than employ place as "narrative engine," *Nashville* draws from and seeks to increase its host city's spatial capital by providing both narrative and touristic destinations.

In this essay I offer a dual-focused approach that interrelates text and context to illustrate how the mutually beneficial alliance between city and series alternately foregrounds and marginalizes communities, lifestyles, and neighborhoods in an effort to appeal to a desirable demographic according to the standards of network executives and tourism officials: affluent millennial to middle-aged white women. Though the primary story arcs develop from conventional melodramatic tropes (love triangles, deception, tragic accidents, and so on), others develop from contemporary issues that the locally specific country music industry faces, including sexism, toxic masculinity, homophobia, and, more generally, the conservative aversion to social change. Through its creative blend of fact and fiction, *Nashville* ultimately imagines a better future featuring more female power players and LGBTQ stars. Yet the series rarely plumbs the city's socioeconomic complexities for storylines and maintains a blind spot toward race, a troubling omission for a show deeply concerned with the authenticity of blues-influenced roots music, set in a southern city where the vestiges of segregation remain. While *Nashville*'s racial problem may accurately reflect the country music industry, the exclusion takes on greater significance when reinforced through a fictional series that the executive director for the Tennessee Entertainment Commission, Bob Raines, calls "an excellent marketing vehicle for Tennessee," worthy of Tennessee taxpayers' support.[11]

Hollywood "Handouts," Televisual Tourism, and the Creative City

Tennessee passed its first film and television production legislation with the Visual Content Act of 2006, shortly after Tennessean Reese Witherspoon won an Academy Award for her portrayal of local legend June Carter Cash in *Walk the Line* (James Mangold, dir., 2005).[12] *Walk the Line* featured several scenes filmed in and around Nashville and Memphis, though the studio work was completed in Los Angeles. Tennessee's Visual Content Act of 2006 followed a wave of similar U.S. state legislation passed in the wake of Canada's 1997 Production Services Tax Credit for international coproductions, which contributed to immediate losses for U.S.-based film and television production. As Michael Curtin and Kevin Sanson have explained, Canada's efforts were part of a global trend during the 1990s when "policymakers began to position their countries as hotspots of the 'creative economy,' reasoning that intellectual and cultural output had become distinguishing features of the world's wealthiest societies."[13] New York passed its first production tax rebate in 2004, citing the need to curb "runaways" heading to Canada.[14] New York City also introduced the "Made in NY" campaign in 2005, conceived as a way to promote the post-9/11 city by offering co-marketing sponsorships with qualified film and television productions that displayed its logo.[15] City and state logos have since become a fixture on film and television end credits and publicity materials. Competition among the largest U.S. production centers—Louisiana, New York, Georgia, and California—has resulted in an exponential increase in available U.S. tax credits in the past twenty years in the United States and abroad (e.g., New York's 10 percent tax refund for "below-the-line costs" introduced in 2004 has since tripled). Evidence that these rebates stimulate local economies and provide reliable employment opportunities remains elusive, at best.[16]

Tennessee does not collect income tax—an additional benefit for production personnel who establish residence—and provides cash grants for up to 25 percent of qualifying Tennessee labor and vendor expenditures from a designated fund, determined annually by the state assembly.[17] Tennessee is also a "right-to-work" state; thus union membership is not a requirement for employment, allowing for flexible specialization and lower labor costs. Criticisms of production tax breaks have paralleled those made about creative economy initiatives more generally. Vicki Mayer, a vocal critic of Louisiana's generous "handouts," has argued that the regional production competition fueled by tax breaks incentivizes local and state governments to offer a multibillion-dollar industry a financial break while social services dependent on tax revenue remain severely underfunded.[18] Louisiana, Tennessee, and other so-called right-to-work states also weaken unions and workers' bargaining power, contributing to Hollywood's global "race to the bottom" in search of the biggest tax break paired with the lowest labor cost.[19] Furthermore, while most U.S. production credits and rebates are funded at the state level, the benefits in terms of employment and representation are rarely felt outside major urban centers.

Tennessee's production fund is not substantial enough to compete with major television production centers such as New York, Louisiana, and Georgia, which can subsidize a greater number of projects through tax credits, offer larger and more experienced labor pools, and provide better studio infrastructure. The primary focus of Tennessee's Visual Content Act is to keep Tennessee stories in Tennessee. After losing several high-profile Tennessee-set films and TV series to neighboring states with better tax incentives—including *Get Low* (Aaron Schneider, dir., 2009), the TNY series *Memphis Beat* (2010), and, most notably, *The Blind Side* (John Lee Hancock, dir., 2009)—Tennessee increased rebates for "Qualified Tennessee Expenditures" from 17 percent to 25 percent and decreased the production budget minimum from $1 million to $200,000.[20] Tennessee's Visual Content Act specifies that the film fund should support productions "in all areas of the state" and encourage "independent productions" and "minority participants" to apply.[21] Yet *Nashville*, which started filming shortly after the

2012 increase, became the primary beneficiary of the fund, receiving the six largest individual grants.[22] The rebates provided to *Nashville* amounted to more than 65 percent of the total dispensed by the commission between 2015 and 2018 for film and television.[23]

The Beacon Center of Tennessee, a conservative think tank that opposes all forms of "corporate welfare," released a damning report in 2018 that cited *Nashville* as a particularly egregious example of wasted taxpayer money on film and television "flops."[24] According to the report, "*Nashville* also serves as an example of how corporations and sports teams hold cities and states hostage after receiving taxpayer money."[25] But city and state representatives and business leaders have repeatedly defended their investment in the series. One 2014 survey conducted by the Nashville Convention and Visitors Corporation found that 20 percent of overnight visitors named the series as one of the reasons for their visit, and those same visitors stayed longer and spent more money than those who had not seen the show.[26] The TDECD estimates that the show has generated $486.7 million in revenue from tourists who "indicated the show as their motivating factor to visit Nashville."[27] Butch Spyridon, chief executive of the Nashville Convention and Visitors Corporation, said of the series, "We couldn't have bought what we got. We couldn't have asked for any better treatment of Nashville."[28]

Much like HBO's *Sex and the City* (1998), which predated New York State's tax credit but set the benchmark for television representation as urban branding, *Nashville* is intended to appeal to the well-heeled, presumably white, female viewer with the means to visit as-seen-on-TV landmarks, restaurants, and shops. The series also courts the millennial audience through storylines featuring young Nashville transplants exploring off-the-beaten-track corners of the city. Neither as cosmopolitan as *Sex and the City* and CW's *Gossip Girl* (2007), or as hipster as HBO's *Girls* (2012), *Nashville* recalibrates the postfeminist, postracial urban television fantasy to celebrate the roots-y charm of the revitalized southern city. Though the musical melodrama is markedly different in style and tone from its New York City predecessors, it similarly presents a weekly visual love letter to its city, presented as a site for (white) female exploration and economic empowerment. Therefore, an analysis of how *Nashville* seeks to represent the creative class and urban revitalization in the Music City also invites an examination of the socioeconomic and geographic consequences of transposing creative city strategies envisioned for dense, vertical cities to a rapidly growing southern capital defined by sprawl.

Honky-Tonk Women

Nashville seeks to construct a televisual presence for its namesake city through recurrent and contrasting imagery of bucolic landscapes and sleek downtown architecture. In bridging the urban-rural divide, the show presents an ideal city that can cater to the cosmopolitan elite, the urbane hipster, and the good ol' boy alike. The show's greatest challenge in rendering the city on-screen parallels the difficulty for the city of Nashville to construct a coherent urban brand for a sprawling metropolitan area. However, the absence of either internationally recognizable landmarks or a distinctively cinematic skyline also provides an opportunity for show creators to visually construct a distinctive iconicity for the city associated with the stories and characters of the series. *Nashville* showcases the city's growth and revitalization efforts as part of its mise-en-scène and emphasizes the benefits of a more socially progressive, entrepreneurial city through several central character arcs. At the same time, the series foregrounds Nashville's desire to highlight—and market—its cultural heritage through its emphasis of the city's legendary performers, venues, and songwriting traditions.

Narratively, the conflict over what constitutes *real* country music is dramatized through a rivalry between two female country superstars, Rayna Jaymes and Juliette Barnes. Rayna, a Faith Hill/Martina McBride type, is beloved by older women but needs to appeal to a younger demographic to stay relevant. Juliette, with stylistic similarities to Carrie Underwood and Taylor Swift, tops the digital download charts, thanks to her rabid preteen fan base, but envies the critical success that Rayna has achieved. When Rayna's arena tour fails to sell, the top brass at her music label humiliatingly suggests that she open for their best-selling artist, Juliette, setting in motion a bitter competition between the two women in the pilot episode. However, the "cat fight" scenario is ultimately a bait-and-switch. Khouri, the show's creator and the screenwriter of *Thelma and Louise* (Ridley Scott, dir., 1991), favors female bonds and unlikely alliances, often cultivated through a mutual desire to stop male predators and exploiters. Rather than conform to industry expectations, Rayna sets up her own label, Highway 65—named after the interstate that runs through the city—as a safe haven for herself, Barnes, and, eventually, all of the other young characters in the ensemble cast to develop and grow as artists.

Rayna, the only main character *from* Nashville, provides a matriarchal symbol for the city. Her image is explicitly tied to the city center through

9.1 The country duo Rayna Jaymes (Connie Britton) and Deacon Claybourne (Charles Esten) meet on the John Seigenthaler Pedestrian Bridge in the premiere episode of *Nashville*. Screen grab.

its most distinctive feature, the John Seigenthaler Pedestrian Bridge, formerly the Shelby Street Pedestrian Bridge (figure 9.1). Though the touristic footbridge is an unlikely place for celebrities to frequent, Rayna's favorite spot in town offers a fantastic sunset view of the downtown skyline over the Cumberland River. In the pilot episode, Rayna meets her bandmate and former lover Deacon Claybourne (Charles Esten) at a lookout site on the bridge, setting up central conflicts that will drive the next six seasons of the series: their love, their music, his alcoholism, and her declining record sales. The scene also secures a visual anchor from which to build an iconicity for Nashville's epicenter, reinforced through recurrent aerial-view establishing shots and through a return to the bridge for scenes of heightened narrative and emotional significance over the course of six seasons. As Rayna eschews the trappings of aging female stardom to become a singular independent label head in a male-dominated industry, the city itself becomes associated with female economic power and entrepreneurial spirit.

While Rayna confidently guides viewers through Nashville's elite neighborhoods and established venues, several of the younger characters provide a more aspirational perspective. This includes Juliette, who, despite her enormous success, gazes longingly at the stage of the Bluebird, a famed no-frills songwriters club in a strip mall on the south side of town. Juliette's desire to receive an invitation to play at the Bluebird illustrates the show's thematic privileging of artistic integrity over popular success while establishing a landmark to symbolize the series and the city's commitment to authentic country/Americana music that visitors can experience for themselves. (While the pilot was shot at the venue, an identical replica was constructed on a soundstage for subsequent episodes.) Several not-yet-famous characters similarly strive for recognition at notable touristic venues while also leading viewers to off-the-beaten-path East Nashville locations as they meet in local coffee shops, shop at vintage stores, and perform in small to mid-size music clubs. With the exception of Rayna and her daughters, all of the main characters move to Nashville from more remote southern towns with little more than talent and ambition. Though they play different styles of music, from southern-tinged indie rock (Avery Barkley) to radio-friendly country songs about beer and romance (Will Lexington), all find personal fulfillment and career success in the Music City.

In short, *Nashville* features characters who are successful entertainers, producers, and entrepreneurs, which reflects, reinforces, and celebrates the real-life "rise of the creative class" in Nashville over the past decade.[29] The well-documented boom has resulted in an estimated one hundred new residents a day and skyrocketing rents.[30] An article published in *Forbes* in 2017 claimed that Nashville owed its recent turn as a hotspot for young entrepreneurs and venture capitalists to finally shaking off its "hee-haw, honky-tonk image."[31] And yet it is the traditions of the Music City that provide its aura of authenticity, a valuable commodity for the neoliberal city, as the urban theorist Sharon Zukin has demonstrated.[32] The challenge, then, for the city and the TV show that bears its name has been not to erase Nashville's country music legacy, but to repackage it as a cultural commodity for a younger, more socially progressive demographic.

Nashville Pride

One way in which the show attempts to broaden its appeal beyond the "honky-tonk" set is through storylines that interrogate long-standing conservative values associated with the country music genre and its fan base. While episodes regularly acknowledge industry sexism and the objectification of women in important ways, Chris Carmack's portrayal of the gay singer-songwriter Will Lexington offers one of the show's most compelling and extended explorations of mainstream country music's strictly imposed heteronormativity. Initially brought on for a limited story arc, Carmack was promoted to series regular in the second season, which allowed his character to move beyond the familiar tropes associated with gay characters.[33] In the first season, Will engages in self-hating and dangerous sexual behavior to remain closeted as he simultaneously struggles with coming out. As his story progresses in later seasons, he more interestingly works through the challenges of being the first openly gay country musician.

Though Will's storylines remain secondary to the central dramas and heterosexual romances, his development complements Rayna's as they both challenge the establishment, breaking industry barriers based on gender and sexuality. Will's story also focuses on industry dynamics, but the depiction of progress extends to the city itself. In an early episode, Will is beaten mercilessly during an attempt to cruise a city park, suggesting that Nashville is no better than the small rural town he left behind. However, in the following season, Will's first boyfriend, who finds Will's secrecy and shame regressive, introduces him to Nashville's activist LGBTQ community. After establishing a local support network, Will is empowered to come out on a nationally televised broadcast. Will's relationship dramas figure more heavily in the final seasons, when he becomes serious with the Silicon Valley entrepreneur Zach Welles (Cameron Scoggins), the new partner investor of Highway 65. Although Zach is first perceived as an outsider threat to the local label, his financial backing and entrepreneurial expertise ultimately save Rayna's company and, by association, Nashville's musical integrity.

In the final episode, Will and Zach are seen walking across the Seigenthaler Pedestrian Bridge, fingers intertwined, securing the future of Rayna's legacy and symbolizing—through the figure of the cowboy and the tech guru—a reconciliation of the city's southern traditions with its global city aspirations (figure 9.2).

Though Rayna dies in the fifth season (Britton left the series shortly after CMT picked it up), a return to the bridge in the final episode brings closure to her story while suggesting that the changes she has set in motion in the city and its music industry will carry on to the next generation. Rayna's daughter Maddie (Lennon Stella) also walks the bridge in the episode with her older cousin Scarlett (Clare Bowen)—the former ingénue who had been the first signed to Rayna's label. The newly single women discuss stepping out of the shadows of parents and boyfriends to take ownership of their lives and careers. These satisfying conclusions associate

9.2 The country singer Will Lexington (Chris Carmack) and the tech entrepreneur Zach Welles (Cameron Scoggins) stroll hand in hand across the John Seigenthaler Pedestrian Bridge in the *Nashville* series finale. Screen grab.

southern social progress with increased earning potential and purchasing power for women and gay men in the newly revitalized city. The coupling of the billionaire entrepreneur and star performer promises wealth accumulation and entry into the global economic and cultural elite. Scarlett and Maddie's transformations are humble by comparison, but both women formalize their independence through first-time homeownership. Without providing a counterpoint, the show renders invisible the displacement and economic hardship that working-class, immigrant, and minority populations (including intersectional identities such as women and queer people of color) have experienced as a result of the social and economic progress celebrated onscreen.

Whitewashing the Inner City

The CMT *Nashville* tour seeks to highlight the show's authenticity, as evidenced by its commitment to filming on location; however, location tours inevitably pull back the curtain, revealing the production process, as well as what lies beyond the camera's frame. This becomes readily apparent as soon as the *Nashville* tour bus leaves its dock under the Seigenthaler Bridge, passing over the Cumberland River into East Nashville to visit several key location sites, including Scarlett and Will's first rental share. East Nashville was the city's wealthiest residential community from the late nineteenth century until the East Nashville Fire of 1916 displaced thousands, leading the city's most affluent residents to establish Belle Meade. By the 1930s, the area had been rebuilt as a white working-class community, but suburbanization, desegregation, and white flight of the 1950s and 1960s transformed East Nashville into a low-income area with a predominantly African American population.[34] The tour guide—just before proudly pointing out where Oprah Winfrey graduated high school in 1973—described the area from the 1970s through the late 1990s as "the ghetto, the hood," known by the disparaging nickname "East Nasty." A tornado in 1998 again destroyed a significant number of East Nashville homes and shelters—only this time displacing the city's poorest residents—coinciding with what Richard Florida has called "the rise of the creative class."[35]

Florida's urban planning tome from 2002 helped to popularize the principles of New Urbanism meant to appeal to young professionals (particularly in "creative" tech and media fields) through Jane Jacobs–inspired planning initiatives that favor incentivizing mixed-use urban growth in diverse pedestrian-friendly areas (i.e., gentrification), as opposed to top-down prefabricated urban planning models. Florida has since turned his attention to the increased inequality and segregation created by New Urbanism, or the "new urban crisis."[36] According to Florida, "Nashville has a moderate to potentially severe case of the 'new urban crisis'" created by its recent rise as a "vibrant knowledge creative and tech hub."[37] Due to its transition from "East Nasty" to Nashville's "coolest" neighborhood, East Nashville has become a metonym for the city's revitalization, as well as for its mounting crisis.[38]

Not surprisingly, neither East Nashville's socioeconomic history nor its contemporary housing crisis is referenced in the series, though most of the young characters rotate in and out of a three-bedroom rental home located on East Nashville's Boscobel Street. The area is definitively identified as hipster when Will, in an effort to hide from fans and paparazzi, trades his cowboy hat for a knit skullcap to attend the East Nashville music festival, confident that the crowd will not recognize a mainstream country star. East Nashville also provides coffee shops, rock-and-roll clubs, and a number of specialty businesses (e.g., Blue Sky Café, 5 Spot, Legato Gelato) used as filming locations, where young, not-quite-famous characters meet and perform.

As the *Nashville* Grey Lines tour bus drives past many of these sites, the contradictions among the guide's script, televisual representation, and the view outside the window begin to manifest. For one, markers of East Nashville's gentrification-related inequality become more pronounced as vintage shops and tattooed white women pushing expensive strollers stand kitty-corner from dispossessed minority residents and the city's largest public housing development. The continuous long take offered by the bus window undermines the tour's purpose of selling authenticity by revealing how selective framing and elliptical editing have transformed Nashville into a postracial fantasy, one that is easily disrupted by a four-hour bus tour. Without acknowledging the reversal of white flight or the ongoing territorial contestations, *Nashville* replicates the whitening of the inner city through its representational choices and omissions.

While East Nashville is depicted selectively, other areas, such as the predominantly African American area of North Nashville, never make it on-screen. The show's erasure of African American neighborhoods also extends to the exclusion of central Black characters and a disregard of African American musical traditions. While *The Wire* (2002) actor Robert Wisdom's turn as the mayoral candidate Coleman Carlisle in the first two seasons of *Nashville* could have amounted to a fascinating look at race and politics, the character never develops beyond his role as either foil or sounding board to white counterparts. In fact, racial difference and inequality in the Music City remains unacknowledged until season 5, when Maddie takes a musical and romantic interest in a young African American blues musician named Clay (Joseph David-Jones). In the same season, Juliette befriends a gospel singer named Hallie (Rhiannon Giddens of the Carolina Chocolate Drops). Through Clay, Maddie learns about racism and the African American roots of country music. Hallie teaches Juliette about southern gospel and the musical traditions of the Black church.

Arriving in the nick of time for both the characters and the series, the introduction of Clay and Hallie provides the first recognition of southern racism, racial distinctions, and country music's history of appropriation. But their arrival in season 5 to broaden the show's appeal (following its transition to cable) also comes too late, and the characters' limited roles as saviors and educators to central white protagonists further draws attention to *Nashville*'s racial problem.[39] More troublingly, both characters are geographically dislocated: Hallie lives somewhere on the outskirts of town; Clay lives somewhere downtown. In a series that obsessively identifies destinations for visitors to explore, Black spaces remain off the grid.

Conclusion

Through melodrama, *Nashville* successfully redefines the traditionally conservative, heteronormative local music industry in ways that both reflect and anticipate a cultural change afoot. Its portrayal of empowered women and attractive, sensitive men (both gay and straight) never hit as expected with ABC's target primetime drama demographic—women age thirty-five to forty-nine—but proved surprisingly successful with millennial women age nineteen to thirty-five.[40] During the period when the show aired, the same demographic helped Nashville earn its newfound status as the hottest U.S. destination for bachelorettes.[41] While Nashville's population and tourism boom owe more to the city's real-life revitalization and entrepreneurial growth than to the television series, *Nashville*—developed as a coordinated effort of government, local business, and media—played an important role in showcasing old and new attractions on an international scale through storylines that celebrated the city's social and economic progress.

Helen Morgan-Parmett sees *Nashville* as part of a growing trend toward "site-specific television," referring to series that not only film on location but are also about the places where they film. Placing *Nashville* in conversation with series ranging from *Portlandia* (2011) to *Treme* (2010), Morgan-Parmett argues that television series have increasingly come to play "a constitutive role in new urban regeneration schemes."[42] While the touristic and branding potential of these shows has been widely celebrated by the cities that host them, we might also recognize that they reinforce and contribute to the growing inequality associated with urban revitalization. *Nashville* is still a unique case study, given the level of involvement and assistance from local government and business liaisons, but its production raises vital questions about the relationship between civic boosterism and media production. At what point does government-subsidized production become state-sponsored production? And what, then, is the responsibility of the state to distribute funds in an equitable way in terms of production access and media representation?

PORTLAND AT THE INTERSECTION

Gentrification and the Whitening of the City
in *Portlandia*'s Hipster Wonderland

It took until the last season for *Portlandia* (2011–18), the Independent Film Channel (IFC) series created by and starring Fred Armisen and Carrie Brownstein, to directly address Portland's declining racial diversity. On March 1, 2018, *Portlandia* aired "Most Pro City," featuring a sketch of the fictional Mayor's (Kyle MacLachlan) diversity initiative in response to a negative news headline that calls Portland "America's least diverse city."[1] In the sketch, Carrie (Carrie Brownstein), one of the Mayor's staff members, acknowledges that Portland is majority-white in response to his surprise that Portland is the "least" diverse city in the nation. According to the 2010 U.S. census, Portland, Oregon, at 76 percent white, is the whitest big city in the United States.

Desperate to prove that his liberal administration is diverse compared with the city, the Mayor surveys his staff in search of a person of color. He asks a man on his staff who appears white if he is, in fact, white. The man confirms that he is white and adds that he also is gay. The Mayor is encouraged by that revelation, arguing that his administration is diverse because, in his words, "a rainbow isn't white." Fred (Fred Armisen), another staff member, offers the Mayor another opportunity to assuage his liberal white guilt by announcing that he is not white: he is Korean and Venezuelan. The Mayor makes a joke that he always suspected that Fred is not white but assumed he was "maybe sick or had that thing that Vin Diesel has"—in other words, racial ambiguity. For fans of the show, the joke is a nod to Armisen's notable impressions of Barack Obama and Prince on *Saturday Night Live* and the fact that his mother is Venezuelan and his father is Korean and German.

Fred tells the mayor that he made the discovery of his mixed racial heritage after taking a DNA test. Fred seems to embrace diversity. But by stating that "hardly anyone is 100 percent European" to support his pride in his new nonwhite identity, he adopts the position that whiteness is the standard of society. The Mayor seizes on that strategy to achieve racial diversity and orders DNA testing of the entire city of Portland.

The Mayor, Carrie, and Fred support the diversity initiative because they want to be perceived as do-gooders. At "Portland's Potluck of People," the Mayor announces that, after DNA testing, Portland is no longer 75 percent white. He states, "There is scarcely a white person in Portland. We are more diverse than New York City and even Detroit!" The choice of the word "potluck" in this context is significant because it implies that the Mayor has latched on to any form of diversity as acceptable. For example, the Mayor addresses a journalist for the *Portland Tribune*, who appears to be the only Black person in the room. Fred reads the results of the DNA tests, and we learn that one of *Portlandia*'s fictional white residents is a minority because he is 0.25 percent Jewish and 0.25 percent Black. In addition, Chico, a Black man who, genetically, is predominantly of African descent, is now white because he is partly Scottish.

In response to the absurdity of the Mayor's initiative, the *Portland Tribune* journalist writes a follow-up story titled, "Portland Is the Most Problematic City," and shares a preview with the Mayor for last-minute comment before the story runs the next day. Instead of addressing the structural problems of race in the city, the Mayor, Fred, and Carrie try to come up with other fun stories about Portland to distract readers and residents from the potential negative publicity. In the end, the paper decides not to lead with the journalist's story and instead makes the opening of a new Whole Foods 365 grocery store the front-page headline, confirming that consumerism is more important than antiracist and inclusive initiatives to the fictional denizens of *Portlandia*.

As illustrated in the "Most Pro City" sketch, *Portlandia* uses satire to reveal the absurdity of white hipster culture in Portland. The first six-episode season aired on IFC on January 21, 2011, with the goal of reaching a niche audience of people who lived or wanted to live in other gentrifying hipster places such as Brooklyn and Austin.[2] The show represented a new direction in IFC's rebranding as a network that featured indie or alternative culture. Jennifer Caserta, a programming manager at IFC, stated that the network's viewer was "someone who has a job but DJs on the weekends or loves to go see rock bands."[3] As characters, Carrie and Fred embody the meaning of hipster. Their characters represent the influx of individuals who moved to Portland in the previous ten to fifteen years and mirror the targeted audience and representations of creative professionals on the critically acclaimed satirical comedy.[4] *Portlandia* is a sketch comedy show that features Armisen and Brownstein, sometimes in wigs and costumes, playing recurring characters that appear throughout the series. Often, sketches form micro-narratives that are returned to repeatedly during an episode. The original idea of the show came from Brownstein and Armisen's earlier collaboration, in 2005, on a series of comedy sketches for an online-only show titled *ThunderAnt* that focused primarily on life in Portland.

Although hipsters are represented in the media as embracing progressive counterculture, hipster culture questions only specific forms of consumerism. It does not interrogate the erasure of intersectionality as a theory of power relations but, instead, embraces neoliberal ideologies.[5] Hence, hipsters operate as what Ico Maly and Piia Varis call "neoliberal consumer-citizens," whose identities are wrapped in "the logics of commodity activism, [where] 'doing good' and being a good consumer collapse into one and the same thing."[6] In *Portlandia*, the Mayor tries to do good by the residents of the city in recognizing the diversity of the city, but the sketch falls short as the cultural specificity of the Black characters (the journalist and Chico) is dismissed because "race has been transformed into a marker of visual difference" under the pressures of neoliberal ideology.[7]

In this chapter, I argue that *Portlandia*'s embrace of neoliberalism divorces intersectionality from theories of oppression. From Kimberlé Crenshaw's conception, "Intersectionality refers to the interaction between gender, race, and other categories of difference in individual lives, social practices, institutional arrangements, and cultural ideologies and the outcomes of these interactions in terms of power."[8] Instead, intersectionality is understood as a theory of difference—where everyone recognizes and embraces social identity as multifaceted. The sketch cited earlier illustrates Crenshaw's observation that contemporary discourse on diversity is a form of "intersectional erasure" in which intersectionality is divorced from theories of oppression.[9]

Erasing Intersectionality

Oregon's lack of racial diversity has a long history. It is a deliberate result of the killing and expulsion of Native Americans and laws prohibiting Black migration dating back to the state constitution in 1857. In fact, Oregon was granted statehood in 1859 with a constitution that prohibited Black people from owning property or living or working in the state, even though approximately 75 percent of voters rejected slavery during the 1857 referendum.[10] One voter, John Rogers McBride, who later became a Republican state senator, justified the contradiction at a reunion of the Oregon Pioneer Association in 1898:

> Some believers in the doctrine of abstract human rights interpret this vote against admission of free negroes as an exhibition of prejudices which prevailed against the African who was not a slave, but I have never so regarded it. It was largely an expression against any mingling of the white with any of the other races, and upon a theory that as *we had yet no considerable representation of other races in our midst, we should do nothing to encourage their introduction. We were building a new state on virgin ground; its people believed it should encourage only the best elements to come to us, and discourage others.*[11]

Note the erasure of Indigenous people in the pronouncement that Oregon was founded on "virgin" ground and the recognition of the whiteness of Oregon because of the lack of representation of people of color. It was not until 1926 that the exclusion law was removed from Oregon's Bill of Rights and Black people could legally move to the state, at which point Oregon had already solidified its national reputation as a white utopia. For McBride, it is not racist to want to live in a place surrounded by people who predominantly look like you. *Portlandia* projects the same sentiment through its erasure of intersectionality. Armisen's and Brownstein's characters have free rein in the city with neighbors who look and act like them.

Of course, despite a history of structural racism, Portland has had thriving communities of color in historically Black neighborhoods such as Albina, in the northeastern section of the city. Unfortunately, Portland has become increasingly less diverse due to significant migration from other areas in the United States to the inner core of the city since the late 1990s. *Portlandia* does use satire to spoof Portland's whiteness and is aware of the problems that have emerged as a result of gentrification and hipster culture. However, the show makes the city seem whiter than it actually is through casting that exemplifies color-blindness and an embrace of Portland's neoliberal social-spatial practices that obscure the roots and impact of structural racism. The sociologist Eduardo Bonilla-Silva argues that color-blindness masks the prominent role of racism in neoliberalism.[12] Neoliberalism is an aspect of a "racist society that works to both reinforce the racial structure of society, while also modifying the processes of racialization."[13] *Portlandia* exemplifies color-blindness through its narrative and casting and highlights other neoliberal strategies, such as the colonization of intersectionality, by its representation of gentrification and real estate practices in Portland through the perspective of white, middle-class hipsters.

It would be difficult for an unfamiliar viewer to recognize that many of the filmed locations are in historically Black neighborhoods. For the audience that knows Portland's landscape, the signs, stores, and other landmarks depicted provide contextual clues to actual Portland neighborhoods that are rapidly gentrifying. Many of the scenes are filmed in the Alberta Arts District. Racial diversity in the neighborhood declined approximately 18 percent between 2000 and 2014 as white residents moved in and could afford higher housing costs exacerbated by a lack of renters' rights.[14] *Portlandia* practices a form of color-blindness that whitewashes Portland's historic residents of color and newly arrived gentrifiers of color. In the rare instances when people of color make an appearance in sketches, the show deploys intersectionality to signify difference by casting them in scenes that give the impression that Portland is a postracial utopia. People of color sometimes appear as extras in the background scenes at restaurants, at parties, and on the streets of Portland. For example, in the episode "Mayor Is Missing" (2011), Carrie and Fred search the city for the missing Mayor. They eventually find him and learn his dark secret: he is moonlighting as a bass player in an African American "real roots reggae" band and is forced to come out as "openly reggae." The sketch focuses on the weirdness of a white man secretly playing reggae (i.e., highlighting Portland's favorite slogan, "Keep Portland Weird") instead of the history and lived experience of Black musicians in Portland.

This form of casting is what the media scholar Kristen Warner refers to as plastic representation, which "uses the wonder that comes from seeing characters on screen who serve as visual identifiers for specific demographics in order to flatten the expectation to desire anything more."[15] The only recurring Black actor with a speaking role, Henry Cottrell (Ronald/Ron Moore), like Armisen and Brownstein, plays different roles. Sometimes he plays a neighbor, family/guidance counselor, or coworker; in "One Moore Episode" (2012), he is mistaken for Ronald D. Moore, a writer for the popular science-fiction show *Battlestar Gallatica* (2004–10). The joke lies in the absurdity of Fred and Carrie—as superfans—mistaking Ron for a white television writer and Ron's willingness, despite his wife's objections, to go

along with their request to write a new episode to continue the canceled series. Fred's and Carrie's characters embrace color-blind neoliberalism. The
sketch never recognizes his blackness or uses satire to examine the lived
experience of people of color in Portland. Satire as a genre is political. *Portlandia*'s refusal to address structural racism in a city known as left-leaning
erases intersectionality and, consequently, does nothing to subvert white
privilege.

The Whitening of Portland

Crenshaw gave a talk at Tulane University in 2017 using gentrification
as a metaphor to explain the erasure of intersectionality. She claims that
intersectionality "has been gentrified in the sense that people whom it
initially designed to recognize have been pushed out of the discourse."[16]
I want to extend her argument by examining how *Portlandia*'s neoliberal
discourse about gentrification and embrace of the real estate industry, in
turn, erases intersectionality by pushing people of color out of the narrative. The show denies Portland's complicated racial history and obfuscates
racialized spaces in the city. *Portlandia* depicts the mobility of cultural and
economic capital—in this case, a proxy for whiteness—by mapping the circulation of the hipster lifestyle via gentrification throughout the inner core
of the city. I draw on intersectional theory to explain how existing power
structures that privilege whiteness and middle-class professional lifestyles
through neoliberal ideology are the underlying forces that drive the show.
Portlandia's erasure of intersectionality illuminates whose economic interests are represented and reveals which social identities are absent in the
show's narrative.

The show is filmed on location, and in the diegetic world of *Portlandia*,
street and commercial signage, city landmarks, and residential and commercial exteriors function as narrative place-making devices. It maps fictional narrative spaces that correspond to recognizable places in Portland;
it uses those signifiers to structure the storyline in many of the sketches and
uses them as a form of "locational imaging," in what Tom Conley describes
as the viewer plotting a "sense of time and place in which the fantasies of a
[show] are set."[17] Street signs help viewers navigate the city's terrain and root
certain characters to familiar residential and commercial places. Thus, *Portlandia* maps neoliberal social and economic practices—deployed as satire
on the hipster lifestyle—by visually labeling specific places in Portland and

10.1 Establishing shot of Fred and Carrie's home.

assigning those places specific social practices (e.g., sustainable city farm-
ing, do-it-yourself [DIY] culture, artisanal stores, dog parks, bicycle valet
service, and so on).

    Portlandia also uses labeling of these spaces in the city as a narrative and
place-making device. The show uses an intertitle-esque technique to mark
the beginning of a sketch and identify significant places in the narrative associated with the main characters (figure 10.1). The intertitles use a punch
label font reminiscent of postwar typewriters. The font signifies Portland's
DIY analog culture and hipsters' supposed nostalgia for agrarian/artisan-
based societies of the past.[18] *Portlandia* makes fun of Portland's embrace of
the past, but it is unclear what hipsters and, by extension, viewers are actually nostalgic for: is it "The Dream of the 1990s," of being alive in Portland,
established in the opening sequence of the series in season 1, or is it the
cold-opening start "The Dream of the 1890s" in season 2, episode 5? Is it a
nod to pregentrification Portland of the 1990s or does it go back further—
to the period of Black exclusion laws in Oregon? It is hard to determine
whether Brownstein and Armisen believe the desire for and embrace of the
past is problematic because *Portlandia* treats the past as a sentimental concept, a safe space where mostly white, middle-class, and young individuals
can retreat into a liberal bubble.

    Brownstein and Armisen have directly addressed accusations from the
public (mainly Portland residents) that the show is fueling gentrification
and, consequently, the whitening of Portland. They agree that the city is

changing but argue that the show is not responsible for gentrification as Portland is no different from most popular cities in the United States. In an interview with *The Oregonian*, Armisen states, "We use Portland as a framework. And the rest of it is more what's going on all over the country. We travel, and we use Portland as a backdrop, but it's things that are going on everywhere." Brownstein further explains: "Portland was already in the process of changing, the show only commented on it."[19] Armisen and Brownstein refuse to attribute Portland's popularity to the show, and their acceptance of gentrification as the normal development of the city reflects one of the primary logics of neoliberalism: economic growth equals human progress. Their arguments also reflect one of the central frames of color-blind racism: naturalization. Bonilla-Silva describes naturalization "as a frame that allows whites to explain away racial phenomena by suggesting they are natural occurrences."[20] In this case, gentrification in Portland is not unique, as it is happening in every major city. Armisen and Brownstein are essentially arguing this is "just the way things are," deploying a white universalizing tactic to justify the erasure of difference.

Portlandia not only represents gentrification. It also contributed to it through informal and formal partnerships with the TV and film industries and local businesses. *Portlandia*'s budget for its first season was less than $1 million, which included a 20 percent rebate from the state of Oregon to cover a sixty-eight-location shoot with fifty-six Portland-based crew members.[21] According to Brownstein, the crew and writers were primarily white, until the last season, which seems to be a reaction to the 2016 presidential election and ensuing toxicity.[22] The production company used a local casting company, Simon Max Hill, to hire extras, mostly of whom were local actors.[23] The show actively recruited Portland-based businesses and artists who wanted their products or work featured on the show.[24]

Portlandia also contributed to gentrification through its formal partnerships with the real estate industry. For example, to promote the series and, ultimately, the city, *Portlandia* featured integrated content (also referred to as native advertising) from the real estate company Zillow in a sketch entitled "House for Sale" (season 5, episode 8). In the establishing shot, a house appears with the text "NW Glisan St.," which is located in the Pearl District. Brownstein's and Armisen's characters are completing a kitchen renovation with high-end finishes and other signifiers of wealth, such as a subzero fridge. The couple decides to buy a fixer-upper because they do not have anything left to fix or upgrade in their current home. The sketch makes fun of upper-middle-class renovation culture made popular by HGTV and

10.2 Searching for a new home in the Zillow integration episode.

hints toward a general sense of domestic unease, as their lives seem empty without a project to complete together.[25]

Initially, the couple find what they refer to as a "scary" house for sale on Zillow with an asking price of $205,900 at the fictional address 10005 Cookes Street (figure 10.2). The house appears condemned and occupied by white heroin addicts. The use of a fictional address is significant, as I was able to locate the majority of the locations featured in the sketch, both commercial and residential, using Google Maps and on-the-ground detective work. Contextual clues, such as signs and landmarks, imply that the house is located in the eastern, browner part of the city, where rapid gentrification has taken place. Notably, the term "gentrification" is never used during the episode, and the fictional address does not conform to Portland's postal convention that often employs directional cues with street names. Linking the house to *white* heroin addicts, *Portlandia* deploys signifiers of problematic or undesirable bodies to mark the house as scary and the neighborhood as needing revitalization, thus directly avoiding addressing the intersection of race and class in the practice of gentrification in Portland's historically Black neighborhoods.[26]

The show's integration of real estate marketing extends past this one episode: IFC contracted with BARKBARK, a marketing company based in Atlanta, to create custom "advertainment" vignettes to air during the commercial breaks. In one version, a thirty-second vignette features recurring extras from the show riding a tandem bike to visit houses for sale that they have identified as having their "must-haves" using the Zillow app on their tablets. To establish a link to the show, the white couple rides by the Feminist Bookstore, a controversial place in *Portlandia*'s narrative. The actual bookstore, In Other Words, was featured in many skits during seasons 1–6 but ended its relationship with the show in September 2016 because of what the store considered a last straw: the producers asked the store to take down its Black Lives Matter sign during filming.[27] The staff explained their decision to end their participation in *Portlandia* in an open letter posted on the bookstore's website: "In Other Words is in the heart of a historically Black neighborhood in Northeast Portland. We have Black Lives Matter written on our window. Black Lives Matter Portland meets regularly in our space. But as more and more Black folks and people of color have become involved at In Other Words, Portlandia has only gotten steadfastly more white."[28] Although the city of Portland has promoted the economic benefits of *Portlandia* shooting on location and shining a spotlight on the city, local businesses, such as In Other Words, and community activists within the neighborhoods that *Portlandia* features do not think making fun of economic development that displaces people of color and the working class is a politically effective use of satirical humor.

Portlandia refuses to overtly mock the lack of racial diversity in Portland, even when it takes on gentrification in a storyline. For example, the sketch "No-Fo-O-Fo-Bridge" (2013) directly confronts gentrification in Portland and features anthropomorphic rats using stop-motion animation.[29] The sketch follows the rats' quest to go east to find new neighborhoods to inhabit. The story begins in the Pearl District, a formerly industrial area of the city that witnessed rapid decline before artists moved into the neighborhood in the 1980s and public and private urban planning partnerships redeveloped the area into a commercial and residential neighborhood in the 1990s.[30] The rats complain that the original stores have been replaced with all-wood-toy shops and other signifiers of gentrification, such as the closing of established stores in the neighborhood. The rats whine about the lack of good food, which they later describe as exotic and ethnic (e.g., Indian food), on the streets, exemplifying gentrifiers' engagement with superficial multiculturalism—that is, intersectionality as a theory of difference.

Brownstein and Armisen clearly see gentrification as the enemy, and on the surface this seems like a powerful political message; they depicted gentrification using rats, not their own likeness, as in the majority of the sketches. Here, as in Art Spiegelman's *Maus*, the decision to use animals (and stop-motion animation) "visibly and immediately alerts" the viewer to the constructedness of the sketch.[31] Representations of animals are socially and culturally coded, similar to stereotypes that serve to swiftly communicate specific behavior, characteristics, personality types, or views to the audience.[32] This coded form of communication is often used to advance critiques of human culture and social activities—in this case, gentrification.[33] Perhaps Brownstein and Armisen used rats to represent gentrification because, historically and culturally, the "rat is a highly charged figure that can warn and threaten, yet also bring salvation and good fortune."[34] Rats are vermin, pests that are ubiquitous and hard to eliminate, just like the gentrifiers Brownstein and Arisen target in their satirical criticism.

As viewers, we are compelled to accept that the rats are exploring undiscovered and unnamed neighborhoods, which is the typical narrative of gentrification. Yet there is a missed opportunity to question this often-deployed justification for gentrification. As feminist geographers have argued, "An intersectional approach would enable us to discuss the different and complex ways different axes of oppression cut across each other and are expressed and negotiated through the process of gentrification."[35] Instead, the sketch focuses on the rats' refusal to name or rename the neighborhoods they visit, acknowledging realtors' use of naming to market locales and attract new residents. The rats argue that it would be all over; it would be no longer cool to live there once the place is named. However, at the end of the sketch they toy with the idea of renaming the area near the Burnside Bridge "Bi-Fi," echoing familiar real-estate place-naming conventions that have given us names such as "SoHo" in New York City.[36] The sketch fails to recognize working-class people of color who live in Portland and to confront the city's history of redlining and disinvestment in the historically Black neighborhoods on the other side of the Willamette River.[37]

The audience is in on the joke, even though the rats refuse to acknowledge that they are gentrifiers. However, Brownstein's and Armisen's use of rats to stand in for white gentrifiers only hints at the reality of gentrification in Portland and does not address the structural racism that led to historical disinvestment in the neighborhoods in which the rats are clamoring to live. Black residents were denied opportunities to buy homes in Portland because of government redlining and discriminatory mortgage lending practices from the beginning of white flight from Albina in the 1950s to well into the 1980s.[38] The contrast between what is unsaid/unseen in the sketch and what is represented reveals the mechanisms of neoliberal urban renewal practices in Portland. Because the sketch fails to directly depict whiteness, and by framing choosing a place to live as an individual choice, the audience can identify with the rats and comfortably believe that they are not complicit in engendering racist housing practices. The sketch's erasure of intersectionality fails to highlight racial and economic inequity in the city. Instead, it privileges subjects who can freely move about the city— in this case, the rats that stand in for white gentrifiers.

Conclusion

Portlandia's hipster wonderland is a white neoliberal utopia. The series espouses intersectional erasure by adopting neoliberal practices such as color-blindness and privatization that have replaced overt forms of racism such as intimidation, violence, and discriminatory laws, all of which originally made Portland a white utopia. The show contributes to the collective illusion of the elimination of racism as a social-spatial practice in America through neoliberal ideologies that promote gentrification and false narratives of equality and diversity instead of embracing political solutions to challenge social injustice. By omitting narratives that acknowledge the history of segregation and housing inequity, *Portlandia* keeps audiences in the dark, unable to trace that history to present conditions in Portland. That omission ensures that the audience is comfortable criticizing and laughing at Portland, because viewers see themselves as onlookers and not implicated in social practices that keep racism and economic disparity thriving. *Portlandia* privileges the visibility of specific actors in the narrative and reduces intersectionality to a theory of overlapping identities that embrace difference for difference's sake.

CHAPTER ELEVEN

Erica Stein

CRIMINAL PROPERTIES

Real Estate and the Upwardly Mobile Gangster

The gangster genre plays out narratives of social containment and control through spaces that are deeply intertwined with raced and classed identities. When gangsters attempt to expand their territory beyond their local environments, they also challenge the limitations imposed by race- and class-based marginalization and are punished accordingly.[1] Of all the fatal avenues of escape pursued by gangster protagonists, real estate investment is perhaps the most thematically and spatially rich. In this staple of the genre, the gangster seeks not so much to expand as to transcend his turf by becoming a legitimate businessman through construction contracts, land deals, infrastructure speculation, or other real estate ventures. Such plots allow gangsters to transform their hereditary territory into unbounded flows of capital, succeed in a lawful trade, and access legitimate social standing outside their communities—or try to, before their inevitable failure. An intersectional analysis of the real estate trope demonstrates how its embodiment of criminality, territory, and capital vary directly with individual texts' depiction of race and class. Moreover, such an analysis illuminates the histories of urban real estate development that underlie these depictions, tracing their linkage of the poor and racial minorities to criminal forms of territoriality. I argue that an intersectional analysis of the real estate trope not only demonstrates how the gangster genre reinscribes dominant images of criminality but traces how particular entries in the genre use specific formal tactics to complicate, or even subvert, these images.

In this chapter I use *The Wire* (2002) and *The Long Good Friday* (John Mackenzie, dir., 1979, 1980)[2] to explore the real estate trope and its implications. These case studies diverge from each other in multiple ways. In addition to differences of media, release date, and national origin, *The Wire* is often studied in terms of the American melodrama and social problem genres, while *The Long Good Friday* sits staunchly in the center of the British gangster canon.[3] Perhaps most important, *The Wire* has a claim to a progressive politics through its nuanced representation of the lives of the Black urban underclass and critique of neoliberal institutions. *The Long Good Friday*, by contrast, is often read as nostalgic for a more authentic, less globalized, and more racially heterogeneous Britain.[4] Marsha Kinder, however, has shown that both the series and the film tie their gangster narratives to a larger "systemic analysis of corruption" that questions the central tenets of the genre.[5] Building on Kinder's work, I show that attending to the similar role real estate development plays in both plots while exploring their different treatments of race and class helps surface exactly what kind of corruption these texts are concerned with and how embodied difference helps systematize it.

I first detail *The Wire*'s use of the real estate trope and its depiction of the Black underclass, showing how the third season's doubled plot—which connects a drug dealer's investment in condo construction to a police commander's creation of a zone in which drugs are decriminalized—deconstructs the idea of territory. *The Wire* links territory to institutional expropriation, on the one hand, and redevelopment, on the other, pointing toward the historical processes that have dispossessed Black citizens and criminalized poverty. *The Wire*'s overt invocation of this history through a serialized, intricate plot focalized through racial and economic marginalization helps illuminate the critical potential in *The Long Good Friday*'s attachment of the real estate trope to the white middle class. This group's "proper place" is generally not articulated to territory at all. Rather, it is assumed to have the right to the city as a whole. *The Long Good Friday*'s aesthetics collapse social boundaries and intertwine legal and illegal acts to depict "authentic" middle-class Britain's dependence on Irish and Caribbean immigration. Exploring these texts in tandem elucidates the critical possibilities in their narratives, particularly their ability to represent how the intersectional pressures of race and class construct the social and spatial places that trap the gangster.

Occupied Territory: *The Wire* and Urban Planning

The Wire is set during Baltimore's early twentieth-century population drop and federally funded redevelopment, which left many older, historically Black neighborhoods with increasingly vacant housing stock, even as land values and rents rose precipitously in the Inner Harbor and Downtown areas.[6] At the same time, the rising crime rate led to the adoption of New York City's COMPSTAT and "broken windows" system of law enforcement, along with increased levels of police violence against Black residents.[7] *The Wire* dramatizes these events through the character of Stringer Bell (Idris Elba), the lieutenant/chief financial officer of the Barksdale drug gang. Bell's desire to avoid a war over drug territory on the city's west side, instead profiting from real estate investments and his downtown development project, drives the season. Bell's counterpart is Major Colvin (Robert Wisdom), the police commander in charge of the west side. Where Bell seeks to remake himself in and profit from the Inner Harbor and Downtown, Colvin attempts to claim more of western Baltimore for the police by creating non-enforcement "free" zones and confining the drug trade within them. *The Wire* builds equivalencies between these goals through intertwining plots that question the justness of policing and urban redevelopment in majority-Black cities. The season also allegorically depicts the longer history of housing discrimination, dispossession, and racial discrimination that makes much of the city inaccessible to the Black underclass and life within it precarious for the Black working and middle classes. Mirroring Bell and Colvin allows the season to foreground the systems that underpin the control and economic exploitation of Baltimore instead of presenting each character as an exceptional and tragic figure.

Bell's and Colvin's plots are intertwined from the opening moments of the season, when Mayor Royce (Glynn Turman) oversees the demolition of one of the city's high-rise public housing complexes (figure 11.1). The destruction of the high-rise escalates tension in the drug trade, as the Barksdales must seek new territory to compensate for the loss of business, causing conflict with other gangs. This exacerbates the city's already astronomical murder rate, drawing pressure from the mayor, City Council, and police commissioner to reduce crime statistics, which leads Colvin to come up with his plan. Every major plot point of the season—from Bell's eventual fall, Colvin's firing, to the mayor's declining political fortunes to the dismantling of the Barksdales—derives from this moment. Its omnipresent

11.1 The demolition of high-rise public housing at the start of the season begins *The Wire*'s connection of contemporary gentrification to historical forms of racial housing discrimination.

reach is dramatized in the cloud of dust that results from the terrace's demolition, spilling out from the deserted building onto apparently orderly streets, sending the assembled onlookers—former residents and visiting dignitaries alike—scrambling. The dust cloud embodies the season's insistence that, no matter how much figures such as Bell and Colvin understand the city as legible and salvageable only when criminal territory and the spaces of legitimate capital are kept separate, they are inherently interdependent.

This striking image opens onto an allegorical history that positions Colvin's project as a precursor to Bell's in a microcosm of the history of twentieth-century American housing policy. This allegory narrates the multigenerational theft of wealth from Black citizens. Stan Corkin argues that the opening sequence dramatizes the neoliberal management of real estate: "the projects must be torn down so that gentrification can take hold in their vicinity."[8] The scene also enacts gentrification's tendency to devalue public ownership, collective space, and controlled markets.[9] In addition to this more direct representation of gentrification's structure, the sequence gestures to its prehistory. The areas Colvin identifies as potential free zones fit mid-twentieth-century criteria for slum clearance, the wholesale removal of poor populations and leveling of the built environment. One of the major determining factors for neighborhood selection was the dominance of a minority demographic, especially African Americans, whose presence was treated as evidence of poverty and criminality. This mutual constitution of race and crime, as well as the conflation of race and class, was further tied to national housing and banking policies that made capital accumulation more difficult for even well-off African Americans.[10]

Colvin identifies his free zones, all of which occupy Black residential neighborhoods, through criteria reminiscent of slum clearance policy, based on a lack of services, homeownership, institutions, or a stable population. After disbursing "citizens" (i.e., residents who are not participants in the drug trade or aligned with the police) from the area by leveraging police resources, he forcibly transports a captive population of low-level drug dealers and their customers to the premises and contains them there, mimicking the concentration of poverty and social problems slum clearance helped cause.[11] When this concentration can no longer be contained and spills into adjoining territory, the entire area is razed to the ground, just as the gentrification of the American inner city in the late 1970s and 1980s was ushered in by the demolition of public housing. Colvin is a progressive figure within the series, emblematic of a demilitarized policing that could be achieved if the drug war was abandoned. Yet his project unintentionally reenacts the generational theft of wealth and housing from African Americans by governmental entities. Its status as a series of extralegal actions illuminates the ways in which this theft not only sets the historical preconditions of a rising crime wave but was also in itself a criminal act.

Colvin's experiment was judged a disaster both within the diegesis and in popular coverage of the series.[12] Yet it could be said, from the point of view of gentrification, to have functioned exactly as intended. Colvin transforms a long-turnover area into a short-turnover area and prepares the ground for reclamation by public-private partnerships that can reenter it into the market and exploit its exchange value. As Corkin argues, it is easy to imagine a sign advertising new condos over the barren ground where the free zone once stood.[13] However, the condos we see built in this season are erected not in western Baltimore but rather downtown, and they are erected by Bell. This further entwines drug enforcement with the profits from the trade it supposedly disrupts and contextualizes Bell's actions as the historical sequel to midcentury policies. Bell's company, B&B Enterprises, selects its construction, investment, and development opportunities based on their eligibility for state and federal programs, such as tax-increment financing and empowerment zones. These policies use several of the same criteria as slum clearance and were put in place to "revitalize" the inner city after slum clearance devastated them.[14] Bell repeatedly insists on the legitimacy, the "cleanness," of his real estate business, which is run with much-laundered profits that have only distant ties to the Barksdale drug empire. However, the series' wider historical view implicates this real estate business, as well as the federal investments it courts, as simply a different kind of criminal undertaking.

Bell ultimately fails to secure his federal contract, despite having spent a quarter-million dollars on fees, retainers, and bribes to architects, contractors, and state senators that amount to a "white-collar crime" as much committed against Stringer as it is perpetrated by him.[15] Bell's demise is typical of the gangster protagonist, caused by disputes within the criminal arm of his organization once he has been made more vulnerable and unable to read the shifting terrain of both legitimate and illegitimate power by his failed real estate venture.[16] However, Stringer's failure at real estate, and his inability to access the power and protection of the state, are not due to his criminal status. Throughout the season, multiple other characters occupying both sides of the law request resources from the government. Their success never depends on the legitimacy of their request. Instead, it depends on having secured the patronage of a powerful official. For example, the ex-Barksdale soldier Cutty Wise (Chad Coleman) needs permits to open a gym for at-risk youth but has no success until an assemblyman, Odell Watkins (Frederick Strother), provides support. Watkins asks Cutty, "Did you use my name? Anybody's name?" and explains that he must do so if he expects any positive response from city regulatory bodies. Bell's assumption that bribes and extralegal authority were the only avenue by which the Black underclass could achieve government recognition appears to have been correct; he was simply mistaken in his choice of criminal associates.

Watkins's emphasis on the power of names again aligns the season's criminals with its other characters and criminal territory with luxury property. The drug dispute that eventually causes Stringer's death is about the power of names—specifically, his partner Avon's (Wood Harris) need to have his "name ring out" and elevate his reputation over his rival Marlo's (Jamie Hector). Colvin's plan, likewise, depends on the prominence of the free zones and the preservation of his credibility by "taking corners" from Barksdale. These compulsive ties and parallels between cops and criminals, politicians and developers, suggest that every player considers the city a territory to be controlled, the police simply another gang in competition over corners, with politicians and power brokers conning Bell for federal grants. Bell's Baltimore is a space unified under the banner of illegal activity, one that alibis itself by imputing an inherent illegitimacy to the territory of poor African Americans, the better to transform that territory into real estate and secure its profits for the white developer class in an ongoing property crime that goes unpunished.

Privatizing London from the Docklands to the East End

The Long Good Friday is set at the dawn of the Thatcher era, when extensive deregulation and privatization led to the "big bang" expansion of London's financial district, the City, enabling the rise of London as a global finance hub with extensive ties to both America and Europe. At the same time, many sites within London formerly used for manufacturing and industry sat vacant—notably the Docklands, adjacent to the City. These ruins, the engine of England's nineteenth-century imperial dominance, had become emblematic of the country's postindustrial economic slump.[17] This state of affairs, in conjunction with the Conservative Party's neoliberal policies and one of the more violent periods of the Troubles, gave rise to a far-right nativism that targeted immigrants from the subcontinent, the Caribbean, and Ireland.[18] In this context, the Anglo-Saxon working-class—even its criminals—embodied a "more authentic" England threatened by both poor, nonwhite immigrants and an internationalized upper class.[19] The Long Good Friday details Harold Shand's (Bob Hoskins) efforts to make a deal with the American Mafia to purchase and redevelop extensive portions of the Docklands. As he does so, he is continually stymied by an Irish Republican Army (IRA) campaign of bombing and assassination, on the one hand, and the increasing racial heterogeneity of his territory, on the other. While this premise echoes the nativist rhetoric of the time, the film consistently undercuts it through cinematography, editing, and characterization that places Shand's viciousness on the same level as that of his opponents and ties his redevelopment project to economic and terrorist violence.

In the opening moments of The Long Good Friday, Shand has already succeeded where so many other screen gangsters failed: he has gained control of organized crime across the entire city and heads an immense legitimate real estate business that encompasses construction, pubs, and casinos. Shand's trajectory and air of celebrity resonates with the real-life Kray twins,[20] as well as their plentiful fictionalized counterparts on British screens. However, just as Shand has essentially entered the middle class, he has also shed the signifiers of queerness and Jewishness that attached to and complicated the working-class identity of other Kray screen avatars, from *Performance* (Donald Cammell and Nicholas Roeg, dirs., 1970) to *The Long Firm* (2004). These other depictions, as well as real-life media coverage, associated the Krays with a social outsider status articulated to traditional, inherently malicious working-class neighborhoods.[21] By contrast, Shand is first seen striding through Heathrow Airport on his way to his yacht mooring on the Thames upon his return from New York, having secured funding from the Mafia to complete his next land deal. This sequence begins to unify the different precincts of the city and undo the equation of gangster to territory by associating Shand with London's liminal spaces. Although later in the film he uses the terms "patch" and "manor"—which working-class South London and East London gangs use to describe their territories—we never see him inhabit one; rather, he lives in a palatial West End flat.[22] The opening sequence suggests that Shand has indeed stepped "out of his place" to make every place his. Yet throughout the film, every place remains essentially anonymous and interchangeable. This is crucial to *The Long Good Friday*'s dramatization of the effects of privatization. Every space is disarticulated through breaks in editing continuity, yet each space is fundamentally the same, bound up in and contributing to the same socioeconomic system. This construction of space is echoed by the plot's revelation that there is no legitimate authority, whether that of an "authentic" white English working class or of capital and its legal/financial systems.

This simultaneous atomization and unification of space and criminality is played out in an early scene in which Shand lays out his plans to "make London the economic capital of Europe." Shand's goal is closely aligned with Thatcherite policy and Britain's entry into the European Economic Community. Throughout the film, Shand and his American counterpart—the Mafia don Charlie (Eddie Constantine)—valorize the unimpeded movement of money across national boundaries as the engine of their own cross-class slippage into "legitimacy," here conflating the erasure of spatialized class boundaries with those that separate the illegal from the legal. Shand defines London's potential, and his own, as their blankness: "Having cleared out the past . . . no other city in the world has so much open land right at its center for profitable progress." This "open land" refers to the Docklands and the Isle of Dogs, and the speech is made as the yacht passes by them

11.2 Given in the middle of the Thames, Shand's development pitch embodies the deterritorializing impact of real estate speculation on London's historically working-class spaces.

(figure 11.2). However, they remain almost entirely off-camera, glimpsed only incidentally in a brief reestablishing shot that focuses on the yacht.

Instead, the scene consists of a shot-reverse-shot sequence of Shand standing in the bow of the yacht, alternating between long shots of him framed by the Tower Bridge as he makes his speech and close-ups of various stakeholders in his audience as they sit on the deck. The identities of these stakeholders—a high-ranking detective inspector, Charlie, Shand's lieutenants, and a construction magnate/city councilman—illustrates the intertwining of global finance, organized crime, and state authorities under capital.

The stakeholders are tightly framed, cutting each off from the others, suggesting the fragmented nature of Shand's supporters and reflecting the discontinuities of the privatized space they each profit from and embody. Moreover, each is shot at an angle that reflects their position on the deck of the yacht and their spatial relation to Shand, who stands at the bow. Shand, however, is always depicted in a frontal composition, breaking continuity. Just as the spaces Shand purports to use to save the city are held off-screen, the character himself occupies an impossible space, caught between the river's northern and southern banks, with their vastly divergent economic fortunes, and framed by a clichéd remnant of England's past imperial glories. The cinematography and editing suggest that Shand's plan will fail because it depends on a space that does not really exist. At the same time, the dialogue reducing the Docklands to "[economic] potential," use of disjunctive camera distances, and disarticulation of space through editing reveal that the deterritorializing on which Shand's plan depends is itself a kind of vanishing of space: the obliteration of its past, the nullification of class and ethnic ties within it, and the reduction of it to a pure exchange commodity.

Shand's plans resonate with the real-life redevelopment that displaced working-class Londoners from traditional employment and increased European and American investment in London. They are thwarted by the IRA, which, enraged by a double-cross by Shand's corporation on a recent deal, begins attacking his employees and properties. This inciting incident plays out in the opening images of the film, and the unraveling of Shand's plans (and, indeed, his life) are already inevitable before he makes his speech—even, in fact, before he is first glimpsed on-screen. Every action Shand takes is futile. He is essentially defeated by Northern Ireland's ability to produce coherent identities and communal unity through shared ethnic and class identity akin to the one he himself has forsaken.

The Long Good Friday seems not only to enact the "forgetting your place" narrative typical of the gangster genre, but also to produce Northern Ireland as an entirely Other, archaic space that threatens England and its future. Thematically, Northern Ireland functions as criminal territory and extends that territoriality into London through violent activity. Yet the film's aesthetics incorporate Northern Ireland and the IRA into, and explore them through, commonalities with London. The introductory scenes, set in Northern Ireland, use the same cinematography as the rest of the film, connecting this space to London and rendering the two equivalent. Throughout the film, telephoto lenses, crane shots, and pans convey a sense of surveillance. Establishing shots are static and often depict apparently barren spaces, with the camera positioned behind a car window or fence, moving to track arriving characters as though lying in wait for them. Within scenes, continuity is jettisoned in favor of incongruous extreme long shots and close-ups. The former isolate characters within the frame and make their actions difficult to perceive. The latter, especially in the first scenes, eschew faces and reaction shots for apparently random details of torsos and hands. This framing, which in a typical continuity system would grant access to the entire setting, instead withholds narrative information—amplified by the muffling of dialogue through the barriers that appear in many shots—and evokes both exposure and claustrophobia while complicating traditional audience identification. The result is that the events of the film unfold outside of any character's control; even the apparently omniscient IRA is depicted as being taken by surprise in an opening ambush. These formal elements subvert the claims made by multiple English characters that the IRA "doesn't know the rules," is "unstoppable," and "can't be reasoned with."

Shand's characterization complicates this stance as well. In a climactic scene, Shand learns that the IRA is after him because his lieutenants double-crossed the group on a payment. This payment was related to Shand's legitimate real estate business, which uses Irish construction workers and employs the IRA to keep them from striking or negotiating better wages. This plot twist repositions the Irish workers—whose economic and ethnic threat to the nation were bywords of the Thatcher government and the National Front—as *literally* building the London of the future. Their suppression as organized labor, moreover, requires the government, nationalist groups, and native gangsters to depend on the IRA. Here, the stereotyped figures of the poor Irish immigrant and psychotic Irish terrorist are imploded and depicted instead as mutually serving the political-economic needs of the former empire that proclaims them both existential threats.

Just as the privatized space of London is unified through economic interests that span nations and legality, Shand lacks a "patch" because the idea of a self-contained neighborhood has become impossible. Yet the character continually claims not only power but also moral authority from his affiliation with the "authentic" white working-class areas of the city, even as this also allows him to claim to represent respectable middle-class Englishness itself. Shand's construction of Englishness is founded on its distinction from and superiority to the Italian American Mafia, the IRA, and the Caribbean community that now increasingly lives in Shand's old neighborhood. *The Long Good Friday* deconstructs the claims of white Britain to working-class London neighborhoods and to the city's future with an extended scene set in an unnamed neighborhood that evokes the increasingly immigrant-dominated, soon-to-gentrify areas of Limehouse, Clapham, and the East End. Shand arrives in this neighborhood to question an informant about the bombings and killings. Throughout the scene he directs racist screeds and violence at the inhabitants, most of whom are Black, in ways that echo the underlying logic of the gentrification of which he is a part: that the presence of the poor and people of color is inherently criminal and invasive.

This scene, however, visually and thematically aligns the audience with the neighborhood residents, who are depicted in conventional medium shots that contextualize them in space, and noticeably not with the distancing diegetic barriers that mark the rest of the film. As Shand threatens a young Black man working on his car, his neighbors run over to comfort and protect him. Similarly, the camera dwells on the neat, well-kept, sun-drenched public spaces of the neighborhood so at odds with Shand's description of them. Finally, an interracial group of boys stand guard over the gangster's car and request money for its protection, evoking the communal ties and class solidarity that Shand mourns as lost from his own criminal dealings. In *The Long Good Friday*, Shand's misreading of immigrant neighborhoods is identical to the official Thatcherite narrative. Shand cannot successfully escape his patch for the legitimation and financial bounty of the City or his posh West End flat because there is no difference between criminal territory and the centers of power.

Everything in Its Right Place

Charlotte Brunsdon and Marsha Kinder argue that characters such as Bell and Shand are ultimately killed by the literal and figurative places they forget because, in forgetting them, they also slough off their authenticity, vitality, and ability to read urban social space.[23] Yet in *The Wire* and *The Long Good Friday*, the unwinding of traditional territory, the heightening of global capital's mobility, and class- and race-based restrictions of socioeconomic mobility result in gentrified cities that resist legibility *in general*. Disjunctive editing, surveillance-like cinematography, and extremely complex causal structures suggest that urban illiteracy is not a failing of the upwardly mobile gangster but characteristic of the redeveloped city itself. The aesthetics and plots of the series and the film insist on the city as a unified space in which real estate speculation is comparable to trafficking and racketeering, each equally threatening to the urban ensemble's well-being. As the consummate detective and series conscience Lester Freeman (Clarke Peters) says of Bell in *The Wire*, "He's worse than a drug dealer, he's a developer." Of the same series, Paula Massood asked, "If the gangster genre is as much about acquiring the American dream (in the form of social and economic belonging) as it is about criminality, then what happens when that dream is directly connected to real estate?"[24]

The Wire and *The Long Good Friday*'s use of real estate proposes that there is ultimately no difference between criminality and the conditions that make social and economic belonging possible. That is, on the one hand, title to property and accumulation of wealth through it are prerequisites for socio-economic belonging, and such title and accumulation can be achieved only through criminal acts: the exploitation of African Americans and of immigrants, respectively. On the other, real estate as a spatialized sign of socioeconomic belonging reinscribes its legitimacy through an artificial contrast with territories it constructs as criminal, in large part through the race and class of those territories' inhabitants. By playing out the real estate trope through plot structure, characterization, aesthetic form, and historical intertext, *The Wire* and *The Long Good Friday* demonstrate the extent to which the gangster genre is dependent on separations of legal and criminal space and illuminate the artificiality of those distinctions. The series and film show how the place of the gangster—territory and the complex of race and class for which it serves as a metaphor—exists only in contrast to an idealized, unmarked whiteness and wealth that has proper title to real estate, to all space that is not territory, to the city, and to the law. An intersectional analysis of *The Wire* and *The Long Good Friday* elucidates the unique tactics each uses to contest the naturalization of whiteness and capital inherent in the gangster genre's usual invocation of one's place and the dangers of forgetting it.

IV _ RACE, PLACE, AND SPACE

DRESSING THE PART

Black Maids, White Stars in the Dressing Room

The dressing room is the rare space in classical Hollywood musicals in which we see white and Black actresses sharing the screen. In their scenes together, the women are alternately friends and foes, enjoying camaraderie or engaging in competition. No matter the nature of their relationship, however, these scenes are fundamentally about the power differential between white stars and their Black maids. This essay considers those backstage narratives— and, specifically, backstage musicals of the classical era—in which Black maids appear. Whether silent or vocal, the maid begs attention because of her persistence in dressing room scenes. These are not incidental appearances. Rather, the maid's presence is vital to the intersecting negotiations of race, class, and gender that take place in these narratives. This chapter asks the questions: Why does she appear, and what is her function in the genre?

A subgenre of the musical film, the backstage musical explores the lives of performers, their professional aspirations, and their intimate desires. Bifurcated along the spatial divide of onstage and backstage space, the genre explores the tension between public and private forms of identity. The protagonist is typically a white woman who reveals her private self and prepares for her public role in the dressing room, an enclosed space that harbors the tools of transformation: costumes, makeup, and so on. On hand to assist in this crucial process is her Black maid, a figure of inferiority and servitude. First and foremost, the maid's presence underscores the protagonist's transformation, signaling a conflation of stardom and whiteness. The dressing room, a space of "reality" compared with the fictional world of stage performance, naturalizes that conflation.

The backstage musical's use of the Black maid echoes representations of Black supporting figures in other mediums. Referencing the practice of including Black servants in early modern portrait painting, Peter Erickson notes a dynamic in which the servant "is secondary but nevertheless 'portrayed,'" creating an awkwardness and a "built-in tension" within the text. Similarly, in his analysis of the Black (female) backup singer in popular music, John Corbett argues that her position in the background is essential, but ultimately nameless, support. She "extends the potential" of the (male) lead by the mere presence of her raced and gendered body in the background. Analogous to servants and backup singers who occupy an enclosed "background" space, the maid's inferiority is signaled by her raced body, which then heightens the protagonists' whiteness. And her emplacement in the dressing room renders the space one of interiority, a "claustral" site of confinement that justifies the power relationships it encloses.[1]

But while she extends the potential of whiteness in the musical, the Black maid also constricts the potential of femininity. She functions as a corrective to the female protagonist who has risen too quickly and achieved too much. Typically, these films are set at the turn of the twentieth century and against the backdrop of the Ziegfeld Follies, a popular entertainment form that exalted white femininity at precisely the moment that American racism and nativism were particularly virulent. Florenz Ziegfeld, the entertainment mogul and creator of the Follies, used his position to celebrate his "Ziegfeld girls" according to his own standards of beauty and female decorum.[2] Both exalted and contained, Ziegfeld girls were at once symbolic of women's achievement and men's discipline. In Hollywood, the Ziegfeld Follies appears as an entertainment form that gives the girl her big break (*Glorifying the American Girl* [Millard Webb, dir., 1929], *Easter Parade* [Charles Walters, dir., 1948], *Somebody Loves Me* [Irving Brecher, dir., 1952], *Love Me or Leave Me* [Charles Vidor, dir., 1955], *Funny Girl* [William Wyler, dir., 1968], *Funny Lady* [Herbert Ross, dir., 1975]). The sudden appearance of a Black maid in her luxurious dressing room confirms the girl's success, to the detriment of her moral character and personal relationships. The dressing room literally contains the Black maid while it elevates whiteness, but it also justifies the constriction of women's empowerment and checks women's mobility.

Historically, the dressing room has been a site of female power. In Tita Chico's analysis of eighteenth-century satirical fiction, dressing rooms are spaces where sexual excess, theatrical dissembling, and feminine agency have free rein precisely because of the space's private and transformational qualities. Dressing rooms are at once the focus of men's fascination and critique, preparing "the woman for public display as well as serving as sites of display in their own right."[3] Male intruders into the space justified their actions by demonstrating that women's manipulation and expression required censure and control.

The backstage musical uses the Black maid's femininity and servility to surveil the dressing room. She observes and at times conceals the white woman's secrets. These narratives rely on the Black maid to undergird white racial superiority, but they also enlist her as a cautionary device to deliver critical commentary on white women's achievement outside of the domestic sphere. The maid does this silently and symbolically, which is the norm in the earliest backstage musicals, and vocally and subversively in later examples. In body and in expression she reveals how the genre's meaning and function hinge on the intersectionality of race, class, and gender, employing each modality to define and check the others. After discussing early sound-era examples of this dynamic, I focus the analysis on two postwar films: *Easter Parade* and *Somebody Loves Me*.

Black maids appear in the earliest backstage musicals, including *The Jazz Singer* (Alan Crosland, dir., 1927) and *Glorifying the American Girl*, as the uncredited and silent attendants of Mary Dale (May McAvoy) and Gloria Hughes (Mary Eaton), respectively. While we do not see the interior of Mary Dale's backstage quarters, *The Jazz Singer* signals Dale's stardom by portraying a Black female attendant who escorts her to and from the dressing room. In *Glorifying*, a narrative that charts the rise of Gloria from anonymity to star, we see the appearance of her maid only when Gloria has become "glorified" on the Ziegfeld stage. While *The Jazz Singer* is a rare example in which the narrative focuses on male (and immigrant) stardom, *Glorifying* introduces what would become a convention of the genre in the classical period: the confluence of stage success with opulent dressing rooms and the Black maids who occupy them.

In a dressing room scene near the end of the film, Gloria's maid shakes her hand after a successful performance. The maid quickly recedes into the background until Gloria is ready to exit once again. Her static presence in the dressing room renders it a stable and safe place for Gloria to grapple with her newfound identity as star. Meanwhile, the maid's celebration of Gloria's stardom and attention to her dress makes her a figure of support and comfort, as Corbett notes about the role of the backup singer. The maid stands and works while her mistress sits and self-reflects. She occupies the anterior of the space while Gloria is at the forefront. The maid wears a drab smock while Gloria displays a bedizened gown. And her maid remains silent and nameless while Gloria has free expression and achieves an exalted identity. In this way, the Black maid provides visual evidence of her own fixedness while she marshals the transformative qualities of the dressing room to amplify her mistress's rising social position.[4]

As in a number of backstage musicals, however, the Black maid qualifies the star's choices. In *Glorifying*, Gloria learns that her hometown sweetheart has married someone else in the time that she has spent working toward stardom. Her maid's presence in the background thus communicates both success and sacrifice for the female star. Achievement, these backstage narratives say, comes at a price for the working woman. Similarly, in *42nd Street* (Lloyd Bacon, dir., 1933), Dorothy Brock (Bebe Daniels) suffers the loss of romantic love as a result of pursuing her stage ambitions and the luxuries that come with them, including fine clothes and a Black maid (Pansy [Louise Beavers]). Similarly, in *The Hard Way* (Vincent Sherman, dir., 1943), Katie Blaine (Joan Leslie) regretfully considers her decision to reject her suitor while a Black maid (Libby Taylor) fusses over her. The maids are status-laden figures and the result of women's ambition.

The convention of having the woman pay a price for her success is put into harsh relief by Mae West's *I'm No Angel* (Wesley Ruggles, dir., 1933), a film that offers a notable exception. As with *Glorifying*, the Black maid, Beulah (Gertrude Howard), appears along with the protagonist's elevated social position. Tira (Mae West) goes from being a lowly "kooch" dancer to a star lion tamer. The rise in status comes with the transformation of her dressing room from a dingy tent to a lavish abode. Pamela Robertson argues that Mae West's maids demonstrate how "codes of sex and gender intersect with racial codes."[5] To this I would add class, symbolized by the upgraded dressing room and the sudden appearance of Beulah as her maid. Beulah's arrival is coterminous with the maintenance of Tira's superiority as a white woman, but she also confirms Tira's newfound wealth and social position.

Yet where *I'm No Angel* is in keeping with other films that conflate white women's stardom with the use of Black maids, it departs from that convention when it comes to the portrayal of the Black maid as a silent companion and a symbol of female loss. As Robertson discusses, West engaged in "complicated cross-racial identifications with blackness which are key to her transgressive image." West lends her maids subjectivity, giving them names, dialogue, and, to an extent, movement outside the domestic realm. Robertson points to the homosocial affinity displayed by Tira and her maids as a moment when gender trumps race.[6] They talk about men and desire from their shared position as sexualized female beings. So while

Beulah and the other maids in the film maintain a position of inferiority, communicated by their location in the background of the dressing room, their costumes, their drawling speech, and their work, these scenes are ones of contentment rather than regret. Instead of suggesting that Tira must make sacrifices for her elevated status, the film revels in her enjoyment of it. West, who wrote the script, takes care to reject the idea that she must atone for her character's decadent lifestyle, which includes multiple Black maids, extravagant clothes, and open sexual promiscuity. West goes as far as to place Tira's lifestyle choices on trial. As her own lawyer, Tira exposes the hypocrisy of the men who criticize her for having multiple partners and taking their gifts, arguing, "Who's harassing who? I just want a square deal, that's all." After she wins the case, a reporter asks her what she intends to do, to which she responds defiantly, "Carry on the same as before." The final scene shows her happily ensconced in her lavish apartment, enjoying both the fruits of her labor and the love of a man. Tira, unlike the protagonists in other backstage narratives, is stridently unapologetic and refuses to make a choice between love and ambition. Her maids figure as confidantes, albeit racially inferior ones, rather than social correctives.

Like those in *I'm No Angel*, the maids in the postwar musicals *Easter Parade* and *Somebody Loves Me* have more developed characters. But where West's film gestures toward female companionship, the postwar films feature female betrayal and competition. Though still contained by the logic of racial hierarchy in the genre, the Black maid nevertheless exposes its insecurities by "talking back" to her mistress. These are brief moments of insubordination that, once uttered, are quickly suppressed. Their silencing, both narratively and musically, is part of the censuring and containment of Black and white women as the price of both of their transgressions. Much like the miscegenation narratives of which Susan Courtney writes, the "temporary transgression of one register of difference is negotiated or stabilized through the reassertion of another."[7] In these backstage musicals, the Black maid's misbehavior challenges the authority of her white mistress. The mistress in turn corrects her servant but is ultimately disciplined by male patriarchy and the convention of heteronormative coupling. The backstage musical's fascination with women who eschew domestic life in favor of their careers had particular resonance in the postwar era, when the pressure to domesticate both men and women was acute amid Cold War anxieties of social (and national) dissolution. In the dressing room we witness white and Black women stepping out of bounds and needing to be disciplined in public and private ways.

Jeni LeGon plays the maid in both films, serving Nadine (Ann Miller) in *Easter Parade* and Blossom Seeley (Betty Hutton) in *Somebody Loves Me*. An exceptional tap dancer and singer, LeGon was the daughter of Black migrants to Chicago and danced in all-Black revues before going to Hollywood and eventually earning a long-term contract with MGM, the first Black woman to do so. The contract proved to be limiting, however. In an interview conducted later in life, she tells the story of being denied a role in *Broadway Melody of 1936* (Roy Del Ruth, dir., 1935) because she was "upstaging" Eleanor Powell's dancing. Similarly, while she has prominent billing in the cast of *Easter Parade*, LeGon's one song-and-dance number was cut from the final print of the film, a further indication that producers feared she might have upstaged Ann Miller, Judy Garland, and Fred Astaire, the stars of the film.[8] As Miriam J. Petty argues, notions of "upstaging" and "stealing the show" were frequently applied to African American performance in 1930s Hollywood as a means of circumscribing and devaluing Black performance.[9] LeGon's story certainly fits this model. Frustrated by her relegation to minor roles, she ultimately left the United States for a teaching career in Canada. Her career shows the effect of Hollywood's racial politics on the lives of Black performers. Nevertheless, it would be a mistake to dismiss LeGon's maids as just stereotype if we are to understand how the backstage musical functions. LeGon's characters serve the critical function of checking female vanity in the dressing room. And they highlight her talents while exposing the cinematic mechanisms that keep her in check.

In *Easter Parade*, LeGon plays Essie, Nadine's duplicitous maid. Nadine is a Ziegfeld star who spurns her longtime partner, Don Hewes (Fred Astaire), to pursue a solo career. We quickly come to understand Nadine as a deeply flawed character. While she is beautiful and talented, she is cold, materialistic, and shallow. She orders Essie to spy on Don's show. Essie lies and delivers the message that the show is a flop, gratifying Nadine. Essie returns to Nadine's dressing room and is joined by Johnny (Peter Lawford), friend to both Nadine and Don. Having just returned from watching Don's show, Johnny looks slyly at Essie who is busying herself with Nadine's costumes and says, "Well, Essie, I see you got here before me."

The frame's composition in the scene reveals a spatial geography that signals Nadine's lack of character and Essie's duplicity. The mirror plays a particularly important role in the power dynamics of the room. The scene shows Nadine sitting at her dressing table gazing at Johnny's reflection (figure 12.1). Johnny is positioned off-screen, as is Essie, whose hand and profile occasionally enter the frame from screen left. As Julian Hanich has

12.1 Essie (Jeni Le Gon) occupies the edges of the frame in *Easter Parade*.

argued, these are "complex mirror shots" in which off-screen characters are framed by their reflections, actively alerting the viewer to the possibilities and meanings of off-screen space. In this instance, the two off-screen characters, Essie and Johnny, are bearers of the true narrative: that Don's show was a success. Nadine's two-faced nature is communicated by the two versions of herself that we see: the disingenuous one seen in her reflected look of sympathy, and her real self seated (between the camera and the mirror) at the table. The placement of Johnny's reflection between the two views of Nadine emphasizes the visual split between her true and false personas. Johnny's spatial location allows him to occupy a position of power from which he can deliver judgment on Nadine inside the mirror shot and share in Essie's lie outside of it. In this way he provides the requisite male oversight in this otherwise female space. Essie, who does not have a reflected subjectivity, remains in the off-screen shadows, an indication of her inferior social position and treachery.[10]

While Essie transgresses her role as servant, we nevertheless understand her behavior to be warranted, given Nadine's cold, careerist ambition. It is significant that, just prior to Nadine's dressing room scene, we see Hannah (Judy Garland), Don's new dancing partner, in her own dressing room. The space is well appointed and organized in similar fashion to Nadine's, with the dressing table at the far right of the frame. The glaring difference, however, is that an elderly white maid attends to Hannah's dressing needs. Nadine's employment of Essie appears as one more extravagance of a superficial single woman. The white maid, by contrast, underscores Hannah's humility and openness to romantic love, which she achieves with Don in the end.

Though Nadine's self-image suffers as a result of Essie's betrayal, *Easter Parade* maintains the racial status quo with its musical sequences. Just before Essie visits Hannah and Don's show, Nadine performs the Irving Berlin song "Shaking the Blues Away." Emulating Black dance movements ("Do like the voodoos do, listening to a voodoo melody / they shake their bodies so, to and fro"), Nadine embodies the Black performer, asserting her own dominance in the process.[11] And immediately after Nadine learns of Essie's deception, she goes onstage to perform "The Girl on the Magazine Cover," a Berlin ballad that celebrates white femininity ("She is fairer than all the queens"). So while Nadine's brand of femininity gets checked from below by her Black maid, her superiority as a white woman is ultimately upheld by the performance numbers in the film. *Easter Parade* engages in an interplay of racialized and gendered identity formations that temporarily unsettle but ultimately restore one another according to social norms.

In LeGon's subsequent film, *Somebody Loves Me*, the dressing room and the Black maid become the performance itself. LeGon plays a critical role in a medley of songs sung as part of Blossom Seeley's star turn on the Ziegfeld stage. The number begins with a dressing room scene in which Blossom and Delilah (LeGon) prepare for the show. The curtain closes as Blossom steps forward to sing a duet with her costar. The curtains open again, and she returns to the dressing room, changes costume, and exits once more to sing the final song. While Hutton moves between "backstage" space and onstage space throughout the performance number, LeGon is physically and musically segregated to the dressing room behind the curtain. The song that they sing together has no title and is not included in the credits for the film, effectively erasing LeGon's presence from the soundtrack. Nevertheless, the sequence lends LeGon's character a subjectivity that few Black maids are given and showcases LeGon's talent in direct counterpoint to Hutton's.

The power relationships and tensions of the dressing room, as a site of performance, move from private to public realms and from interiority to spectacle. The space and its inhabitants become iconic representations of archetypes: the white, female star and her Black maid. Blossom performs as herself. It is her story of stardom and privilege that the number celebrates.

As the first curtain rises, we see Blossom standing with her back to the theater's audience, wearing a pink bustier bodysuit and gold high heels, admiring herself in a large mirror studded with lights in the center of the stage. The setting is a hyperfeminine space, decorated with flowers and draperies in pastel colors of white and pink and an elaborate crystal chandelier overhead. There is a tufted table below the mirror that holds the symbols of female vanity, including a hand mirror, brush, and powder-puff. Draperies enclose the space and conceal the closets full of costumes.

Blossom calls for Delilah, whose entrance from one of the closets is punctuated by a change in the orchestration to a burlesque-style trilling of horns. Delilah wears a white lace apron and cap and a short black dress, the uniform of the maid and a symbol of her servility. But the two women share in the project of the dressing room: to prepare the star for her performance. They stand together in the center of the stage, squatting in time. Delilah sings, "Heard ya callin', heard ya callin', Miss Blossom / Ain't this dressin' room a pretty sight? / Watcha need, watcha wearin', Miss Blossom? / Do ya want a dress that's comfy or tight?" Like that of a backup singer, Delilah's function is to soothe and amplify the lead performer. When Blossom returns to the dressing room later in the medley, Delilah gratifies her employer's ego, saying, "That was really something special, Miss Blossom. Betcha Mr. Ziegfeld had a smile." The sequence performs the reliance of white women on Black ones to effectively dress the part of the star.

Spatially, the archetype of the white female star traverses both narrative and performance, and the Black maid remains an enclosed entity. While she and Blossom occasionally perform the same movements, Delilah is always positioned a step behind Blossom, reinforcing Blossom's superior social position. Her anterior location becomes all the more apparent when the spotlight turns on and the curtain closes on Delilah, an action that is repeated twice in the medley; as our view of the dressing room closes, so does Delilah's access to the space of performance outside. Blossom moves outside the dressing room to sing two duets as different characters—an elegant lounge singer in "Rose Room" and a sexy jazz singer in "Way Down Yonder in New Orleans"—while Delilah remains fixed in place and in identity.

Delilah challenges this fixity in subversive ways. Before hanging Blossom's pink boa in the closet, she quickly tries it on, shimmying with it while Blossom has her back turned. This brief indiscretion warrants a look of rebuke and the order to hurry with the next costume. Delilah hands her the new dress and belts the line, "And you've got every other singer beat, by a long, long mile." Singing "long, long," Delilah improvises and elongates the

12.2 Delilah (Jeni Le Gon) competes for center stage in *Somebody Loves Me*.

words so as to showcase the low and high registers of her voice. The lyrics she sings fulfill her role as support to Blossom, but the manner in which she sings them constitutes a challenge (figure 12.2). Delilah finishes her impromptu solo, looking pleased with herself and smiling at the camera. Blossom responds with an angry expression and a quick "thanks" before she exits the dressing room once more. At this point, the curtain never reopens to reveal Delilah. Instead, the end of the number is marked by Blossom and her male costar taking bows in front of the audience.

While Delilah's subordinate status is firmly established, spatially and formally, she uses these same techniques of cinematic language to break free from her constraints, if only for a moment. As in *Easter Parade*, LeGon's character in *Somebody Loves Me* performs the stereotype of the insubordinate Black servant. She wears Blossom's boa and co-opts a line in the song in order to showcase her own vocal prowess. But these moments of Black transgression are liberatory. LeGon's characters are transgressive and wily, constantly threatening to overturn the balanced system of power in the dressing room. Delilah claims the spotlight and reveals that her own talents match, and potentially exceed, those of her mistress. She exposes the power differential in the dressing room as a construction, like the dressing room number itself, and one that can be easily challenged. For a brief moment, Delilah claims the dressing room as a space of mobility for herself.

Ultimately, however, the film contains both Black and white women's transgressions with the musical numbers that appear adjacent to the dressing room sequence. The song that immediately follows Delilah's misbehavior is one in which Blossom stages her own act of stealing from the Black performer. She sings of the "Creole babies" whose "flashing eyes softly whispering tender sighs" provide comfort and enjoyment "way down yonder." The number confirms her white dominance and perpetuates the fiction of the docile Black body, a myth that Delilah has just proved to be false. In the second instance, she embodies the Black performer by wearing blackface and singing a medley of "Mr. Banjo Man" and "Dixie Dreams," two songs that situate the "antebellum idyll" (as opposed to the modern city) as the rightful home for Black people.[12] Again, Delilah's very sophisticated performance in the dressing room provides a corrective to this belief, rendering the film's multiple representations of blackness discontinuous.

Like earlier musicals in which Black maids appear, the film is invested in using gender to re-establish the boundaries of race. These, however, also use heteronormative systems of control to discipline gender. While Blossom contains Delilah's transgressions, it is Blossom's love interest and eventual husband, Benny Fields (Ralph Meeker), who disciplines her. The timing of the dressing room number—which exalts but, with the use of Delilah, also qualifies Blossom's stardom and talent—is significant. It occurs just after she has met Benny and already attempted to control him by offering him an inferior part in her show. The number both confirms Blossom's identity as star inasmuch as it relegates Benny to the role of secondary player. They marry, but Benny gets tired of being "Mr. Seeley." He divorces Blossom and strikes out on his own. It is not until Blossom decides to give up her own career in support of his that the film allows the couple to reunite. As she tells the audience upon making the decision, "I've got the billing I've always wanted, Mrs. Benny Fields." In the end, she performs the role of wife, erasing her professional identity as star in the process.

The backstage musical is a genre that allows for the exploration of women working in the public sphere, charting the rise of aspiring performers and exploring the private lives of stars. Of all backstage spaces, the dressing room is where the cinematic audience understands what is at stake for these women. As an enclosed, quasi-domestic space that protects the woman from the public sphere, but also readies her to occupy it, the dressing room is a critical site of female character development. The Black maid is crucial in this project, for she renders the dressing room a site of comfort and support for the white star, highlighting the transformational and liberatory qualities of whiteness with her own lack of social mobility and spatial fixity. With the exception of *I'm No Angel*, Black maids in film also serve as a corrective for the female lead, checking the elevated status that comes with stardom. As I have shown, the Black maid's earliest representation as a symbol of extravagance transitions into open subversion in LeGon's postwar roles. While the films quickly curb these transgressions, they nevertheless reveal the inherent tensions in a genre that seeks to both celebrate women's achievement and curtail it. Inside the dressing room, the genre's real performance takes place.

CHAPTER THIRTEEN

Sarah Louise Smyth

"I DO NOT KNOW THAT I FIND MYSELF ANYWHERE"

The British Heritage Film and Spaces of Intersectionality in Amma Asante's *Belle* (2013)

In a key moment in Amma Asante's British heritage film *Belle* (2013), Chief Justice Lord Mansfield (Tom Wilkinson) asks his great-niece Dido Elizabeth Belle (Gugu Mbatha-Raw), a wealthy multiracial woman born to a Black African slave mother and a white British naval officer father in eighteenth-century England, about the book she is reading. She replies that it is *A Gentleman Named Thomas Day*, which "speaks of a slave who agrees to marry an English lady; a voice for people, people like my mother, who do not have one." When Lord Mansfield asks whether she finds herself in such writing, Dido replies: "I do not know that I find myself anywhere."

In this chapter, I investigate this issue of placelessness. Narratively foregrounding the complexity of Dido's identity, *Belle* offers a significant opportunity for an intersectional analysis of race, class, and gender representations in British heritage cinema.[1] Moreover, as the first British heritage film with a multiracial woman as its lead protagonist, *Belle* enables an explicit interrogation of the British heritage film's whiteness.[2] As I demonstrate, within heritage film studies little work has been done to interrogate the ubiquity of white representations or the presence—or absence—of people of color, particularly Black and multiracial people, within British heritage cinema. Centering my analysis on *Belle's* representation of the country house—a symbol of white, patriarchal authority—I examine how Asante stages her wealthy multiracial protagonist. Arguing that the film's use of this space paradoxically upholds and challenges the hegemonic whiteness of the genre, I argue that *Belle* provides a complex representation of a woman of color's subjectivity in a genre that so often marginalizes, ignores, or erases her existence.

Race and the British Heritage Film

In film studies, the British heritage film has often been conceived as a high-quality historical or romantic costume drama (often a literary adaptation) that reproduces nostalgic and reductive images of national history and identity. Andrew Higson canonized the term in academic studies, where he links a cycle of films to the cultural-industrial moment of Margaret Thatcher's government (1979–90). The films, he argues, articulate a nostalgic and conservative pastiche of the values and lifestyles of imperialist upper-class Britain through both their textual visual display and their links to the heritage industry, where the past becomes a commodity for consumption.[3] Since then, academics have complicated and broadened the term, suggesting that the heritage film is a flexible critical category connected to a network of cultural and industrial practices that relate to the construction of collective memory, often using the term synonymously with period drama, costume drama, or historical film.[4] In this chapter, I take up the term "heritage film" deliberately to question whose history is being remembered—or, to quote Stuart Hall, "Who is Heritage *for*?"[5]

For Hall, the answer in Britain is clear: heritage "is intended for those who 'belong'—a society which is imagined as, in broad terms, culturally homogeneous and unified."[6] As John Corner and Sylvia Harvey argue, "Working behind every use of 'heritage' . . . there is necessarily a sense of an *inheritance* which is rhetorically projected as 'common' whilst at the same time it is implicitly or contextually closed down around particular characteristics of, for instance, social class, gender and ethnicity."[7] For Hall, British heritage is deeply intertwined with histories of colonization, slavery, and empire. However, these histories are subject to selective amnesia and disavowal and represented as an "external appendage" to British history and culture.[8] If heritage is constructed along racialized, gendered, and classed lines and continues to marginalize histories of colonialism within the dominant national narrative, then certain groups are left out of the sense of national belonging, including, but not limited to, people of color, particularly women of color; transgender, nonbinary, genderqueer, and gender-nonconforming people; disabled people; queer people; people from Britain's former or current colonies; and members of the working class.

Scholars have made various attempts to interrogate on-screen representations of British heritage in terms of race, gender, class, and sexuality.[9]
Much has been written about (white) women's representation, for, as Claire
Monk observes, heritage films often exhibit an overt concern with sexuality and gender.[10] Likewise, Richard Dyer has demonstrated how heritage
films provide fertile ground for representations of queer histories.[11] Little
has been done, however, to investigate the presence—or absence—of people
of color, particularly Black or multiracial people, within British heritage
cinema.[12] Of the small work done, Stephen Bourne provides a survey of
Black representation, arguing that the Black British presence is invisible
to the extent that "whiteness [is] a specific generic trait of British period
films."[13] Black British actors such as David Oyelowo repeatedly complain
about Britain's "obsession" with the production and consumption of heritage films to the exclusion and detriment of Black British narratives and
talent.[14] However, a number of British heritage films have emerged recently
that investigate nonwhite stories within narratives about colonial histories,
such as *A United Kingdom* (Amma Asante, dir., 2016), *Victoria & Abdul* (Stephen
Frears, dir., 2017), and *Viceroy's House* (Gurinder Chadha, dir., 2017), or that
cast Black actors in roles conventionally offered to white actors, such as
Wuthering Heights (Andrea Arnold, dir., 2011) and *Lady Macbeth* (William
Oldroyd, dir., 2016). This cultural and industrial trend offers a new opportunity with which to interrogate what we mean by British heritage. *Belle*
provides a unique example as the first and, currently, only British heritage
film to have a multiracial woman as its lead protagonist, opening up new
possibilities of intersectional analysis in British heritage cinema studies.

The Country House: Visibilities and Invisibilities

In this chapter, I examine one central space of the heritage film: the country house. As Madge Dresser and Andrew Hann argue, "The British country
house, that symbol of refinement, connoisseurship and civility, has long been
regarded not only as the jewel in the nation's heritage crown, but as an iconic
signifier of national identity."[15] The country house often links the heritage
film and heritage industry as both the place where films are set and shot and
key tourist attractions run by the National Trust or English Heritage. However, in this chapter I move away from an analysis of what Amy Sargeant
identifies as "the marketing and consumption of Britain's cultural heritage
as a tourist attraction" to investigate the textual representation of the

country house in *Belle*, considering how this mediates the representation of classed, racialized, and gendered bodies in the film.[16] I follow Julianne Pidduck's argument that the country house is a contentious place for (middle-class white) women in heritage cinema, particularly Austen adaptations: as a representational space of women's limited agency; as a contested site of subjecthood through property ownership, inheritance, and marriage; and as a place symbolizing romantic heterosexual desire and longing.[17] Asante's staging of her wealthy multiracial female protagonist in the country house centralizes issues of nation, race, and class as they intersect with gender, both suggesting the limits of Pidduck's argument and opening up new maps of inquiry within the spatial configurations of heritage cinema.

When *Belle* first reveals the country house—Kenwood House in Hampstead Village (now Hampstead Heath, north London)—the idyll of the white stately home, nestled into the picturesque pastoral landscape, is emphasized by glorious sunshine and a swelling orchestral score (figure 13.1). Higson, rather reductively, argues that the heritage film constructs a nostalgic gaze that resists visual ironies, social critiques, and political tensions and instead turns images and objects, including the country house, into an excessive spectacle to be admired.[18] In *Belle*, the first shot of Kenwood House—a panning shot from an objective and omniscient point of view—certainly encourages the pleasures of looking through the emotive music and beautiful landscape, contrasting sharply with, for example, the audience's first look at Mansfield Park in the postcolonial reworking of Austen's novel in Patricia Rozema's 1999 adaptation.[19] However, although the film situates us within the familiar generic milieu of the heritage film, Asante also destabilizes the images through both oblique and direct references to colonialism and slavery.

In the preceding scene, Captain Sir John Lindsay (Matthew Goode), a white British naval officer, arrives at a port to collect young Dido (Lauren Julien-Box), his daughter born to a Black slave mother who has since died. The opening frame—a long shot of an English port—shows the hustle and bustle of seafaring life, with rows of ships lined up in the foreground and background of the shot. The ship, Pidduck argues, represents the "spectre of colonial space" just outside of the frame of heritage films, particularly Austen adaptations.[20] Asante explicitly situates us in this historical colonial context through the film's opening title card, which reads, "The year is 1769. Britain is a colonial empire and a slave trading capital." However, Asante also explicitly made an "Austenesque" film.[21] Therefore, although the film attempts to interrogate the financial underpinnings of this society,

KENWOOD HOUSE
HAMPSTEAD VILLAGE

13.1 The country house in *Belle* both conforms to and challenges heritage cinema's generic conventions.

following Austen's narratives slaves are not visible. If spatiality is "a powerful tool of cinema that can reveal aesthetic, political, social and historical meanings of the cinematographic image," the extent of what is made visible or invisible becomes significant.[22] Dido's mother, for example, is never seen, although the film identifies "Belle" as Dido's mother's name, indicating her important structural (if not visible) presence. Moreover, *Belle* elides any ethical questioning of the relationship between Captain Lindsay and Belle or the terms under which Dido was conceived, even cutting a line from Lord Mansfield, who describes Captain Lindsay's relationship with Belle as "sheer lack of 'self-control.'"[23] Some aspects of slavery and colonialism, it seems, are "too much" to reveal in a heritage film, particularly one imitating an Austenesque romance.

Following a brief exchange at the port, Captain Lindsay takes Dido to his carriage to begin their journey to Kenwood House. If colonialism constitutes "a shadowy yet essential aspect of an audiovisual economy of restraint and movement," then this journey from one part of England to another marks the absent (or "shadowy") journey of wider transatlantic journeys and exchanges through which Dido was conceived and brought to England.[24] Asante frames the arrival of Captain Lindsay and Dido at the house from the perspective of Dido's young white cousin, Elizabeth (played as a child by Cara Jenkins and as an adult by Sarah Gadon); an over-the-shoulder shot with Elizabeth in the extreme foreground of the frame shows the carriage pulling up and Dido being lifted out before Asante cuts to a medium close-up shot of Elizabeth's quizzical look at Dido. Framing this moment through Elizabeth's gaze, Asante emphasizes the "strangeness" of this arrival for the white inter- and extratextual onlooker. The film may

situate us in the familiar iconography of the county house, with an Austenesque gesture to the history of colonialism and slavery that is just out of
frame, but Asante also makes clear that this is also a perspective of history
and heritage with which we are unfamiliar: the perspective of an aristo-
cratic woman of color.

The Country House: Longing and Belonging

Like the feminist critiques of white patriarchal property ownership by Sally
Potter, by way of Virginia Woolf, in *Orlando* (1992) and Emma Thompson,
by way of Austen, in *Sense and Sensibility* (Ang Lee, dir., 1995), Asante uses
the country house to focalize Dido's intersecting axes of privilege and oppression and the conflicting notions of "belonging" they reflect. Lady Mansfield (Emily Watson) makes clear that Dido is not to marry because "any
gentleman of good breeding would be unlikely to form a serious attachment
to Dido, and a man without would lower her position in society." Indeed,
rather than being offered the limited social agency afforded to middle-class
married women, Dido is given the keys to take over the household duties at
Kenwood—not a symbol of property ownership, but a reminder of her low
social and domestic position.

Moreover, just as the interiors of country houses in heritage films evoke,
as Pidduck argues, "the claustrophobic weight of history, oppressive patriarchal laws of inheritance, and the strict codes of comportment," which
goes beyond their representations as what Higson calls "museum pleasures,"
Asante demonstrates how they further destabilize Dido's sense of belonging.[25] At several moments in the film, Dido gazes at paintings around the
house depicting Black servants and their white masters—a tacit reminder
of Dido's racialized position and the histories of colonialism and slavery on
which the wealth of her ancestors was built.[26] Later in the film, Dido is to be
painted, offering her a representative "place" within the house. The actual
painting, upon which this moment is based, suggests the significance of
Dido's subjectivity, which inspired Asante to make the film: "[The painting]
said: I am here. I'm relevant. I'm a lady. I'm brown."[27] The painting and the
film both indicate the importance of reexamining material history through
an intersectional, racialized lens—the paintings, after all, function more
than Pidduck's gendered assertion that interiors evoke oppressive patriarchal laws of inheritance—and pose broader questions of (national) belonging, both inside the country house and outside of it.[28]

However, the portrait is not enough. Once the painting is shown to her, Dido continues to wonder where her "place" is, leading Lord Mansfield to ask Dido: "What do you want?" Pidduck argues that female desire is encapsulated by the trope of the woman looking out of the window in heritage cinema as she longs for romance, heterosexual courtship, and marriage, which are inextricable from the question of historical property relationships: "In this sense, the gaze from the window may also be read as a retrospective yearning for middle-class entitlements of citizenship denied Austen's female protagonists by accident of sex."[29] Despite being told she will not marry, Dido does secure a match in Oliver Ashford (James Norton), a second-born son in a high-ranking family whose attraction to her inheritance outweighs the potential shame her race would bring to him and his family. His brother, James Ashford (Tom Felton), however, disapproves of the match and assaults Dido while accusing her of destroying "the entire order of our family." In the scene following this incident, Dido looks out the window, with the camera cutting from a long shot of her silhouette in the window frame to a close-up shot of her contemplative face—a suggestion of her interiority. Dido's look out of the window refracts Pidduck's affective female longing through the further intersection of race and class, offering a potent reminder that the yearnings for "entitlements of citizenship" mean something very different to Dido than to analogous white women.

Pidduck suggests what is at stake for people of color's subjecthood in heritage films, particularly Austen adaptations, via Toni Morrison's reading of the interdependence of slavery and freedom in Mark Twain's *Huckleberry Finn*: "To tease out the contemporary yearnings afoot in the Austen adaptations is to bring forward the supporting characters of servants and countryfolk—and to consider the structuring absences of colonial peoples and places just outside the frame."[30] In other words, the middle-class white woman's yearnings for personhood, social mobility, and corporeal and sexual freedom is always in relation to other social groups who do not have any, such as slaves. In another scene, Dido gazes out the window again, and this follows both a romantic development (this time a genuine moment of desire with Mr. Davinier [Sam Reid], the man Dido eventually marries, as he touches her hand affectionately) and a moment of political awakening for Dido. Dido compels Mr. Davinier, who is working with Lord Mansfield as he prepares to rule on the *Zong* case, to tell her what he believes happened on the *Zong* ship. As he outlines the details of the case—that slaves were deliberately thrown overboard because they were diseased and therefore "worth more as dead insured merchandise than as alive spoiled goods"—Dido's eyes fill with tears. The cut to the next scene, where Dido looks out of the window, brings forth the gendered, racialized, and classed structures of feeling. Dido is a financially privileged woman, but she is one intimately imbricated in the history of slavery, colonialism, and the *Zong* trial. The window, then, becomes a place where Dido contemplates her complex position as a wealthy woman of color who desires heterosexual love and marriage and a claim to citizenship—a longing for belonging—not afforded to her due to her status as a multiracial woman born to a slave mother.

The Dining Table

In this way, Asante inverts Pidduck's claim that heritage film's pervasive trajectory of female becoming is constructed "*against* fraught backgrounds of class and colonial struggle" by demonstrating how Dido's strive for subjectivity plays out *within* these struggles.[31] Asante centralizes the trope of the dining table both to make explicit Dido's position within the house and wider social structures and to mount an intersectional feminist critique against this positioning. When the Mansfields receive guests, Dido is told she will not dine with the family, prompting her to ask Lord Mansfield, "Papa, how may I be too high a rank to dine with the servants and too low to dine with my family?" The dining table here functions as a class and race marker that prevents Dido from integrating into upper-class social life and finding a potential romantic suitor.

In another scene, after being served breakfast by Mabel (Bethan Mary-James), the Mansfields' Black servant, Dido asks the family whether Mabel is a slave. After Lord Mansfield informs her that Mabel is "free and under our protection," Dido curtly responds, "Oh, like me," before further antagonizing her uncle by asking how the *Zong* trial is going, which she calls a "fraud appeal." Through her challenge to Lord Mansfield's white patriarchal rule, Dido (and, by extension, Asante) function here as Sara Ahmed's intersectional figure of the feminist killjoy.[32] Seated around the family table (figure 13.2), Ahmed's feminist killjoy becomes tense as the conversation turns to something she finds problematic yet cannot challenge without disrupting the apparent happiness of this family image. Asante transmutes Dido's moments of affective longing at the window into the willful act of exposing, and therefore posing a problem, at the table. The table symbolizes and enacts intersectional feminism as an "object of feeling"—as a way

13.2 While Dido (Gugu Mbatha-Raw) takes up the role of feminist killjoy at the table, Mabel (Bethan Mary-James), the servant, is not welcome at the table at all.

of relating to and making sense of the world—which allows us to see what the picture at the table does not and will not reflect.[33] Although Lady Mansfield attempts to restore the happy family image by telling Dido to desist discussing the "vulgar subject," which, in turn, vocalizes the broader silencing of slavery and race relations in Austen's work and heritage cinema, Dido/Asante's challenge turns them into willful subjects: "*a refusal to look away from what has already been looked over,*" whether this is Lord Mansfield's refusal to consider the racial politics at play at home and work or British heritage cinema's broader marginalization of slavery and the history of people of color.[34]

But to assume a feminist is a killjoy at the table is to assume, of course, that she has a place at the table in the first place. Dido is not always welcome at the dining table, but Mabel, as a Black servant, is not welcome at the table at all. Although Asante suggests that Mabel and Dido are, to some extent, comparable in their blackness—race, after all, is what compels Dido to compare herself to Mabel and to become a killjoy in this moment— Dido's status as an heiress to a fortune gained through colonialism offers her a tenuous privilege never afforded to Mabel. Yet the film also offers a moment of affinity between Mabel and Dido at another table—the dressing table—when Dido struggles to brush her hair and Mabel, taking pity on her, shows her how to do it. Although Mabel is still performing labor for Dido (and, indeed, Mabel would not be welcome to sit at the dressing table, either), Asante presents this as a moment of Black female solidarity by framing the two women looking at each other in the mirror. (Elizabeth, standing in the background, is tellingly out of focus.) In addition to gesturing to the symbolic significance of hair to Black and multiracial women's identities, this moment enacts what bell hooks calls the "process of mirrored recognition" and the "shared gaze of . . . solidarity" between women of color in the struggle to represent Black women's subjectivity.[35] Also inserting the maternal figure (Mabel tells Dido that her "mam" taught her how to brush her hair), Asante locates this moment of Black female subject formation across a generational and class struggle, even if this is constrained by class positionings that cannot be overcome.

Beyond the Country House

Ultimately, Asante/Dido's literal and figurative spatial challenge within the house is limited. To stake her claim as a full legal subject, Dido furthers her involvement in the *Zong* case by stealing evidence from Lord Mansfield's study and giving it to Mr. Davinier to make it known in a court of law; her spatial transgressions can go (literally) only so far. The film culminates in Lord Mansfield's ruling in the *Zong* case (that the slaves were purposefully thrown overboard and should be considered human beings, not cargo) and Dido and Mr. Davinier's declaration of love for each other. The romantic conclusions of heritage films, particularly Austen adaptations, frequently have been read as indicative of the postfeminist moment in which feminine subjectivity is linked to romance and consumption.[36] Indeed, Dido's confirmation into this white world via marriage could be read as the postfeminist and postracial demand for the multiracial subject to "transcend" their blackness to arrive at a state of success—a figure in opposition, yet related, to the "tragic mulatto."[37] However, in *Belle* multiracial female subjecthood depends on more than a depoliticized heterosexual marriage script.

As Lord Mansfield presides over court, Asante cuts between shots of him reading his verdict with shots of Dido sneaking out of the house and breaking into the public gallery, overlaying the gallery with Lord Mansfield's speech in voice-over. Linking these moments, Asante positions Dido as a woman of color for whom the verdict will have enormous ramifications for her own freedom. This is not to suggest that Dido's journey, personal autonomy, and freedoms are the same as the slaves'. Rather, this rebellious and transgressive journey is the culmination of Asante's challenge to heritage cinema and a statement on the importance of Dido's subjecthood for her to marry Mr. Davinier as his "equal." So Mayer argues that *Belle* reconfigures the courtroom as a place of celebration and marriage as a route to freedom. Citing Kara Keeling's delineation of the doubled meaning of the word "representation" (meaning both "depicted," for example as a visual or embodied representation, and "empowered to speak for," such as in legal proceedings), Mayer observes that both meanings are at stake in *Belle*.[38] For just as the film centralizes Dido's position within a wider eighteenth-century society through the legal implications of Lord Mansfield's deliberation and eventual ruling over the *Zong* case, so it also begins to correct cinematic representation's staggering lack of people of color, particularly in heritage cinema.

Asante's challenge to heritage cinema can be situated within a broader history of transnational women's filmmaking that reexamines national history and memory through race and colonialism, such as Jane Campion's *The Piano* (1993) and Julie Dash's *Daughters of the Dust* (1991). This also includes the films with British female authors already mentioned, such as *Mansfield Park, Sense and Sensibility, Orlando, Viceroy's House, A United Kingdom*, and *Wuthering Heights*. The growing number of these films perhaps suggests that the whiteness of (British) heritage films is being interrogated and that women's filmmaking presents an acute example of what Stuart Hall calls "rewrit[ing] the margins into the centre."[39] This spatial metaphor is appropriate for my analysis of *Belle*. I have argued in this chapter that the country house is a key feature in heritage cinema, both for the familiar generic milieu it offers and for the image of upper-class, patriarchal whiteness it maintains. However, in *Belle*, Asante foregrounds the house as a place where a challenge against this authority can be mounted and a space in which a woman of color's intersectional subjectivity can be explored and negotiated. Doing so within the "familiar" framework of the heritage film, particularly an Austenesque film, Asante interrogates the genre's role in the formation of British history and cultural memory. After Dido's concern that "I do not know that I find myself anywhere," Asante's intervention in the constructions and histories of multiracial womanhood opens up new spaces for explorations of race, gender and class in heritage cinema and beyond.

QUEERNESS, RACE, AND CLASS
IN THE MIDCENTURY SUBURB FILM
CRIME OF PASSION (1956)

This chapter addresses the intersection of queerness, race, and class in the mid-twentieth-century suburb cycle film *Crime of Passion* (Gerd Oswald, dir., 1956) in creating an "interlocking system of oppression" for its major female protagonist, Kathy Ferguson (Barbara Stanwyck).[1] It explores Hollywood's effort to contain Kathy's difference through prescriptive ideologies concerning gender and sexual identity, restrictive and racialized suburban structures and practices, and class entrapment in what George Lipsitz terms a "white spatial imaginary."[2] In accord with most midcentury Hollywood suburb cycle films, such as *The Desperate Hours* (William Wyler, dir., 1955), *Man in the Grey Flannel Suit* (Nunnally Johnson, dir., 1956), and *Bigger than Life* (Nicholas Ray, dir., 1956), the inhabitants are almost uniformly white and middle-class because of what Richard Dyer and a host of other scholars regard as "the invisibility of whiteness as a racial position" and because whiteness became synonymous with suburban identity.[3] I identify how *Crime of Passion*'s Kathy Ferguson registers queerness and masculine femininity in her negotiations of the new suburban house, which is also racialized as white and gendered as feminine in midcentury America. Women were ushered back to the home front after World War II, where they were expected to provide a nurturing atmosphere, attend to domestic tasks, and raise a family.[4] Kathy is further constrained by the mutually constitutive categories of race and class, struggling against normative, white middle-class expectations as shown in her efforts to secure a more upscale private abode through her husband's professional advancement, evidencing her adherence to a "possessive investment in whiteness."[5]

In spite of her multipronged entrapment, queer-coded characters such as Kathy transgress the traditional home spaces and gendered room arrangements as a form of resistance and redolent of her queerness. But ultimately, Hollywood renders queerness in *Crime of Passion* as maladjustment to hegemonic gender and class expectations and a resistance to dominant spatial habits at home and at work while opening a space for alternative identities to surface in domestic space.

The Expulsion of Difference in Midcentury Suburbia

The spaces of postwar American suburban communities and their individual dwellings were constructed predominantly to accommodate white heterosexual, middle-class nuclear families after the housing shortage occasioned by World War II. The new midcentury postwar suburb thus served as an intersectional space, suggestive of hegemonic ideas on race, gender, sexual identity, and class. Just as cities such as New York and San Francisco were more accepting of Otherness, suburban places were marshaled for their eradication. Lynn Spiegel notes, "At the center of suburban space was the young, upwardly mobile middle class family; the suburban community was, in its spatial articulations, designed to correspond with and reproduce patterns of nuclear family life. . . . Older people, gays and lesbian people, homeless people, unmarried people, and people of color were simply written out of these community spaces and relegated back to the cities."[6]

Elaine May asserts that the return to traditional domesticity resulted from postwar feelings of insecurity and as a bulwark against Cold War fears of communism. Conservative politicians believed that communism could be controlled on the home front, May argues, by preventing so-called subversives, including foreigners, gays and lesbians, and nonconformists, from "spreading their poisonous influence through the body politic."[7] Gill Valentine concurs, referring to the idea of sexual citizenship and the manner in which spaces are regulated by the nation-state.[8]

Single domestic dwellings were built primarily as the most basic form of white, heterosexual American territory, an analogue to the country, indicative of its values of private ownership, homogeneity, and exclusivity, from whose boundaries putative dangerous forces must be kept at bay. Middle-class suburbs were racialized environs, constructing whites and "Others" through spatial inclusions and exclusions. From the 1940s to the 1960s in America, as Michael Omi and Howard Winant argue, the prevalent belief was that racial and ethnic strife could be assuaged by "assimilationism," which stressed the homogenizing role of both ideological and material culture.[9] Most postwar American suburbs were such adaptive spaces, as Dianne Harris has demonstrated, where "nonwhite" ethnics who were formerly relegated to discrete urban neighborhoods were admitted with provisional white identities and expected to acclimatize to its norms.[10] She locates a "pervasive iconography of white middle-class domesticity," which was inscribed in the architecture of the "little white houses" of the suburbs and crucial to the formulation of white identity. Real estate agents and loan officers sold the suburbs by underscoring their selectivity and separation from the "blighted" cities, employing coded adjectives such as "secure," "stable," and "private" for middle-class prosperity and heteronormative whiteness.[11] Concurrent with the inclusion of would-be white ethnics, African Americans, Asian Americans, and Latinx were still marked as other and barred from the majority of suburban spaces and the American Dream by a complex, well-documented nexus of legal barriers and government policies, including restrictive racial covenants; the federal government's discriminatory loan practices, supported by private banks, that dispensed home loans only to white male breadwinners; and redlining, racial zoning, steering, blockbusting, and myriad other policies practiced by realtors.

The equally coterminous pressure to be middle class also inflected these normalized, post–World War II white suburbs. The housing expert Charles Abrams claimed in 1955 that the suburban middle-class denizen was told to be "homogeneous", not to mix with the rich or poor, and to use "restrictions" to keep the wrong people out."[12] Undesirables were also associated with the underprivileged, who supposedly harmed a neighborhood's stability and social and economic standing. As Abrams shows, the word "homogeneous" began to appear with frequency in official and unofficial Federal Housing Administration (FHA) publications. The author of the book *How to Buy or Build Your Home Wisely* (1941), echoing FHA policies, claims that "inharmonious racial, national or income groups" were detrimental to a neighborhood and led to a decrease in property values."[13] Since poverty was associated with heterodox, "blighted" cities, Becky Nicolaides and Andrew Wiese point to the "two warring images of suburban abundance and urban decline" that persisted in midcentury America, which were a result of segregation policies, echoing what Eric Avila calls "the vanilla suburbs of homogeneity, certainty, and containment versus the chocolate cities of danger, and heterosociality."[14]

White domestic isolation and purposeful separation not only meant the buttressing of white racial, heterosexual, and class hegemony; for LGBTQ citizens, the policy was also one of domestic exclusion and expulsion. As Andy Medhurst opines, "It is perhaps sexual dissidents who are the most rigorously policed victims of the suburban cult of conformity. Of all the hegemonies of suburbia, it is the hegemony of heterosexuality that cuts deepest, bites hardest."[15] Despite the paucity of scholarship on the indignities perpetrated against queer Americans in suburbia during the Cold War, the example of Ocean Beach on Fire Island in New York serves as an exemplar. An alliance of convenience composed of white Christians and summer-vacationing Jews (who were themselves the previous victims of discrimination on Fire Island) objected to the infiltration of homosexuals and sought to rid the island of the "blemish."[16] We can extrapolate further concerning the treatment of queer Americans in the suburbs from Cold War federal government policies, which purged homosexuals from jobs with more frequency and venom than communists. An influential Senate report of 1950 concluded that homosexuals were morally weak and had a "corrosive influence" on other employees. Senators referred specifically to homosexuals' putative effects on physical space, charging that they "could pollute an entire office." Employing a domestic metaphor that could easily be applied to the suburbs, "The Republican Party campaign slogan, 'Let's Clean House,' promised to rid the federal bureaucracy of Communism, corruption, and sexual perversion." The inclusion of the term "sexual perversion" in the Republicans' platform was a new addition and served as a code word for homosexuality.[17]

Whiteness, Class, and Sexual Difference in the Cinematic Suburbs

The suburb's white heteronormativity and putative class oppressiveness are registered in *Crime of Passion* as soon as Kathy moves from San Francisco to the San Fernando Valley of Los Angeles. Introduced by a downward tilt shot of intersecting, collage-like rooftops to underscore claustrophobia, the scene serves to augur the human relationships of its residents. The script describes the desultory suburban surroundings as made up of cheaply constructed houses, which appear "to push each other, as though struggling for breathing space."[18] This negative view of the suburbs was instantiated by a host of mid-century social critics, such as David Riesman in *The Lonely*

Crowd (1950), whose class critique blamed consumer-oriented, "outer-directed" types who sought happiness in the purchase of commodities.[19] The camera then fixes on the residence tightly sandwiched between two identical generic houses before proceeding to the street below, emphasizing the class confinement of its new resident, the former Kathy Ferguson. The modest, lowbrow valley home belongs to Bill Doyle (Sterling Hayden), a Los Angeles Police Department (LAPD) detective who recently married Kathy, a gutsy, former newspaper columnist, after she helped him and his partner, Captain Alidos (Royal Dano), apprehend the murderess Mary Dana. After their unlikely, whirlwind romance, Kathy relocates to Doyle's mediocre suburban neighborhood, which is far below her class expectations. But before she leaves her job and acquiesces to Bill's proposal, she informs him that a woman's putative fulfillment through marriage is nothing more than "propaganda," continuing: "For marriage, I read life sentence. For home life, I read TV nights, beer in the fridge and second mortgage. For me, life has to be something more than that."[20] Kathy's reference to marriage and its gendered, carceral suburban spaces portends poorly for any adjustment to her new locale while foreshadowing her ultimate imprisonment at the film's denouement.

The film's rows of generic white stucco houses that were shot on location in the San Fernando Valley neighborhood represent the modest hopes of families seeking the American Dream, and their suburban designs are meant to encourage conformity to the white heterosexual nuclear family. For example, kitchens faced the front of the house so mothers could supervise their children. Indeed, numerous youngsters are seen playing in an enclosed cul-de-sac in the film, a form of midcentury suburban planning that was often confounding and purposely intended to keep "undesirable" elements at bay. The architectural historian Barbara Miller Lane argues further that such dwellings and, indeed, the entire suburban layout—the picture-windowed houses facing one another in circular cul-de-sacs, including expanded front lawns without boundary fencing—are configured to promote outdoor social intercourse with one's similar neighbors while keeping others out. They also facilitate surveillance and, hence, an adherence to normative heterocentric and racial ideologies through spatial enforcement.[21]

Obviously not cut out for the gendered feminine and class position that she is expected to occupy, Kathy begins to plan her escape, first by establishing an opportunistic liaison with Alice (Fay Wray), the wife of her husband's boss, Anthony "Tony" Pope (Raymond Burr), the chief inspector of the LAPD, then by carrying on an illicit affair with the powerful inspector himself. When the inspector refuses to promote Bill, Kathy eventually kills him in his magisterial abode in a final attack on suburban space. But the film's eponymous crime of passion, the murder of Tony Pope, has been brewing for a long time and is prompted by Kathy's intersectional oppression—hatched in the newsroom, where she is forced to work on a female-centered advice column because of her sex while unacknowledged by her male supervisor, and fueled in the spatial confines of the stultifying suburbs, where she is expected to adhere to heterocentric white ideals, before finally combusting in an act of violence that is redolent of both Kathy's queer containment and her frustrated class aspirations. Yet the other crime of passion the film instantiates is the manner in which her desire—a journalism career, hence, her voice—is destroyed by patriarchal ideology that, in turn, prompts her fateful decision to renounce an offer of professional advancement in New York for married suburban life.

The small, white generic Doyle residence is typical of the Levittown-like dwellings that sprang up all over the country, with a restrictive interior that is seen from Kathy's point of view and underscores her middle-class oppression. The production designer, Leslie Johnson, fashioned the tightly confining living room, which abuts the front door, to mimic the typical, small, 800–1,000-square-foot postwar suburban dwelling and to associate the house's lack with Kathy's growing class dissatisfaction; thus the house is a trap for her difference. Decorated with a horror vacui of floral-patterned wallpaper that clashes with a checkered couch and easy chair, the drab, lowbrow accouterments are stultifying, a mismatched arrangement, much like the Doyles' relationship. So tightly is the house configured that their marital bed is visible from the living room; it is surmounted by the Mexican artist Diego Rivera's painting *The Flower Carrier* (1935), which acts like a pall over the Kathy and Bill's newly formed heterosexual union. The painting features a woman behind a stooped, anonymous male peasant carrying a heavy basket, witnessing or exacerbating his backbreaking burden.[22]

Despite Kathy's dissatisfaction with her suburban abode and her gendered outlier position, she nevertheless adheres unknowingly to a "possessive investment in whiteness," believing that she is entitled to certain property rights and economic advantages. Even though she is now the joint owner of a private, albeit unexceptional, suburban residence, she almost immediately covets a baronial dwelling in the tony Westwood neighborhood, a means to ensure her class rise and buttress her white privilege. One such house, which belongs to Inspector Pope, is introduced in a low-angle

shot from Kathy's point of view to underscore its elevated hillside presence
and vertical girth—and to register her mid-twentieth-century consumerist
gaze and class envy. Westwood is occupied by majestic neocolonial resi-
dences situated on ample plots with manicured lawns, outward signifiers
of upper-class white privilege, privacy, and exclusivity. Kathy is further
ensconced in what George Lipsitz has termed a "white spatial imaginary,"
which structures "feelings and institutions" and their concomitant material spaces. The white spatial imaginary promotes a quest for individual
escape rather than encouraging democratic deliberations about social
relations that affect everyone. Lipsitz singles out isolated, self-contained
suburbs as engines of "self-interest imbued with moral value," which are
valorized by their separation from racialized, ethnic, and queer denizens,
especially in midcentury America. Individuals, according to Lipsitz, view
houses as investments for the production of exchange value; hence, "trading up" to an upscale neighborhood was, and still is, a sign of one's worth
and social status associated with whiteness and the accumulation of generational wealth.[23] Thus, although Kathy strains against the midcentury
gender ideology to which she is consigned, which demanded that she give
up her profession for that of a domestic helpmate, she supposes that happiness can be obtained by her benefits as a white, married woman.

But Kathy realizes that her husband's lack of drive will never satisfy her
or get them to Westwood, prompting the savvy former newspaperwoman
to use her skills to achieve upward mobility through disruption and subter-
fuge. She insinuates herself into the upscale neighborhood by orchestrat-
ing an automobile accident near the Pope home, thereby increasing the
chances of her husband's promotion. Soon Kathy makes herself indispens-
able to the gentle but sickly Alice Pope, initially gaining entry to the expensive interior by concealing her real identity (the wife of an underling of
Pope's in the LAPD), an indication of her willingness to both dissemble and
commit illicit acts. Her ruse—the storming of forbidden spaces—is a reverse
of the expulsion of queer characters from actual domestic spaces, but it also
identifies her as a queer disrupter of middle-class suburban equanimity.

Feminine Masculinity in Queer San Francisco

Single, middle-aged, and childless, Kathy is coded at the film's outset as
a queer outlier who works in a masculine, gender-segregated newsroom
in San Francisco. Alexander Doty argues that even in ostensibly hetero-

centric texts, queer elements may emerge at various moments to unravel sexual and gender hegemony.[24] Harry Benshoff and Sean Griffin add that Hollywood filmmakers found strategies to suggest that certain characters might even be "connotative homosexuals" or queer through "subtle mannerisms, costuming or speech patterns," and, one might add, owing to casting choices, coded dialogue, and decisions about a character's location and spatial behavior.[25]

Kathy is thus associated with the place San Francisco, which became a mecca for queer servicemen after military discharges were carried out in the port city following World War II. As a result, the city developed a reputation for tolerance, which, combined with its liberal state laws, led to its emergence as a lesbian- and gay-friendly city.[26] Kathy writes the "Your Heart and Mine" newspaper column for a community of women in San Francisco, alluding to her queer-coded allegiances.

In the script, Kathy is described as outfitted in a "severely cut, but chic tailored suit," a stereotype of professional masculine attire and one of the standard uniforms of queer female characters, according to Dyer.[27] In concert with her appearance, she is rendered as a sufferer of a midcentury "masculinity complex," a diagnostic label invented by the psychiatrist Helene Deutsch and popularized in Ferdinand Lundberg and Marilyn Farnham's best seller *Modern Woman: The Lost Sex* (1947). Characterized by the adoption of so-called masculine behavior, this women's syndrome led inexorably, the authors claimed, to psychiatric and physical illness and "the destruction of the home," the title of one of the book's most important and lengthy chapters.[28]

Kathy's "female masculinity" is further manifested in her forceful commandeering of space, introduced when the towering LAPD detectives arrive at the newsroom to instruct reporters not to interfere in their homicide investigation of the Dana crime. Jack Halberstam's theorization of gender aptly describes this scene's unorthodox gendered confrontation: "Sometimes female masculinity coincides with the excesses of male supremacy and sometimes it coincides with a unique form of social rebellion, often female masculinity is a sign of female alterity, but occasionally it marks heterosexual variation."[29] Kathy's challenge is emphasized by a low-angle shot to enhance the discrepancy in scale between the protagonists— the diminutive, but fearless female columnist strides up to the arrogant lawmen, loudly asserting that she will not be deterred from her job. Captain Alidos underscores Kathy's abnormality, goading her to return to the domestic sphere to raise a family and thus challenging her right to the public workplace. Valentine points out that such "heterosexing of space," like gender, is continually reproduced by repetition and regulated, often by aggressive means, such as Captain Alidos's injunction.[30] Kathy's forceful challenge to his authority and the law, in turn, prompts his threat to arrest her for interfering in his investigation, but Kathy undermines his authority anew by sending him to the wrong address to locate Mary Dana, the murderess.

Casting Stanwyck as queer—a professional woman unwilling or unable to fit normative standards of domestic femininity—accords with her star persona. It had long been thought that she was gay and in a "lavender marriage" (1939–51) with Robert Taylor, although the rumor was never corroborated. Thus, casting her as the two-timing housewife and scheming murderess in *Double Indemnity* (Billy Wilder, dir., 1944), the ruthless heiress in *The Strange Love of Martha Ivers* (Lewis Milestone, dir., 1946), the unhinged corporate board member in *Executive Suite* (Robert Wise, dir., 1954), and the professional designer and potential home-wrecker in *There's Always Tomorrow* (Douglas Sirk, dir., 1955) accord with her putative dual identity. In addition, Stanwyck appeared in seven Westerns in the 1950s, a genre that cemented her queer persona, especially the film *Forty Guns* (Samuel Fuller, dir., 1957), in which, as Elaine Lennon points out, she appears riding her horse while brandishing a gun, running the town as her personal fiefdom while encompassing both masculine and feminine traits and desires.[31] At the level of reception, and due to her dual gender traits, Stanwyck has held a particular queer appeal. Her biographer Dan Callahan claims that as she aged and her voice got lower, the actress could send out subliminal suggestions to women.[32] Thus before Kathy capitulates to the domestic position she abhors in *Crime of Passion*, her successful career in progressive San Francisco allows her to provide guidance to a diverse community of women. When we first encounter her at the film's inception, her assistant is reading aloud a letter from a seventeen-year-old advice seeker who is having an affair with a married man. Kathy's reply to the young woman—and, indeed, her demeanor and sartorial appearance— are coded as queer: "Forget the man. Run away with the wife," she quips to her subordinate.

The secondary, often-anonymous San Francisco–based characters that inhabit the margins of the cinematic narrative also underscore Kathy's queer difference, serving as her anonymous sisterhood. Patricia White maintains that "asexual" characters are often defined against the leading lady and "are as close as Hollywood gets to indicating 'deviant' gender

14.1 Queer San Francisco taxicab drivers.

presentations and the sexual identities they sometimes imply."[33] Significantly, the film offers up these nonhegemonic, alternative feminine identities and varied women-centered experiences in San Francisco's tolerant environs to counter those of the traditional suburban homemaker, a role that Kathy ultimately rejects. These women are introduced after Kathy is assigned to cover the case of the fugitive murderess Mary Dana, who foreshadows her own crime of passion. Kathy employs her newspaper column to prompt Dana's surrender to the police while simultaneously addressing her female readership. "I write to you from the heart of one woman to another," Kathy begins her column as if writing a love letter to the murderess. A montage sequence follows that focuses on varied female subscribers hungrily devouring her address to Dana to show that the message resonates with each one at a time before the networking opportunities provided by social media. Notably, only one is shown in a traditional, albeit unhappy heterosexual relationship: a bathrobed woman in hair rollers who is sitting up in bed reads, "When we are alone" and "tortured by fate" as the camera moves to a sleeping husband beside her, implying that their marriage—and the husband, in particular—are the sources of her suffering. On a movie date in a theater, another woman reads to a female companion who is leaning on her shoulder, "Where can we turn except to the heart and understanding of another woman who knows what you are suffering?" "I suffer with you," says a cocktail waitress as her unsympathetic male supervisor looks on. "In a world made by men for men," resumes a "hefty" female taxi driver who is reading to a compatriot as the couple rest their "meaty seats on the front fender of a cab" and share the *San Francisco Post* (figure 14.1). "Let me stand by your side in your fight for justice and compassion," the butch taxi driver continues, a comment that may serve as a coded plea for gay and lesbian rights.[34] "I will join you by your side," continues Kathy to the criminal Dana, which portends the former's subsequent murder of Inspector Pope. In every vignette in the montage, Kathy reaches the heart of a woman, a place men are unable to comprehend.

Transgressions in the White Suburbs

Kathy's ability to make an affective connection with a group of diverse women is stymied in the racialized suburbs, however, where whiteness, feminine homogeneity, and class conformity prevail, further highlighting her dissimilarity and bitterness. Kathy's failure to adjust to such white standards of heteronormativity, gender, and class allegiance is shown by contrasting her with the more conventional female cohorts with whom she is expected to socialize, thus identifying them as the counterparts of their generic white houses. The all-white female suburban group is unlike her mixed colleagues in the lunchroom of the San Francisco newspaper office, where a sign reads, "Treat this like your own home" and scrawled on the door "Do not feed the animals," and a subsequent discussion about an unclaimed bagel-and-lox sandwich disclose San Francisco's ethnic diversity and strangeness. In contrast, the party at the suburban Doyle residence is composed solely of Bill's white colleagues and their spouses. The male and female guests are situated in different parts of the house, echoing the separate-sphere ideology of 1950s America, yet Kathy belongs to neither group, emphasizing her alterity. These obligatory social get-togethers are always presided over by Sara Alidos (Virginia Grey), whose husband had earlier tried to relegate Kathy to the domestic sphere. The group of similar white spouses all kowtow to queen bee Sara in identical, high-pitched, echolalic voices, telling her what a wonderful man her husband is and claiming that this always reflects well on "the wife," which underscores their own and Kathy's subordination. A low-angle shot features Sara on the left; the line of like-minded, seated sycophants on the right; and a stony Kathy at the apex of the cinematic frame, echoing the disconnection from her female suburban peers. A sculpture of a bull positioned behind her echoes her simmering resentment and acts as a further cipher of her female masculinity.

Kathy's gender and class resentments are exacerbated at a similar party at her home a few days later, when she can barely tolerate the women's bathetic conversation about diets, hors d'oeuvres, and the size of their newly acquired television sets, emphasizing their lowbrow consumerist values. The camera tracks Kathy to the cramped, traditionally feminized kitchen, where the husbands are playing cards while engaged in an equally classed-inflected debate on future pension benefits, which consigns them to careers and suburban lives as entrapping as the room (figure 14.2). In contrast to these weakened men, Kathy rebels in this traditionally feminized space, thereby queering the kitchen and signaling her refusal to be confined to its boundaries or that of the female domesticated living room.

Valentine claims that most public and even private spaces are heterocentrically configured and regulated but argues that queer citizens have the ability to undermine these spatial regimes through covert and overt disruption.[35] Jack Halberstam agrees, arguing that in such circumstances, "Failing, losing, forgetting, unmaking, undoing, and unbecoming" may offer different rewards for the oppressed.[36] The only other times that we see Kathy in the kitchen is when she picks a useless fight with the docile Bill or briefly fixes an alcoholic drink for Inspector Pope while her husband is away on department business; we never see her there as a compliant wife. She paces the kitchen's confines like a caged animal, twisting her wedding ring in discomfort; the room's size is linked to her limiting marriage. She finally bursts when one of the men credits Alidos with being correct on the pension issue, smiling mockingly while simultaneously challenging the male pecking order and the secondary status of women: "Of course Charlie is right. That always speaks so well for the wife, doesn't it? You know the old saying, 'The apple never falls far from the tree.'" Thus, through her misuse of the kitchen and by staging its failure for women, Kathy challenges the punishing norms that discipline conventional gendered behavior.

Most of Kathy's queer and class-inflected suburban spatial transgressions occur in the Popes' commodious Westwood abode at the various social gatherings that she has organized and over which she now presides, achieving the vicarious white upper-class status that she covets. In marked contrast to her displaced, outcast status at her own gender-segregated get-togethers,

14.2 Kathy (Barbara Stanwyck) queers the kitchen.

here she holds court with a mixed-gender audience in the Popes' living room bar, which the final script describes as having the appearance of "a tavern tap room."[37] Such bars became a common feature of postwar suburban dwellings due to the new focus on entertaining in the home rather than in distant urban locales.[38] In an earlier scene, Kathy transgresses another gendered spatial boundary: Tony's masculinized study, filled with books and other professional accouterments, an improper gesture for a married woman in 1950s America.[39] In significant ways, the new domestic bars loosened the separate-sphere notions of propriety and their concomitant gender expectations, leading commentators to note an uptick in suburban affairs.[40] Such is the case with the standout Kathy, who draws the attention of the home's owner, Inspector Pope, who recognizes her as a kindred spirit. Their initial meeting in a suburban home bar is thus suggestive and cheapens their interaction, foreshadowing their short-lived liaison. Indeed, Kathy and Tony's final confrontation occurs in the same darkened living room bar in one of the film's penultimate scenes. A reverse-angle shot shows Tony before its multiple well-stocked shelves, a modern-day vanitas image lined with shimmering glasses and a cipher of Kathy's upper-class pretensions. Immune to Kathy's pathetic injunctions not to promote Alidos over her husband, he exacerbates her humiliation. The camera shifts from a close-up of Kathy's distraught face to the gun discharging, before crosscutting to a low-angle shot of Tony's dead body trapped within the

14.3 Kathy (Barbara Stanwyck) kills Inspector Tony Pope.

sharp angular metal legs of two modernist bar stools, suggesting that the domestic taproom events have served as a just punishment for his illicit deeds (figure 14.3).

Yet the Doyles' small house is the site of Kathy's queer home-wrecking and the most egregious violation of heteronormativity and its expected class alignments—that one should remain in one's own economic cohort— to avoid disturbing the ecology of suburban homogeneity. The wealthy Inspector Pope, who conveniently sends Bill on out-of-town assignments so he can visit Kathy, orchestrates their meeting. Kathy and Tony's transgressions are not only an affront to marriage and class mixing. The illicit couple violate the spatial function of the living room, which is marked as a site of wholesome familial engagement, by succumbing to a sexual act on its premises. Late one night while she is alone in her marital bed and both spouses are conveniently away, a car awakens Kathy as it pulls into the driveway. Scantily clad, she hastily dons a bathrobe and answers the door, where she finds Tony. She invites him, inappropriately but without hesitation, into her darkened living room, which suggestively abuts the bedroom, then proceeds to the kitchen to prepare alcoholic drinks, rendering her own living room a bar-like locale, just like the Popes'. The intimacy of the small, darkened room prompts him to confide that he is about to retire due to Alice's illness. Fixing on Kathy's face, the camera shows the announcement's significance for her husband's career and her insatiable desire for upward class mobility and her own vicarious professional advancement. With drink in hand, she moves within several inches from Tony on the couch and proposes "Inspector Doyle, Inspector William Doyle," to replace him. A jazzy saxophone score signals Tony's awareness of Kathy's close physical proximity, which prompts him to embrace her passionately before they jointly sink downward and consummate their relationship, the defilement of her suburban house and home now complete.

Conclusion

Kathy's spatial transgressions and disruptions of the "normal" gendered spaces of the white suburbs, which she views as a trap, lead ineluctably to her act of uncontrolled passion. Hollywood blames her class greed, signified by her attempt to trade up her tacky suburban home for the likes of Tony and Alice Pope's Westwood colonial. Her unrestrained, antisocial behavior is also indicative of her internalized white privilege, masculine femininity, and queerness. Kathy believes that the only way she can express herself in her conventional marriage, in the stultifying heteronormative suburbs that she has grown to abhor, is through artifice and illicit acts, thus unmaking its spatial regimes and gendered and classed ideological underpinnings. Never suited for the suburban way of life or its material and psychic privations, this cosmopolitan woman finally snaps and seeks revenge for her multiple humiliations, her feminine masculinity further signified by the prosthetic gun, which she now wields to exact her revenge. It is noteworthy that when her husband calls from the precinct to inform her that Pope has been murdered, unaware that she is the perpetrator, he asks her to look after her kindly friend Alice, who will need her support. It is only then—when she considers her injury to another woman—that Kathy feels remorse for her crime. Ironically, but perhaps ineluctably, the violent act's outcome ultimately transfers Kathy from one trap to another, from the incarcerating suburban house to the penitentiary. But the murderous deed has additional significance if we recall the former newswoman's promise to join the murderess Mary Dana "by her side," marking the film's queer unconscious or subtext, which ultimately will occur through ellipsis in a symbolic coupling in prison.

FAIR PLAY

Race, Space, and Recreation in
Black Media Culture

In the late 1980s, Phylicia Rashad, Malcolm-Jamal Warner, and Keshia Knight Pulliam—members of television's most popular family, the Huxtables—appeared in a series of commercials for Walt Disney World. Although theme parks were the Walt Disney Company's most profitable division, attendance had stumbled in the early months of 1988, and the endorsement of *The Cosby Show* (1984) cast members surely bolstered this lagging enthusiasm.[1] As the Disney marketing executive Thomas Elrod told *Black Enterprise* magazine at the time, "Being the world's most popular family vacation destination, we wanted to portray the feeling of the world's most popular family, which happens to be the Cosby family. . . . We felt that a mother and her kids was the right combination for us. Frankly, we never thought about race."[2] Elrod's claims seem especially incredible considering that one of the commercials features the family spiritedly singing "Zip-a-Dee-Doo Dah" from the now unavailable *Song of the South* (Wilfred Jackson, dir., 1946), including a rap performance by Warner. Undoubtedly, the appeal of the cast members to Disney emerged not only in the show's high ratings, but also in the family's cross-racial, cross-class appeal. The advertisements tacitly work to reinscribe established codes of race, gender, and class while championing Disney World as a place in which such codes are rendered invalid. Indeed, theme parks often position themselves as escapist fantasies, yet cultural politics remains deeply ingrained in their design, maintenance, and exploitation.

This chapter explores this idea in greater depth through the lens of cultural studies work interrogating neoliberalism and media culture. In particular, I am interested in how Black media culture—that is, culture predominantly produced by Black creators and for predominantly Black viewers—employs the theme park as a narrative setting. Steven Miles asserts that theme parks provide "a non-conflictual environment promoting the riches of a consumer society within what is in actual fact a highly uniform and controlled setting."[3] As commercialized spaces for recreation and social gathering, theme parks stage the tension between the public and the private, work and play, and appropriate and improper conduct. These sites, both real and represented, allow us to understand the hegemonic control of society while also examining how space, recreation, and personal conduct are endowed with the politics surrounding race, gender, and class. Therefore, an analysis of characterological and spatial representation cannot isolate any one category. Instead, it must explore all three simultaneously. In fact, a deeper understanding of how Black media culture participates in and pushes against neoliberal politics necessitates such rigorous intersectional analysis.

Despite rich interdisciplinary work on theme parks as a cultural phenomenon, little scholarship has been done on the representation of theme parks within popular media and the surrounding discourses' investment in racial and class politics. Through a close textual analysis of episodes set in theme parks of *The Boondocks* (2008) and *Black-ish* (2014), two prominent Black-cast sitcoms, I aim to show how the theme park provides rich insights into Blacks as consumers, citizens, and pleasure seekers. In turn, such consideration also reveals how space, personal conduct, and play are closely monitored and policed within a society controlled by a select number of corporations and individuals, many of whom are white and wealthy. This analysis, I hope, will further studies not only of theme parks, but of mediated spaces more broadly, to understand the ways in which individuals and space itself are deeply imbued with the politics of identity and culture.

The Theme Park as Cultural Space

Before discussing the representation of theme parks in Black media culture, it is necessary to historicize and theorize the theme park as a cultural and spatial phenomenon. The theme park emerges from the amusement park, which itself comes from the European tradition of pleasure gardens, carnivals, and fairs. Over the past two hundred years, amusement parks have served a vital role in introducing the public to technological innovation through mechanical thrills. Thus, these places of play facilitated many Americans' acclimation to industrialization, urbanization, and national belonging in the late nineteenth century.[4] Denmark's Tivoli Gardens and the United States' Coney Island exemplified these trends, and both parks served as models for Walt Disney in the creation of Disneyland in the mid-1950s. But Disney was also concerned with propriety and respectability. The development of cities meant amusement parks became part of the cityscape rather than retreats on the outskirts. As a result, they "acquired new reputations as habitats for urban decay and haunts for urban criminals," leading to drug deals, gang-related violence, and racial tension.[5] Disney sought to distance his company from these social ills and negative impressions. The construction of highways (in this case, the Santa Ana Freeway) and the rise in automobile ownership among the emerging middle class allowed him to build a theme park set off from major cities and accessible only to those with the means.[6] The theme parks' position outside of the city and its invocation of other places, extant or imagined, further exacerbates the distancing visitors may feel from reality.[7]

Whereas the amusement park of the nineteenth century and early twentieth century had celebrated technological change and modernity, Disneyland capitalized on a wistful nostalgia for small-town America—specifically, Disney's hometown of Marceline, Missouri, one of the models for Main Street, U.S.A. In the process, Disneyland became "an oasis of cleanliness, order, and efficiency."[8] But that was not Disney's only theme, as his park also included Fantasyland, Frontierland, Tomorrowland, and Adventureland. Rather than offering some kind of utopia beyond identity politics, these fictional themes were wholly raced and classed. Accessing the park, geographically and financially, required a certain degree of privilege in the form of expendable income. Disney's entertainment presumed a white, middle-class audience, and his parks imagined a theme park space lacking in the alcohol, overt sexuality, and revelry common to earlier incarnations of the amusement park. In creating such a place, he established a standard many theme parks follow to this day: a safe, family-friendly environment that celebrates a fictitious past while imagining an idealized future. In short, he was providing the perfect atmosphere for respectable white, middle-class leisure.

As private, commercialized land encouraging public usage for an admission fee, theme parks provide an important opportunity for examining capitalism, consumerism, and neoliberalism. In one of the earliest meditations on the cultural form, Susan Davis acknowledges that theme parks are costly ventures that nevertheless provide lucrative revenue streams for their corporate overseers, as well as easy entry into the tourism industry and "seemingly limitless opportunities to cross-promote goods and imagery" for conglomerates.[9] Walt Disney conceived of Disneyland, the theme park, and *The Magical World of Disney* (1954), the ABC television series, as integrated industrial entities that would promote each other and the Disney brand, a strategy he referred to as "total merchandising."[10] With their wholesome vision steeped in a nostalgic Americana, the series and the theme park together reinforced a national identity steeped in whiteness and middle-class respectability. It also encouraged young consumers of Disney entertainment to imagine themselves as Americans and customers, a notion Sarah Banet-Weiser refers to as "consumer citizenship." As she explains, "Our sense of ourselves as national citizens emerges *from* (not in spite of) our engagement with the popular media."[11] By building a theme park and narratively structuring his television show around the themes of that park, Walt Disney positioned his audience as media citizens who would hold Disneyland up as the paradigm of an extension of perfect American entertainment.

Theme parks provide an illuminating microcosm of society, both mirroring and altering it in the process. They do not suspend social order; rather, they implicitly uphold it through their investment in expectations surrounding common understandings of family-friendliness, appropriateness, and respectability. A certain decorum always remains, reinforced by security guards, surveillance equipment, and the judging gaze of other patrons. Respectable behavior is expected because of the implicit expectation that this space is for children—or, at the very least, does not actively exclude children. In the name of children, therefore, the level of celebration tolerated at carnivals and even early amusement parks becomes inappropriate, even lewd. Theme parks may welcome play, but only a safe, carefully controlled version. As Janet Wasko describes Disney parks, the "layouts, as well as most rides and exhibits, are designed to control the visitors' activities and experiences."[12] The roller-coasters have been engineered and tested to ensure they do not injure the rider. Stunts within live shows have been meticulously choreographed, while the parades have been planned in detail. Even the characters are highly regulated, even surveilled, to ensure the brand is maintained. In short, any sense of liberation and freedom is largely manufactured and wholly illusory.

Theme parks today are very often a subsidiary of the global conglomerate, where they continue to generate income while championing a range of media products created by their holding company. Therefore, the theme park itself becomes a product, as does the experience it offers. Both commodities imagine a preferred customer, and in the effort to reach and maintain that relationship, other potential customers may be excluded. The theme park alludes to the promise of the commons one might find in a public park, but its private, commercial nature and somewhat isolated location quite intentionally undermine easy access. Pricing is also used to maintain a certain clientele, excluding perceived undesirables through cost-prohibitive entry fees. Like all commercial spaces, the theme park is highly charged with the politics of class. The theme park is unique, however, as a space that also capitalizes on notions of play, propriety, and community, reinforced by its immersive narrative experience.[13] Thus, Black media creators have invoked this space to alternately champion and chastise neoliberal values and the subsequent reimagining of individual, family, and leisure in the process. In what follows, I closely analyze *The Boondocks* and *Black-ish* to demonstrate the spatial politics of theme parks as a cultural space, as well as how we may understand such spaces as deeply embedded in cultural politics, economic policies, and hegemonic values of U.S. society.

The Theme Park as Neoliberal Nightmare

The Boondocks, an animated series based on Aaron McGruder's comic strip of the same name, aired during Cartoon Network's Adult Swim programming block for four seasons between 2005 and 2014. The show's airing on cable television and in an adult-targeted time slot afforded it a certain degree of autonomy to develop a distinctive, even radical, point of view on current events. McGruder named his protagonist Huey Freeman (Regina King), after Huey P. Newton, cofounder of the Black Panthers, and the show often espoused radical politics, described by Robin Means Coleman and William Lafi Youmans as "1970s Black nationalism . . . mediated through hip hop music," in line with McGruder's own political allegiance.[14] Other characters represent alternative strains of Black thought and activism, mostly depending on their age. Having grown up during the Civil Rights Movement, Granddad (John Witherspoon) has mellowed in his advanced age to become more reserved and accommodationist than his grandson, while Huey's younger brother, Riley (also Regina King), embodies a hiphop generation perceived to be largely indifferent to the ongoing urgency of social justice. Uncle Ruckus (Gary Anthony Williams) performs a grotesque sycophancy, loudly defending "the white man" as well intentioned and condemning the Black community as ungrateful and violent. As both a sitcom and an animated series, *The Boondocks* has shrewdly satirized not only racial inequality in U.S. society but also the ongoing tensions within the Black community itself.

"Freedomland" (season 4, episode 7) was written and produced after McGruder's departure at the end of the third season. Nevertheless, it maintains his scathing commentary on the continuing subjugation of Black people in the United States. *The Boondocks* offers a fierce rebuttal to the postracial political discourse that surged following the election of President Barack Obama in 2008, but it does not cower from also criticizing Obama's benign public image. Indeed, the show is quick to call out the ongoing humiliation, manipulation, and exploitation of Black people. The "Freedomland" episode stages this critique within a living-history theme park owned by a white businessman, Eddie Wuncler (Ed Asner). Since Granddad is indebted to Wuncler, Wuncler coerces Granddad, Huey, and Riley to "play" slaves in this new theme park (reminiscent of Disney's failed attempts to build an American history theme park near Manassas, Virginia). In so doing, the show launches an assault on the diabolical ways in which white-dominated corporate America perpetuates neoslavery practices and structures in the twenty-first century, taking advantage of Black labor to generate huge profits while offering its workers no opportunities for social and economic advancement.

The episode begins with Uncle Ruckus, who is all too happy to accommodate his white employer, demanding that Granddad follow him to Mr. Wuncler's office, even implying he will handcuff him to get him there. Instead, Granddad handcuffs Ruckus and throws him out of the house. This gratifying dismissal is undercut when the police arrive to escort Granddad to Wuncler, implying law enforcement's complicity in corporate America's demands. White supremacy stands as a pervasive problem in *The Boondocks*, manifesting itself across institutions and going as far as to effectively brainwash Ruckus.

In the office, the audience learns of the establishment of a slavery theme park:

Wuncler: I opened a living history theme park.

Riley: Boring.

Wuncler: Brings the nineteenth century to life.

Huey: You're forcing Black people to reenact the most painful period in our history?

Wuncler: But with cotton candy and a merry-go-round! And come on, Huey, not just Black people. I'm progressive enough to force all races to reenact your painful history if they owe me money. Even Jews! Isn't it wonderful?

Wuncler's callous indifference reveals the shameless pursuit of profits fostered under capitalism, in which corporations privilege revenues over human lives in general, and over Black lives in particular. Huey attempts to resist by drawing attention to how demoralizing such an endeavor would be for the Black community, but Wuncler's focus remains on the attractions and concessions. The profit potential is far too great to worry about histori-cal accuracy or social consequences. The show demonstrates its trademark satirical tone, excoriating the racism and greed of corporate America. The sheer audacity of the scene would be dumbfounding, but the idea has not gone unexplored by other corporations—all under the benevolent guise of "history" and "education."[15]

The biting tone continues in the park's Williamsburg-esque décor, com-plete with a colonial village. Wuncler names the park "Freedomland," the irony of which is presumably not lost on the viewers. The park offers its primarily white consumer base a range of racially offensive activities, in-cluding a watermelon-shaped carousel, a Fishin' for Crack Babies stand, and a Welfare Queen for a Day exhibit, all of which are predominantly staffed by Black "employees." Of course, the freedoms espoused under the Declaration of Independence and the Constitution were wholly predicated on the enslavement and exploitation of Black bodies. *The Boondocks* draws this historical through line to underscore the American freedoms that were undercut by the existence of chattel slavery. This reality is not only raced but classed, since freedom was always a luxury of the middle and upper classes rather than of the working classes.

What remains missing is a consideration of how gender factors into these power dynamics. In a survey of two hundred *Boondocks* comic strips, Sheena Howard found the Black female voice absent.[16] This trend continues in the "Freedomland" episode, where Black women are represented as background figures (e.g., in the Whack-a-Mammy game [figure 15.1]) but provided no op-portunity to express their agency in any meaningful way besides participat-ing in the climactic rebellion, in which the slaves revolt against Wuncler, the patrons, and park security. Indeed, the episode's racial and economic commentary surprisingly evades any deeper observation on the role of gen-der in this marginalization and dehumanization, aside, perhaps, from the

15.1 Women of different races within the Whack-a-Mammy game rise up to join the ensuing rebellion.

emasculating effects on the three male characters. While a half-hour series can develop its social criticism only so far while still offering some form of narrative entertainment, the absence of women, especially Black women, stands as a glaring omission.

Although the episode avoids an engaged gender commentary, it does offer a rare window into political hostilities within the Black community, as Uncle Ruckus proudly serves Wuncler, even if it means violently punishing Granddad, Riley, and Huey. Granddad encourages Huey to acquiesce, but Huey refuses to yield to Ruckus's terror. The conflict between Ruckus and Huey personifies the perceived social tension between Blacks who willingly participate in neoliberalism as a means to get ahead (even if it means stepping on others to do so) and Blacks who refuse to participate in capitalist exploitation, regardless of the consequences. Huey's perspective is clearly presented as noble, whereas Ruckus's slurred speech and slovenly appearance imply his shortcomings not only physically, but ethically, as well. *The Boondocks* makes no room for compromise, because such negotiations demoralize the Black community. Freedom instead must be achieved, as Huey explains (via Malcolm X), "by any means necessary." Threatened with dismemberment before a gawking mob, Huey launches a rebellion that throws Freedomland into chaos and eventual ruin. This destruction stands not only as a catharsis but as a model for Black liberation.

The theme park as a represented space allows the episode's creators to engage various concerns within Black politics, culture, and daily life. A history theme park emphasizes the historical continuity of oppression and

inequality between whites and Blacks. The economic nature of this violent exploitation is transposed from an agrarian context to a corporate one.
While the nature of the labor changes, the abuse does not. Furthermore, by
staging this critique within a theme park, *The Boondocks* indicts the naïve,
reductive, and casual relationship between the public and American history. Rather than being a complex narrative, rife with violence and corruption, it is simplified and commodified into "edutainment." The willingness
of the largely white, middle-class patrons to seek recreation at the expense
of Black slave labor underscores the enduring legacy of slavery today that
perpetuates in corporate contexts, including popular music and professional sports.[17] After all, how can African Americans find recreation in the
exploitative re-creation of their painful ancestral past? As Huey states at
the episode's uncompromising conclusion, Freedomland is a farce until
freedom exists for all, not just for those who can afford to play there.

The Theme Park as Neoliberal Utopia

One of the most critically acclaimed Black series on network television as
of 2019 is *Black-ish*, a family sitcom airing on ABC, created by Kenya Barris
and starring Anthony Anderson and Tracee Ellis Ross. *Black-ish* continues *The Cosby Show*'s legacy of presenting the Black middle class as a practical strategy for reaching a cross-racial audience, though the series distin-
guishes itself in its wavering between light satire and, at times, a didactic
"Very Special Episode" approach to race and current events. Dre (Anthony
Anderson) is a successful business executive (specializing in "urban marketing"), while his wife Rainbow (Tracee Ellis Ross) is a medical doctor.
Dre's roots are decidedly working-class, and his parents, Pops (Laurence
Fishburne) and Ruby (Jenifer Lewis), feel somewhat out of place with their
son's newfound success. While they resent his propriety, they are more
than willing to take advantage of his newly earned wealth.

In "VIP" (season 3, episode 1), Dre posits a trip to Disney World as an
opportunity to "ball out." It also marks his arrival into a specific echelon of
bourgeois respectability that is clearly raced white. *Black-ish* is produced by
ABC Television Entertainment and airs on the ABC network, both of which,
like Disney World, are major holdings of the Walt Disney Company. This
episode's crude cross-promotion departs from the safe but undeniable social consciousness present in most episodes. Setting an episode of *Black-ish*
within a theme park, unlike doing so in *The Boondocks*, does not so much

criticize as obscure the race, gender, and class dynamics that inform corporatized cultural spaces and recreation more broadly.

In the voice-over narration at the outset of the episode, Dre argues that special treatment is "as American as apple pie." Taking his family to Disney World, complete with VIP treatment, signifies the personal success he has achieved as both a businessman and a father. On the one hand, it signals to the audience that the Disney parks are excellent vacation destinations for families, especially Black families such as the Johnsons. On the other hand, though, it tacitly perpetuates a dangerous myth that wealth not only provides special access but erases the realities of being Black in the United States. Flashbacks to Dre's childhood, where his parents had to steal to get him into Disneyland and bring packed lunches to avoid purchasing from the expensive concessions, are presented for humorous effect. Racial difference becomes irrelevant within the park because in a culture informed by neoliberalism, consumerism—and access to substantial capital—provides one with the freedom central to the American dream by way of buying power. The episode acknowledges race rather passively: Dre suggests he "owns" the (white) tour guide, much to the guide's discomfort, and a white guest at the park later confuses Dre for the football player Marshawn Lynch, which Drew dismisses as a flattering form of racism. But since Dre can pay for VIP access, his family experiences the parks in a way that mostly renders their racial difference moot.

Of course, the show cannot traffic in such crass consumerism alone, though one easily can read the episode as an extended endorsement of one of its conglomerate's signature products. As the preeminent arbiter of family entertainment, Disney has long found its success in perpetuating hackneyed moral lessons through its media narratives. In this instance, Dre's attempt to give his family an exclusive experience backfires when his children become arrogant and elitist, rudely dismissing the other patrons as inherently inferior to themselves. Dre originally welcomes this confidence as a sign his family has achieved a new stratum of success, but when their VIP access expires and they must return to "gen pop" (a term that originated in prison culture) like everyone else, the children become indignant and ungrateful. Meanwhile, Dre's parents, who leave the VIP tour to take up residence in a bar on Dre's dime, are eventually wooed by the Disney World experience. They stare in amazement while riding Soarin' around the World at Disney's Epcot theme park, and they cheerfully dance on a parade float (figure 15.2). This rather abrupt shift in their characterization rings false, and the normally defensive, curmudgeonly roles that Fishburne

15.2 Rainbow (Tracee Ellis Ross), Pops (Laurence Fishburne), and Ruby (Jenifer Lewis) "reluctantly" join the parade at Disney World.

and Lewis play become unintentionally comical as they try to convince viewers that their characters have been transformed by the "magic" of Disney. Ruby wears a Minnie Mouse shirt, while Pops dons Goofy ears. By the end of the episode, Dre reconciles with his kids and his parents, all of whom have transitioned from selfish individuals into appreciative family members. Dre and his father stare lovingly at the fireworks as "When You Wish upon a Star" plays the episode out. The lesson here is clear: Disney World not only brings families together; it makes them better people: loving, humble, grateful. The family's priorities are realigned, and their rather conventional values are strengthened by the trip. In fact, Dre even admits that one (perhaps the viewing audience itself?) can have a special experience without VIP status. Indeed, this theme park fantasy of family reunification is seemingly available to all viewers—if they can afford it.

Furthermore, the episode also presents gender as irrelevant to one's ability to partake in the Disney park experience. Rainbow is pregnant with the couple's fifth child, leading the tour guide to lament that she will be unable to ride many of the park's attractions. Her husband initially commiserates— "Wow, babe, that's a lot you can't do"—before undercutting it with a regretful, "Kinda wish I didn't pay extra for you now," and proceeding onto the ride without her. Rainbow's disappointing exclusion motivates her arc for the episode. She meets up with her ornery in-laws, and together they halfheartedly explore the park. Riding the Soarin' over the World attraction, patronizing the gift shops, and joining the parade (where they sing and dance along to "Be Our Guest" from *Beauty and the Beast* [Kirk Wise and Gary Trousdale, dirs., 1991]), all three realize that the Disney magic can win anyone over, regardless of their attitude or physical ability. Disney World welcomes everyone: Black and white, old and young, male and female. Rainbow meets up again with her husband, who has abandoned their children because of their ungrateful behavior. Since she herself has been won over, she consoles her husband as their children return, laughing and in good spirits. As Rainbow assures Dre, his tantrum—and, of course, Disney World—"gave them the space to actually enjoy each other." The family is reunited, and their loving bond is reinforced, thanks to Disney magic.

Disney theme parks have inspired other Black creators. *Family Matters* set an episode in Disney World in 1995, a year before Disney purchased ABC, the network that broadcast the sitcom in its Friday night line-up. *Bébé's Kids* (Bruce Smith, dir., 1992), the first animated feature written and directed by Black creators and featuring an all-Black cast, was set in Fun World, an obvious proxy for Disney World, by which the film launches a clever but uneven anticonsumerist satire.[18] But *Black-ish*'s use of Disney World is particularly unapologetic in how uncritical it is. The series champions neoliberal family values—consumer citizenship, the pleasure and power of the privatized commons, family reunification via consumption—in service of its conglomerate owners' best interests, even if the experiences showcased here are unavailable to the vast majority of Americans for geographical, financial, and physical reasons. The surprise departure of *Black-ish*'s showrunner Kenya Barris in 2018, following Disney's decision not to air an episode critical of Donald Trump, testifies to how the agency of Black creators remains largely compromised in an era of media culture produced by conglomerates.[19] (It is worth mentioning that Jonathan Groff, one of the show's white executive producers, received credit for writing the "VIP" script.) *Black-ish* may laud itself as a Black-led, Black-cast sitcom, but its narrative and (especially political) content is closely monitored by the predominantly white Disney executives who oversee it.

Conclusion

While *The Boondocks* points to the continuing oppression Blacks face in U.S. society, *Black-ish* minimizes it, and even ignores it completely. If one can pay, one can access this world where race and class dynamics do not function in the same way that they operate in the so-called real world. This postracial fantasy, increasingly championed by conservatives in recent years, ultimately evades those who cannot afford it. Furthermore, race may seem irrelevant in Disney World, but its influence remains present in the vision of America—and America's past—that it celebrates. This fantasy becomes particularly insidious in the way in which recreation becomes coded as a safe, secure location where one is "protected" by location, security, and surveillance from dangerous elements, presumably "outsiders"—quite often, people of color who are excluded by virtue of economic disadvantages imposed on minority groups by white hegemony. Rather than illustrating this injustice, *Black-ish* perpetuates it under the guise of a family-friendly morality play.

What I hope to have shown here is how theme parks provide a productive "text" to analyze and theorize within media culture, especially, in this instance, narratives produced by Black creators for Black audiences. On the one hand, they move beyond the representation of character to show how race and class also structure space and place. The focus does not rest on bodies explicitly, yet the way in which bodies are regulated, controlled, and understood is implicit in how these spaces are regulated, controlled, and understood. The design of such place is always already endowed with deeper political and ideological meanings. And recreation—the *not* serious—nevertheless becomes quite serious when we consider who these places are for, how they be should used, and how they work to exclude certain people and certain behavior.[20] Thus, close studies of the politics of space reveal how hegemony controls bodies both directly and indirectly through its manipulation of power.

V _ STYLE AND/AS INTERSECTIONALITY

THE TOXIC INTERTWINING OF
SMALL-TOWN LIVES IN *HAPPY VALLEY*

In her foundational essay on intersectionality, Kimberlé Crenshaw uses several spatial metaphors or analogies to describe how a "single-axis" approach to antidiscrimination law fails to protect the rights of those whose identities comprise more than one class subject to discrimination—Black women, specifically, but by extension those who may be marginalized by combinations of such other factors as sexuality, class, disability, and so forth. One example involves actual intersections of roads: "Discrimination, like traffic through an intersection, may flow in one direction, and it may flow in another. If an accident happens in an intersection, it can be caused by cars traveling from any number of directions and, sometimes, from all of them." Determining how and why a victim "is harmed because she is in the intersection" must consider all these identity factors simultaneously.[1]

In constructing the woman at its center, Catherine Cawood (Sarah Lancashire), the BBC1 police procedural *Happy Valley* (2014) depicts diegetic intersectional realities—of inhabitants of small communities, of criminal acts traced through highway encounters and alleyways that lead to hidden victims, of the lived social experience of a Northern England hollowed out by globalism—as constitutive of this female, working-class uniformed police sergeant, the mother of a daughter raped by one of the many disempowered, violent men in the region. Cawood's various disadvantaged identities place her at the crossroads for buffeting from all directions, literalized in the near-fatal beating she suffers in season I. Yet the program ultimately dwells so firmly within her psyche that its apparent realities become untethered to actuality and make sense only as metaphors for her troubled consciousness.

Happy Valley maps its diegetic setting onto its geographic region. Its title is an ironic metonymy of that setting—Cawood's jurisdiction—the Calder River Valley, West Yorkshire, Northern England, where the show films on location. The program's creator, Sally Wainwright, is a working-class native of nearby Huddersfield; she decided to fictionally chronicle the valley's dysfunction when she saw a 2009 documentary about rampant substance abuse and suicide there.[2] A valley shown to be more miserable than merry, the upper Calder's sobriquet originates with those who police the large proportion of residents perpetually high on drugs or alcohol, seeking to feel some joy. Cawood lives in Hebden Bridge and works at the Norland Road police station in Sowerby Bridge, Calderdale. Her duties take her to places such as Elland, Overden, Ripponden, and Halifax (pop. 90,000), the nearest city.

Although the region includes moorland farms, with Cawood's team often called on to investigate crimes against sheep, *Happy Valley* replaces picturesque rural villages with various small towns where industrial brick buildings predominate over stone cottages. Often shot from above, the various structures, whether horizontal industrial plants, high-rise apartments, or detached or attached homes, share red-brown exteriors topped by dark slate or tile roofs. Streets, roads, and alleyways are winding and narrow, giving the impression of overall sameness; adjacency of the architecture creates a sense of crowded intimacy and connection. And because the setting is a valley, ground-level shots usually show a horizon of hillsides dotted with additional dwellings.

Such a location places *Happy Valley* within the subgenre of the small-town or rural detective show. Isolated villages well serve the purposes of the "cozy" British mystery. Inhabitants within these small spaces intersect geographically and historically. Feuds and resentments fester for generations; ancient land rights come up against poachers and predatory developers; gossip circulates to make everyone feel that they know everything about everyone else (even as buried secrets elude the assumed communal knowledge). A staple of detective novels throughout the twentieth century, the village procedural struck gold for the British broadcaster ITV in 1997 when it adapted novels by Caroline Graham as *Midsomer Murders*.[3] The program tracks investigations by the Criminal Investigation Department (CID) of the fictional Midsomer County in Southwest England. Working out of the county town of Causton, Detective Chief Inspector (DCI) Barnaby—first

Tom (John Nettles), then his cousin John (Neil Dudgeon)—solves increasingly baroque killings in villages with colorful names such as Badger's Drift and Midsomer Mallow. Eccentric characters with fetishistic attachments to local traditions abound, as the program winks at its own absurdities and stays just on the far side of camp. The recipient of critical scorn as "picturesque, conservative and atavistic," portraying "an England of villages, vicars, blackmail and black magic (but no Black people)", as of its twentieth season in 2018 *Midsomer Murders* remains wildly popular both domestically and internationally.[4]

Midway through those two decades, however, new village procedurals that were anything but cozy began to proliferate. Influenced by the gray color palette and equally gray moral atmosphere of Nordic noir, these series highlighted the landscapes and mores of specific regions of the United Kingdom: Yorkshire (*D.C.I. Banks*, 2010), Northumberland (*Vera*, 2011), Dorset and Somerset (*Broadchurch*, 2013), the Shetland Islands (*Shetland*, 2013), and West Wales (*Hinterland*, 2014). These additions to the subgenre illustrate what Les Roberts calls the "spatial" or "locative turn," described as "a shift towards a broader cultural economy of landscape, space and place whereby television productions have engaged with and invested in *location*."[5] Ruth McElroy attributes this turn to several factors: the interest of regional channels and production companies in showcasing their localities, the advent of high-definition cinematography that makes dramatic landscapes more visually arresting, and "providing audiences with a sense of place [as] one way in which regional television producers can create visual distinction in the crowded marketplace of television crime drama."[6] Charlotte Brunsdon finds that, as fighting terrorism replaces a law-and-order approach to routine crimes, "the officers are either armed, female, or living and policing in remote, often picturesque non-metropolitan centres."[7]

In any twenty-first-century procedural, the lead detective will inevitably stand before a "murder board" that displays photos of all the people involved in the crime under investigation and challenge his or her team to figure out what connects them. As contrasted to the atomized existences lived in large urban areas, the nature of the small town multiplies such interconnectivity.[8] Another feature of the village subgenre involves the amount of driving undertaken by police to reach the various locations occupied by crime scenes, victims' survivors, witnesses, and suspects. "Given the topographic and locative nature of much television procedural drama—the detective being essentially a *mobile* subject: a figure whose procedural enquiries take her or him to and from specific location points as s/he goes about trying to piece together bits of the narrative puzzle—it is a genre that has much to offer for the purposes of spatial analysis," Roberts writes.[9]

An Intersectional Village Variant

Happy Valley adapts the spatial economy of the village procedural to create a closed system through which social ills circulate among the populace, often giving rise to crimes that likewise have widely dispersed effects. The Calder Valley is like an organism fighting off an infection, with the police as overmatched antibodies. The program consequently pays more attention to distinctions of gender and class than is common in the subgenre. These distinctions start with the construction of Cawood as protagonist. Most village procedurals—indeed, most police dramas in the United Kingdom over the past decade—feature detective partners who investigate the crimes being dramatized. Usually they are a DI (detective inspector) and his or her junior, a DS (detective sergeant). Both Barnabys and their revolving DSs on *Midsomer Murders* are men, but the more recently debuting programs cast the partners as a male-female pair.[10] Catherine occasionally takes other members of her team on a call, most reliably Police Constable (PC) Shafiq Shah (Shane Zaza). Very often, however, she is either behind her desk as supervising sergeant or patrolling solo. That she is also a uniformed officer, not a member of the CID, brings in a professional class dynamic that intersects with the socioeconomic makeup of the population.

While Cawood diverges from the typical protagonist of the subgenre, she also stands out as the protagonist in a narrative about her region (figure 16.1). Kristyn Gorton argues that Cawood as a character is inseparable from the specific place she inhabits: "Her identity, her sense of self, is woven into her sense of place, of being Northern. In this way she is intimately linked to the happy valley she comes from and belongs to."[11]

Gorton places the program's literal setting in its historical context as the screen North from the 1960s on: "The 'North' is often used within British cinema and television as both a reference point geographically and as an allusion to a particular style."[12] She singles out social realism; themes of bleakness, coldness, industry, decay; and social dysfunction as characteristics of the on-screen North. Protagonists are usually angry men who feel trapped in a region that offers no gainful employment and therefore no way they can maintain the respect of the women in their lives. Their anger thus turns often into misogyny. This is also the case in *Happy Valley*, but

16.1 Catherine Cawood (Sarah Lancashire) stands at the intersection of her region, class, and gender.

now a woman's point of view predominates. And from a female perspective, the fact that alienated men take out their frustrations on the women they have failed receives a priority that male-focused narratives elide, for the intersectional disadvantage of the northern woman differs from that of the northern man.

The lyrics to Jake Bugg's "Trouble Town," the song that plays over *Happy Valley*'s opening credits, sum up the region's despair as the male speaker complains that "all you's got's your benefits / And you're barely getting by" while "stuck in speed bump city / where the only thing that's pretty is the thought of getting out."[13] In this regard, the North has proved to be the canary in the coal mine. In the wake of globalization, trouble towns have emerged throughout Europe and the United States, giving rise to epidemics of opioid addiction and suicide and to populist, anti-immigrant, nationalist movements. West Yorkshire voted "Leave" on Brexit. Although *Happy Valley* does not touch on the politics, it does portray social conditions common to areas throughout the global West, especially after 2008. Reviewing data from the United States, Canada, Europe, and Australia, Walter DeKeserdy and his coauthors determined that "major social and economic transformations occurring throughout US rural communities and elsewhere are fueling increases in non-violent crime and a myriad of other social problems such as suicide, poverty, and violent male responses to the termination of intimate relationships."[14] They add that "many rural men have peers who view wife beating, rape and other forms of male-to-female victimization as legitimate and effective means of repairing 'damaged patriarchal masculinity.'"[15]

With its female protagonist and woman-dominated creative team, *Happy Valley* may reorient the male-centered northern narrative, but it still focuses on the kind of damaged rural patriarchal masculinity DeKeserdy and his colleagues reference and the collateral damage to women that results from it. That female perspective does, however, reveal a clear distinction between the ways each sex responds to the many stressors and misfortunes that befall all residents of the valley. Gorton claims that Wainwright's women "work through the anger resonant with the male protagonists of social realism. Their emotional labour, the affective working through of their feelings, leads them to find a sense of harmony with their lives, the land they come from and live in."[16] Gorton, I believe, exaggerates how widespread women's achievement of this harmony is in *Happy Valley*'s first season; in the second, which she had not seen when writing her article, the picture becomes bleaker, even for Catherine Cawood. The gender divide in the program rather hinges on women's greater ability to rebound from the troubles found in the trouble town. Emblematic are Catherine and her sister Clare (Siobhan Finneran), who have both been flattened at various points in their lives. Catherine had a mental breakdown after daughter Becky's rape and suicide; Clare is a recovering alcoholic and heroin addict. Yet both manage to regain sanity and sobriety to protect the community and create a home for Becky's son Ryan (Rhys Connah.)

Women's resilience and refusal to remain defeated separate them from the men. Almost all men featured crumble when obstacles occur, letting themselves spiral out of control, sometimes irreversibly. In her review of *Happy Valley*, the *New Yorker* television critic Emily Nussbaum notes that each criminal act it portrays is "an act of weakness, not power."[17] Men often target the women close to them, blaming their troubles on them and railing against them as bitches and whores. They never take responsibility for their own misdeeds; it is always someone else's fault. As the adulterous murderer John Wadsworth (Kevin Doyle) realizes his guilt will soon come to light, he drives to an empty Tesco car park and lets out a primal scream of "What have I done?" Appearing at first to be a realization of the wrongs he has committed, his soliloquy soon becomes a bitter complaint to the heavens about how he could possibly deserve the fate that awaits him.

Moreover, *Happy Valley*'s men present a sorry spectacle even if they have not broken the law. At the beginning of the first episode, Cawood confronts Liam Hughes (James Burrows), a twenty-three-year-old unemployed man whose girlfriend has just left him. Despairing and drunk, he stands on a playground climbing apparatus, soaked in petrol, holding a cigarette lighter, threatening to immolate himself. Unable to talk him down, she foams him with a fire extinguisher. Liam becomes the model for most of the men of the happy valley. Setbacks large and small propel them into substance abuse, infidelity, abandonment of or by their families, and financial distress. Endemic to *Happy Valley*, the characteristics of toxic masculinity—a stoic demeanor, mastery over women, and avoidance of any behavior marked as feminine— curdle within men who cannot maintain them. The character arc of the most toxic male in the series, the psychopathic multiple rapist and murderer Tommy Lee Royce (James Norton), illustrates this phenomenon. By the time Cawood corners him, he is ill, desperate, and threatening to set fire to himself, just like the pathetic Liam of the first scene.

The many aerial and crane shots in the program eschew the dramatic scenes of stark cliffs and rushing waters of many regional productions to repeatedly show how rolling moorlands encircle the built environments in the valley, from terrace houses to tower blocks and suburban bungalows. It is as if the inhabitants are the show's relentlessly consumed tea within the landscape's cup. The curdled masculinity of so many fragile men, if I may extend the metaphor, is the sour milk that sickens many in the populace, its toxins sometimes proving fatal. The program itself provides an alternative metaphor when a pack of dogs mauls an escaped sheep and the vet must put it down with a lethal injection; the dogs return to feast on the carcass, only to perish themselves from the drug.

When class intersects with regional and gender disadvantages, *Happy Valley*'s depiction aligns with Catherine's working-class sympathies, which trump her identification with women more broadly. A fierce ally of sex workers and trafficked women, she also grants working-class men some mitigation for their transgressions that she—and Wainwright—deny middle-class individuals of either sex. Many women of this class do not bring harmony and healing but act on "the frustrated aspirations of a character aggrieved at having been denied the symbolic trappings of a coveted bourgeois lifestyle."[18] Vicky Fleming (Amelia Bullmore) seduces married men and then revenges herself on them by blackmailing them with sexually compromising photos when they try to break things off. Jenny Weatherill (Julia Ford), initially presented as vulnerable because of her multiple sclerosis, counsels her husband, Kevin (Steve Pemberton), on how best to launder the money when he reveals his involvement in an extortion scheme, then drops him cold once he is caught and imprisoned. The wives of other middle-class criminal actors berate and humiliate them. These portrayals come perilously close to the patriarchally authored "castrating bitch" trope.

In context, the drug use and small-time thievery of hapless "scrotes" from the council estates are to Cawood more understandable than the grasping behavior of women such as Jenny Weatherill or Vicky Fleming. That she, however, dissolved her marriage to a middle-class journalist and gave up her job as DI to return to uniform grants her a working-class moral authority. The distinction between uniformed officers and plainclothes detectives mirrors the class divide between working class and middle class. Catherine complains that detectives share no information with the officers who first respond to crimes, merely leaving them to clean up the mess. Similarly, Shafiq expresses his frustration that CID "tossers" expect PCs like him to do the scut work while they sit on their rear ends counting paper clips.

Happy Valley also shows that class resentments can get in the way of women's solidarity. Catherine has to reprimand two female officers who did not take seriously a prostitute's claim of rape by a client whom she refused to service without payment. But Catherine cannot tolerate the "bitch," DI Jodie Shackleton (Katherine Kelly), whose father is a Chief Constable—"So guess how she skinned her way up the greasy pole." Shackleton, however, must put up with just the sort of dismissive condescension and discounting of her investigative insights from Deputy Superintendent Andy Shepherd (Vincent Franklin) that Catherine receives from her male superiors.

All Roads Lead to Cawood

As a police procedural, *Happy Valley* in its two seasons follows the same narrative structure. A systemic criminal network runs throughout the valley, selling drugs in season 1 and sexually exploiting women in season 2. Catherine routinely investigates cases stemming from these activities, usually low-level offenses involving working-class perpetrators. They eventually tie in to the central crime the diegesis tracks, showing its every step to viewers before the police have any inkling of what is going on. In both instances, a respected but desperate middle-aged, middle-class man responds to economic pressures by turning to crime, leaving one, accountant Kevin Weatherill, in prison and the other, Detective John Wadsworth, a suicide. Their crimes in turn become entangled with serial murders and rapes connected to Catherine's *bête noire*, Royce. He is part of the crew Weatherill hires to abduct Ann Gallagher (Charlie Murphy) for ransom. His mother is one of the victims of a serial killer of prostitutes that Wadsworth copycats to rid himself of Vicky Fleming and her blackmail. Catherine happens to be the officer who discovers the body of Royce's mother. In fact, nearly every crime she investigates intersects with every other in some way. Because of Catherine's personal and professional roots in the valley, she is often the point of intersection. In one of several chains of connection, a Croatian sex worker, Ilinka (Ivana Basic), who escapes human traffickers to report their activities to Catherine at Norland Road, is friends with another trafficked woman, whom the serial killer of prostitutes has murdered and raped with a broken bottle.

In the long tradition of small-town British crime dramas, the circulation of acquaintanceships and information in such settings creates narratively compelling links that would seem preposterous if portrayed in larger, urban settings. It is natural that the investigator with local roots would reconnect with family friends or former colleagues. As Roberts notes, the procedural genre and "hinterlands" settings can provide for symbiotic blendings of narrative and landscape because "the detective is a

16.2 Catherine Cawood (Sarah Lancashire) confronts her daughter's rapist, Tommy Lee Royce (James Norton).

figure whose procedural journeys—at their best—are often as much about divining and re-tracing the contours of space and place as they are about solving the murder."[19]

Some of the plot intersections nevertheless inspire eye rolls. Kevin Weatherill lives on the same street as Richard Cawood (Derek Riddell)? The old college chum Clare encounters and begins dating a few days before John Wadsworth murders Vicky is none other than Neil Ackroyd (Con O'Neill), a man Vicky previously tormented? "Halfway through the first episode of rapidly accumulating coincidences, I was shrieking, 'Enough, now!' at the screen," Jenny Diski writes.[20] Helen Piper more thoughtfully notes that "coincidence, in fact, is a key narrative strategy in *Happy Valley* to link the individual with the broader social fabric."[21] Yet the narrative resides so centrally in Cawood's psychic space that the broader social fabric the diegesis has constructed in effect collapses into a virtual projection of her existential trauma.

Gorton notes, "Her grief is not only part of the performance, but is located, by Wainwright, through choosing to show Catherine sitting by her daughter's gravesite."[22] Catherine's psychic reality lives always in her grief over her daughter's death and guilt over failing to make Royce pay for it (figure 16.2).

The central crimes of the two seasons, I would suggest, first allow Catherine to work through her inability to protect Becky from Royce and, second, reflect her fears that Ryan, the result of Becky's assault, may have inherited his father's criminal inclinations. Yet one mystery of *Happy Valley* remains unsolved: the cause of Becky's suicide six weeks after she had Royce's baby. Catherine blames the brutal rape only. Statements by her family, and some of her own admissions, suggest the matter is not so cut and dried. Becky ran wild because she was her mother's favorite. She got in with the wrong crowd and became infatuated with Royce. She feared her mother's wrath and so hid the pregnancy until an abortion was not possible. Catherine's insistence that she raise Ryan placed this reminder of her trauma before Becky every day. Thus, Catherine's guilt may attach not only to incapacity to bring Royce to justice but also to complicity in her daughter's death. Her admonition to the young female officers she mentors that "I'm not your mother" may reflect this ambivalence.[23] Ann Gallagher's kidnapping and rape in season 1 first force Catherine to reexperience her possible failures and then to remedy them.

As Catherine obsessively seeks the whereabouts of Royce, just released from prison after serving time on drug charges, he runs over and kills Officer Kirsten McAskill (Sophie Rundle) when she pulls over the van transporting Ann. The day before, Catherine, whom Kirsten idolizes, has dressed her down for bungling the drunk driving arrest of a city councilor and has not contradicted Kirsten's lament that she is shit at being a police officer. Kirsten's boyfriend, Ollie (Luke Williams), later blames Catherine for Kirsten's putting herself in a dangerous situation to regain her mentor's approval. The parallels to Becky's tragedy hit uncomfortably close to home.

Ann Gallagher is another Becky figure, whom Catherine does not fail. When Catherine learns of Ann's abduction, Clare says that at least investigating the kidnapping will take her mind off her obsession with Royce. Unknown to them, of course, Royce is at the heart of the Gallagher case, and it is only Catherine's search for him that allows her to find Ann and free her. Ann, in turn, rescues Catherine from the severe beating Royce inflicts on the sergeant. Previously an aimless and spoiled rich girl, Ann emerges from her ordeal with renewed resolve and purpose, becoming a police officer who, with Catherine's support and guidance, is well on her way to becoming a detective. With Royce sent to prison for rape and murder, the Gallagher case symbolically closes the case also on the maternal missteps Catherine made with Becky.

Although the first season puts some ghosts of the past to rest, it does not alleviate Catherine's worries about Ryan's future. Despite her efforts, Royce and son come together eventually and dangerously. At the end of the second season, Ryan has begun secretly writing to his father in prison. As with Becky, Catherine's conduct toward her grandson raises concerns. Insisting that she could not see the infant, whose criminal conception is not his fault, go into care may have triggered his mother's suicide and keeps him in an environment where knowledge of his origins circulates freely. The boy acts out repeatedly at school, and Catherine worries that he may have inherited Royce's violent nature, going as far as to call Ryan a psychopath in a particularly fraught moment. She hopes to inculcate a moral framework by telling him, "Don't blame other people for the decisions you've made." But is that even possible for a boy growing up in the valley of curdled, blame-denying men?

The resolution to the serial-killer storyline reflects on Catherine's worst fears for Ryan. The perpetrator, Daryl Garrs (Robert Emms), is an awkward, often bullied man-child; he, too, was born of rape, but also of incest, of his father/grandfather's abuse of his own daughter. When he confesses to his mother, Allison (Susan Lynch), she shoots him in the head to spare him the rigors of imprisonment. Relating this awful story to Clare at Becky's gravesite in the program's final scene, Catherine finds parallels between Allison's situation and her own: "She brought up this kid, this child, this aberration, that she loved and hated, because what else could she do?" As they and Ryan climb up the hill from the churchyard, the boy lobbies for a dog, mentioning only large, fierce breeds. Catherine watches Ryan as he picks up a tree branch and begins slicing at the long grass. The music, the slow-motion photography, and the concern on her face reflect her fear. Is she observing the natural tendency of young boys to turn sticks into imaginary weapons, or may she one day, if not put him down like a vicious dog, clap on the handcuffs as she has done to so many lads she has known since childhood who grow into curdled men in the trouble town?

Here we see that everything that happens in the happy valley folds back into the complex psychic space Catherine herself occupies. And this is a space in which the intersectionalities of region, gender, and class the program delineates do not apply. It is solely the terrain of Catherine's perpetual obsession with the evil of Royce—and eventually of his reciprocal obsession with her. Despite the horrors of Royce's "awful childhood," his being raised in "chaos and squalor" without love, Catherine gives him none of the empathy she shows for the scrotes and prostitutes who have had "shit lives." Ann's mother, Helen (Jill Baker), is regarded as a saint for giving addicts and ex-convicts second chances, for never ceasing to search for the good in everyone; when his disturbed prison "fiancée" Frances Drummond

(Shirley Henderson) articulates the same philosophy toward Royce, she appears as a deluded stalker.[24] True, Royce's crimes are well beyond the norm (and we see them in excruciating detail), but that does not prevent *Happy Valley* from giving an extremely sympathetic portrayal to the vicious serial killer/rapist Daryl Garrs, primarily by never showing him anywhere near his victims while detailing the bullying he suffers. Likewise, Becky lacked the resilience of the other women featured, succumbing to the suicidal despair that otherwise afflicts only male characters.

No matter how many streams of disadvantaging traffic converge to smash the metaphorical victim of discrimination Crenshaw proposes, she intends that victim to stand in for a whole class of people. In the end, *Happy Valley* presents Catherine Cawood as a character whose particular identity reduces all intersectionalities to a single vanishing point. Perhaps this is all to say that the systemic patterns analyzed in the particularized presence of this region disappear when grief and guilt dwell only in the absence marked by a gravestone.

CHAPTER SEVENTEEN

Kirsten Moana Thompson

TATTOOED LIGHT AND EMBODIED DESIGN

Intersectional Surfaces in *Moana*

Released for the first time in three Pacific languages (Māori, Hawaiian, and Tahitian), Disney's *Moana* (John Musker and Ron Clements, dirs., 2016) has been promoted as a form of support for languages defined by the United Nations Educational, Scientific and Cultural Organization (UNESCO) as "endangered" or "vulnerable." When combined with Disney's marketing of the film as an educational lesson on the Pacific, this strategy offered the imprimatur of cultural and linguistic authenticity while monetizing that very indigeneity under the Disney brand.[1] Part of Disney's shift in its representational practices away from the dominant versions of white femininity with which it has long been associated, *Moana* offers a fictional solution to an anthropological mystery known as "the Long Pause," a thousand-year halt to precolonial settlement in the Pacific, through Disney's contemporary narrative formula: a bold feminist heroine breaks the conventions of her isolationist father and village and ventures out beyond the reef to initiate the return of interisland voyaging.[2] While achieving commercial success and popular acclaim as one of the few Disney films to feature a Polynesian character in a leading role, *Moana* was also extensively criticized in the Pacific for its representational practices.[3] Critics have questioned the film's ethnographic authenticities in light of the enormous linguistic, cultural, and topographical diversity of Pacific nations and peoples; challenged the depiction of mythological figures such as Maui as an obese buffoon; and protested the studio's appropriative and, at times, deeply offensive promotional strategies, including the notorious marketing of a Maui "skinsuit" as a children's costume, decried as Buffalo

Maui Costume for Kids - Disney Moana

$44.95 - $49.95   Item No. 2844041217P.

★ ★★★★ Be the first to write a review.

Handsome voyage
Your little one will set off on adventures in this Maui Costume featuring the
demigod's signature tattoos, rope necklace and island-style skirt. Plus, padded
arms and legs for mighty stature! See more

Quantity: 1   Add to Bag

Size   Size Chart   ♡ Add to Favorite

Select a Size   ⌄

17.1 Brown skin as skinsuit? Maui's "Buffalo Bill"–like Halloween costume.

Bill–like (figure 17.1).[4] While well taken, I do not wish to redeploy these arguments here but instead to explore what I believe was insufficiently addressed in these critiques to better understand the powerful and affective appeal of *Moana*. As my argument suggests, Disney's reification of brown skin and tattoos in its marketing was by no means an isolated occurrence, but rather was an extension of the logic of the film's wider aesthetic strategies.[5] Indeed, from the glittering shells of crustaceans to the scintillating constellations of stars above the Pacific, and from *tapa* cloth to tattooed skin, *Moana* is a film fundamentally concerned with the aestheticization of material surfaces. In exploring the ways in which these aestheticized surfaces are also liminal and hybrid, I suggest that the film's attention to surface aesthetics materially articulates, often in self-reflexive form, a politics of intersectionality.

A refusal to remain temporally fixed in their assigned social identities characterizes all three of *Moana*'s principal characters—Maui (Dwayne Johnson), Tamatoa (Jermaine Clement), and Moana (Auli'i Cravalho)—while the spatial dimensions of their boundary crossing are exemplified by the film's heightened attention to skin, shell, and water surfaces in the mise-en-scène. In spatiotemporal terms, their liminality can be understood as not only that which relates "to a transitional or initial stage of a process," but also that which occupies "a position at, or on both sides of a boundary or threshold."[6] Whether it be the vainglorious shapeshifter and trickster Maui, who places himself at the center of every narrative ("You're Welcome"), or the glam crab Tamatoa, whose bling is based on his desire to be "shiny, like a wealthy woman's neck," these characters' boundary crossings are signaled not only through the traditional spatial signifiers of the coral reef or beach that intersect ocean and island, but also through the hybrid or composite nature of the principal characters. They, like our eponymous heroine ("How Far I'll Go"), reinvent and sing about themselves as figures of mobility, metamorphosis, and transformative exchange.

Moana's aestheticization of surface is explored through three specific sites, with particular attention to the racial and gendered intersections they articulate. The first is Maui's tattoos, which come to life as animated "films within the film," as drawings that are distinctively embodied. The second is the scintillating gold surfaces of the glitzy collector crab Tamatoa ("Shiny"). And the third is the mirror-like figures of light in sea and sky that represent a continuum between Moana and those who have gone before her, such as her grandmother Tala and the ancestor navigators, the Wayfarers. The film's architectonic light and contiguous reflective surfaces visualize the Samoan philosophical and spiritual concept of *va*, or that which refers to the space between, where va is understood not as emptiness, but as connectedness or relationality: "the space that is context."[7] Through these examples, I explore the ways in which scintillating light and embodied design powerfully visualize and reimagine the Pacific as a cosmopolitan space of exchange, in which Moana, Maui, and Tamatoa are shape-shifting, boundary-crossing figures of transformation who are distinctively animated.

Moana's aesthetics draw on and further reiterate what I elsewhere name "tiki aesthetics," borrowing not only from a long-standing Pacific Orientalism with roots in settler visual culture, but also, more recently, from a form of vernacular American modernism that has a particular graphic or cartoon-like stylization.[8] This tiki aesthetic also influenced Disney theme park and hotel architecture, exhibits, and merchandising. As a form of what Stéphane Martin has termed "synthetic exoticism," the fusion of Pacific and Californian graphic motifs has been mapped by popular historians such as Sven A. Kirsten as first emerging in the early twentieth century, shaped by cinema, literature, painting, and music, such as the popularization of Hawaiian ukulele music through performance troupes at the Panama-Pacific International Exposition in 1915.[9] Characterized by American appropriations of both Melanesian and Polynesian design motifs in carving and tapa cloth and cited across the bamboo and rattan architecture and interior design of Trader Vic's and Don the Beachcomber bars in

the 1920s and 1930s, the tiki aesthetic was an American popularization of
Pacific design elements used to construct exoticized spaces of recreation,
hospitality, and food services.[10] By the 1940s, the Pacific war had inten-
sified this American fascination, with wartime construction of wharves,
roads, and airfields creating the infrastructure for postwar mass tourism
in the region while also stimulating or reviving the Indigenous production
of and trade in artisanal handcrafts with American soldiers and sailors.[11]
Further catalyzed by James Michener's Pulitzer Prize–winning *Tales of
the South Pacific* (1947), Rodgers and Hammerstein's smash Broadway musical *South Pacific* (1949), and subsequent film adaptation *South Pacific* (Joshua
Logan, dir., 1958), the height of the tiki craze became a vernacular marker
of American postwar prosperity and recreational play, appearing in hotels,
bars, bowling alleys, and restaurants and across a range of social practices,
from luau parties to fruity rum cocktails.[12]

Tiki Animation

While tiki design certainly had its genealogical roots in the neoprimitivist
appropriations of European modern art in the 1920s, what has not yet been
critically considered are the ways tiki art also became fused with the simplified forms of midcentury animated aesthetics. Thick black outlines, bold
flat colors, and recurring graphic shapes such as the triangle, diamond,
A-frame, and oval were the leitmotifs of both Indigenous Pacific designs
and the cartoons of United Productions of America (UPA), an animation
studio formed by breakaway Disney artists who had been fired after the
strike in 1941. Influenced by midcentury trends in advertising and graphic
design, UPA's new technique of limited animation featured a self-reflexive
engagement with the line, angular rather than curvilinear characters, stylized movement, minimalist backgrounds, and planes of flat color to create mood or stand in for lighting or spatial effects in innovative cartoons
such as *Gerald McBoing Boing* (Robert Cannon and John Hubley, dirs., 1950)
and *Rooty Toot Toot* (John Hubley, dir., 1951).[13] The Disney studios were
also influenced by these trends in graphic design and tiki aesthetics, creating theme park architecture and exhibits, including Disneyland's 1963
Enchanted Tiki Room; the New Zealand, Australian, and Pacific sections
of the *It's a Small World* exhibit at the 1964 New York World's Fair (which
later moved to Disneyland); and the Polynesian Village Resort at Disney-
world in 1971. After several decades of shuttered hotels and tiki bars, tiki

aesthetics have shown more recent revival in American popular culture.[14] Disney opened the Aulani Resort in Hawaii in 2011, launched the comic book *Enchanted Tiki Room* in 2016, and hired the retro artist Shag to create promotional artwork for the fiftieth anniversary of its eponymous exhibit. More recently, Disney added a Trader Sam's Enchanted Tiki Bar at Disneyland Hotel and Trader Sam's Grog Grotto in Orlando.[15] Given this nostalgic renaissance of all things tiki, it is not surprising that white supremacists were holding tiki torches at Charlottesville. Indeed, the bizarre evocation of Nuremberg rallies through a cheap symbol of suburban recreation uncovers a nostalgia for a normative whiteness in postwar American popular culture, in which cultural appropriation and exoticized racial fantasy were embedded in tiki's mise-en-scène of bars, restaurants, hotels, and drinks.

Tiki design not only shaped Disney's theme parks and hotels; it was also a key element of *Moana*'s aesthetic development, including concept art, location, and character design. From tiki-like totems and vibrant turquoise and purple in the concept art of James Finch and the hot pink, black, and teal paintings of Kevin Nelson, both designing the underwater world of Lalotai, to the stylized coconut-armor-wearing Kakamora characters of Leighton Hickman, tiki aesthetics persist.[16] They are particularly evident in the two-dimensional tapa design used as a storytelling device within Tala's tale, the film's opening prologue, which introduces us to the legend of Maui and its young auditor, Moana. The film foregrounds the graphic surfaces of its medium through a mixed-modal approach, joining computer animation of Maui and Moana in collaged combination with cel drawings, exemplifying an intersectional mediality that self-reflexively draws attention to skin and surface. We shift from tapa cutouts to 3D Maui and then back again to 2D drawings held by the opening storyteller, now revealed to be Moana's grandmother, Tala. Mixed media formally aligns with the characters who are voyagers, border crossers, and shape-shifters and is most extensively deployed in Maui's song "You're Welcome."

Throughout the film, Maui, an immodest demigod, interacts with the tattoos on his body (named "Mini Maui" by Disney artists), which function as a Greek chorus, suggesting narrative paths for him and ironically commenting on those that are taken. The surfaces of Maui's body act as an expanded screen-within-the screen, drawing upon a long tradition in animated storytelling in which drawings come to life.[17] Remarking on his tattoos' status as graphic decoration and animated design, Maui boasts, "The tapestry here on my skin / is a map of the victories I win" (figure 17.2). We see close-ups of Mini Maui, with each tattoo coming to life, in turn, to

17.2 Maui's intersectional surfaces: "The tapestry here on my skin / is a map of the victories I win."

demonstrate Maui's epic deeds as masculine display on his biceps and triceps: lassoing the sun to create daytime, stealing fire from the underworld, harnessing the wind, creating the coconut tree by beheading the eel, and defeating an eight-eyed fruit bat. As Maui sings, "Honestly I can go on and on / I can explain every natural phenomenon," he opens a tapa cloth, and with a match cut he and Moana enter into a flat graphic universe, within and between colorful cutouts of coconuts, flying fish, fruit, and tapa backdrop. As he taps out the rhythm on a coconut ("I killed an eel / I buried its guts / Sprouted a tree, now you got coconuts"), we get an abbreviated allusion to one of the many legends of Maui. As 3D Maui vanquishes a 3D eel, it now becomes a paper cutout, with shifts in animation modes instantiating narrative transformations into mythic or legendary status (the origin story of the coconut in the Samoan legend Sina and the Eel), while also being a self-congratulatory song about Maui's own celebrity status ("I know it's a lot: the hair, the bod! / When you're staring at a demi-god").[18] In other words, Maui's tattoos are an intersectional genealogy of his own identities, mapping the ways in which he has reinvented himself: disavowing his mother's shameful abandonment of him as a child (a story hidden under his hair on his back), animating his superhero achievements, and undercutting his masculine braggadocio.

Maui's unconventional character design was modeled on a square shape that did not follow human proportions, with legs half the normal length of his torso. This squat rectangularity, coupled with a plastic quality to his skin surface that lacks the detailed shading and color gradations of human skin, seems to suggest that Maui is already toy-like: an aesthetic transformation of the character's body that is in keeping with an emphasis on his corporeal surface as screen and that gives visual precedence to his torso and arms over the rest of his body.[19] This emphasis on skin as an expanded screen was noted by the director John Musker, who acknowledged that "[Maui] is a walking billboard of his great deeds, which is a great storytelling device for us."[20]

In contrast to Maui's graphic simplicity, the strutting collector crab Tamatoa is a robber pirate who has physically reinvented himself ("I was a drab little crab once"), the surfaces of his shell now glittering with gold and mother-of-pearl and the flotsam of human wreckage, including embedded boat skeletons in his shell. Tamatoa's lair lies deep in the underwater world of Lalotai, where scale is reversed, so that he has become gargantuan and Maui and Moana are tiny. In its glam rock homage to David Bowie, Tamatoa's song "Shiny" reimagines the ocean deeps as a Diamond Dog extravaganza of gold and ultraviolet light. Presumably reflected by Tamatoa's shell, which acts as a disco ball in the inverted world of Lalotai, we see dozens of rotating golden lights. The effect of this illuminated background is a hallucinatory one for the viewer, spectacularizing Tamatoa as sparkly performer and queer superstar as it immerses us in his underwater auditorium. This is Tamatoa's moment, and he is enjoying every minute of it: "Watch me dazzle like a diamond in the rough / strut my stuff / my stuff is so shiny." The transporting effects of the counterclockwise camera movement and Tamatoa's own performance, coupled with the transformation of the underwater world into a nightclub, only intensifies when the scene shifts suddenly into black light, spatially disorienting us with its ultraviolet world of blacks, deep blues, hot pinks, and neon greens. Now Tamatoa's golden shell has become like the night sky: a silvery constellation of glittering gems. Overhead shots of Tamatoa spinning around in an illuminated Hollywood-like bowl that now appears like the deepest reaches of the galaxy demonstrates how *Moana*'s mise-en-scène inverts and transforms space. This inversion in scale between human and crab echoes the ways in which *Moana*'s intersectional surfaces also duplicate, mirror, or invert, creating parallel universes: between Maui and his tattoos, between the ordinary and the mythic, between the living and the ancestors, between sea and sky, and, ultimately, between Earth and universe.

In contrast to Tamatoa's sparkly self-assurance, Maui is a shape-shifting demigod whose metamorphoses do not always work out. In frequent attempts to turn himself into a giant hawk, Maui instead cycles through a comical sequence of embarrassing failures (from tiny fish to iguana, man shark, reindeer Sven from *Frozen*, and a pig) before defeatedly returning to his normal form. Tamatoa mocks him for these performative failures, giving particular attention to Maui's diminutive scale, "Well, well, well, Little Maui's having trouble with his look / You little semi-demi-mini-god / Ouch! What a terrible performance." Although Maui's balloony plastic surface and toy-like dimensions differ visibly from Tamatoa's reflective hard shell, the characters are paralleled in that they are both boastful narcissists whose bodies reflect their literal remediation and reconstruction of themselves. Their mobile graphic or sculptural autobiographies are a different form of taxidermy. After all, it takes one to know one, as Tamatoa sings to Maui, "For just like you, I made myself a work of art."[21]

But while Maui and Tamatoa are emboldened boundary crossers in their pursuit of fame and fabulousness, the principal narrative agent who forges paths across liminal spaces is, of course, Moana, singing, "See the line where the sky meets the sea? It calls me / and no one knows how far it goes" in "How Far I'll Go," her desires signaled through the elongated phrasing and musical notation of "it—calls—me." From the film's very first song "Where You Are," the tension between Moana's aspirations and the isolationism of her father, Chief Tui (Temuera Morrison), is evident. Where Tui imagines the reef as a kind of cordon sanitaire and as "the one rule that keeps us safe"—singing, "The island gives us what we need"—Moana's yearning gaze to the horizon line and her constant movement toward the beach and into the water as a toddler prefigure her later transgressive desire to cross the reef as Motonui's outermost boundary. Physically unsettled, in movement like Moana herself, the phrase "there you are" both echoes and linguistically opposes the fixity of her father's "where you are." The relay from Tui to Tala to Moana, who take up different verses of the song in turn, also animates the significance of the song's title: the "Where" of the song's title is on the move. Beginning with Tui, the song is then taken up by Gramma Tala, a liminal figure, as she notes, through her position as the village "crazy lady." She sings, "The water is mischievous (ha!) / I like how it misbehaves / The village may think I'm crazy / Or say that I drift too far." Like her granddaughter, Tala is spatially aligned with the beach and the ocean of the stingray, whose tattoo Tala bears and whose bioluminescent spirit form she becomes after death. As Tala's verse begins, we see that her mobile sense of self affirms Moana's own aspirations: "I like to dance with the water / The undertow and the waves." Thus, even though the beach is within the protective boundary of Tui's reef, it is also, like Tala, a marker of connection and relationality that faces outward to the Pacific Ocean and to the other islands beyond Motunui, an epistemological marker of va as intersectional site that, as Epeli Hau'ofa reminds us, understands the Pacific as a "sea of islands," of connected spaces in Oceania, and not as isolated islands far from (Western) sites of power.[22]

When Moana enters the Cave of the Wayfarers upon Tala's encouragement, it is clear that there are other border crossers who have gone before and whom we come to recognize as Moana's ancestors. Here the temporal dimension of liminality is foregrounded through the film's sound and music. The Cave of the Wayfarers is bounded on one side by a waterfall, which is not only a spatial location of water flowing over a rock edge but also a temporal marker of the duration of that unending flow. This spatio-temporal dimension of the Cave is underscored by the way in which the beating of a drum by Moana seems to reawaken the spirits of the Wayfarers, as the torches magically light themselves and voices are heard. As we pan past a fleet of sails, we look more closely with Moana and jump-zoom into a sail's detail of the lead boat. Suddenly on the next drum beat, the film match-cuts to what appears to be a flashback: a color daytime shot of the Wayfarers riding the ocean and who segue fully into the song "We Know the Way." Moana and her voyaging ancestors are brought together through montage, collapsing past and present into one relational continuum that transcends time and space. We return to this song at the end of the film for a climactic narrative reprise, when Moana is joined by the Wayfarers and her spirit grandmother Tala as bioluminescent figures of light that figure va as radiant continuum.

Moana is most interested in the interstitial spaces between water and air and between sky and sea, marked by a liminal boundary between the ocean's surface and the light from the stars. The indeterminacy of this boundary is emphasized through a number of shots that deliberately disorient the viewer as trompe l'oeil, where the camera presents a shot that is only later revealed to be a reflection in the water. Thus, on the eve of Moana's confrontation with Te Ka, Tala appears to her granddaughter and offers her counsel. In this scene, we pan up from Moana and Tala to the night sky, then resume panning, only to reveal a new, inverted, and impossible image of Moana and Tala that appears to be a reflection in the sky. This Escher-like structure elsewhere echoes the forward- and backward-facing dimension of the film's narrative metaphysics. Instructed in navigation by Maui, Moana is reminded that "it's called wayfinding, princess. It's not just sails and knots," and this wayfinding requires "knowing where you are by knowing where you've been." To navigate, Moana must use her body as an astronomical instrument, her hand marking the distance between the ho-

17.3 Wayfinding: "Knowing where you are by knowing where you've been."

rizon line and Orion's Belt, with one star in the belt visible above her index finger, showing that she is facing east, and that the star is 21 degrees above the horizon line (figure 17.3). Maui, Tamatoa, and Moana are each sites of corporeal remediation: where Maui is graphic line springing to life, Tamatoa is reflective surface, a sparkling galaxy who remediates the celestial sky as a glittering stage. Like Tamatoa, Moana animates herself through light, her body becoming the line. She must find her way by looking back to her ancestor navigators and the light of the stars, in order to map her way forward across the ocean.

The contemporary screen has recently been described as a site of mediation and projection on which surface luminosity and textural hapticity are foregrounded by the materiality of the image. Theorists such as Giuliana Bruno have pointed to the spectacular role of light in contemporary media, such as the Cuban artist Carlos Garaicoa's *On How the Earth Wishes to Resemble the Sky* (2005), in which the screen acts "as if it were a canvas, a material in which holes have been made, through which a shining light is made to shimmer."[23] Bruno suggests that new forms of "connectivity and relationality" are enabled by the contemporary moving image as an illuminated and permeable surface, but this is something with which animation has long been engaged and that *Moana*'s aesthetics foreground. Indeed, the film's architectonic light and reflective surfaces literalize a conception of va that approaches navigation through the world as a spatiotemporal continuum. Va is embodied through the bioluminescent light of Tala (as stingray) and Moana's voyaging ancestors. As the emission of light by living organisms, bioluminescence collapses the boundaries between light and

17.4 Va: The space that is context.

color and between the organism and the natural environment in which
its light is contextualized. But *Moana*'s bioluminescent light also signals
animated magical powers and metaphysical realms, from Tamatoa's location in the underworld Lalotai to Maui's magical transformations, marked
by his glowing tattoos and fishhook filigreed by light, and the presence of
Moana's forebears, who mark the way for her across the ocean and sky in a
spray of bioluminescent light (figure 17.4).

As Hannah Goodwin's work on cinema and cosmology reminds us, the
night sky is akin to a movie theater. As in cinema, there is a temporal delay
between the originating event and the image seen, where the emission of
light from a distant star and our sight of its glimmer is shaped by the speed
of light but delayed by the millions of miles over which it must travel. Sharing two fundamental ontological similarities "as repositories of light from
the past and as surfaces for the projection of human desires, aspirations,
dislocations and uncertainties," cinema, like the night sky, makes us voyagers, bringing the indexical light from the past into our present.[24]

By imagining the bowl of the night sky and the reflective surface of the
black ocean as this intersectional continuum, a tattoo of light whose boundaries cannot be discerned, the film's surfaces are simultaneously a constel-
lational map of Moana's voyage across the Pacific, a site of reunification with

her grandmother Tala, and a shared and reanimated space with the ancestors who sing "We Know the Way" as they voyage again with Moana:

> Aue, aue, we are explorers reading every sign
> We tell the stories of our elders
> In a never-ending chain.

For Moana and even the bragging Maui and Tamatoa are animated figures of mobility and exchange; their corporeal reinventions call emotional witness to, and insist upon, a fundamental cosmopolitan understanding of the Pacific.

VAGUELY VISIBLE

Intersectional Politics in Bertrand
Bonello's *Nocturama* (2016)

Bertrand Bonello's *Nocturama* (2016), which concerns a mass terrorist attack perpetrated by a group of ten youths across Paris, contains a split-screen
sequence that momentarily propels the film into reflexive terrain.[1] The first
half of the film is dedicated to the depiction of characters preparing and
executing these attacks as they bomb a series of symbolic targets, including the Ministry of the Interior, the Tour Total skyscraper in La Défense,
and the city's HSBC headquarters, and set Frémietthe's bronze statue *Jeanne
d'Arc* ablaze.[2] After showing each attack separately, the film proceeds in reverse, cycling through a series of static shots of Paris that appear earlier in
the film and ending with the final image, split four ways, that displays the
events happening simultaneously (figure 18.1).

This brief rewinding of the "film within the film" asks the viewer to con-
template the cumulative power of the actions of this group as a cluster of
spectacular images. The split-screen sequence also serves as a second means
of giving expression to the film's networked structure within the space of a
single screen. The network narrative, described by a multiplicity of scholars,
including David Bordwell, Leisa Rothlisberger, and Wendy Everett, features
multiple narrative trajectories that are interwoven and yet retain a certain
distinctiveness that encourages spectators to take notice of how the stories
of the film are told.[3] The network narrative holds this tension between sameness and difference in place through multistrand narrative trajectories characterized by simultaneity, chance, intersectionality, and relationality. *Nocturama* interweaves the trajectories of its central characters, who range in age,
gender, religious affiliation, and race, while punctuating their activities with

18.1 Split-screen image depicting the acts of terror inflicted by the protagonists simultaneously.

flashback sequences that provide a modicum of narrative information concerning who they are and, crucially, why they band together to mount these attacks. What unites these characters is a generalized malaise that is directed at the French state. The most cited line of dialogue from *Nocturama*, raised in reviews as the only hint of an explanation for these attacks, is articulated during a flashback sequence, when one character, André (Martin Petit-Guyot), tells another, Sarah (Laure Valentinelli), "Civilization appears as a sufficient condition for the rupture of civilization."[4]

The film generates what we can term an "intersectional style," resulting from its adherence to the conventions of the network narrative and the heterogeneous composition of its characters with respect to their identities. The genealogy of intersectionality, as a mode of being and a method of analysis, can be traced to its activist roots as a way to identify and grapple with the real-world effects of often unrecognized, compounding difference. Kimberlé Crenshaw, in her pioneering essays on the term, evokes the spatial metaphor of the street intersection as analogous to the way in which differences related to race, gender, sexuality, and class intersect and inform one another in the formation of identities.[5] In this vein, Vivian May describes intersectionality as "matrix" rather than "single-axis" thinking.[6] As Stuart Hall puts it more broadly, difference "entails a recognition that we all speak from a particular place, out of particular history, out of particular experience, a particular culture."[7] Difference, for Hall, is always "positional, conditional and conjunctural."[8]

This essay subjects Bonello's gestures toward an intersectional politics to close scrutiny. More precisely, I argue that *Nocturama* inadvertently succumbs to what the sociologist Sirma Bilge refers to as "ornamental intersectionality."[9] For Bilge, the ornamental version of intersectionality reduces difference to a series of market values deployed by institutions interested in "diversifying" without having to implement significant structural changes.[10] Thus, the language of diversity is often aligned with a tokenistic understanding of difference. *Nocturama*'s nod toward an intersectional politics signifies as ornamental in more than one register. While Bilge uses the concept to name a superficial instance of the practice, the ornament is also a matter of display as an accessory or decoration. As I demonstrate, *Nocturama* asks us to read the bodies of the characters as they intersect and interact with one another as the primary site of difference, reducing intersectionality to a matter of corporeal surfaces put on display for the viewer. Furthermore, it is my contention that Bonello's penchant for the abstraction and leveling of certain forms of difference undermines the film's attempts at intersectionality, transforming such gestures into a vague universalism. Both forms of ornamentalism lead to a series of broader questions. Does *Nocturama* tap into the political circumstances of the present day, marked by ever-increasing turns toward divisiveness that are evenly matched by movements toward greater homogenization? How does Bonello's project fare when situated within a historical trajectory of identity politics within both a French and a broader European context?

"Problematic on Purpose": Intersectionality or Terrorist Utopia

Nocturama's networked structure fittingly begins on the Paris Metro, as Bonello gradually intersperses the trajectories of many of its central characters on the city's own underground network.[11] Bonello places emphasis on signage in the Metro and eventually zooms in on a Metro Map so that the character's movements across Paris are relayed in all of their specificity. Some of these characters meet on Metro lines, often without acknowledgment, and then disperse individually or in smaller groups, as they make their way to their targets. A time code occasionally flashes on the screen, a device that not only suggests that these characters are connected but that they are inching toward a time-specific goal. The manner in which these characters behave, which includes the taking of selfies in certain locations, the dumping of cell phones, and surreptitious glances, quickly situates the film within the context of "terrorist cinema," broadly conceived. The first half of the film is heavily indebted to Alan Clarke's made-for-television film

Elephant (1989), which features a series of lone men, often followed closely from behind, as they execute eighteen others situated across a variety of spaces. *Elephant* does not offer any context for these killings, though it is well known that the film is "about" the so-called Troubles in Northern Ireland. Bonello's homage to *Elephant* includes the execution-style murders eventually committed by some of the characters and the use of a Steadicam when following these characters from different angles, occasionally showcasing the backs of their heads in classic *Elephant* fashion.

Within this context, a striking feature of *Nocturama* is the composition of this group in terms of racial and gendered identities, and as the film goes on, more details emerge involving questions of religion and sexuality. This is especially the case in the wake of the mainstream predilection to ascribe all acts of domestic and international terror to "Muslim" extremists. This holds true even in the face of Bonello's claims that the film was written before the *Charlie Hebdo* and Bataclan attacks in Paris, as a heightened tendency toward Islamophobia emerges in the West in the wake of 9/11, and thus predates recent events. Bonello groups characters together in the early sections of the film in ways that encourage an intersectional reading. These groupings can be viewed as the aesthetic variant of Hall's conception of the positional and conditional nature of difference. Yacine (Hamza Meziani) is the first character to appear on the Metro, riding in a car. In the following shot, he stands at Châtillon station, boards a train, and sits down near Mika (Jamil McCraven), Sabrina (Manal Issa), and Samir (Ilias Le Doré), who, we come to realize, are the four characters of color in the film. On the basis of surface appearances, it is clear that the characters in this scene are marked by differences related to gender and ethnicity. A second example includes Yacine, Sarah, and David (Finnegan Oldfield) as they sit on a train destined for La Défense, adding two white characters—one male and the other female—to the group.

Other groupings of characters raise the issue of class in its intersection with race. André and Mika are both stationed at the Ministry of the Interior. While André takes a meeting with the minister in a full suit, during which they discuss André's father and his education, Mika roams the hallways in jogging gear, hides in a closet, and eventually sets up the bomb. There are two scenes—one in the street in front of the Ministry, and the other in the building itself—where these two characters pass each other, making their differences palpable. During a flashback sequence in which all of the characters are brought together to plan the attacks, we learn that Sabrina is to use a false name to obtain a room in a hotel that is adjacent to Frémietthe's

Jeanne d'Arc, which she will set on fire. When she is told she needs to pay 300–400 euros per day, she remarks that the room is very expensive, and she could put that money to better use by buying other things. While she quickly notes that she is joking, the question of class is once again in the air. Thus, it is the combination of identities across this group of ten that lends itself to an intersectional interpretation, as differences related to class, race, and gender are raised while all characters are linked together through their commitment to performing their respective acts of terror.

There is, then, the question of whether or not these differences transcend their initial status as ornamental, rendered simply through visual appearances, as the film progresses. "Ornamental" is also a term that encompasses what some critics have pointed to as the stylish and photogenic nature of this group, who make terrorism "look cool."[12] To return to the central dialectic of the network narrative, which manifests tensions between sameness and difference, the network structure of *Nocturama* unveils a number of significant differences among members of the group while shrouding others in vagueness. Flashback sequences provide suggestions of a backstory, at least for some of the characters. During the flashback sequence that features the coffee meeting between Sarah and André, Sarah says that they will both end up like their fathers if she attends a school that André graduated from, which solidifies the link between the two on the basis of class affiliation. In this scene, they are served by Yacine, thereby establishing a contrast along class- and race-based lines. The mastermind of the group, Greg (Vincent Rottiers), who also provides the Semtak bombs for the attacks, is presented as working-class. Our first encounter with him is at a surveillance firm during a flashback sequence, where he is to be interviewed for a job he has performed before. During this scene, we learn that Yacine's friend Fred (Robin Goldbronn), who is also part of the plot, has been unable to find work for a year. This particular series of flashbacks explicitly addresses class difference, tethered not only to the notion of "old" money in the case of André and Sarah but also to the conditions of neoliberal France, marked by high levels of unemployment.[13]

There also is a flashback sequence in which Sabrina, Yacine, Mika, and Samir spend time together outdoors, thus establishing their friendship as one that precedes their involvement in the attacks. The setting resembles a typical *banlieue* (Paris suburb), particularly at the start of the scene in which Sabrina is filmed against the backdrop of the bottom half of a series of square tower buildings typical of HLM blocks built in the 1960s. As Kristin Ross has famously argued, the distinction between Paris and its banlieue, home mostly to populations who have descended from former French colonies such as Algeria and other North African nations, is akin to a "frozen temporal lag" that fixes in place relations of inequality along the lines of race and class.[14] Unlike other locations in *Nocturama*, this one is never specified, either in terms of its location or whether it is, in fact, a banlieue. Rather, it is the presence of four individuals of color in a space that is clearly not central Paris that suggests they are from a banlieue.

If the promise of the flashback sequence resides in the revelation of key elements of narrative, this promise is only partially fulfilled in *Nocturama*. Moments of sparing detail, related to issues of class and race, do very little to transcend the parameters of an ornamental intersectionality; characters are akin to citations in this film, as their presence alludes to the broader context of identity politics within a French context. It comes as little surprise that one reviewer glibly refers to them as "multicultural terrorists."[15] However, Bonello's assertion of class distinction, at the level of characterization, is grounded within his explicit critique of capitalist abstraction in evidence across numerous facets of the film. Thus, class difference is granted a certain weight and breadth in the film. According to Bonello, what is new about the contemporary period is a growing sense of equivalency, where one can happen upon a young person is who as "fascinated by terrorism as by consumerism."[16] The two halves of the film—one depicting acts of terrorism performed by these characters, and the other transpiring in a mall where the characters take refuge in the aftermath of the attacks— speak to his claim.[17] The second half of the film serves as a continuation of its networked structure, only at a much slower pace. While the film's first half pays tribute to *Elephant*, the film's second half is indebted to George Romero's *Dawn of the Dead* (1978). While Romero's mall is of the suburban variety, Bonello's mall is the abode of the elite of Paris, where characters wander through a series of enclaves dedicated to the wares of top designers. Bonello's debt to Romero may extend to the very impetus for this section of the film. In *Dawn of the Dead*, Peter (Ken Foree) explains to his group of escapees that perhaps it is nostalgia that draws the zombies to the mall. Something similar is at work in *Nocturama* as the characters find themselves in thrall to its luxurious surfaces, suggesting that the building of the new world is harder than it appears.[18]

In contrast, questions of race, religious affiliation, and gender are raised through the presence of characters, but they are not subject to exploration or further elaboration. One inadvertent reaction on the part of critics to Bonello's mode of ornamental differentiation is homogenization, or a desire to flatten difference in the face of difference. A number of reviews are telling in this regard. The critic Justin Chang refers to Omar (Rabah Nait Oufella), a security guard at the mall involved in the plot, as a "brash kid from Middle Eastern descent," while David Ehrlich describes Yacine and Samir as brothers "who have brown skin and appear to be members of France's Muslim popula- tion."[19] A. O. Scott asserts that a number of the group "appear to be children of immigrants from suburban housing projects."[20] He also notes that one of the characters is "a Muslim who doesn't drink alcohol and believes he will be welcomed in Paradise as a martyr."[21] The character is question is Samir, and Scott invents a crucial detail in his review: after Samir declares that they are going to Heaven when they are hiding in the mall, he *accepts* a glass of cognac from Yacine, who is drinking himself into oblivion in a bathtub. Yacine asks Samir to join him, and he simply says that he does not feel like it. At this point, it is also clear that the characters are not brothers.

Scott's invention is not merely a matter of careless viewing or misre- membering; it results from an assumption that if one states that violent actions constitute a direct route to Heaven, one must be a "Muslim" of "Middle Eastern descent" who embodies all characteristics a "Muslim" is thought to possess. In fact, an earlier sequence not mentioned by Scott could be called on to solidify his reading. During the flashback sequence that reveals the previous friendship of Samir, Yacine, Sabrina, and Mika, Sabrina tells Samir that he must go home because his mother has found unspecified material on his computer that has prompted her to yell and to cry. Although Samir claims this material is for school, the exchange re- calls a host of such stories in the popular press that narrate "the moment of belated discovery," where families realize that their children have been harboring "fanatic" or "extremist" views. In recent years, these stories have been linked specifically to jihadist-inspired activity. Ehrlich, by contrast, reads the surfaces of characters' skin for evidence of their "Middle Eastern Muslim-ness," which suggests brotherly love rather than same-sex desire. Thus, race and religion, both presented in the most tokenistic of ways, meld into one in his review.

Bonello takes a calculated risk in this particular sequence between Samir and Yacine, but one that yields few results. The composition of the scene suggests that Bonello anticipates a particular reading of the characters' ac- tions vis-à-vis their appearances and attempts to complicate it by having Samir consume alcohol and not express revulsion toward Yacine's quasi- sexual advance. Yet the popular and populist association between "Muslim fanaticism" and martyrdom that Bonello himself evokes overpowers any nuances that he introduces. To refer to characters as "Muslim," as these reviewers do, is also troubling. As David Theo Goldberg asserts, to "standardize the figure of the Muslim" is to effectively deny that any differences do exist among individuals and groups who may subscribe to numerous variations of the Muslim faith.[22]

While Bonello asks viewers to consider the question of how they see what they see, in keeping with the parameters of the network narrative as form, this strategy crumbles when it comes to the intersectional politics of the film. All the characters of color are primarily linked to one another, and there is little sense of how we might differentiate them on the basis of race, sexuality, or religion. There is the suggestion that these four characters originate from a similar class bracket, and again, it appears that class is the only category of difference that Bonello feels comfortable asserting with some degree of explicitness. Bonello's variant of the network narrative establishes—and, in fact, privileges—relations of similarity among all of its characters. Thus, *Nocturama* provides us with nothing less than a veritable terrorist utopia, where characters surmount a range of differences to mount a devastating and spectacular act of mass violence (figure 18.2).

The characters also meet the exact same fate as each is gunned down by heavily armed police. My reading of a number of reviews suggests that this utopia comes at the very particular cost of a nuanced portrayal of its Muslim characters at a time of heightened Islamophobia around the globe.

As May argues, the analytical value of intersectionality rests on its ability to bring hidden forms of oppression into the light.[23] Thus, intersectionality is rarely a matter of surface; to grasp its dynamics, one must dig deeper. For scholars such as May and Bilge, to universalize an intersectional politics for ornamental purposes is to engage in its depoliticization. The universalizing tendency of Bonello's project both neutralizes the film's orientation toward intersectionality while also encouraging viewers to conflate surface appearances with facets of one's identity that are not always subject to visibility. For this reason, the film's intersectional style fails to yield an intersectional politics.

Ornamental Intersectionality: Today and Yesterday

Bonello's version of an ornamental intersectionality seems as tailored to present-day circumstances as much as it also appears to be entrenched in the past. It is a film, then, that speaks to tensions between a previous world order and the current one. If viewed within a contemporary context, the

18.2 Last group embrace by the protagonists before they embark on their acts of terror the following day.

sense of equivalency among disparate things—a notion that governs Bonello's pairing of terrorism with shopping—can be taken as a sign of the times. The philosopher Alain Badiou, for example, views Donald Trump's electoral win as part of the growing homogenization of global politics, where other figures associated with the far right, including Theresa May, Narendra Modi, and Vladimir Putin, are united in their commitment to the continued success of neoliberal capitalism.[24] As Badiou argues, the obvious differences among these figures and their regimes have become abstracted by the mantra of "no alternatives."[25] Greater homogenization has been met with an opposing and yet similar pull toward greater differentiation. Nowhere is this more apparent than in the tendency toward Islamophobia that is transpiring the world over. To return to the French context and to the terrorist attacks that Bonello refuses to name, the media coverage in the wake of the *Charlie Hebdo* attacks sought to establish the banlieues as bastions of radical Islamic extremism, as two of the attackers claimed residence in two different banlieues.[26] As Matthew Moran writes, "Demonised in political and popular discourse, the suburbs are widely perceived as a place apart, a sociocultural anomaly that is far removed from idealized notions of the Republic."[27]

On the one hand, we can advance the claim that Bonello wholeheartedly succumbs to the tendency toward greater homogeneity in this film, made evident in his diluted brand of intersectionality. On the other hand, Bonello's embrace of a certain exorbitance regarding the reason for the actions undertaken by this group of ten, in conjunction with his suggestion that *anyone* is capable of executing an act of mass terrorism, can be read in a progressive light. In opting for vagueness, Bonello refuses to submit to the extreme version of either pole while simultaneously mounting a pointed critique of neoliberalism and capitalist abstraction.

And yet Bonello's inability to address differences pertaining to race and its intersection with religion can be viewed in a historical light, starting with the question of how intersectionality has been taken up within Europe specifically. As Bilge explains, intersectionality in a European academic milieu is often subjected to theoretical abstraction or to "whitening," which involves decentering race as a central factor in the foundations of the term, as well as marginalizing the contributions to discourses or debates on the topic that originate from women (queer and straight) of color. She writes, "This reflects a dominant tendency among European scholars: disallowing race as an analytical category, instead framing problems through categories such as ethnicity, culture and religion."[28] As noted previously, religion is treated in problematic terms by Bonello, dovetailing with David Theo Goldberg's assessment of the status of the figure of the Muslim in contemporary Europe. Tackling the question of a growing Islamophobia in Europe during the time of writing, Goldberg's observations remain relevant to the present juncture, where Islamophobia is reaching something of an apogee in Europe and far beyond. As Goldberg writes, the figure of the Muslim, stripped of all variations, has come to stand not only for the lack of freedom and civility, but also for death. Death in this case pertains not only to physical loss but also to a growing anxiety about the death of Europe itself, as though the continent is under threat of being swallowed up whole by those who were never allowed to fully belong.[29] To return to *Nocturama*, the readings of the exchange between Samir and Yacine by critics mentioned previously illustrates a central tenet of the image of the Muslim in circulation today; *he* is the chief emblem of "fanaticism, fundamentalism, female suppression, subjugation and repression."[30] Race, however, never transcends its ornamental designation in the film. As a result, race and religion are conflated within the film itself, as it appears only Bonello's characters of color also have clear religious affiliations.

Debate about the relevance of race as a category to Europe has a long and difficult history, stemming from a widely held assertion that colonialism was an experience that was external to Europe and to its present-day constitution. Bilge briefly evokes Goldberg's work in this regard. Goldberg argues that the Holocaust assumes the point of centrality in the European post-war imaginary, often at the expense of a reckoning with the legacies of European colonialism though the two were imbricated in disturbing ways.[31] Narrowing our focus to a French context, scholars such as Kristin Ross and Étienne Balibar, among many others, have articulated the ways in which colonization and decolonization could never have been external to the rise of a modern, postwar France. In "Borderland Europe and the Challenge of Migration," Balibar relays an anecdote dating back to the colonial period, where French maps adorning classroom walls contained a double border. While one border demarcated the boundaries between the French nation and the rest of Europe, the other established boundaries between the French empire and its colonies. For Balibar, since the double border was a fact of numerous European empires, "an implicit opposition between Europe and the rest of the world, between the natural residence of the 'Europeans' and that of the 'non-Europeans' (commonly qualified as 'indigenous peoples') was drawn."[32] Border making in this instance is a key manifestation of how European nations such as France established colonialism as an external affair.

Ross's seminal and much-cited arguments in this regard pivot on a dialectical relationship between presence and absence, between what is visible and what remains hidden in plain sight. The presence of Algerian migrants and their descendants in France constitutes the strongest marker of colonial history that persists within the folds of the former imperial nation. France in the postwar period also entered into a wave of modernization, which for Ross operated as a substitute for the lost glory of imperial era.[33] A new surface splendor took hold of France in this period in the form of cars, luxury goods, and the modernization of the city, which bury all traces of the former imperial life of the nation.[34] This brief detour into the historical terrain of colonialism and its enduring legacies enables us to tie the ornamental presence of race in *Nocturama* back to a broader interpretive context that continues to hold purchase today. The problem of race has no place within a certain imaginary of Europe as European Union, which basks in the image of itself as tolerant and civilized.[35] But as Ross details, the Parisian bourgeoisie retreated inward, dwelling in the comfort of the commodified surfaces of home, the department store, and so on while inequalities were perpetuated in the separation between Paris and its banlieue along the lines of race (and class), though not considered a problem *of* race.[36] Bonello's characters similarly retreat inward, losing themselves in the sites of bourgeois splendor that they sought to eradicate. But so does Bonello in his inability to address race with any of the nuance, however slight, that is reserved for his treatment of class difference. The flatness of his intersectional politics constitutes a trace of this history that continues to thrive in the contemporary moment. Consequently, Bonello's vagueness about the racial identities of his characters acquires reams of specificity when viewed historically.

INTRODUCTION

1 De Certeau, *The Practice of Everyday Life*, 91–98.
2 De Certeau, *The Practice of Everyday Life*, 94. "Given the wide variety of possible urban experience," the sociologists John R. Logan and Harvey L. Molotoch understate, "the lives of urban people must come to differ": Logan and Molotoch, *Urban Fortunes*, 103.
3 Lefebvre, *The Production of Space*, 82–83.
4 Quart, "Woody Allen's New York," 16–19.
5 Massood, *Black City Cinema*, 130.
6 Massood, *Black City Cinema*, 130.
7 Kracauer, *Theory of Film*, 46, 53–54.
8 Wanzo, "Precarious-Girl Comedy," 27–28. See also Sobande, "Praising, Erasing, Replacing and Race-ing Girls."
9 Taylor, "When Seams Fall Apart."
10 *The Elder Scrolls: Arena*, Bethesda Softworks, 1994, MS-DOS.
11 *The Elder Scrolls: Skyrim*, Bethesda Game Studios, 2011, PlayStation 3.
12 Nash, "Intersectionality and Its Discontents," 119.
13 Collins, "The Difference That Power Makes," 19.
14 May, *Pursuing Intersectionality, Unsettling Dominant Imaginaries*, 4.
15 Crenshaw, "Demarginalizing the Intersection of Race and Sex," 149.
16 Crenshaw, "Demarginalizing the Intersection of Race and Sex," 151.
17 The spatial imagining of intersectionality continues in Crenshaw's follow-up essay, "Mapping the Margins," where she "maps" the "location of women of color at the intersection of race and gender": Crenshaw, "Mapping the Margins," 1245.
18 For a summary of prominent writings on the city and film, see Wojcik, "The City in Film."
19 See Haenni, *The Immigrant Scene*; Massood, *Black City Cinema*; Schleier, *Skyscraper Cinema*; Stewart, *Migrating to the Movies*; Wojcik, *Fantasies of Neglect*.
20 Corbin, *Cinematic Geographies and Multicultural Spectatorship in America*; Fullwood, *Cinema, Gender, and Everyday Space*.
21 Matos, "Something's Flaming in the Kitchen."

CHAPTER ONE: "WHERE DO ALIENS PEE?"

1 Steve Pile writes that spaces make "possible or impossible certain forms of resistance and . . . resistance makes other spaces—other geographies—possible or impossible": Pile, "Opposition, Political Identities and Spaces of Resistance," 2.

2 Kristen Schilt and Laurel Westbrook write that when it is applied to nondiscrimi-
nation ordinances, the term "bathroom bills" frames all trans rights as a threat to
cisgender women and girls: Schilt and Westbrook, "Bathroom Battlegrounds and
Penis Panics," 28.

3 Westbrook and Schilt, "Doing Gender, Determining Gender," 34–35; Keegan,
"On Being the Object of Compromise," 152.

4 Halberstam, *Female Masculinity*, 24.

5 Robert McRuer writes that "compulsory able-bodiedness" is produced by institutions, both physical and social, and as a result disability activists work toward "a
newly imagined and newly configured public sphere where full participation is
not contingent upon an able body": McRuer, *Crip Theory*, 30.

6 Cavanagh, *Queering Bathrooms*, 26.

7 Brown, *States of Injury*, 75.

8 As Reina Gossett notes, increased visibility also produces increased vulnerability,
particularly for trans women of color: Gossett, "What Are We Defending?"

9 National Center for Transgender Equality, "The Discrimination Administration"; Page, "Why Are Some Feminists in the U.K. Freaking Out about Trans
Rights?"

10 Selfie sticks also produce more distant framing; as a result, they similarly emphasize location alongside identity.

11 Clifton, "This Selfie Campaign Shows the Sheer Absurdity of Anti-Trans Bathroom Bills"; Peters, "Brae Carnes' Restroom Selfie Campaign Shows Just How
Ridiculous Anti-Trans Restroom Bills Are."

12 Kellaway, "Trans Folks Respond to 'Bathroom Bills' with #WeJustNeedToPee
Selfies"; Kohner, "Trans Man behind #WeJustNeedtoPee Isn't Selfie-Centered";
Williams, "I Don't Belong in Here!," 32.

13 Indeed, Hughes's selfies resemble transphobic advertising campaigns that feature
images of threatening men entering women's bathrooms: Gersen, "Who's Afraid
of Gender-Neutral Bathrooms?"

14 Cavanagh, *Queering Bathrooms*, 84.

15 See, e.g., Bay-Cheng, "When This You See"; Giroux, "Selfie Culture in the Age of
Corporate and State Surveillance."

16 Ubelacker, "Trans Community Seeking Beefed-Up Human Rights Protection."

17 Renda, "La protesta della trans Brae Carnes contro la proposta di legge canadese";
"In Protest of Bill C-279"; Ubelacker, "Seeking Reform through the Selfie."

18 John Berger writes that "men look at women. Women watch themselves being
looked at. . . . Thus she turns herself into an object—and most particularly an
object of vision: a sight": Berger, *Ways of Seeing*, 47.

19 Crockett, "The Bizarre History of Bathrooms Getting in the Way of Equal
Rights."

20 Plaskow, "Embodiment, Elimination, and the Role of Toilets in Struggles for
Social Justice," 56.

21 Keegan, "On Being the Object of Compromise," 152.

22 Cavanagh, *Queering Bathrooms*, 31.

23 Cavanagh, *Queering Bathrooms*, 37–38. Following Catherine Ingraham's work, the straight lines and right angles of public bathroom design can also be understood as an attempt to ward off the animality and abjection of elimination: Ingraham, "The Burdens of Linearity," 68–70.

24 Foucault, *The History of Sexuality*, 27–28.

25 Cavanagh, *Queering Bathrooms*, 177–78.

26 Cavanagh, *Queering Bathrooms*, 172–73.

27 Cavanagh, *Queering Bathrooms*, 26.

28 Quoted in West, "PISSAR's Critically Queer and Disabled Politics," 163.

29 West, "PISSAR's Critically Queer and Disabled Politics," 167.

30 See, e.g., Booth, "Camp Toi!"; Piggford, "Who's That Girl?"; Robertson, "What Makes the Feminist Camp?"

31 Robertson, "What Makes the Feminist Camp?" 271.

32 Robertson, "What Makes the Feminist Camp?" 272.

33 At times, the argument for gender-neutral bathrooms is supported by the fact that professional networking often takes place in bathrooms, which frequently disadvantages those using the women's bathroom. However, the series refuses to argue for a better bathroom in order to merely preserve the status quo in other areas of life, such as capitalistic norms.

CHAPTER TWO: THE QUEERNESS OF SPACE

1 Giddings, *Gameworlds*, 9. "Gameworld" is a term commonly used to describe video games that "involve exploration of, or orientation in, a simulated topography."

2 For insightful and rigorous analyses of how *Zelda* games are structured using the principles of nonlinear design, see Mark Brown, "Boss Keys."

3 Nintendo, *The Legend of Zelda: Hyrule Historia*, 69. For decades, fans of the *Zelda* series have often tried to fit the games within a neat timeline even though they sometimes resist chronological organization. This changed, however, when Nintendo published an official timeline in the *Hyrule Historia*. This timeline is tentative and could be subject to revision according to where future games in the series fit (or do not fit) within this chronology.

4 *The Legend of Zelda*, Nintendo, 1986, Family Computer Disk System.

5 *The Legend of Zelda: Breath of the Wild*, directed by Hidemaro Fujibayashi, Nintendo, 2017, Nintendo Switch; Nintendo, "Top Selling Title Sales Units."

6 Juul, "The Open and the Closed," 327. Juul points out that "progression structures are heavily pre-controlled by the game, whereas emergence structures allow for much variation and improvisation that was neither anticipated by the game designer, nor is easily derivable from the rules of a game." Note, however, that games with an emergence structure are bound to rules, and "events can still be determined."

7 Pugh, "The Queer Narrativity of the Hero's Journey in Nintendo's *The Legend of Zelda* Series," 226.

8 Pugh, "The Queer Narrativity of the Hero's Journey in Nintendo's *The Legend of Zelda* Series," 227.

9 Ruberg, *Video Games Have Always Been Queer*, 1.

10 Ruberg, *Video Games Have Always Been Queer*, 2.

11 Chen, *Animacies*, 11, 104.

12 Ruberg, *Video Games Have Always Been Queer*, 7.

13 *The Legend of Zelda: Twilight Princess*, Nintendo, 2006, Nintendo Wii.

14 *The Legend of Zelda: A Link between Worlds*, Nintendo, 2013, Nintendo 3DS.

15 Sullivan, "Transmogrification," 561.

16 Sullivan, "Transmogrification," 562.

17 *The Legend of Zelda: Ocarina of Time*, Nintendo, 1998, Nintendo 64; *The Legend of Zelda: Majora's Mask*, Nintendo, 2000, Nintendo 64. All quotes, descriptions, and gameplay elements discussed here refer to the remake of the game *The Legend of Zelda: Ocarina of Time 3D*, Nintendo, 2011, Nintendo 3DS, and the remake of *The Legend of Zelda: Majora's Mask 3D*, Grezzo and Nintendo, 2015, Nintendo 3DS. The remakes retain most of the narrative elements present in the original version, with updated graphics, gameplay controls, and minor content revisions.

18 Players have modified *Zelda* games to alter aspects such as Link's gender identity. Mike Hoye, for instance, gained both recognition and infamy for reprogramming Link's pronouns in *The Legend of Zelda: The Wind Waker* (2002). For more on this mod, see Hoye, "Flip All the Pronouns."

19 Bogost, "The Rhetoric of Video Games," 136.

20 Consalvo, "Hot Dates and Fairy-Tale Romances," 180.

21 *The Legend of Zelda: Ocarina of Time*; *The Legend of Zelda: Ocarina of Time 3D*.

22 Pugh, "The Queer Narrativity of the Hero's Journey in Nintendo's *The Legend of Zelda* Series," 239.

23 *The Legend of Zelda: Ocarina of Time*; *The Legend of Zelda: Ocarina of Time 3D*.

24 *The Legend of Zelda: Ocarina of Time*; *The Legend of Zelda: Ocarina of Time 3D*.

25 Giddings, *Gameworlds*, 96.

26 For an in-depth look at how these dungeons are designed and structured, see Brown, "Boss Keys."

27 Consalvo, "Hot Dates and Fairy-Tale Romances," 180.

28 Stockton, *The Queer Child*, 11.

29 Sherlock, "Three Days in Termina," 126.

30 *Zelda* games often implement the term "race" when referring to in-game groups such as the Hylians and Gerudo, the aquatic Zoras, the rock-eating Gorons, and the plant-like Deku scrubs. Although all of these groups are bipedal and speak common languages, there are major physical, cultural, theological, and social differences between these groups. *MM* further stresses the notion that beings such as Deku scrubs are "not human," therefore indicating that the term "race"

is being used synonymously with the term "species." My discussion consciously uses the term "beings" to avoid conflating in-game uses of the term "race" with real-world applications.

31 *The Legend of Zelda: Majora's Mask; The Legend of Zelda: Majora's Mask 3D.*

32 *The Legend of Zelda: Majora's Mask; The Legend of Zelda: Majora's Mask 3D.*

33 Sherlock, "Three Days in Termina," 130.

34 Sullivan, "Transmogrification," 562.

35 Garner, "Becoming," 31.

36 For a more nuanced discussion of *Breath of the Wild*'s development, its physics engine, and the series' return to an open-world format, see GDC Entertainment, "Breaking Conventions with the *Legend of Zelda: Breath of the Wild.*"

37 Hines, "*Zelda: Breath of the Wild* Makes Open-World Games Exciting Again."

38 Otero, "*The Legend of Zelda: Breath of the Wild* Review."

39 Jones, *The Meaning of Video Games*, 15.

40 Pugh, "The Queer Narrativity of the Hero's Journey in Nintendo's *The Legend of Zelda* Series," 46.

41 Ruberg, *Video Games Have Always Been Queer*, 15.

CHAPTER THREE: THE DIGITAL FLÂNEUSE

1 Davey Wreden and William Pugh, *The Stanley Parable*, mod for *Half-Life 2*, Galactic Café, 2011, personal computer; Davey Wreden and William Pugh, *The Stanley Parable*, stand-alone release, Galactic Café, 2013, personal computer; Dan Pinchbeck, *Dear Esther*, mod and stand-alone release, Chinese Room, 2012, personal computer; Steve Gaynor, *Gone Home*, Fullbright Company, 2013, personal computer; Auriea Harvey and Michaël Samyn, *Sunset*, Tale of Tales, 2015, personal computer; Olly Moss and Sean Vanaman, *Firewatch*, Campo Santo, 2016, personal computer; Variable State, *Virginia*, 505 Games, 2016, personal computer; Ian Dallas, *What Remains of Edith Finch*, Annapurna Interactive, 2017, personal computer.

2 Vanderhoef, "Casual Threats"; Kubik, "Masters of Technology."

3 Adams, *Geographies of Media and Communication*; Falkheimer and Jansson, *Geographies of Communication*.

4 Flanagan, "[domestic]."

5 Graham Relph, *The Forest*, Phipps Associates, 1983, ZX Spectrum; Graham Relph, *Explorer*, RamJam Corporation and Electric Dreams Software, 1986, ZX Spectrum; Clark, "A Brief History of the 'Walking Simulator.'"

6 Mason, "The Origins of the Walking Simulator."

7 Mason, "The Origins of the Walking Simulator," para. 10.

8 Fullerton et al., "A Game of One's Own," sec. 2, para. 6. See also Butler, *Gender Trouble*.

9 Ryan Green, Amy Green, and Josh Larson, *That Dragon, Cancer*, Numinous Games, 2016, personal computer.

10 Galloway, *Gaming*, 68–69.

11 Galloway, *Gaming*, 69.

12 Clark, "A Brief History of the 'Walking Simulator,'" para. 17.

13 Kagen, "Walking Simulators, #Gamergate, and the Gender of Wandering."

14 #Gamergate emerged as a hashtag and rallying cry circa 2014 for angry gamers who felt threatened by social and cultural critiques of gaming culture by journalists, critics, and academics. After an ex-boyfriend of the game designer Zoe Quinn accused her of using her contacts in gaming journalism to garner positive reviews of *Depression Quest*, a contingent of self-identified gamers marshaled a campaign of hatred and harassment against her—and eventually against many other female, queer, and transgender game critics and designers. This campaign, which claimed righteousness under the guise of "ethics in games journalism," eventually found its rallying moniker after the actor Adam Baldwin named the controversy #gamergate on the social media service Twitter. Despite the fact that the campaign was based entirely on misconceptions, falsehoods, and interpersonal matters most would consider unequivocally private, the #gamergate mob continued its campaign to discredit and terrorize Quinn and others, going as far as to publish Quinn's home address so she was forced to move. For more, see Chess and Shaw, "A Conspiracy of Fishes."

15 Kagen, "Walking Simulators, #Gamergate, and the Gender of Wandering," 277.

16 Kagen, "Walking Simulators, #Gamergate, and the Gender of Wandering," 291.

17 Benjamin, *The Arcades Project*.

18 Debord, "Theory of the Dérive."

19 Bowlby, "Walking, Women and Writing."

20 Bruno, *Atlas of Emotion*, 17.

21 Bill Gardner, *Perception*, Feardemic, 2017, personal computer.

22 Bogost, "Perpetual Adolescence."

23 Bogost, "Video Games Are Better without Stories."

24 Donnelly, "*Gone Home* Prevents *Tacoma* from Being Judged on Its Own."

25 Samyn and Harvey, "And the Sun Sets . . ."

26 Fraterrigo, "Pads and Penthouses," 80–104.

27 Davis, "Afro Images."

28 The term "apartment plot" comes from Wojcik, *The Apartment Plot*. For more on *Jeanne Dielman, 23, quai du Commerce, 1080 Bruxelles* as an apartment plot, see Jagose, "Housework, Sex Work."

29 Shaw, "Are We There Yet?," 77.

30 Shaw, "Are We There Yet?," 78.

31 Nakamura, "Head-Hunting on the Internet," 526; "Race in/for Cyberspace: Identity Tourism and Racial Passing on the Internet," *Work and Days 13* (1995): 181–93.

32 D'Anastasio, "Why Video Games Can't Teach You Empathy."

CHAPTER FOUR: BLURRING BOUNDARIES

1 Crenshaw, "Demarginalizing the Intersection of Race and Sex," 149–51.

2 Rabinovitz, *Points of Resistance*, 97.

3 The films were intended as a broad reflection on the American experience. Clarke arranged the filmmakers' raw footage according to themes, including cities, leisure, education, and employment. Averaging two and a half minutes each, the films were "projected from behind shaded viewing frames mounted on the walls of the pavilion. Screens [were] of different sizes and shapes to conform with various displays": "Film at Brussels," 30.

4 "Unfinished Business" focused on "America's view of the problems [urban conditions, natural resources, and segregation] it expects to face in the next decade and how we [the government] envisage their solution": Krenn, "Unfinished Business," 595–96.

5 Nilsen, *Projecting America, 1958*, 144.

6 Nilsen, *Projecting America, 1958*, 100. The American Pavilion did feature some jazz performances as part of its broader musical programming, including the Benny Goodman Band and the Sidney Bechet Sextet. Of the former, Nilsen suggests that it "was not a performance that was in anyway challenging or experimental." The author describes Bechet's band as "saving the day" for the music programming: Nilsen, *Projecting America, 1958*, 139.

7 The film fuses fragmented images of New York City's bridges into a visual choreography that turns man-made objects into something new, like, suggests Clarke in another context, Rene Clair's "hats dancing in the wind in *A Nous la Liberte*": Clarke, quoted in Thompson, "Shirley Clarke."

8 "Film at Brussels," 30.

9 The Barrons composed the electronic score to the film *Forbidden Planet* (Fred M. Wilcox, dir., 1956), and there was concern that *Bridges-Go-Round* overlapped with the MGM film. Clarke secured rights to the Barron composition in 1968, and the film has been screened subsequently as a seven-minute short that juxtaposes the two pieces of music.

10 Breitrose, "Films of Shirley Clarke," 57.

11 For more on Helen Levitt's *In the Street*, see Wojcik, *Fantasies of Neglect*; Massood, *Making a Promised Land*.

12 Bebb, "The Many Media of Shirley Clarke," 4.

13 Milestone Film and Video, *The Connection*.

14 The play includes two cameramen who have been commissioned to film events. As the producer suggests to Leach and the others, "It just means more money. For you and for me. Besides, we aren't going Hollywood. They're making an avant-garde movie": Gelber, *The Connection*, 24.

15 Koutsourakis, "From Post-Brechtian Performance to Post-Brechtian Cinema," 145.

16 Barron, "Truthmovies Are Just Beginning," 64.

17 Clarke, quoted in Bebb, "The Many Media of Shirley Clarke," 3.

18 Some of Ornitz's B films suggest thematic connections to *The Connection*. *The Pusher* (1960), for example, is a low-budget detective story about a dead heroin addict.

19 Milestone Film and Video, *The Connection*

20 Milestone Film and Video, *The Connection*. See also Barron, "Truthmovies Are Just Beginning," 74.

21 Barron, "Truthmovies Are Just Beginning," 64.

22 "The First Statement of the New American Cinema Group," 80. The statement originally appeared in *Film Culture* 22–23 (Summer 1961): 131–33.

23 Mekas, "Notes on the New American Cinema," 87–88. The inclusion of censorship may have been influenced by Clarke's experience with *The Connection*, which was banned in the United States for a year after its release.

24 Like Clarke's, Rogosin's later films became more experimental and more attuned to American race relations. For more on Rogosin's *On the Bowery* and *Black Fantasy* (1972), see Massood, "Dans la rue, sous les draps."

25 Dienstfrey, "The New American Cinema."

26 Rabinovitz, *Points of Resistance*, 117–19.

27 Milestone Film and Video, *The Connection*.

28 As Nilsen suggests, most Europeans praised the original exhibition, while American tourists and politicians (particularly from the South) were its harshest detractors: Nilsen, *Projecting America, 1958*, 130.

29 After its premiere in 1961 at the Cannes Film Festival, the film was banned initially from being shown in New York, Clarke's hometown. While its subject matter may have been threatening on a number of fronts, the state's film-licensing board opposed its vulgar language, particularly the word "shit." Clarke and Allen fought the decision, which was overturned by the New York State Court of Appeals in 1962.

CHAPTER FIVE: CINEMATIC CRUISING

Epigraph: Benjamin, *The Arcades Project*, 88.

1 The title translates into English as "The Week of the Murderer." A different version of the film was distributed in English under the title *The Cannibal Man*. I have used the Spanish title throughout this chapter, as I refer to the original Spanish version of the film and script unless noted otherwise.

2 Bruno, *Atlas of Emotion*, 271.

3 Wojcik, *The Apartment Plot*, 77.

4 Paul Julian Smith considers de la Iglesia's cinema representative of the Spanish Transition in multiple senses, writing, "It chronicles the historical period of the shift from dictatorship to democracy; it exploits the distribution hiatus between the end of censorship and the legalization of pornography; and it depicts in the

struggles of the homosexual hero the emergence of a new figure in Spanish film: the gay man who was to speak for and of himself": Smith, *Laws of Desire*, 162. *La semana del asesino* represents the beginnings of this larger body of work.

5 Carabancheleando, *Diccionario de las periferias*, 24–25.

6 Smith, *Laws of Desire*, 159.

7 The term *quinqui* derives from the Spanish word *quinquillero*, or *quincallero*, which translates into English as scrap metal collector. The term is often used as a pejorative to describe someone who makes a living through petty theft and informal street dealings. Whittaker, *The Spanish Quinqui Film*, is the first English-language monograph on the *quinqui* cycle.

8 In a script annotation that was surely added to appease censors, de la Iglesia explicitly disavows any "hint of homosexuality" in *La semana del asesino* and instead compares Nestor's voyeuristic interest to James Stewart's character in Alfred Hitchcock's *Rear Window* (1954): de la Iglesia and Fos, *La semana del asesino*, 1.

9 Smith, *Laws of Desire*, 127.

10 Crenshaw, "Demarginalizing the Intersection of Race and Sex," 149.

11 The Spanish Civil War began as a military uprising in 1936 and continued through 1939, when Francisco Franco's forces succeeded in overthrowing the government of the Second Republic. Franco's ensuing military dictatorship lasted from 1939 until his death in 1975.

12 Montoliú Camps, *Enciclopedia de Madrid*, 72.

13 Franco's end-of-the-year speech in 1954 called for "una cruzada de la vivienda" (a housing crusade). This militaristic terminology illustrates how the regime's wartime rhetoric closely mirrored the rhetoric used to refer to civil society after the war.

14 For a fine analysis of the subversive function of humor in *The Executioner*, see Marsh, *Popular Spanish Film under Franco*. For an in-depth analysis of *The Tenant* in the context of the housing crisis, see Larson, "The Spatial Fix."

15 De la Iglesia argues that films such as Nieves Condes's *The Tenant* belong to a Christian or Falangist radicalized cinema—a cinematic tradition that, in the end, was not far from cinema informed by Marxism: de la Iglesia, "Visceralidad y autoría," 110–11.

16 Montoliú Camps, *Enciclopedia de Madrid*, 73, my translation.

17 Gutiérrez-Albilla, *Queering Buñuel*, 29. Gutiérrez-Albilla writes in the context of Luis Buñuel's Mexican film *The Young and the Damned* (1950), which portrays the sharp contrasts between Mexico City's slums and its bourgeois modernity.

18 Lázaro Reboll, "Masculinidades génericas," 174. Like de la Iglesia, Grau exposed the problems of the housing crisis. His propagandistic documentary short *Ocharcoaga* (1961) exposes the dismal living conditions in the shantytowns of Bilbao. However, the film was produced by the Ministry for Housing and ultimately serves as a panegyric of the dictatorship's well-known housing project in the neighborhood of the same name.

19 Aguilar, "Fantasía española," 30.

20 For an in-depth analysis of the differences between the international and domestic versions of the film, see Gómez, "Efectos subversivos de la perversión."

21 Censorship was officially lifted in 1977. Despite this, de la Iglesia, as one of the first directors to explore the representation of gay men in Spanish cinema, was subjected to a great deal of criticism from the press during the post-dictatorship transition period. For an account of the homophobic abuse de la Iglesia received in the press, see Smith, *Laws of Desire*, 130–32.

22 De la Iglesia, "Visceralidad y autoría," III.

23 Ruiz, *Franco's Justice*, 50.

24 Graham, *The War and Its Shadow*, 116.

25 Richards, *A Time of Silence*, 67.

26 Matanza celebrations are a popular rural tradition surrounding the slaughter of livestock and the ensuing communal distribution of food. The celebration makes explicit the links among nutrition, economy, and society, which are obscured in the modern model of industrialized slaughter: see Labrador Méndez, "The Cannibal Wave," 245.

27 Gómez, "Efectos subversivos de la perversión," 87, my translation.

28 Willis, "The Spanish Horror Film as Subversive Text," 173.

29 Willis, "The Spanish Horror Film as Subversive Text," 171–72.

30 The text of the law is available at https://www.boe.es/buscar/doc.php?id=BOE-A-1970-854.

31 Smith, *Laws of Desire*, 10, emphasis added.

32 Losilla, "En los limites de la realidad," 52, my translation.

33 Wojcik, *The Apartment Plot*, 91. The juxtaposition of the high-rise and the shantytown spaces represents a contrast not just between high and low class, but also between modernity and tradition. Similar to de la Iglesia's later film *Hidden Pleasures* (1977), homosexuality, represented by the figure of Néstor, could be read as "the essence of modern, secular society in opposition to the old Spain of family and religion": Smith, *Laws of Desire*, 139.

34 This is not the last time de la Iglesia would rely on the built environment of Madrid to illustrate socioeconomic divides. His film *Colegas* (1984) prominently featured the social housing building known as Las Colmenas to "almost metaphorically underscore the oppression faced by the characters": de la Iglesia, "Visceralidad y autoría," 151, my translation.

35 De Certeau, *The Practice of Everyday Life*, 92.

36 De Certeau, *The Practice of Everyday Life*, 93.

37 Mirzoeff, *The Right to Look*, 4.

38 De Certeau, *The Practice of Everyday Life*, 92.

39 Although there is no reverse-shot eye-line match with Marcos in this opening sequence, there are two shots in the film where Marcos "looks back," or looks up. These low-angle shots suture the gaze of Marcos, the audience, and the camera. The first—an extreme low-angle spinning shot—occurs on Gran Vía in central Madrid and transmits a feeling of urban anxiety. The second occurs when Marcos

returns home after visiting Néstor's apartment and realizes he can be seen clearly from Néstor's balcony.

40 De Certeau, *The Practice of Everyday Life*, 101.

41 Robbins, *Crossing through Chueca*, 7.

42 Crenshaw, "Demarginalizing the Intersection of Race and Sex," 139.

43 "[A] new precinct begins like a step into the void—as though one had unexpectedly cleared a low step on a flight of stairs": Benjamin, *The Arcades Project*, 88.

44 Chisholm, *Queer Constellations*, 46.

45 Chisholm, *Queer Constellations*, 46.

46 Bruno, *Atlas of Emotion*, 265.

47 Bruno, *Atlas of Emotion*, 268.

48 Muñoz, *Cruising Utopia*, 18, 189.

49 Muñoz, *Cruising Utopia*, 189.

50 Muñoz, *Cruising Utopia*, 125.

51 De la Iglesia, "Visceralidad y autoría," 111.

52 Muñoz, *Cruising Utopia*, 39.

53 Muñoz, *Cruising Utopia*, 18. Muñoz builds on Oscar Wilde's famous quotation, "A map of the world that does not include Utopia is not worth glancing at."

CHAPTER SIX: ENCOUNTERS AND EMBEDDEDNESS

1 King, *Indie 2.0*; Canet, "The New Realistic Trend in Contemporary World Cinema"; Miner, "Ghostly Trajectories"; Roger Ebert, review of *Man Push Cart*, accessed January 5, 2015, http://www.rogerebert.com/reviews/man-push-cart-2006; Scott, "Neo-Neo Realism."

2 Porton, "A Sense of Place," 44–48.

3 May, *Pursuing Intersectionality, Unsettling Dominant Imaginaries*, 42.

4 May, *Pursuing Intersectionality, Unsettling Dominant Imaginaries*, 24–26.

5 Hibbins and Pease, "Men and Masculinities on the Move," 1–19.

6 Hopkins and Noble, "Masculinities in Place," 814.

7 Pease, "Immigrant Men and Domestic Life."

8 Keith and Pile, "Introduction."

9 Massey, "A Global Sense of Place."

10 Nashashibi, "Ghetto Cosmopolitanism."

11 Marciniak, *Alienhood*.

12 Nashashibi, "Ghetto Cosmopolitanism," 245–46.

13 This is similar to what Mark Shiel speaks of when he writes about Los Angeles as a microcosm of First World–Third World relations: Shiel, "Cinema and the City in History and Theory," 7.

14 Jaffe, "Talkin' 'bout the Ghetto."

15 Jaffe, "Talkin' 'bout the Ghetto," 676.

16 Massey, "A Global Sense of Place," 244.

17 Pred, *Making Histories and Constructing Human Geographies*.

18 Augé, *Non-Places*, 76–78.

19 Shah, *Contagious Divides*, 13–14.

20 Casey, *Getting Back into Place*, 290–92.

21 Porton, "A Sense of Place," 45.

22 Foucault, "Of Other Spaces," 24.

CHAPTER SEVEN: PERPETUAL MOTION

This essay benefited tremendously from comments by Yannis Tzioumakis, Michael Lawrence, and Karen Lury at the "Retrenching/Entrenching Youth: Mobility and Stasis in Youth Culture Representation on Screen" conference, University of Liverpool, June 4–5, 2018, and by Dana Polan.

1   Klein, *American Film Cycles*, 4.

2   Standing, *The Precariat*, 22–23.

3   Standing, "The Precariat," 11.

4   Standing, *The Precariat*, 76–77; Means, "Generational Precarity, Education, and the Crisis of Capitalism," 339.

5   Standing, *The Precariat*, 74.

6   Berlant, "Slow Death," 754.

7   Slow death relates to what Rob Nixon has described as "slow violence"—that is, "a violence that occurs gradually and out of sight, a violence of delayed destruction that is dispersed across time and space, an attritional violence that is typically not viewed as violence at all": Nixon, *Slow Violence and the Environmentalism of the Poor*, 2. Nixon links slow violence especially to environmental violence, though he also links slow violence to certain patterns of abuse. Slow death seems somewhat more apt a term for the films I am discussing because of its sense of the grind of everyday life, which may encompass violence but is not limited to it.

8   While my analysis focuses on hypermobility, its opposite—stasis and endless waiting—is another, equally important feature of life under late capitalism. In Scott Bukatman's gloss of a talk given by Dana Polan, the "traumatic can become banal" through both "endless waiting" and "ineffectual movement." *Wendy and Lucy* combines hypermobility—long tracking shots, a sense of placelessness—with slow scenes of waiting, and long takes: Bukatman, "A Day in New York," 40. See also Polan, "Urban Trauma and the Metropolitan Imagination."

9   Shortell and Brown, "Introduction," 1.

10 Laurie's and other female characters' destinies are not noted, a misogynistic absence pointed out in Brickman, *New American Teenagers*, 42–70.

11 Driscoll, *Teen Film*, 11–12.

12 Creswell, *On the Move*, 2.

13 Creswell, *On the Move*, 1–2.

14 Creswell, *On the Move*, 25.

15 Shortell and Brown, "Introduction," 5.

16 As Nixon reminds us, the picaro, hero of the picaresque, is typically a "canny, scheming social outlier(s) . . . drawn from polite society's vast impoverished margins, [who] survive by parasitism and by their wits . . . the picaro embodies everything the socially remote privileged classes . . . seek to contain, repress, and eject": Nixon, *Slow Violence and the Environmentalism of the Poor*, 55.

17 Creswell, *On the Move*, 45–46.

18 Baker explicitly aligns *The Florida Project* with *Wild Boys of the Road*, as well as *The Little Rascals, Our Gang, The Kid*, and *The Little Fugitive*: see Porter, "Life on the Margins," 23. *Tramps* invokes tramp films in its title, and *Wendy and Lucy* features an early scene at a hobo camp near freight lines and ends with Wendy hopping a freight train.

19 Creswell, *The Tramp in America*, 15–16, 19.

20 Lizotte, "Review of *Lean on Pete*," 70.

21 Means, "Generational Precarity, Education, and the Crisis of Capitalism," 350. See also Semuels, "Poor at 20, Poor for Life."

22 Berlant, "Slow Death," 761.

23 Berlant, "Slow Death," 760.

24 Means, "Generational Precarity, Education, and the Crisis of Capitalism," 351; Semuels, "Poor at 20, Poor for Life"; "Precarity Talk," 166.

25 Creswell, *The Tramp in America*, 20.

26 Semuels, "Poor at 20, Poor for Life"; "Richest 1 Percent Bagged 82 Percent of Wealth Created Last Year"; Means, "Generational Precarity, Education, and the Crisis of Capitalism," 341.

CHAPTER EIGHT: GRAY POWER ACTIVISM

I thank Pamela Wojcik, Paula Massood, and Angel Daniel Matos for their shrewd comments and edits. During our conversations in person and over email, Lynne Littman shared valuable information and many riveting stories about her career in Los Angeles and collaborations with Barbara Myerhoff. Deep gratitude goes to Mark Quigley at the UCLA Film and Television Archive, who offered insights about Venice-related films and made material available for viewing. Special thanks to Claude Zachary, Susan Hikida, and Louise Smith at USC Special Collections for providing generous access to the Barbara Myerhoff Papers. Sherri Kadovitz at the Israel Levin Senior Adult Center filled in the backstory of the institution and helped provide a sense of how Venice had changed in recent decades. *Number Our Days* is streaming on the Internet Archive and is available for DVD purchase through Direct Cinema Limited. This essay expands on material from Glick, *Los Angeles Documentary and the Production of Public History*.

1 Gelya Frank has written an overview of Myerhoff's relation to cinema but provides little cultural context concerning the production and reception of *Number*

Our Days: Frank, "The Ethnographic Films of Barbara G. Myerhoff." See also Stanton, *Venice, California*; Lipton, *The Holy Barbarians*; Shiel, *Hollywood Cinema and the
Real Los Angeles*, 69–127; Wolfe, "From Venice to the Valley." The Gray Panthers
were started by Maggie Kuhn in 1970 with the aim of confronting ageism in U.S.
society. Issues concerning health care and housing were particularly important.

2 Deener, *Venice*, 8–18.

3 Valentine, "Theorizing and Researching Intersectionality," 19; Grzanka, "Space,
Place, Communities, and Geographies," 104.

4 Given some of her past fieldwork in Mexico, Myerhoff considered doing an ethnography on elderly Chicanos in East Los Angeles. While they supported her interests in advocating for marginalized communities, they suggested she research
her own ethnic group: Kirshenblatt-Gimblett, "Foreword," ix–xiv; Myerhoff,
Number Our Days, 10–13.

5 Collins and Bilge, *Intersectionality*, 42.

6 Shevitz, "Jewish Space and Place in Venice," 67–68, 70–71; Moore, *To the Golden
Cities*, 1–52.

7 See, e.g., Monahan, "Los Angeles Studies"; Soja, *Postmodern Geographies*, 190–221.

8 Adler, *A History of the Venice Area*; Deener, *Venice*, 31–43, 146–53; Myerhoff, *Number
Our Days*, 3–18.

9 Harmon, "Don't Look Now, but Venice Is Coming Back!," 59; Squire, "Venice,"
64–65; Faris, "Neighbors Unite to Fight Soaring Taxes," WSI; Takei, "Eviction
of Elderly," 4; Torgerson, "Venice"; Luther, "Venice Property Values Skyrocket";
Ferderber, "Outsized Rents Put Elderly to Flight," WSI; Schmidt-Brummer, *Venice
California*, 20–30.

10 Meyer, "The Los Angeles Woman's Building and the Feminist Art Community";
Myerhoff and Metzger, "The Journal as Activity and Genre," 351–56.

11 Lynne Littman, quoted in Murphy and Bentsen, "Coming to Grips with the Issue
of Power." See also Murphy, "AFI Women"; Joshua Glick, interview with Lynne
Littman, February 13, 2012, New York City.

12 Myerhoff and Ruby, "Intro."

13 MacDougall, "Beyond Observational Cinema," 120–29.

14 Rouch, "The Camera and the Man," 89.

15 Myerhoff, "Life History among the Elderly," 240.

16 Hoover, "Old Jews of Venice."

17 "Muscle artists" in Venice were also on display in *Pumping Iron* (George Butler,
dir., 1977). The documentary depicts bodybuilders working out on Muscle Beach
and in Gold's Gym.

18 Gentrification did not, of course, affect the different Venice communities in the
same way: Deener, *Venice*, 44–163.

19 Margulies, "Venice Jews in TV Documentary"; O'Connor, "TV"; Tone "Telefilm
Review," *Variety*, October 4, 1976, 6; Kerr, "How to Win an Oscar with a $30,000
Budget"; "Number Our Days"; advertisement in *Chicago Tribune*, May 8, 1977, J14;
Geyer, "Prof's Film Available for Screening."

20 Myerhoff, "Surviving Stories"; Glick interview.

21 Fan mail to the Israel Levin Center, box 92, folder 0275. For other forms of correspondence, see Letters 1979–81, box 114, folder 0275; requests for *Number Our Days*, box 93; fan mail 1976–77, box 92, folder 0275; all in Barbara Myerhoff Papers, Special Collections, Doheny Memorial Library, University of Southern California, Los Angeles.

22 Littman soon after made the theatrically released fiction film *Testament* (1983). For statistics on the staggeringly low representation of women in the film and television industry in the late 1970s, see Lee, "Where Are the Women Directors?"

23 Myerhoff, "Life not Death in Venice," 265–66.

24 Leviton, "Numbering Their Days," 23–26.

25 May, *Pursuing Intersectionality, Unsettling Dominant Imaginaries*, 53–60.

CHAPTER NINE: MUSIC CITY MAKEOVER

1 Although the series finale aired in July 2018, the locations tour was still in operation as I was writing.

2 The first officially branded *Walking Dead* studio and locations tour in winter 2018, though unofficial tours have operated for years.

3 "Motion Picture (Industry Cluster)."

4 Paulson, "As 'Nashville' Says Goodbye, It Leaves a Mark on the Real Music City."

5 Rau, "ABC's 'Nashville' Cancelled after Four Seasons."

6 Andreeva, "Update."

7 See Mayer and Goldman, "Hollywood Handouts." See also Curtin and Sanson, *Precarious Creativity*.

8 Brembilla, "Thank God I'm a Country Series," 159. Please see Brembilla's chapter for an industry studies perspective on *Nashville*, focusing on the series' season 5 transition from ABC to CMT.

9 McNutt, "Narratives of Miami in *Dexter* and *Burn Notice*," 74.

10 McNutt, "Narratives of Miami in *Dexter* and *Burn Notice*," 78–83.

11 Hodak, "Still Hope for 'Nashville' Fans after ABC's Cancellation?"

12 "Our Purpose," n.d., accessed August 15, 2018, http://tennesseeentertainment alliance.org/purpose.

13 Curtin and Sanson, *Precarious Creativity*, 3.

14 Collins, "Plan to Boost Film Industry in New York."

15 McPherson, "Meet the Woman behind 'Made in NY.'"

16 DeMause, "New York Is Throwing Money at Film Shoots, but Who Benefits?"

17 TN Code §4-3-4903 (2017), Visual Content Act of 2006, https://law.justia.com /codes/tennessee/2017/title-4/chapter-3/part-49/section-4-3-4903.

18 Mayer and Goldman, "Hollywood Handouts."

19 Curtin and Sanson, *Precarious Creativity*, 3.

20 Ridley, "Tennessee Has Lights and Cameras"; "Film Incentives," Transparent Tennessee, accessed August 15, 2018, https://www.tn.gov/transparenttn/jobs -economic-development/openecd/film-incentives.html.

21 TN Code §4-3-4903 (2017).

22 Shultis, "Calling Cut on Film Incentives."

23 Wilson, "Performance Audit Report," 8; Department of Economic and Community Development, "TFEMC Report."

24 Shultis, "Calling Cut on Film Incentives," 7.

25 Shultis, "Calling Cut on Film Incentives," 7.

26 "Motion Picture (Industry Cluster)."

27 "Motion Picture (Industry Cluster)."

28 Quoted in Paulson, "As 'Nashville' Says Goodbye."

29 Florida, *The Rise of the Creative Class*.

30 Taylor, "Nashville Is One of America's Hottest Cities Right Now, and It's Not Just the Hockey."

31 Taylor, "Nashville Is One of America's Hottest Cities Right Now."

32 Zukin, *Naked City*, 18.

33 Goldberg, "'Nashville' Promotes Three to Series Regular."

34 Bliss, "East Nashville Reborn after 1916's 'Fire of the Century.'"

35 Florida, *The Rise of the Creative Class*.

36 Florida, *The New Urban Crisis*.

37 Plazas, "Is Nashville in an Urban Crisis?"

38 Marcus, "East Nasty." For an extended critical assessment of the effects of gentrification in East Nashville, see Lloyd, "East Nashville Skyline."

39 Bethonie Butler provides concise yet considered overview of the "Magical Negro" trope in "'Nashville' Still Doesn't Know What to Do with Black People."

40 James, "ABC's 'Nashville' Poses a Viewership Riddle."

41 Cain, "Bachelorettes in Boots Take on Nashville."

42 Morgan-Parmett, "Site-Specific Television as Urban Renewal," 42.

CHAPTER TEN: *PORTLANDIA*'S HIPSTER WONDERLAND

1 This fictional headline seems to be a response to actual negative media stories about Portland, Oregon, that have circulated since the show started in 2011.

2 Mesh, "Mock Star."

3 Levine, "IFC Bets the House on Hipsters."

4 Levine, "IFC Bets the House on Hipsters."

5 Maly and Varis, "The 21st-Century Hipster," 650.

6 Banet-Weiser and Mukherjee, "Introduction," 12.

7 Warner, *The Cultural Politics of Colorblind TV Casting*, 2.

8 Davis, "Intersectionality as Buzzword," 68.

9 Kimberlé Crenshaw, interview with the author, Columbia Law School, New York, June 8, 2017, https://www.law.columbia.edu/pt-br/news/2017/06/kimberle-crenshaw-intersectionality.

10 Oregon Pioneer Association, *Transactions of the Annual Reunion*.

11 Oregon Pioneer Association, *Transactions of the Annual Reunion*, 42.

12 Bonilla-Silva, *Racism without Racists*.

13 Roberts and Mahtani, "Neoliberalizing Race, Racing Neoliberalism," 250.

14 Portland Housing Bureau, "State of Housing in Portland."

15 Warner, "In the Time of Plastic Representation," 35.

16 Fornof et al., "Kimberlé Crenshaw."

17 Conley, *"The 39 Steps,"* 132.

18 For more information about Portland's long history of counterculture movements and emphasis on self-sufficiency embodied by DIY culture, see Kopp, *Eden within Eden*. In its present form, Portland's DIY culture embraces nostalgia by rejecting digital culture. This is evident in the preference for so-called analog technologies and industries, such as vinyl records, film cameras, and home-brewed beer. For further discussion of the history of the analog-digital binary and the cultural rise of nostalgic media, see Stern, "Analog"; Lizardi, *Nostalgic Generations and Media*.

19 Turnquist, "'Portlandia' in Portland."

20 Bonilla-Silva, *Racism without Racists*, 76.

21 Mesh, "Mock Star."

22 In response to a question asking how *Portlandia* has made space for the other, Brownstein replied, "We made very purposeful changes to make sure the writers' room, the crew, the casting was more intersectional." Brownstein went on to explain that she realized that, as a producer and writer for the show, she needed to be "actively anti-racist" to make any meaningful change and provide access to more women, people of color, and members of the LGBTQ+ community: Thomson, "Carrie Brownstein Puts Her Last Bird on 'Portlandia.'"

23 "Fifteen Things You Probably Didn't Know about Portlandia."

24 See, e.g., Turnquist, "Portland Artists and Extras Wanted for 'Portlandia' Season 2"; see Parmett, "Media as a Spatial Practice," for a discussion of the central role of media in neoliberal urban renewal practices.

25 For further discussion, see White, "A House Divided."

26 This scene also signifies the problem of opioid abuse among white residents in Portland.

27 The open letter also accused Armisen and Brownstein of being trans-antagonistic and trans-misogynist. In the Feminist Bookstore sketches, Fred Armisen is depicted in a wig and a dress. The staff argued that the representation of trans-women "is a deeply shitty joke whose sole punchline throws trans femmes under the bus by holding up their gender presentation for mockery and ridicule": Hughes, "Feminist Bookstore from 'Portlandia' Accuses Show of Transmisogyny, Gentrification and Whitewashing."

28 Hughes, "Feminist Bookstore from 'Portlandia' Accuses Show of Transmisogyny, Gentrification and Whitewashing."

29 The anthropomorphic rats also appear in two other episodes in seasons 2 and 3. Both sketches indirectly address gentrification by depicting rat and human social interactions.

30 Jurjevich et al., "Destination Portland."

31 Hathaway, "Reading Art Spiegelman's 'Maus' as Postmodern Ethnography," 252.

32 DeMello, *Speaking for Animals*, 74.

33 For further discussion of how images of animals are deployed in the media, see Wells, "Stop Writing or Write like a Rat," 96–97.

34 Burt, *Rat*, 49.

35 Sakizhoglu, "Rethinking the Gender-Gentrification Nexus," 219.

36 The practice of naming and renaming places on maps and establishing neighborhood boundaries is an erasure of history and the materiality of space. Renaming neighborhoods evokes earlier, colonial practices of cartography in that naming places and establishing boundaries on maps promotes and assists European expansion and, ultimately, furthers imperialism. Gentrification, like colonialism, assumes a blank slate, a territory that can be taken by right because the inhabitants are considered insignificant: see Basset, "Cartography and Empire Building in Nineteenth-Century West Africa."

37 For a detailed history of Portland's African American communities, see Portland Bureau of Planning, "History of Portland's African American Community."

38 Gibson, "Bleeding Albina," 3.

CHAPTER ELEVEN: CRIMINAL PROPERTIES

1 Massood, "We Don't Need to Dream No More," 174.

2 *The Long Good Friday* is completed in 1979, plays at festivals in late 1980, has a very limited UK release in 1981, and a worldwide release in 1982.

3 Massood, "We Don't Need to Dream No More," 174. *The Long Good Friday*, especially as it relates to national identity, is central to discussions of the genre in multiple chapters of Chibnall and Murphy, *British Crime Cinema*. The film also features in Charlotte Brunsdon's work on London cinema, particularly the East End: Brunsdon, *London in Cinema*, 160–70.

4 For a review of this discourse on the series, as well as a complication of it through the lens of melodrama, see Williams, *On The Wire*. For *The Long Good Friday*'s nostalgia, see Pike, "Afterimages of Victorian Culture," 261–62.

5 Kinder, "Re-wiring Baltimore," 51–52.

6 Corkin, *Connecting The Wire*, 79–85.

7 COMPSTAT stands for "compare statistics," and is an influential form of statistics and data-driven policing that compares statistics over small increments of time as well as between districts within a given city. Its proponents claim it helps

police to recognize and reverse upward trends in crime and reward or punish unit commanders accordingly. Its critics claim that it rewards discriminatory policies like stop-and-frisk while discouraging longer-term investigations and community-based policing.

8 Corkin, *Connecting* The Wire, 123.

9 Brenner and Theodore, "Cities and the Geographies of Actually Existing Neoliberalism," 3–8.

10 Pritchett, "The Public Menace of Blight," 22–26.

11 Millington, *Race, Culture, and the Right to the City,* 66–67, 105.

12 See O'Rourke, "Behind *The Wire*"; Owen, "Is Hamsterdam Realistic?"; Sepinwall, *The Revolution Was Televised*, 89–90.

13 Corkin, *Connecting* The Wire, 141.

14 Weber, "Extracting Value from the City," 533–35.

15 Massood, "We Don't Need to Dream No More," 175.

16 Massood, "We Don't Need to Dream No More," 175.

17 Fraser, "London Docklands."

18 "The Troubles" refers to armed conflict in Northern Ireland between unionists (who want to remain part of the UK) and nationalists (who want to join the Republic of Ireland). The former group is largely Protestant and the latter largely Catholic. The Troubles reached their most sustained and violent period between 1968 and 1998, when they were largely ended by the Good Friday Agreement.

19 McGuirk, "London Black and/or White," 127–32.

20 The Kray Twins (Ronnie and Reggie) were East End gangsters in the 1950s and 1960s who operated several nightclubs. They became venerated by parts of the counterculture in 1960s "swinging London," which admired their fashion sense, flamboyant violence, working-class authenticity, and Ronnie's unapologetic queerness.

21 Jenks, "Watching Your Step," 154–56. One of Shand's henchmen is instead explicitly depicted as gay, which allows Shand to display his more liberal characteristics through his acceptance of him as a friend.

22 Jenks, "Watching Your Step," 153.

23 Brunsdon, *London in Cinema*, 152; Kinder, "Re-wiring Baltimore," 51.

24 Massood, "We Don't Need to Dream No More," 170.

CHAPTER TWELVE: DRESSING THE PART

1 Erickson, "Invisibility Speaks," 24; Corbett, *Extended Play*, 63–64.

2 Mizejewski, *Ziegfeld Girl*, 3.

3 Chico, *Designing Women*, 14.

4 Corbett, *Extended Play*, 63.

5 Robertson, "Mae West's Maids," 395.

6 Robertson, "Mae West's Maids," 396, 398.

7 Courtney, *Hollywood Fantasies of Miscegenation*, 4.
8 *Jeni LeGon: Living in a Great Big Way* (Grant Greschuk, dir., National Film Board of Canada, 1999). In the same on-camera interview, LeGon details how her fellow actors were kind to her on the set, but would not acknowledge her around the studio. For the reference to LeGon's cut musical number from *Easter Parade*, see "With Eye on Box Office Hollywood Plans Several Mixed Pictures."
9 Petty, *Stealing the Show*.
10 Hanich, "Reflecting on Reflections," 131.
11 The same song returns in *Love Me or Leave Me* (1955) just before its performer, Doris Day, returns to her Ziegfeld dressing room, where her black maid waits.
12 Massood, *Black City Cinema*.

CHAPTER THIRTEEN: BRITISH HERITAGE FILM

Many thanks to my generous readers, including Shelley Cobb, Catherine Paula Han, Sarah Hill, and Linda Ruth Williams.
1 I follow Kimberlé Crenshaw's definition of intersectionality, where axes of gender, race, and class, among others, are interlaced and mutually reinforcing, and must be examined simultaneously: Crenshaw, "Demarginalizing the Intersection of Race and Sex," 140.
2 Following Ralina L. Joseph, I use the term "multiracial" rather than "biracial" or "mixed-race": see Joseph, *Transcending Blackness*, 10.
3 Higson, "Representing the National Past," 93.
4 For an overview of the debates, see Vidal, *Heritage Film*.
5 Hall, "Whose Heritage?," 24.
6 Hall, "Whose Heritage?," 24.
7 Corner and Harvey, "Mediating Tradition and Modernity," 49.
8 Hall, "Whose Heritage?," 25.
9 Although Higson questions in a later work whose heritage is being projected in British heritage cinema, interrogating this problematic racial narrative is not his primary concern: Higson, *English Heritage, English Cinema*, 26.
10 See Monk, "Sexuality and the Heritage Film." See also Cook, *Fashioning the Nation*; Pidduck, *Contemporary Costume Drama*; Vidal, "Playing in a Minor Key."
11 Dyer, *The Culture of Queers*.
12 Some work has been done regarding Britain's colonial history with India: see Ali, "Echoes of Empire."
13 Bourne, "Secrets and Lies," 49.
14 Singh, "Why No Black Actors in Period Dramas?"
15 Dresser and Hann, "Introduction," 13.
16 Sargeant, "Making and Selling Heritage Culture," 301.
17 See Pidduck, *Contemporary Costume Drama*, 26–37.

18 Higson, "Representing the National Past," 99.

19 For an analysis, see Gibson, "Otherness, Transgression and the Postcolonial Perspective," 56.

20 Pidduck, *Contemporary Costume Drama*, 35. Pidduck's reading recalls Edward Said's famous argument in which references to the British colony in Antigua in Austen's *Mansfield Park* "stand for a significance 'out there' that frames the genuinely important action *here*": Said, *Culture and Imperialism*, 93.

21 Asante, "Belle."

22 Da Silva and Cunha, "Introduction," 2.

23 Sagay, *Belle*.

24 Pidduck, *Contemporary Costume Drama*, 35.

25 Pidduck, *Contemporary Costume Drama*, 29.

26 See Dresser and Hann, *Slavery and the British Country House*. For an analysis of Dido's uneasy legacy at Kenwood House, see Bressey, "Contesting the Political Legacy of Slavery in England's Country Houses," 114–22.

27 Kellaway, "Amma Asante."

28 For a history and analysis of the portrait, see Byrne, *Belle*.

29 Pidduck, *Contemporary Costume Drama*, 27.

30 Pidduck, *Contemporary Costume Drama*, 27.

31 Pidduck, *Contemporary Costume Drama*, 16, emphasis added.

32 Ahmed's figure of the feminist killjoy can point out multiple and overlapping forms of discrimination, including sexism, racism, and homophobia: Ahmed, "Feminist Killjoys (and Other Willful Subjects)."

33 Ahmed, "Feminist Killjoys (and Other Willful Subjects)."

34 Ahmed, "Feminist Killjoys (and Other Willful Subjects)."

35 See Thompson, "Black Women, Beauty, and Hair as a Matter of Being"; Root, "Mixed-Race Woman," 163; hooks, "The Oppositional Gaze," 272.

36 Hill, *Young Women and Contemporary Cinema*. See also Vidal, *Heritage Film*, 104–10.

37 Joseph, *Transcending Blackness*, 6.

38 Mayer, *Political Animals*. See also Keeling, *The Witch's Flight*.

39 Hall, "Whose Heritage?," 31.

CHAPTER FOURTEEN: QUEERNESS, RACE, AND CLASS

1 Grzanka, *Intersectionality*, xv.

2 Lipsitz, *How Racism Takes Place*, 13, 28–41.

3 Dyer, *White*, 33.

4 According to Gwendolyn Audrey Foster, "Kathy is unable to perform gender or heterosexuality in the fashion dictated by cultural norms of the fifties": Foster, "Housewife with a Gun," 6.

5 Lipsitz, *The Possessive Investment in Whiteness*.

6 Spiegel, *Welcome to the Dream House*, 33.

7 May, *Homeward Bound Families in the Cold War Era*, 16.

8 Valentine, "Queer Bodies and the Production of Space," 146.

9 Omni and Winant, *Racial Formation in the United States*, 22.

10 Harris, *Little White Houses*, 32.

11 Harris, *Little White Houses*, 12, 37.

12 Abrams, *Forbidden Neighbors*, 163.

13 Roland K. Abercrombie, *How to Buy or Build Your Home Wisely* (New York: Macmillan, 1941), quoted in Abrams, *Forbidden Neighbors*, 163.

14 Nicolaides and Wiese, *The Suburb Reader*, 372; Avila, *Popular Culture in the Age of White Flight*, 4–6.

15 Medhurst, "Negotiating the Gnome Zone," 266.

16 Abrams, *Forbidden Neighbors*, 202.

17 Johnson, *The Lavender Scare*.

18 Eisinger, "Crime of Passion," 30.

19 Riesman et al., *The Lonely Crowd*.

20 Eisinger, "Crime of Passion," 20.

21 Lane, *Houses for a New World*, 9–15, 24–27.

22 The same painting hangs in Dixon Steele's apartment in the film *In a Lonely Place* (Nicholas Ray, dir., 1950), which is also the site of a failed heterosexual relationship.

23 Lipsitz, *Racism Takes Place*, 29.

24 Doty, *Making Things Perfectly Queer*, 72–73.

25 Benshoff and Griffin, *Queer Images*, 9.

26 Valentine, "Queer Bodies and the Production of Space," 146.

27 Eisinger, "Crime of Passion," 3; Dyer, "Homosexuality and Film Noir," 58.

28 Lundberg and Farnham, *Modern Woman*, 90–117.

29 Halberstam, *Female Masculinity*, 9.

30 Valentine, "Renegotiating the 'Heterosexual Street,'" 146–47.

31 Lennon, "Steers, Queers, and Pioneers" (pt. 2), 31–32. See also Lennon, "Steers, Queers, and Pioneers" (pt. 1).

32 Callahan, *Barbara Stanwyck*, 169.

33 White, *Uninvited*, xxii.

34 Eisinger, "Crime of Passion," 12.

35 Valentine, "Queer Bodies and the Production of Space," 153–55.

36 Halberstam, *The Queer Art of Failure*, 1–2, 4; Matos, "Something's Flaming in the Kitchen," 119–32.

37 Eisinger, "Crime of Passion," 53.

38 "The Origins of the Home Bar," Home Bar Company, accessed October 23, 2018, http://thehomebarcompany.co.uk/home-bar-origins; Getson, "Great American Home Improvement."

39 Foy and Schlereth, *American Home Life*, 53.

40 Keats, *The Crack in the Picture Window*, 99–100.

CHAPTER FIFTEEN: FAIR PLAY

I thank the editors for drawing my attention to the fascinating moment in Disney marketing that opens this essay.

1 Shiver, "Star Struck," 50–51.
2 Quoted in Shiver, "Star Struck," 51.
3 Miles, *Spaces for Consumption*, 142.
4 Rabinovitz, *Electric Dreamland*, 21–22.
5 Rabinovitz, *Electric Dreamland*, 163–64.
6 Watts, *The Magic Kingdom*, 385.
7 Phillips, "Narrativised Spaces," 106.
8 Rabinovitz, *Electric Dreamland*, 164.
9 Davis, "The Theme Park," 405–6.
10 Anderson, *Hollywood TV*, 134.
11 Banet-Weiser, *Kids Rule!* 2.
12 Wasko, *Understanding Disney*, 166.
13 In "Narrativised Spaces," Phillips examines the function of narrative within theme parks.
14 Means Coleman and Youmans, "Graphic Remix," 117–18.
15 In 1994, the Walt Disney Company announced plans for a theme park near Manassas, Virginia, which would feature a slavery exhibit "to make you feel what it was like to be a slave," as one Disney imagineer observed. The park folded amid protests over the park's location and intention as well as the lack of generous state tax incentives. Consult Styron, "Slavery and Disney."
16 Howard, "Gender, Race, and *The Boondocks*," 160.
17 See, e.g., Rhoden, *Forty Million Dollar Slaves*.
18 For an in-depth discussion of *Bébé's Kids*, its production, and its satire, see Kunze, "We Don't Die, We Multiply."
19 See Rose, "*Black-ish* Creator Kenya Barris Breaks Silence on That Shelved Anti-Trump Episode."
20 Huizinga, *Homo Ludens*, 5.

CHAPTER SIXTEEN: SMALL-TOWN LIVES

1 Crenshaw, "Demarginalizing the Intersection," 149.
2 White, "The REAL Happy Valley Might Look like a Pretty Village."
3 Turnbull, *The TV Crime Drama*, 10.
4 Bignell, "Cars, Places and Spaces in British Police Drama," 126; Brunsdon, "Bad Sex, Target Culture and the Anti-Terror State," 28. A controversy arose when the producer Brian True-May justified *Midsomer*'s overwhelming whiteness as a function of its essential "Englishness." This led to increasing representation of people of color in that program and others, but few of them, including those

in *Happy Valley*, pay any real attention to race as a component of intersectional identity.

5 Roberts, "Landscapes in the Frame," 365.

6 McElroy, "Introduction," 13.

7 Brunsdon, "Bad Sex, Target Culture and the Anti-Terror State," 30.

8 The towns at the centers of these rural jurisdictions vary in size. *Vera* and *DCI Banks* are hybrids, with rural crimes investigated by police units headquartered in larger cities (Newcastle, Leeds), as the name of *Vera*'s fictional Northumberland and City Police implies.

9 Roberts, "Landscapes in the Frame," 370–71. See also Bignell, "Cars, Places and Spaces in British Police Drama."

10 Wainwright created one of the few urban detective dramas to have all female leads, *Scott & Bailey* (2011).

11 Gorton, "Feeling Northern," 82.

12 Gorton, "Feeling Northern," 75.

13 Jake Bugg, "Trouble Town," Genius Lyrics, n.d., accessed November 3, 2018, https://genius.com/Jake-bugg-trouble-town-lyrics.

14 DeKeserdy et al., "Thinking Critically about Rural Gender Relations," 307.

15 DeKeserdy et al., "Thinking Critically about Rural Gender Relations," 305.

16 Gorton, "Feeling Northern," 76.

17 Nussbaum, "Brief Encounters."

18 Piper, "*Happy Valley*," 185. Her essay presents a more expansive treatment of how class operates in the program.

19 Roberts, "Landscapes in the Frame," 381.

20 Diski, "On the Sofa," 16.

21 Piper, "*Happy Valley*," 184.

22 Gorton, "Feeling Northern," 82.

23 Amanda Greer uses this line for the title of her examination of the maternal role in recent police dramas: see Greer, "I'm Not Your Mother!"

24 See Piper, "*Happy Valley*," 189. She attributes these contradictions to Catherine's unerring moral compass, whereas I see a blind spot resulting from her all-consuming hatred of Royce.

CHAPTER SEVENTEEN: INTERSECTIONAL SURFACES

1 Inefuku, "Casting Underway for Hawaiian-Language Version of *Moana*"; Kroulek, "The Languages of *Moana*." The definition of an endangered language is a complex one: see Eberhard, Simons, and Fennig, *Ethnologue*, accessed July 17, 2020, https://www.ethnologue.com/guides/how-many-languages-endangered.

2 On the Long Pause, see Kirch, *On the Road of the Winds*, 191–98.

3 *Moana*'s gross revenue was $248,757,044 in the United States and $394,574,067 internationally: see Box Office Mojo, n.d., accessed December 2, 2017, http://

www.boxofficemojo.com/movies/?id=disney1116.htm. *Lilo and Stitch* (Dean DeBlois and Chris Sanders, dirs., 2002) was the only other Disney film to feature a Polynesian lead character.

4 Andrews, "Brown Skin Is Not a Costume"; Roy, "Disney Depiction of Obese Polynesian God in Film *Moana* Sparks Anger." Vicente Diaz criticized the film's neoprimitivist romanticism, while Tina Ngata critiqued Disney's merchandising of collectable *Moana* toys, whose plastic content only further contributes to the great garbage gyres of the Pacific Ocean: see Diaz, "Don't Swallow (or Be Swallowed by) Disney's 'Culturally Authenticated Moana'"; Ngata, "Maui Skin Suit Isn't the End of *Moana* Trouble." For a recent and nuanced response to these critics' allegations of cultural appropriation, see Tamaira and Fonoti, "Beyond Paradise?"

5 Although the Maui costume was withdrawn, hoodies and sweatshirts licensed by Disney with tattooed skin designs are still for sale. See, e.g., the ecommerce page for AmzBarley's *Moana* boy's pajamas, Amazon.com, accessed January 12, 2019, https://www.amazon.com/stores/page/DD374A7B-BA4A-4403-B118 -3F102C2BA5A2?store_ref=SB_A03616341Y5YU3DGMH11S&pf_rd_p=3ff6092e -8451-438b-8278-7e94064b4d42&hsa_cr_id=8449907810101&lp_slot=auto -sparkle-hsa-tetris&lp_asins=B075ZP4DVM,B075VKSNQD,B0769HW7HP& lp_mat_key=maui&lp_query=maui%20sweatshirst&sb-ci-n=textLink&sb-ci-v =Relive%20the%20adventure%20of%20Moana%20for%20Boys. At D23 (2013), a biennial expo for Disney fans, visitors could photograph themselves against a board that featured Tinkerbell's wings with traditional Samoan male (*pe'a*) tattoo designs.

6 *Oxford English Dictionary*, 3d ed. (New York: Oxford University Press, 2014), accessed January 13, 2019, http://www.oed.com.

7 Wendt, "Tatauing the Post-colonial Body."

8 I explore this tiki aesthetic in Thompson, "Light, Color and (E)Motion." This chapter is a revised version of parts of that essay.

9 Stéphane Martin was the curator of the Tiki Pop exhibition at Quai Branly, France: see Kirsten, *Tiki Pop*, 7, 49–58. See also Kirsten, *The Book of Tiki*; Kirsten and von Stroheim, *The Art of Tiki*.

10 *Tapa* is a term derived from the Cook Islands and Tahiti that describes a papyrus-like material created by softening and beating the bark of the mulberry tree and then dyeing it in different colors. It is also called *siapo* in Samoa, *kapa* in Hawai'i, and *hiapo* in Tonga.

11 Mallon, "War and Visual Culture"; Mallon, "Tourist Art and Its Markets."

12 American popular culture also influenced tourism and marketing in the Pacific: Thompson, "The Construction of a Myth."

13 For more on midcentury modernist animation, see Amidi, *Cartoon Modern*.

14 See "The Doorway, Part 1," season 6, episode 1, and "The Doorway, Part 2," season 6, episode 2, *Mad Men*, directed by Scott Hornbacher, aired April 7, 2013; "Enchanted Tiki Dreams," episode 145b, season 7, *SpongeBob SquarePants*, directed by Alan Smart,

written by Aaron Springer, aired June 29, 2010; Kirsten, *Tiki Pop*, 367–83. For examples of recent tiki expos, see the website for Otto and Baby Doe Von Stroheim's Tiki Oasis 2020 festival at http://tikioasis.com and the website for Sandy Bottom Productions' Tiki Kon, now rescheduled for 2021, at http://www.tikikon.com.

15 Harker, "Walt Disney's Enchanted Tiki Room Fiftieth Anniversary Event at the Disneyland Resort"; Miller, "First Look."

16 Julius and Malone, *The Art of Moana*, 110–11 (on Finch), 114 (on Hickman), 122, 136 (on Nelson).

17 Julius and Malone, *The Art of Moana*, 96–99. The directors recycled this idea from their earlier film *Hercules* (1997), which featured flat silhouette figures painted on Grecian vases that come to life.

18 For this and other legends of Maui, see Steubel and Brother Herman, *Tala o le Vavau*.

19 After an initial concept drawing of Maui as bald was rejected by the Oceanic Trust, Disney's consultant group, this inflated shape was chosen to represent Maui's *mana* through his size and long hair: Julius and Malone, *Art of Moana*, 87.

20 Oguschewitz, "Behind the Scenes for Disney's *Moana*."

21 "Taxidermy," from the Greek *taxis* "to move," "to arrange," and *derma*, "skin": see the *Oxford English Dictionary*.

22 Hau'ofa, "Our Sea of Islands," 7.

23 Bruno, *Surface*, 6.

24 Goodwin, "Modern Astronomy," 2. "Modern Astronomy" is an expansion of Goodwin's "Archives of Light, Cinematic and Cosmological Time," PhD diss., University of California, Santa Barbara, 2017.

CHAPTER EIGHTEEN: VAGUELY VISIBLE

1 This technique is frequently employed across his celebrated biopic *Saint Laurent* (2014).

2 The film was released mere months after the *Charlie Hebdo* and Bataclan attacks in Paris, and as is clear, the film does not allude to either event. In the aftermath of the attacks, Bonello chose to change the title of the film from *Paris Is Happening* or *Paris Is a Party* to *Nocturama*, taken from a Nick Cave album. Rumor has it that the film was not screened at Cannes because of its uncanny resemblance to the Paris attacks. The film was released in France in August 2016: see Goodfellow, "Bertrand Bonello on Politically Charged Thriller *Nocturama*."

3 See Bordwell, *Poetics of Cinema*, 191–221; Everett, "Fractal Films and the Architecture of Complexity"; Rothlisberger, "*Babel*'s National Frames in Global Hollywood."

4 For example, the film scholar Erika Balsom also argues that this particular line in the film offers an implicit explanation for the characters' act of mass violence: see Corless et al., *Certain Women, Elle, Moonlight and Nocturama*.

5 See Crenshaw, "Demarginalizing the Intersection of Race and Sex"; Crenshaw, "Mapping the Margins."

6 May, *Pursuing Intersectionality, Unsettling Dominant Imaginaries*, 5.

7 Hall, "New Ethnicities," 272.

8 Hall, "New Ethnicities," 272.

9 Bilge, "Intersectionality Undone," 408.

10 Bilge, "Intersectionality Undone," 408.

11 Hampton, "Blank Generation."

12 See Brody, "The Ideological Mad Libs of 'Nocturama'"; Ehrlich, "'*Nocturama* Is *Elephant*' for the Age of ISIS-TIFF Review"; Hoffman, "*Nocturama* Review."

13 There is a brief moment in the film in which Greg looks at his computer and the viewer sees a story pertaining to a massive layoff at HSBC's headquarters in Paris.

14 Ross, *Fast Cars, Clean Bodies*, 151–52.

15 Hampton, "Blank Generation."

16 Dillard, "Interview."

17 The mall sequences are shot at La Samaritane, once a famous Parisian department store and now a shooting location.

18 In fact, we may even view the mall in the film as a contemporary "ruin of the bourgeoisie" in the way that Benjamin discusses in his canonical essay "Paris, the Capital of the Nineteenth Century."

19 Chang, "Bertrand Bonello's *Nocturama* Is a Haunting Portrait of Young French Terrorists in Action"; Ehrlich, "'*Nocturama* Is *Elephant*' for the Age of ISIS-TIFF Review."

20 Scott, "A Terror and Shopping Spree."

21 Scott, "A Terror and Shopping Spree."

22 Goldberg, "Racial Europeanization," 349–50.

23 May, *Pursuing Intersectionality, Unsettling Dominant Imaginaries*, vii–viii.

24 Badiou, "Reflections on the Recent Election."

25 Badiou, "Reflections on the Recent Election."

26 Moran, "Terrorism and the *Banlieues*," 322.

27 Moran, "Terrorism and the *Banlieues*," 323.

28 Bilge, "Intersectionality Undone," 414.

29 Goldberg, "Racial Europeanization," 345–46.

30 Goldberg, "Racial Europeanization," 346.

31 As Goldberg writes, "This is a radically anti-relational presumption, one failing to understand how much modern and contemporary Europe has been made by its colonial experiences, how deeply instrumentalities of the Holocaust such as concentration camps were products of colonial experimentation, how notions such as racial hygiene can be traced to racially predicated urban planning around sanitation syndromes by colonial regimes, how the operations of emergency law worked out in colonies like India were re-imported into European contexts such as Ireland and later Nazi Germany": Goldberg, "Racial Europeanization," 337.

32 Balibar, "Borderland Europe and the Challenge of Migration."

33 Ross, *Fast Cars, Clean Bodies*, 78.

34 Ross, *Fast Cars, Clean Bodies*, 11,

35 Europe continues to hold fast to such imagery while in the midst of fortifying its
    borders against boatloads of people arriving and often drowning in the Mediter-
    ranean Sea. Currently framed as a "migrant crisis" stemming from the Syrian
    War and other global conflicts, much of Europe has either closed off its borders
    or heavily regulates the flow of migrants in this time of emergency.

36 Ross, *Fast Cars, Clean Bodies*, 11.

Abrams, Charles. *Forbidden Neighbors: A Study of Prejudice in Housing*. New York: Harper and Brothers, 1955.

Adams, Paul C. *Geographies of Media and Communication*. Somerset, UK: Wiley-Blackwell, 2009.

Adler, Patricia. *A History of the Venice Area*. Los Angeles: Department of City Planning, 1969.

Aguilar, Carlos. "Fantasía española: Negra sangre caliente." In *Cine fantástico y de terror español*, edited by Carlos Aguilar, 11–73. San Sebastián, Spain: Donostia Kultura, 1999.

Ahmed, Sara. "Feminist Killjoys (and Other Willful Subjects)." *Polyphonic Feminisms* 8, no. 3 (2010). Accessed August 10, 2018. http://sfonline.barnard.edu/polyphonic/print_ahmed.html.

Ali, Yasmin. "Echoes of Empire: Towards a Politics of Representation." In *Enterprise and Heritage: Crosscurrents of National Culture*, edited by John Corner and Sylvia Harvey, 194–211. London: Routledge, 1991.

Amidi, Amid. *Cartoon Modern: Style and Design in Fifties Animation*. San Francisco: Chronicle, 2006.

Anderson, Christopher. *Hollywood TV: The Studio System in the Fifties*. Austin: University of Texas Press, 1994.

Andreeva, Nellie. "Update: ABC's 'Nashville' Staying Put in Music City with $8 M[illion] Incentives Package." *Deadline Hollywood*, May 16, 2014. https://deadline.com/2014/05/nashville-renewal-talks-zero-in-on-order-size-727820.

Andrews, Travis M. "Brown Skin Is Not a Costume: Disney Takes Heat for *Moana* Halloween Costume." *Washington Post*, September 20, 2016. https://www.washingtonpost.com/news/morning-mix/wp/2016/09/20/brown-skin-is-not-a-costume-disney-takes-heat-for-moana-halloween-costume/?utm_term=.442a7b9e32d7.

Asante, Amma. "Belle: Talks at Google." YouTube video at 49:31, May 23, 2014. https://www.youtube.com/watch?v=CApscmt3XE0.

Augé, Marc. *Non-Places: Introduction to an Anthropology of Supermodernity*. London: Verso, 1995.

Avila, Eric. *Popular Culture in the Age of White Flight Fear and Fantasy in Suburban Los Angeles*. Los Angeles: University of California Press, 2006.

Badiou, Alain. "Reflections on the Recent Election." *Verso* (blog), November 15, 2016. https://www.versobooks.com/blogs/2940-alain-badiou-reflections-on-the-recent-election.

Balibar, Etienne. "Borderland Europe and the Challenge of Migration." *Open Democracy*, September 8, 2015. https://www.opendemocracy.net/can-europe -make-it/etienne-balibar/borderland-europe-and-challenge-of-migration.

Banet-Weiser, Sarah. *Kids Rule! Nickelodeon and Consumer Citizenship.* Durham, NC: Duke University Press, 2007.

Banet-Weiser, Sarah, and Roopali Mukherjee. "Introduction: Commodity Activism in Neoliberal Times." In *Commodity Activism: Cultural Resistance in Neoliberal Times*, edited by Roopali Mukherjee and Sarah Banet-Weiser, 1–17. New York: New York University Press, 2012.

Barron, Ted. "Truthmovies Are Just Beginning: American Independent Cinema in the Postwar Era." In *The Wiley-Blackwell History of American Film*, edited by Cynthia Lucia, Roy Grundmann, and Art Simon, 62–84. Boston: Blackwell, 2012.

Bassett, Thomas J. "Cartography and Empire Building in Nineteenth-Century West Africa." *Geographical Review* 84, no. 3 (1994): 316–35.

Bay-Cheng, Sarah. "'When This You See': The (Anti) Radical Time of Mobile Self-surveillance." *Performance Research* 19, no. 3 (2014): 48–55.

Bebb, Bruce. "The Many Media of Shirley Clarke." *Journal of the University Film and Video Association* 34, no. 2 (Spring 1982): 3–8.

Benjamin, Walter. *The Arcades Project.* Translated by Howard Eiland and Kevin McLaughlin. Cambridge, MA: Harvard University Press, 1999.

Benshoff, Harry M., and Sean Griffin. *Queer Images: A History of Gay and Lesbian Film in America.* Lanham, MD: Rowman and Littlefield, 2005.

Berger, John. *Ways of Seeing.* New York: Penguin, 1977.

Berlant, Lauren. "Slow Death (Sovereignty, Obesity, Lateral Agency)." *Critical Inquiry* 33, no. 4 (Summer 2007): 754–80.

Bignell, Jonathan. "Cars, Places and Spaces in British Police Drama." In *Contemporary British Television Crime Drama: Cops on the Box*, edited by Ruth McElroy, 123–36. Routledge: Milton Park, 2017.

Bilge, Sirma. "Intersectionality Undone: Saving Intersectionality from Feminist Intersectional Studies." *Du Bois Review* 10, no. 2 (Fall 2013): 405–24.

Bliss, Jessica. "East Nashville Reborn after 1916's 'Fire of the Century.'" *The Tennessean*, March 19, 2016. https://www.tennessean.com/story/news/2016/03 /19/fire-century-ripped-through-east-nashville-1916/80573322.

Bogost, Ian. "Perpetual Adolescence: The Fullbright Company's *Gone Home*." *Los Angeles Review of Books*, September 28, 2013. http://lareviewofbooks.org/essay /perpetual-adolescence-the-fullbright-companys-gone-home.

Bogost, Ian. "The Rhetoric of Video Games." In *The Ecology of Games: Connecting Youth, Games, and Learning*, edited by Katie Salen, 117–40. Cambridge, MA: MIT Press, 2008.

Bogost, Ian. "Video Games Are Better Without Stories." *The Atlantic*, April 25, 2017. https://www.theatlantic.com/technology/archive/2017/04/video-games-stories /524148.

Bonilla Silva, Eduardo. *Racism without Racists: Color-blind Racism and Racial Inequality in Contemporary America*. Lanham, MD: Rowman and Littlefield, 2010.

Booth, Mark. "Camp Toi! On the Origins and Definitions of Camp." In *Camp: Queer Aesthetics and the Performing Subject: A Reader*, edited by Fabio Cleto, 66–79. Ann Arbor: University of Michigan Press, 1999.

Bordwell, David. *Poetics of Cinema*. London: Routledge, 2008.

Bourne, Stephen. "Secrets and Lies: Black Histories and British Historical Films." In *British Historical Cinema: The History, Heritage and Costume Film*, edited by Claire Monk and Amy Sargeant, 47–65. London: Routledge, 2002.

Bowlby, Rachel. "Walking, Women and Writing: Virginia Woolf as Flâneuse." In *New Feminist Discourses: Critical Essays on Theories and Texts*, edited by Isobel Armstrong, 26–47. Routledge: London, 1992.

Breitrose, Henry. "Films of Shirley Clarke." *Film Quarterly* 13, no. 4 (Summer 1960): 57–58.

Brembilla, Paola. "Thank God I'm a Country Series: Interacting Environments and Networks in Nashville." In *Reading Contemporary Serial Television Universes: A Narrative Ecosystem Framework*, edited by Paola Brembilla and Ilaria A. De Pascalis, 157–76. New Brunswick, NJ: Routledge, 2018.

Brenner, Nick, and Nik Theodore. "Cities and Geographies of Actually Existing Neoliberalism." In *Spaces of Neoliberalism: Urban Restructuring in North America and Western Europe*, edited by Nick Brenner and Nik Theodore, 1–32. London: Wiley-Blackwell, 2012.

Bressey, Caroline. "Contesting the Political Legacy of Slavery in England's Country Houses: A Case Study of Kenwood House and Osborne House." In *Slavery and the British Country House*, edited by Madge Dresser and Andrew Hann, 114–22. Swindon, UK: English Heritage, 2013.

Brickman, Barbara. *New American Teenagers: The Lost Generation of Youth in 1970s Film*. New York: Bloomsbury Academic, 2014.

Brody, Richard. "The Ideological Mad Libs of 'Nocturama.'" *New Yorker*, August 21, 2017. https://www.newyorker.com/culture/richard-brody/the-ideological-mad -libs-of-nocturama.

Brown, Mark. "Boss Keys." Game Maker's Toolkit, YouTube playlist, June 11, 2016–present, https://www.youtube.com/playlist?list=PLc38fcMFcV _ul4D6OChdWhsNsYY3NA5B2.

Brown, Wendy. *States of Injury: Power and Freedom in Late Modernity*. Princeton, NJ: Princeton University Press, 1995.

Bruno, Giuliana. *Atlas of Emotion: Journeys in Art, Architecture, and Film*. London: Verso, 2002.

Bruno, Giuliana. *Surface: Matters of Aesthetics, Materiality, and Media*. Chicago: University of Chicago Press, 2016.

Brunsdon, Charlotte. "Bad Sex, Target Culture and the Anti-Terror State: New Contexts for the Twenty-First Century British Television Police Series." In

Contemporary British Television Crime Drama: Cops on the Box, edited by Ruth
McElroy, 27–39. Routledge: Milton Park, 2017.

Brunsdon, Charlotte. *London in Cinema*. London: British Film Institute, 2007.

Bukatman, Scott. "A Day in New York: *On the Town* and *The Clock*." In *City That
Never Sleeps: New York and the Filmic Imagination*, edited by Murray Pomerance,
33–48. New Brunswick, NJ: Rutgers University Press, 2007.

Burt, Jonathan. *Rat*. London: Reaktion, 2005.

Butler, Bethonie. "'Nashville' Still Doesn't Know What to Do with Black People."
Washington Post, January 20, 2017. https://www.washingtonpost.com/news/arts
-and-entertainment/wp/2017/01/20/nashville-still-doesnt-know-what-to-do
-with-black-people/?utm_term=.300a54e350e5.

Butler, Judith. *Gender Trouble: Feminism and the Subversion of Identity*. New York:
Routledge, 1990.

Byrne, Paula. *Belle: The True Story of Dido Belle*. London: William Collins, 2014.

Cain, Stephanie. "Bachelorettes in Boots Take on Nashville." *New York Times*,
June 13, 2018, https://www.nytimes.com/2018/06/13/fashion/weddings
/bachelorettes-in-boots-take-on-nashville.html.

Callahan, Dan. *Barbara Stanwyck: The Miracle Woman*. Jackson: University of
Mississippi Press, 2012.

Canet, Fernando. "The New Realistic Trend in Contemporary World Cinema:
Ramin Bahrani's *Chop Shop* as a Case Study." *Acta Universitatis Sapientiae, Film
and Media Studies* 7, no. 1 (2014): 153–67.

Carabancheleando. *Diccionario de las periferias: Métodos y saberes autónomos desde los
barrios*. Madrid: Traficantes de sueños, 2017.

Casey, Edward S. *Getting Back into Place: Toward a Renewed Understanding of the
Place-World*. Bloomington: Indiana University Press, 1993.

Cavanagh, Sheila L. *Queering Bathrooms: Gender, Sexuality, and the Hygienic Imagination*.
Toronto: University of Toronto Press, 2010.

Chang, Justin. "Bertrand Bonello's *Nocturama* Is a Haunting Portrait of Young
French Terrorists in Action." *Los Angeles Times*, August 14, 2017. http://www
.latimes.com/entertainment/movies/la-et-mn-nocturama-review-20170814
-story.html.

Chen, Mel Y. *Animacies: Biopolitics, Racial Mattering, and Queer Affect*. Durham, NC:
Duke University Press, 2012.

Chess, Shira, and Adrienne Shaw. "A Conspiracy of Fishes, or, How We Learned
to Stop Worrying about #Gamergate and Embrace Hegemonic Masculinity."
Journal of Broadcasting and Electronic Media 59, no. 1 (2015): 208–20.

Chibnall, Steven, and Robert Murphy, eds. *British Crime Cinema*. London: Routledge,
2005.

Chico, Tita. *Designing Women: The Dressing Room in Eighteenth-Century English Literature and Culture*. Lewisburg, PA: Bucknell University Press, 2005.

Chisholm, Dianne. *Queer Constellations: Subcultural Space in the Wake of the City*.
Minneapolis: University of Minnesota Press, 2004.

Clark, Nicole. "A Brief History of the 'Walking Simulator,' Gaming's Most Detested
    Genre." *Salon*, November 11, 2017. https://www.salon.com/2017/11/11/a-brief
    -history-of-the-walking-simulator-gamings-most-detested-genre.
Clements, Ron, and John Musker, dirs. *Moana,* 2016. Burbank, CA: Walt Disney
    Pictures, 2017, DVD. Blu-ray Disc, 1080p HD.
Clifton, Derrick. "This Selfie Campaign Shows the Sheer Absurdity of Anti-Trans
    Bathroom Bills." Mic.com, March 11, 2015. https://mic.com/articles/112440/this
    -selfie-campaign-shows-the-sheer-absurdity-of-anti-trans-bathroom-bills#
    .Sig6tjCTP.
Collins, Glenn. "Plan to Boost Film Industry in New York." *New York Times,*
    August 17, 2004, B1.
Collins, Patricia Hill. "The Difference That Power Makes: Intersectionality and
    Participatory Democracy." *Investigaciones Feministas* 8, no. 1 (1989): 19–39.
Collins, Patricia Hill, and Sirma Bilge. *Intersectionality.* Cambridge: Polity, 2016.
Conley, Tom. "*The 39 Steps* and the Mental Map of Classical Cinema." In *Rethinking
    Maps: New Frontiers in Cartographic Theory,* edited by Martin Dodge, Rob
    Kitchin, and Chris Perkins, 131–48. Abingdon, UK: Routledge, 2011.
Consalvo, Mia. "Hot Dates and Fairy-Tale Romances: Studying Sexuality in Video
    Games." In *The Video Game Theory Reader,* edited by Mark J. P. Wolf and
    Bernard Perron, 171–94. New York: Routledge, 2003.
Cook, Pam. *Fashioning the Nation: Costume and Identity in British Cinema.* London:
    British Film Institute, 1996.
Corbett, John. *Extended Play: Sounding Off from John Cage to Dr. Funkenstein.* Durham,
    NC: Duke University Press, 1994.
Corbin, Amy Lynn. *Cinematic Geographies and Multicultural Spectatorship in America.*
    New York: Palgrave Macmillan, 2015.
Corkin, Stanley. *Connecting* The Wire*: Race, Space, and Postindustrial Baltimore.* Austin:
    University of Texas Press, 2017.
Corless, Kieran, with Erika Balsom, Henry K. Miller, and Catherine Wheatley.
    Certain Women, Elle, Moonlight and Nocturama—Four 2016 Highlights, Debated.
    Podcast audio, January 5, 2017. https://www.bfi.org.uk/news-opinion/sight
    -sound-magazine/podcast-certain-women-elle-moonlight-nocturama-2016
    -london-film-festival.
Corner, John, and Sylvia Harvey. "Mediating Tradition and Modernity: The
    Heritage/Enterprise Couplet." In *Enterprise and Heritage: Crosscurrents of National
    Culture,* edited by John Corner and Sylvia Harvey, 45–75. London: Routledge,
    1991.
Courtney, Susan. *Hollywood Fantasies of Miscegenation: Spectacular Narratives of Gender
    and Race, 1903-1967.* Princeton, NJ: Princeton University Press, 2005.
Crenshaw, Kimberlé. "Demarginalizing the Intersection of Race and Sex: A Black
    Feminist Critique of Antidiscrimination Doctrine, Feminist Theory, and
    Antiracist Politics." *University of Chicago Legal Forum* 156, no. 1 (1989):
    139–67.

Crenshaw, Kimberlé. "Mapping the Margins: Intersectionality, Identity Politics, and Violence against Women of Color." *Stanford Law Review* 43, no. 6 (July 1991): 1241–99.

Creswell, Tim. *On the Move: Mobility in the Modern Western World.* New York: Routledge, 2006.

Creswell, Tim. *The Tramp in America.* London: Reaktion, 2001.

Crockett, Emily. "The Bizarre History of Bathrooms Getting in the Way of Equal Rights." Vox.com, December 30, 2015. https://www.vox.com/2015/12/30 /10690802/bathrooms-equal-rights-lgbtq.

Curtin, Michael, and Kevin Sanson. *Precarious Creativity: Global Media, Local Labor.* Berkeley: University of California Press, 2016.

D'Anastasio, Cecilia. "Why Video Games Can't Teach You Empathy." *Motherboard,* May 15, 2015. https://motherboard.vice.com/en_us/article/mgbwpv/empathy -games-dont-exist.

Da Silva, Antônio Márcio, and Mariana Cunha. "Introduction." In *Space and Subjectivity in Brazilian Cinema,* edited by Antônio Márcio da Silva and Mariana Cunha, 1–22. Basingstoke, UK: Palgrave Macmillan, 2017.

Davis, Angela. "Afro Images: Politics, Fashion, and Nostalgia." *Critical Inquiry* 21, no. 1 (1994): 37–45.

Davis, Kathy. "Intersectionality as Buzzword: A Sociology of Science Perspective on What Makes a Feminist Theory Successful." *Feminist Theory* 9 (2008): 67–85.

Davis, Susan G. "The Theme Park: Global Industry and Cultural Form." *Media, Culture and Society* 18 (1996): 399–422.

Debord, Guy-Ernest. "Theory of the Dérive." In *Situationist International Anthology,* edited by Ken Knabb, 5–8. Berkeley, CA: Bureau of Public Secrets, 1981.

De Certeau, Michel. *The Practice of Everyday Life.* Translated by Steven Rendall. Berkeley: University of California Press, 1984.

Deener, Andrew. *Venice: A Contested Bohemia in Los Angeles.* Chicago: University of Chicago Press, 2012.

DeKeserdy, Walter, Joseph F. Donnermeyer, Martin D. Schwartz, et al. "Thinking Critically about Rural Gender Relations: Toward a Rural Masculinity Crisis/ Male Peer Support Model of Separation/Divorce Sexual Assault." *Critical Criminology* 15, no. 4 (December 2007): 295–311.

De la Iglesia, Eloy. "Visceralidad y autoría. Entrevista con Eloy de la Iglesia" (interview by Carlos Francisco Llinas). In *Conocer a Eloy de la Iglesia,* edited by Carlos Aguilar, 97–173. San Sebastián, Spain: Filmoteca Vasca, 1996.

De la Iglesia, Eloy, and Antonio Fos. *La semana del asesino.* Film script. Madrid: Filmoteca Española, 1971.

deMause, Neil. "New York Is Throwing Money at Film Shoots, but Who Benefits?" *Village Voice,* October 11, 2017. https://www.villagevoice.com/2017/10/11/new -york-is-throwing-money-at-film-shoots-but-who-benefits.

DeMello, Margo. *Speaking for Animals: Animal Autobiographical Writing.* New York: Routledge, 2015.

Department of Economic and Community Development. "TFEMC Report Ending December 31st, 2019," January 22, 2020. https://www.tn.gov/content/dam/tn /transparenttn/documents/reports/tec/December%2031st,%202019%20%20 TFEMC%20%20Bi%20Annual%20Report.pdf.

Diaz, Vicente, M. "Don't Swallow (or Be Swallowed by) Disney's 'Culturally Authenticated Moana.'" *Indian Country Today*, November 13, 2016. https:// newsmaven.io/indiancountrytoday/archive/don-t-swallow-or-be-swallowed-by -disney-s-culturally-authenticated-moana-9NFXz7ZqJEa9h-I3120lrQ.

Dienstfrey, Harris. "The New American Cinema." *Commentary Magazine*, June 1, 1962. Accessed July 20, 2018. https://www.commentarymagazine.com/articles /the-new-american-cinema.

Dillard, Clayton. "Interview: Bertrand Bonello on *Nocturama*, Pop Culture and Terrorism." *Slant Magazine*, August 7, 2017. https://www.slantmagazine.com /features/article/interview-bertrand-bonello-on-nocturama-pop-culture-and -terrorism.

Diski, Jenny. "On the Sofa." *London Review of Books*, vol. 36, no. 13, July 3, 2014, 16.

Donnelly, Joe. "*Gone Home* Prevents *Tacoma* from Being Judged on Its Own, Says Creator Steve Gaynor." *PC Gamer*, October 3, 2017. https://www.pcgamer.com /gone-home-prevented-tacoma-from-being-judged-on-its-own-says-creator -steve-gaynor.

Doty, Alexander. *Making Things Perfectly Queer: Interpreting Mass Culture.* Minneapolis: University of Minnesota Press, 1993.

Dresser, Madge, and Andrew Hann. "Introduction." In *Slavery and the British Country House,* edited by Madge Dresser and Andrew Hann, 13–16. Swindon, UK: English Heritage, 2013.

Dresser, Madge, and Andrew Hann, eds. *Slavery and the British Country House.* Swindon, UK: English Heritage, 2013.

Driscoll, Catherine. *Teen Film: A Critical Introduction.* New York: Berg, 2011.

Dyer, Richard. *The Culture of Queers.* London: Routledge, 2002.

Dyer, Richard. "Homosexuality and Film Noir." In *The Matter of Images: Essays on Representations,* by Richard Dyer, 50–70. London: Routledge, 2002.

Dyer, Richard. *White: Essays in Race and Culture.* London: Routledge, 1997.

Eberhard, David M., Gary F. Simons, and Charles D. Fennig (eds.). 2020. *Ethnologue: Languages of the World,* 23rd edition. Dallas: SIL International.

Ebert, Roger. "Sisyphus in New York." Rogerebert.com, October 19, 2006. http:// www.rogerebert.com/reviews/man-push-cart-2006.

Eco, Umberto. "Travels in Hyperreality." In *Travels in Hyperreality: Essays by Umberto Eco,* translated by William Weaver, 1–58. New York: Harvest, 1986.

Ehrlich, David. "'*Nocturama* Is *Elephant*' for the Age of ISIS-TIFF Review." *Indiewire,* September 8, 2016. https://www.indiewire.com/2016/09/nocturama-review -bonello-tiff-2016-1201724755.

Eisinger, Jo. "Crime of Passion." Final screenplay, May 21, 1956, folder 28, Virginia Grey Papers, Academy of Motion Pictures Arts and Sciences, Los Angeles.

Erickson, Peter. "Invisibility Speaks: Servants and Portraits in Early Modern Visual Culture." *Journal for Early Modern Cultural Studies* 9, no. 1 (Spring–Summer 2009): 23–61.

Everett, Wendy. "Fractal Films and the Architecture of Complexity." *Studies in European Cinema* 23 (2005): 159–71.

Falkheimer, Jesper, and Andre Jansson, eds. *Geographies of Communication: The Spatial Turn in Media Studies.* Gothenburg, Sweden: Nordicom, 2006.

Faris, Gerald. "Neighbors Unite to Fight Soaring Taxes." *Los Angeles Times*, August 17, 1975, WS1.

Ferderber, Skip. "Outsized Rents Put Elderly to Flight." *Los Angeles Times*, March 23, 1975, WS1.

"Fifteen Things You Probably Didn't Know about Portlandia." IFC, December 29, 2014. Accessed February 13, 2017. http://www.ifc.com/2014/12/15-things-you -probably-didnt-know-about-portlandia.

"Film at Brussels." *Business Screen* 19, no. 4 (1958): 30.

"The First Statement of the New American Cinema Group." In *Film Culture Reader*, edited by P. Adams Sitney, 79–83. New York: Cooper Square, 2000.

Flanagan, Mary. "[domestic]." Interactive exhibit. dLux MediaArts, Sydney.

Florida, Richard. *The New Urban Crisis: How Our Cities Are Increasing Inequality, Deepening Segregation, and Failing the Middle Class.* New York: Basic, 2017.

Florida, Richard. *The Rise of the Creative Class.* New York: Basic, 2002.

Fornof, Emily, Nile Pierre, and Canela Lopez. "Kimberlé Crenshaw: Race Scholar Speaks on Erasure of Women of Color." *Tulane Hullabaloo*, October 4, 2017. https://tulanehullabaloo.com/30450/intersections/kimberle-crenshaw-3.

Foster, Gwendolyn Audrey. "Housewife with a Gun: Gender Instabilities in *Crime of Passion.*" Paper presented at the Annual Conference of the Society for Cinema and Media Studies, Vancouver, BC, March 3, 2006.

Foucault, Michel. *The History of Sexuality, Volume 1: An Introduction.* Translated by Robert Hurley. New York: Vintage, 1990.

Foucault, Michel. "Of Other Spaces." Translated by Jay Miskowiec. *Diacritics* 16, no. 1 (Spring 1986): 22–27.

Foy, Jessica H., and Thomas Schlereth. *American Home Life, 1880–1940.* Knoxville: University of Tennessee Press, 1994.

Frank, Gelya. "The Ethnographic Films of Barbara G. Myerhoff: Anthropology, Feminism, and the Politics of Jewish Identity." In *Women Writing Culture*, edited by Ruth Behar and Deborah A. Gordon, 211–32. Berkeley: University of California Press, 1995.

Fraser, Murray. "London Docklands." *Literary London* 5, no. 1 (March 2007). http:// www.literarylondon.org/london-journal/march2007/fraser.html.

Fraterrigo, Elizabeth. "Pads and Penthouses: *Playboy*'s Urban Answer to Suburbanization." In *Playboy and the Making of the Good Life in Modern America*, 80–104. Oxford University Press, 2009.

Fullerton, Tracy, Jacquelyn Ford Morie, and Celia Pearce. "A Game of One's Own: Towards a New Gendered Poetics of Digital Space." *Fibreculture Journal* 11 (2008). http://eleven.fibreculturejournal.org/fcj-074-a-game-of-one%E2%80%99s-own-towards-a-new-gen.

Fullwood, Natalie. *Cinema, Gender, and Everyday Space: Comedy, Italian Style.* New York: Palgrave Macmillan, 2015.

Galloway, Alexander. *Gaming: Essays on Algorithmic Culture.* Minneapolis: University of Minnesota Press, 2006.

Garner, T. "Becoming." *Transgender Studies Quarterly* 1, nos. 1–2 (2014): 30–32.

GDC Entertainment. "Breaking Conventions with the Legend of Zelda: Breath of the Wild." YouTube, March 10, 2017. https://www.youtube.com/watch?v=QyMsF31NdNc.

Gelber, Jack. *The Connection: A Play.* New York: Grove, 1957.

Gersen, Jeannie Suk. "Who's Afraid of Gender-Neutral Bathrooms?" *New Yorker*, January 25, 2016. https://www.newyorker.com/news/news-desk/whos-afraid-of-same-sex-bathrooms.

Getson, Eli M. "Great American Home Improvement: The Old School Basement Bar." *Selvedge Yard*, January 1, 2010. https://selvedgeyard.com/2010/01/01/great-american-home-improvement-the-old-school-basement-bar.

Geyer, Anne. "Prof's Film Available for Screening." *Daily Trojan*, April 18, 1978, C3.

Gibson, Karen J. "Bleeding Albina: A History of Community Disinvestment, 1940–2000." *Transforming Anthropology* 15 (2007): 3–25.

Gibson, Pamela Church. "Otherness, Transgression and the Postcolonial Perspective: Patricia Rozema's *Mansfield Park*." In *Janespotting and Beyond: British Heritage Retrovision since the Mid-1990s*, edited by Eckart Voigts-Virchow, 51–64. Tübingen, Germany: Narr Dr. Gunter, 2004.

Giddings, Seth. *Gameworlds: Virtual Media and Children's Everyday Play.* New York: Bloomsbury, 2014.

Giroux, Henry A. "Selfie Culture in the Age of Corporate and State Surveillance." *Third Text* 29, no. 3 (2015): 155–64.

Goldberg, David Theo. "Racial Europeanization." *Ethnic and Racial Studies* 29, no. 2 (2006): 331–64.

Goldberg, Leslie. "'Nashville' Promotes Three to Series Regular." *Hollywood Reporter*, July 8, 2013, https://www.hollywoodreporter.com/live-feed/nashville-season-2-lennon-maisy-stella-chris-carmack-581705#:~:text=ABC's%20Nashville%20is%20adding%20three,Hollywood%20Reporter%20has%20learned%20exclusively.

Gómez, Carlos. "Efectos subversivos de la perversión: Sexualidad y construcción social en *La semana del asesino*." *L'Atalante*, no. 23 (2017): 81–94.

Goodfellow, Melanie. "Bertrand Bonello on Politically Charged Thriller *Nocturama*." *Screen Daily*, September 8, 2016. https://www.screendaily.com/features/bertrand-bonello-on-politically-charged-thriller-nocturama/5109186.article.

Goodwin, Hannah. "Modern Astronomy: Cinematic Cosmologies, 1896–1962," unpublished ms., University of California, Santa Barbara.

Gorton, Kristyn. "Feeling Northern: 'Heroic Women' in Sally Wainwright's *Happy Valley* (BBC One, 2014–)." *Journal for Cultural Research* 20, no. 1 (2016): 73–85.

Gossett, Reina. "'What Are We Defending?': Reina's Talk at the INCITE! COV4 Conference." ReinaGossett.com, April 6, 2015. http://www.reinagossett.com /what-are-we-defending-reinas-talk-at-the-incite-cov4-conference.

Graham, Helen. *The War and Its Shadow: Spain's Civil War in Europe's Long Twentieth Century.* Brighton, UK: Sussex Academic Press, 2012.

Greer, Amanda. "'I'm Not Your Mother!': Maternal Ambivalence and the Female Investigator in Contemporary Crime Television." *New Review of Film and Television Studies* 15, no. 3 (2017): 327–47.

Grzanka, Patrick R. *Intersectionality: A Foundations and Frontiers Reader.* Boulder, CO: Westview Press, 2014.

Gutiérrez-Albilla, Julián Daniel. *Queering Buñuel: Sexual Dissidence and Psychoanalysis in His Mexican and Spanish Cinema.* London: Tauris Academic Studies, 2008.

Haenni, Sabine. *The Immigrant Scene: Ethnic Amusements in New York, 1880–1920.* Minneapolis: University of Minnesota Press, 2008.

Halberstam, Jack [Judith]. *Female Masculinity.* Durham, NC: Duke University Press, 1998.

Halberstam, Jack [Judith]. *The Queer Art of Failure.* Durham, NC: Duke University Press, 2011.

Hall, Stuart. "New Ethnicities." In *Writing Black Britain 1948–1998: An Interdisciplinary Anthology*, edited by James Proctor, 82–94. Manchester, UK: Manchester University Press, 2000.

Hall, Stuart. "Whose Heritage? Un-settling 'The Heritage', Re-imagining the Post-Nation." In *The Politics of Heritage: The Legacies of "Race,"* edited by Jo Littler and Roshi Naidoo, 23–35. London: Routledge, 2005.

Hampton, Howard. "Blank Generation." *Film Comment*, May–June 2017. https://www .filmcomment.com/article/nocturama-bertrand-bonello.

Hanich, Julian. "Reflecting on Reflections: Cinema's Complex Mirror Shots." In *Indefinite Visions: Cinema and the Attractions of Uncertainty*, edited by Martine Beugnet, Allan Cameron, and Arild Fetveit, 131–56. Edinburgh: Edinburgh University Press, 2017.

Harker, Michelle. "Walt Disney's Enchanted Tiki Room 50th Anniversary Event at the Disneyland Resort." *Disney Parks Blog*, February 28, 2013. https://disneyparks .disney.go.com/blog/galleries/2013/02/walt-disneys-enchanted-tiki-room-50th -anniversary-event-at-the-disneyland-resort.

Harmon, Ginger. "Don't Look Now, but Venice Is Coming Back!" *Los Angeles Magazine*, October 1974, 59.

Harris, Dianne. *Little White Houses: How the Postwar Home Constructed Race in America.* Minneapolis: University of Minnesota Press, 2013.

Hathaway, Rosemary V. "Reading Art Spiegelman's 'Maus' as Postmodern Ethnography." *Journal of Folklore Research* 48, no. 3 (September 2011): 249–67.

Hau'ofa, Epeli. "Our Sea of Islands." In *A New Oceania: Rediscovering Our Sea of Islands*, edited by Epeli Hau'ofa, V. Naidu, and E. Waddell, 1–16. Suva, Fiji: University of the South Pacific, 1993.

Hibbins, Raymond, and Bob Pease. "Men and Masculinities on the Move." In *Migrant Men: Critical Studies of Masculinities and the Migration Experience*, edited by Mike Donaldson, Raymond Hibbons, Richard Howson, and Bob Pease, 1–19. New York: Routledge, 2009.

Higson, Andrew. *English Heritage, English Cinema: Costume Drama since 1980*. Oxford: Oxford University Press, 2003.

Higson, Andrew. "Representing the National Past: Nostalgia and Pastiche in the Heritage Film." In *Fires Were Started: British Cinema and Thatcherism*, 2d ed., edited by Lester D. Friedman, 91–109. London: Wallflower, 2006.

Hill, Sarah. *Young Women, Girls and Postfeminism in Contemporary British Film*. London: Bloomsbury Academic, 2020.

Hines, Zach. "*Zelda: Breath of the Wild* Makes Open-World Games Exciting Again." *Engadget*, April 2, 2017. https://www.engadget.com/2017/04/04/zelda-breath-of -the-wild-open-world-games.

Hodak, Brittany. "Still Hope for 'Nashville' Fans after ABC's Cancellation?" *Forbes*, May 13, 2016. https://www.forbes.com/sites/brittanyhodak/2016/05/13/still-hope -for-nashville-fans-after-abcs-cancellation/#63b270e68d05.

Hoffman, Jordan. "*Nocturama* Review—Attention-Grabbing Hipster Terrorism in Paris." *The Guardian*, September 9, 2016. https://www.theguardian.com/film /2016/sep/09/nocturama-review-bertrand-bonello-paris-terrorism-toronto-film -festival-tiff.

hooks, bell. "The Oppositional Gaze: Black Female Spectators." In *Reel to Real: Race, Class and Sex at the Movies*, by bell hooks, 253–74. New York: Routledge, 2009.

Hoover, Eleanor. "Old Jews of Venice." *Los Angeles Times*, September 26, 1976, C1.

Hopkins, Peter, and Greg Noble. "Masculinities in Place: Situated Identities, Relations and Intersectionality." *Social and Cultural Geography* 10, no. 8 (December 2009): 811–19.

Howard, Sheena C. "Gender, Race, and *The Boondocks*." In *Black Comics: Politics of Race and Representation*, edited by Sheena C. Howard and Ronald L. Jackson II, 151–68. New York: Bloomsbury, 2013.

Hoye, Mike. "Flip All the Pronouns." *Blarg?* November 7, 2012. http://exple.tive.org /blarg/2012/11/07/flip-all-the-pronouns.

Hughes, Josiah. "Feminist Bookstore from 'Portlandia' Accuses Show of Transmisogyny, Gentrification and Whitewashing." *Exclaim!* September 29, 2016. http://exclaim.ca/film/article/feminist_bookstore_from_portlandia_parts _ways_with_show_over_concerns_about_transmisogyny_gentrification_and _whitewashing.

Huizinga, Johan. *Homo Ludens: A Study of the Play-Element in Culture*. London: Routledge and Kegan Paul, 1949.

Inefuku, Terri "Casting Underway for Hawaiian Language Version of *Moana.*" *Khon 2*, November 2, 2017. Accessed November 13, 2017. http://khon2.com/2017/11/02 /casting-underway-for-hawaiian-language-version-of-moana.

Ingraham, Catherine. "The Burdens of Linearity: Donkey Urbanism." In *Architecture and the Burdens of Linearity*, by Catherine Ingraham, 62–86. New Haven, CT: Yale University Press, 1998.

"In Protest of Bill C-279." *The Star*, April 16, 2015. https://www.thestar.com/photos /from_the_photo_desk/2015/04/in-protest-of-bill-c-279.htm.

Jaffe, Rivke. "Talkin' 'bout the Ghetto: Popular Culture and Urban Imaginaries of Immobility." *International Journal of Urban and Regional Research* 36, no. 4 (2012): 674–88.

Jagose, Annemarie. "Housework, Sex Work: Feminist Ambivalence at 23 Quai de Commerce, 1080 Bruxelles." In *The Apartment Complex: Urban Living and Global Screen Cultures*, edited by Pamela Robertson Wojcik, 105–25. Durham, NC: Duke University Press, 2018.

James, Meg. "ABC's 'Nashville' Poses a Viewership Riddle." *Los Angeles Times*, January 11, 2013. http://articles.latimes.com/2013/jan/11/entertainment/la-et-ct -abc-nashville-poses-viewership-riddle-20130111.

Jenks, Chris. "Watching Your Step: The History and Practice of the *Flâneur.*" In *Visual Culture*, edited by Chris Jenks, 142–60. London: Routledge, 1995.

Johnson, David K. *The Lavender Scare: The Cold War Persecution of Gays and Lesbians in the Federal Government.* Chicago: University of Chicago Press, 2004.

Jones, Stephen E. *The Meaning of Video Games: Gaming and Textual Strategies.* New York: Routledge, 2008.

Joseph, Ralina L. *Transcending Blackness: From the New Millennium Mulatta to the Exceptional Multiracial.* Durham, NC: Duke University Press, 2013.

Julius, Jessica, and Maggie Malone. *The Art of Moana.* San Francisco: Chronicle, 2016.

Jurjevich, Jason R., Greg Schrock, and Jihye Kang. "Destination Portland: Post–Great Recession Migration Trends in the Rose City Region." *America on the Move*, 2017. http://works.bepress.com/jurjevich/60.

Juul, Jesper. "The Open and the Closed: Games of Emergence and Games of Progression." In *Proceedings of Computer Games and Digital Cultures Conference*, edited by Frans Mäyrä, 232–329. Tampere, Finland: Tampere University Press, 2002.

Kagen, Melissa. "Walking Simulators, #Gamergate, and the Gender of Wandering." In *The Year's Work in Nerds, Wonks, and Neocons*, edited by Jonathan P. Eburne and Benjamin Schreier, 275–300. Bloomington: Indiana University Press, 2017.

Keats, John. *The Crack in the Picture Window.* New York: Houghton Mifflin, 1956.

Keegan, Cáel M. "On Being the Object of Compromise." *Transgender Studies Quarterly* 3, nos. 1–2 (May 2016): 150–57.

Keeling, Kara. *The Witch's Flight: The Cinematic, the Black Femme, and the Image of Common Sense.* Durham, NC: Duke University Press, 2007.

Keith, Michael, and Steve Pile. "Introduction: The Politics of Place." In *Place and the Politics of Identity*, edited by Michael Keith and Steve Pile, 1–21. London: Taylor and Francis, 1993.

Kellaway, Kate. "Amma Asante: 'I'm Bi-Cultural, I Walk the Division That Belle Walked Every Day.'" *Observer*, May 18, 2014. https://www.theguardian.com/film/2014/may/18/amma-asante-belle-bicultural-ghanaian-british-director-grange-hill.

Kellaway, Mitch. "Trans Folks Respond to 'Bathroom Bills' with #WeJustNeedToPee Selfies." Advocate.com, March 14, 2015. http://www.advocate.com/politics/transgender/2015/03/14/trans-folks-respond-bathroom-bills-wejustneedtopee-selfies.

Kerr, Jennifer. "How to Win an Oscar with a $30,000 Budget." *Washington Star*, May 8, 1977, G6.

Kinder, Marsha. "Re-wiring Baltimore: The Emotive Power of Systemics, Seriality, and the City." *Film Quarterly* 62, no. 2 (Winter 2008–9): 50–57.

King, Geoff. *Indie 2.0: Change and Continuity in Contemporary American Indie Film*. New York: Columbia University Press, 2014.

Kirch, Patrick Vinton. *On the Road of the Winds: An Archaeological History of the Pacific Islands before European Contact*. Los Angeles: University of California Press, 2017.

Kirshenblatt-Gimblett, Barbara. "Foreword." In *Remembered Lives: The Work of Ritual, Storytelling, and Growing Older*, edited by Marc Kaminsky, ix–xiv. Ann Arbor: University of Michigan Press, 1992.

Kirsten, Sven A. *The Book of Tiki: The Cult of Polynesian Pop in Fifties America*. Köln: Taschen, 2003.

Kirsten, Sven A. *Tiki Pop: America Imagines Its Own Polynesian Paradise*. Cologne, Germany: Musée du Quai Branly/Taschen, 2014.

Kirsten, Sven A., and Otto von Stroheim. *The Art of Tiki*. San Francisco: Last Gasp, 2017.

Klein, Amanda. *American Film Cycles: Reframing Genres, Screening Social Problems, and Defining Subcultures*. Austin: University of Texas Press, 2011.

Kohner, Claire-Renee. "Trans Man behind #WeJustNeedToPee Isn't Selfie-Centered." Advocate.com, March 17, 2015. https://www.advocate.com/politics/transgender/2015/03/17/trans-man-behind-wejustneedtopee-isnt-selfie-centered.

Kopp, James J. *Eden within Eden: Oregon's Utopian Heritage*. Corvallis: Oregon State University Press, 2009.

Koutsourakis, Angelos. "From Post-Brechtian Performance to Post-Brechtian Cinema: Shirley Clarke's Adaptation of the Living Theatre's *The Connection*." *International Journal of Performance Arts and Digital Media* 7, no. 7 (2011): 141–54.

Kracauer, Siegfried. *Theory of Film: The Redemption of Physical Reality*. Princeton, NJ: Princeton University Press, 1997.

Krenn, Michael L. "'Unfinished Business': Segregation and U.S. Diplomacy at the 1958 World's Fair." *Diplomatic History* 20, no. 4 (October 1996): 591–612.

Kroulek, Alison. "The Languages of *Moana*." *K International: The Language Blog*, October 2, 2017. Accessed December 2, 2017. http://www.k-international.com /blog/the-languages-of-moana.

Kubik, Erica. "Masters of Technology: Defining and Theorizing the Hardcore/ Casual Dichotomy in Video Game Culture." In *Cyberfeminism 2.0*, edited by Radhika Gajjala and Yeon Ju Oh, 135–52. New York: Peter Lang, 2012.

Kunze, Peter C. "'We Don't Die, We Multiply': *Bébé's Kids*, Hip-Hop Aesthetics, and Black Feature Animation." *Black Camera* 8, no. 2 (Spring 2017): 226–42.

Labrador Méndez, Germán. "The Cannibal Wave: The Cultural Logic of Spain's Temporality of Crisis (Revolution, Biopolitics, Hunger, and Memory)." *Journal of Spanish Cultural Studies* 15, nos. 1–2 (2014): 241–71.

Lane, Barbara Miller. *Houses for a New World: Builders and Buyers in the American Suburbs, 1945–1965*. Princeton, NJ: Princeton University Press, 2012.

Larson, Susan. "The Spatial Fix: Censorship, Public Housing, and the Altered Meanings of *El Inquilino*." In *Capital Inscriptions: Essays in Hispanic Literature, Film and Urban Space in Honor of Malcolm Compitello*, edited by Benjamin Fraser, 123–36. Newark, DE: Juan de la Cuesta, 2012.

Lázaro Reboll, Antonio. "Masculinidades genéricas: Tomas criminales en *La semana del asesino* (1971)." *Dossiers Feministes*, no. 6 (2002): 171–86.

Lee, Grant. "Where Are the Women Directors?" *Los Angeles Times*, June 20, 1980, G1.

Lefebvre, Henri. *The Production of Space*. Translated by Donald Nicholson-Smith. Oxford: Blackwell, 1991.

Lennon, Elaine. "Steers, Queers, and Pioneers: Barbara Stanwyck's Westerns, Part 1: Anthony Mann's *The Furies*." *Offscreen* 17, no. 12 (December 2013): 1–17. https:// offscreen.com/view/stanwyck-part-1.

Lennon, Elaine. "Steers, Queers, and Pioneers: Barbara Stanwyck's 1950s Westerns: Part 2, Post–*The Furies*." *Offscreen* 17, no. 12 (December 2013): 18–42. Accessed May 15, 2019. https://offscreen.com/view/stanwyck-part-2.

Levine, D. M. "IFC Bets the House on Hipsters: The Indie Film Network Is Remaking Itself with Original Programming." *Adweek*, December 7, 2011. Accessed January 11, 2019. https://www.adweek.com/tv-video/ifc-bets-house -hipsters-136903.

Leviton, Mark "Numbering Their Days." *USC Chronicle*, October 1980, 23–26.

Lipsitz, George. *How Racism Takes Place*. Philadelphia: Temple University Press, 2011.

Lipsitz, George. *The Possessive Investment in Whiteness: How White People Benefit from Identity Politics*. Philadelphia: Temple University Press, 1998.

Lipton, Lawrence. *The Holy Barbarians*. New York: Messner, 1959.

Lizardi, Ryan. *Nostalgic Generations and Media: Perception of Time and Available Meaning*. Lanham, MD: Lexington, 2017.

Lizotte, Chloe. "Review of *Lean on Pete*." *Film Comment* 54, no. 2 (March–April 2018): 69–70.

Lloyd, Richard. "East Nashville Skyline." *Ethnography* 12, no. 1 (2011): 114–45.

Logan, John R., and Harvey L. Molotoch. *Urban Fortunes: The Political Economy of Place*, 20th anniversary ed. Berkeley: University of California Press, 2007.

Losilla, Carlos. "En los límites de la realidad: La marginalidad y el arte burgués." In *Conocer a Eloy de la Iglesia*, edited by Carlos Aguilar, 49–77. San Sebastián, Spain: Filmoteca Vasca, 1996.

Lundberg, Ferdinand, and Marilyn Farnham. *Modern Woman: The Lost Sex*. New York: Harper and Brothers, 1947.

Luther, Claudia. "Venice Property Values Skyrocket." *Los Angeles Times*, July 17, 1975, WS3.

MacDougall, David. "Beyond Observational Cinema" (1974). In *Principles of Visual Anthropology*, edited by Paul Hockings, 120–29. New York: Mouton de Gruyter, 2003.

Mallon, Sean. "Tourist Art and Its Markets, 1945–1989." In *Art in Oceania: A New History*, edited by Peter Brunt, Nicholas Thomas, Sean Mallon , et al., 384–407. London: Thames and Hudson, 2012.

Mallon, Sean. "War and Visual Culture, 1939–1945," In *Art in Oceania: A New History*, edited by Peter Brunt, Nicholas Thomas, Sean Mallon, et al., 326–47. London: Thames and Hudson, 2012.

Maly, Ico, and Piia Varis. "The 21st-Century Hipster: On Micro-Populations in Times of Superdiversity." *European Journal of Cultural Studies* 19 (2016): 637–53.

Marciniak, Katarzyna. *Alienhood: Citizenship, Exile, and the Logic of Difference*. Minneapolis: University of Minnesota Press, 2006.

Marcus, Lilit. "East Nasty: This Is Nashville's Coolest Neighborhood." *Vogue*, July 26, 2016. https://www.vogue.com/article/east-nashville-travel-guide.

Margulies, Lee. "Venice Jews in TV Documentary." *Los Angeles Times*, October 4, 1976, E13.

Marsh, Steven. *Popular Spanish Film under Franco: Comedy and the Weakening of the State*. Basingstoke, UK: Palgrave Macmillan, 2005.

Mason, Graeme. "The Origins of the Walking Simulator." *Eurogamer*, November 13, 2016. http://www.eurogamer.net/articles/2016-11-13-the-origins-of-the-walking-simulator.

Massey, Doreen B. "A Global Sense of Place." In *Space, Place, and Gender*, by Doreen Massey, 146–56. Minneapolis: University of Minnesota Press, 1994.

Massood, Paula J. *Black City Cinema: African American Urban Experiences in Film*. Philadelphia: Temple University Press, 2003.

Massood, Paula J. "Dans la rue, sous les draps: Le New York de Lionel Rogosin." *Decadgrades* 37–38 (2017): 12–27.

Massood, Paula J. *Making a Promised Land: Harlem in 20th Century Photography and Film*. New Brunswick, NJ: Rutgers University Press, 2013.

Massood, Paula J. "'We Don't Need to Dream No More. We Got Real Estate': *The Wire*, Urban Development, and the Racial Boundaries of the American

Dream." In *The Apartment Complex: Urban Living and Global Screen Cultures*, edited by Pamela Robertson Wojcik, 168–86. Durham, NC: Duke University Press, 2018.

Matos, Angel Daniel. "Something's Flaming in the Kitchen: Exploring the Kitchen as a Stage of Gay Domesticity in *Queer as Folk*." *Queer Studies in Media and Popular Culture* 2, no. 1 (2017): 119–32.

May, Elaine. *Homeward Bound Families in the Cold War Era*, 20th anniversary ed. New York: Basic, 2008.

May, Vivian A. *Pursuing Intersectionality, Unsettling Dominant Imaginaries*. New York: Routledge, 2015.

Mayer, So [Sophie]. *Political Animals: The New Feminist Cinema*. London: I. B. Tauris, 2016.

Mayer, Vicki, and Tanya Goldman. "Hollywood Handouts: Tax Credits in the Age of Economic Crisis," *Jump Cut* 52 (2010). http://www.ejumpcut.org/archive/jc52 .2010/mayerTax/text.html.

McElroy, Ruth. "Introduction." In *Contemporary British Television Crime Drama: Cops on the Box*, edited by Ruth McElroy, 1–23. Routledge: Milton Park, 2017.

McGuirk, Bernard. "London Black and/or White: *My Beautiful Laundrette*." In *"New" Exoticisms: Changing Patterns in the Construction of Otherness*, edited by Isabel Santaolalla, 127–34. Amsterdam: Rodopi, 2000.

McNutt, Myles. "Narratives of Miami in *Dexter* and *Burn Notice*." *International Journal of TV Serial Narratives* 3, no. 1 (Spring 2017): 73–86.

McPherson, Susan. "Meet the Woman Behind 'Made in NY.'" *Forbes*, June 8, 2015. https://www.forbes.com/sites/susanmcpherson/2015/06/08/meet-the-woman -behind-made-in-ny/#f64615f21cae.

McRuer, Robert. *Crip Theory: Cultural Signs of Queerness and Disability*. New York: New York University Press, 2006.

Means, Alexander J. "Generational Precarity, Education, and the Crisis of Capitalism: Conventional, Neo-Keynesian, and Marxian Perspectives." *Critical Sociology* 43 no. 3 (2017): 339–54.

Means Coleman, Robin R., and William Lafi Youmans. "Graphic Remix: The Lateral Appropriation of Black National in Aaron McGruder's *The Boondocks*." In *The Blacker the Ink: Constructions of Black Identity in Comics and Sequential Art*, edited by Frances Gateward and John Jennings, 117–34. New Brunswick, NJ: Rutgers University Press, 2015.

Medhurst, Andy. "Negotiating the Gnome Zone: Versions of Suburbia in British Popular Culture." In *Visions of Suburbia*, edited by Roger Silverstone, 240–68. London: Routledge, 1997.

Mekas, Jonas. "Notes on the New American Cinema." In *Film Culture Reader*, edited by P. Adams Sitney, 87–107. New York: Cooper Square, 2000.

Mesh, Aaron. "Mock Star." *Willamette Week*, November 3, 2010. https://archive.is /20130105194914/http:/www.wweek.com/editorial/3652/14707/?SOURCE=RSS.

Meyer, Laura. "The Los Angeles Woman's Building and the Feminist Art Community, 1973–1991." In *The Sons and Daughters of Los: Culture and Community in L.A.*, edited by David James, 39–62. Philadelphia: Temple University Press, 2003.

Michener, James A. *Tales of the South Pacific* (1947). New York: Dial, 2014.

Miles, Steven. *Spaces for Consumption*. London: Sage, 2010.

Milestone Film and Video. *The Connection* (press kit). 2012. http://www.projectshirley .com/connection.html.

Miller, Steven. "First Look: Enchanted Tiki Room Comic Series from Disney Kingdoms." *Disney Parks Blog*, September 5, 2016. https://disneyparks.disney.go .com/blog/2016/09/first-look-enchanted-tiki-room-comic-series-from-disney -kingdoms.

Millington, Gareth. *Race, Culture, and the Right to the City: Centres, Peripheries, Margins*. London: Palgrave, 2011.

Miner, Kyle. "Ghostly Trajectories: Neorealism and Urban Movement in Ramin Bahrani's 'American Dream' Trilogy." *Jump Cut: A Review of Contemporary Media* 59 (Fall 2019). https://www.ejumpcut.org/currentissue /MinerBahraniTrilogy/index.html.

Mirzoeff, Nicholas. *The Right to Look: A Counterhistory of Visuality*. Durham, NC: Duke University Press, 2011.

Mizejewski, Linda. *Ziegfeld Girl: Image and Icon in Culture and Cinema*. Durham, NC: Duke University Press, 1999.

Monahan, Torin. "Los Angeles Studies: The Emergence of a Specialty Field." *City and Society* 2 (2002): 155–84.

Monk, Claire. "Sexuality and the Heritage Film." *Sight and Sound* (October 1995): 32–34.

Montoliú Camps, Pedro. *Enciclopedia de Madrid*. Barcelona: Planeta, 2002.

Moore, Deborah Dash. *To the Golden Cities: Pursuing the American Jewish Dream in Miami and L.A.* Cambridge, MA: Harvard University Press, 1994.

Moran, Matthew. "Terrorism and the *Banlieues*: The *Charlie Hebdo* Attacks in Context." *Modern and Contemporary France* 25, no. 3 (2017): 315–32.

Morgan-Parmett, Helen. "Media as a Spatial Practice: Treme and the Production of the Media Neighbourhood." *Continuum* 28, no. 3 (June 2014): 286–99.

Morgan-Parmett, Helen. "Site-Specific Television as Urban Renewal: Or How Portland Became Portlandia." *International Journal of Cultural Studies* 21, no. 1 (April 2017): 42–56.

"Motion Picture (Industry Cluster)," n.d. http://tennesseeentertainmentalliance.org /motion-picture-industry-cluster/.

Muñoz, José Esteban. *Cruising Utopia: The Then and There of Queer Futurity*. New York: New York University Press, 2009.

Murphy, Mary. "AFI Women: A Camera Is not Enough." *Los Angeles Times*, October 27, 1974, 1.

Murphy, Mary, and Cheryl Bentsen. "Coming to Grips with the Issue of Power." *Los Angeles Times*, August 16, 1973, E1.

Myerhoff, Barbara. "Life History among the Elderly." In *Remembered Lives: The Work of Ritual, Storytelling, and Growing Older*, edited by Marc Kaminsky, 231–48. Ann Arbor: University of Michigan Press, 1992.

Myerhoff, Barbara. "Life not Death in Venice." In *Remembered Lives: The Work of Ritual, Storytelling, and Growing Older*, edited by Marc Kaminsky, 257–76. Ann Arbor: University of Michigan Press, 1992.

Myerhoff, Barbara. *Number Our Days: A Triumph of Continuity and Culture among Jewish Old People in an Urban Ghetto*. New York: Simon and Schuster, 1978.

Myerhoff, Barbara. "Surviving Stories." In *Remembered Lives: The Work of Ritual, Storytelling, and Growing Older*, edited by Marc Kaminsky, 277–304. Ann Arbor: University of Michigan Press, 1992.

Myerhoff, Barbara, and Deena Metzger. "The Journal as Activity and Genre." In *Remembered Lives: The Work of Ritual, Storytelling, and Growing Older*, edited by Marc Kaminsky, 341–60. Ann Arbor: University of Michigan Press, 1992.

Myerhoff, Barbara, and Jay Ruby. "Intro." In *A Crack in the Mirror: Reflexive Perspectives in Anthropology*, edited by Jay Ruby, 322–40. Philadelphia: University of Pennsylvania Press, 1981.

Nakamura, Lisa. "Head-Hunting on the Internet: Identity Tourism, Avatars, and Racial Passing in Textual and Graphic Chat Spaces." In *Popular Culture: A Reader*, edited by Raiford Guins and Omayra Cruz, 520–33. Thousand Oaks, CA: Sage, 2005.

Nash, Jennifer. "Intersectionality and Its Discontents." *American Quarterly* 69, no. 1 (March 2017): 117–29.

Nashashibi, Rami. "Ghetto Cosmopolitanism: Making Theory at the Margins." In *Deciphering the Global: Its Scales, Spaces and Subjects*, edited by Saskia Sassen, 243–64. New York: Routledge, 2007.

National Center for Transgender Equality. "The Discrimination Administration: Trump's Record of Action against Transgender People," n.d. https://transequality.org/the-discrimination-administration.

Ngata, Tina. "Maui Skin Suit Isn't the End of *Moana* Trouble." *Honolulu Civil Beat*, September 27, 2016. http://www.civilbeat.org/2016/09/maui-skin-suit-isnt-the-end-of-moana-trouble.

Nicolaides, Becky, and Andrew Wiese. *The Suburb Reader*, 2d ed. Abington, UK: Taylor and Francis, 2016.

Nilsen, Sarah. *Projecting America, 1958: Film and Cultural Diplomacy at the Brussels World's Fair*. Jefferson, NC: McFarland, 2011.

Nintendo. *The Legend of Zelda: Hyrule Historia*. Milwaukie, OR: Dark Horse, 2011.

Nintendo. "Top Selling Title Sales Units." *Nintendo IR Information*, June 30, 2019. https://www.nintendo.co.jp/ir/en/finance/software/index.html.

Nixon, Rob. *Slow Violence and the Environmentalism of the Poor*. Cambridge, MA: Harvard University Press, 2011.

"Number Our Days." *Washington Post*, May 5, 1977, D14.

Nussbaum, Emily. "Brief Encounters: 'The Night Manager,' 'Happy Valley,' and the Six-Episode Drama." *New Yorker*, May 30, 2016. https://www.newyorker.com /magazine/2016/05/30/the-night-manager-and-happy-valley.

O'Connor, John J. "TV: Moving Study of the Elderly." *New York Times*, May 10, 1977, 46.

Oguschewitz, Mark. "Behind the Scenes for Disney's Moana—Researching Pacific Lore." Adventures by Daddy, September 7, 2016. http://www .adventuresbydaddy.com/2016/09/07/disneys-moana.

Omi, Michael, and Howard Winant. *Racial Formation in the United States*, 3d ed. New York: Routledge, 2015.

Oregon Pioneer Association. *Transactions of the Annual Reunion of the Oregon Pioneer Association*. Salem: Oregon Pioneer Association, 1875.

O'Rourke, Meghan. "Behind *The Wire*." *Salon*, December 1, 2006. http://www.slate .com/id/2154694/pagenum/all/#page_start.

Otero, Jose. "*The Legend of Zelda: Breath of the Wild* Review." IGN Entertainment, March 2, 2017. http://www.ign.com/articles/2017/03/02/the-legend-of-zelda -breath-of-the-wild-review.

Owen, Paul. "Is Hamsterdam Realistic?" *The Guardian*, October 12, 2009. https:// www.theguardian.com/media/organgrinder/2009/oct/13/wire-drugs-season-3 -episode-9.

Page, Morgan M. "Why Are Some Feminists in the U.K. Freaking Out about Trans Rights?" BuzzFeed News, July 9, 2018. https://www.buzzfeednews.com/article /morganmpage/why-are-some-feminists-in-the-uk-freaking-out-about-trans.

Paulson, Dave. "As 'Nashville' Says Goodbye, It Leaves a Mark on the Real Music City." Tennessean.com, July 25, 2018. https://www.tennessean.com/story /entertainment/music/2018/07/25/tv-show-nashville-season-6-cmt/789804002/.

Paulson, Dave. "Fans Fight to Bring Back ABC's 'Nashville.'" *The Tennessean*, May 20, 2016. https://www.tennessean.com/story/entertainment/music/2016/05/20 /fans-fight-bring-back-abcs-nashville/84650576/.

Pease, Bob. "Immigrant Men and Domestic Life: Renegotiating the Patriarchal Bargain?" In *Migrant Men: Critical Studies of Masculinities and the Migration Experience*, edited by Mike Donaldson, Raymond Hibbons, Richard Howson, and Bob Pease, 79–95. New York: Routledge, 2009.

Peters, Lucia. "Brae Carnes' Restroom Selfie Campaign Shows Just How Ridiculous Anti-Trans Restroom Bills Are." Bustle.com, March 12, 2015. https://www.bustle .com/articles/69382-brae-carnes-restroom-selfie-campaign-shows-just-how -ridiculous-anti-trans-restroom-bills-are.

Petty, Miriam J. *Stealing the Show: African American Performers and Audiences in 1930s Hollywood*. Berkeley: University of California Press, 2016.

Phillips, Deborah. "Narrativised Spaces: The Functions of Story in the Theme Park." In *Leisure/Tourism Geographies: Practices and Geographical Knowledge*, edited by David Crouch, 91–108. New York: Routledge, 1999.

Pidduck, Julianne. *Contemporary Costume Drama: Space, Place and the Past*. London: British Film Institute, 2004.

Piggford, George. "'Who's That Girl?' Annie Lennox, Woolf's 'Orlando,' and Female Camp Androgyny." In *Camp: Queer Aesthetics and the Performing Subject: A Reader*, edited by Fabio Cleto, 283–99. Ann Arbor: University of Michigan Press, 1999.

Pike, David. "Afterimages of Victorian Culture." *Journal of Victorian Culture: Special Issue on Urban Mobility* 15, no. 2 (August 2010): 254–67.

Pile, Steve. "Opposition, Political Identities, and Spaces of Resistance." In *Geographies of Resistance*, edited by Steve Pile and Michael Keith, 1–32. New York: Routledge, 1997.

Piper, Helen. "*Happy Valley*: Compassion, Evil and Exploitation in an Ordinary 'Trouble Town.'" In *Social Class and Television Drama in Contemporary Britain*, edited by David Forrest and Beth Johnson, 181–97. London: Palgrave Macmillan, 2017.

Plaskow, Judith. "Embodiment, Elimination, and the Role of Toilets in Struggles for Social Justice." *CrossCurrents* 58, no. 1 (2008): 51–64.

Plazas, David. "Is Nashville in an Urban Crisis?" *The Tennessean*, May 28, 2017. https://www.tennessean.com/story/opinion/columnists/david-plazas/2017/05 /28/nashville-urban-crisis/342963001.

Polan, Dana. "Urban Trauma and the Metropolitan Imagination." Presentation, Stanford University, Stanford, CA, May 5–7, 2005.

Porter, Richard. "Life on the Margins: An Interview with Sean Baker." *Cineaste* 43, no. 1 (Winter 2017): 22–25.

Portland Bureau of Planning. *The History of Portland's African American Community (1805 to the Present)*. Portland, OR: City of Portland Bureau of Planning, 1993.

Portland Housing Bureau. "State of Housing in Portland," 2016. Accessed August 3, 2018. https://www.portlandoregon.gov/phb.

Porton, Richard. "A Sense of Place: An Interview with Ramin Bahrani." *Cineaste* 33, no. 3 (Summer 2008): 44–48.

"Precarity Talk: A Virtual Roundtable with Lauren Berlant, Judith Butler, Bojana Cvejić, Isabell Lorey, Jasbin Puar, and Ana Vujanovic." *TDR: The Drama Review* 56, no. 4 (Winter 2012): 163–77.

Pred, Allan. *Making Histories and Constructing Human Geographies: The Local Transformation of Practice, Power Relations, and Consciousness*. Boulder: Westview Press, 1990.

Pritchett, Wendell. "The Public Menace of Blight: Urban Renewal and the Private Uses of Eminent Domain." *Yale Law Review* 21, no. 1 (Winter 2003): 1–52.

Pugh, Tison. "The Queer Narrativity of the Hero's Journey in Nintendo's *The Legend of Zelda* Series." *Journal of Narrative Theory* 48, no. 2 (2018): 225–51.

Quart, Leonard. "Woody Allen's New York." *Cineaste* 19, nos. 2–3 (1992): 16–19.

Rabinovitz, Lauren. *Electric Dreamland: Amusement Parks, Movies, and American Modernity*. New York: Columbia University Press, 2012.

Rabinovitz, Lauren. *Points of Resistance: Women, Power, and Politics in the New York Avant-garde Cinema, 1943–71*. Urbana: University of Illinois Press, 1991.

Rau, Nate. "ABC's 'Nashville' Cancelled after Four Seasons." *The Tennessean*, May 12, 2016, https://www.tennessean.com/story/entertainment/2016/05/12/abcs-nashville-cancelled/84298550/.

Renda, Silvia. "La protesta della trans Brae Carnes contro la proposta di legge canadese. 'Cosa accadrebbe se fossi costretta a utilizzare il bagno degli uomini.'" *Huffington Post*, April 18, 2015. https://www.huffingtonpost.it/2015/04/18/protesta-trans-brae-carnes_n_7092136.html.

Rhoden, William C. *Forty Million Dollar Slaves: The Rise, Fall, and Redemption of the Black Athlete*. New York: Broadway, 2006.

Richards, Michael. *A Time of Silence: Civil War and the Culture of Repression in Franco's Spain, 1936–1945*. Cambridge: Cambridge University Press, 1998.

"Richest 1 Percent Bagged 82 Percent of Wealth Created Last Year—Poorest Half of Humanity Got Nothing." Oxfam International, January 22, 2018. Accessed July 24, 2018. https://www.oxfam.org/en/pressroom/pressreleases/2018-01-22/richest-1-percent-bagged-82-percent-wealth-created-last-year.

Ridley, Jim "Tennessee Has Lights and Cameras—But without Competitive Film Incentives, Where's the Action?" *Nashville Scene*, February 17, 2011. https://www.nashvillescene.com/news/article/13037348/tennessee-has-lights-and-cameras-but-without-competitive-film-incentives-wheres-the-action.

Riesman, David, Nathan Glazer, and Reuel Denney. *The Lonely Crowd: A Study of the Changing American Character*. New Haven, CT: Yale University Press, 1950.

Robbins, Jill. *Crossing through Chueca: Lesbian Literary Culture in Queer Madrid*. Minneapolis: University of Minnesota Press, 2011.

Roberts, David, and Minelle Mahtani. "Neoliberalizing Race, Racing Neoliberalism: Placing 'Race' in Neoliberal Discourses." *Antipode* 42 (2010): 248–57.

Roberts, Les. "Landscapes in the Frame: Exploring the Hinterlands of the British Procedural Drama." *New Review of Film and Television Studies* 14, no. 3 (September 2016): 364–85.

Robertson, Pamela. "Mae West's Maids: Race, 'Authenticity', and the Discourse of Camp." In *Camp: Queer Aesthetics and the Performing Subject: A Reader*, edited by Fabio Cleto, 393–408. Ann Arbor: University of Michigan Press, 1999.

Robertson, Pamela. "What Makes the Feminist Camp?" In *Camp: Queer Aesthetics and the Performing Subject: A Reader*, edited by Fabio Cleto, 266–82. Ann Arbor: University of Michigan Press, 1999.

Root, Maria. "Mixed-Race Woman." In *Race/Sex: Their Sameness, Difference, and Interplay*, edited by Naomi Zack, 157–74. New York: Routledge, 1997.

Rose, Lacey. "*Black-ish* Creator Kenya Barris Breaks Silence on That Shelved Anti-Trump Episode, His ABC Exit and 'Unapologetic' Netflix Plans." *Hollywood Reporter*, September 12, 2018, https://www.hollywoodreporter.com/features/black-ish-creator-kenya-barris-abc-exit-netflix-plans-interview-1141981.

Ross, Kristin. *Fast Cars, Clean Bodies: Decolonization and the Reordering of French Culture*. London and Boston: MIT Press, 1995.

Rothlisberger, Leisa. "*Babel*'s National Frames in Global Hollywood." *Jump Cut* 54
    (Fall 2012): https://www.ejumpcut.org/archive/jc54.2012/RothlisbergerBabel
    /index.html.

Rouch, Jean. "The Camera and Man" (1974). In *Principles of Visual Anthropology*,
    edited by Paul Hockings, 83–102. New York: Mouton de Gruyter, 2003.

Roy, Elinor Ainge. "Disney Depiction of Obese Polynesian God in Film *Moana* Sparks
    Anger." *The Guardian*, June 27, 2017. https://www.theguardian.com/world/2016
    /jun/27/disney-depiction-of-obese-polynesian-god-in-film-moana-sparks-anger.

Ruberg, Bonnie. *Video Games Have Always Been Queer*. New York: New York
    University Press, 2019.

Ruiz, Julius. *Franco's Justice: Repression in Madrid after the Spanish Civil War*. Oxford:
    Oxford University Press, 2010.

Sagay, Misan. *Belle*. Film shooting script, 2012.

Said, Edward. *Culture and Imperialism*. New York: Vintage, 1994.

Sakizhoglu, Bahar. "Rethinking the Gender-Gentrification Nexus." *Handbook
    of Gentrification Studies*, edited by Loretta Lees and Martin Phillips, 205–22.
    Cheltenham, UK: Edward Elgar, 2018.

Samyn, Michaël, and Auriea Harvey. "And the Sun Sets . . ." *Sunset Blog*. Accessed
    August 21, 2018. http://tale-of-tales.com/Sunset/blog/index.php/and-the-sun
    -sets.

Sargeant, Amy. "Making and Selling Heritage Culture: Style and Authenticity in
    Historical Fictions on Film and Television." In *British Cinema, Past and Present*,
    edited by Justine Ashby and Andrew Higson, 301–15. London: Routledge,
    2000.

Schilt, Kristen, and Laurel Westbrook. "Bathroom Battlegrounds and Penis Panics."
    Contexts 14, no. 3 (August 2015): 26–31.

Schleier, Merrill. *Skyscraper Cinema: Architecture and Gender in American Film*.
    Minneapolis: University of Minnesota Press, 2009.

Schmidt-Brummer, Horst. *Venice California: An Urban Fantasy*. English text
    translated by Feelie Lee. New York: Grossman, 1973.

Scott, A. O. "Neo-Neo Realism." *New York Times Magazine*, March 22, 2009.

Scott, A. O. "A Terror and Shopping Spree." *New York Times*, August 11, 2017.

Semuels, Alana. "Poor at 20, Poor for Life." *The Atlantic*, July 14, 2016. Accessed
    July 24, 2018. http://www.theatlantic.com/business/archive/2016/07/social
    -mobility-america/491240.

Sepinwall, Alan. *The Revolution Was Televised*. New York: Touchstone, 2013.

Shah, Nayan. *Contagious Divides: Epidemics and Race in San Francisco's Chinatown*.
    Berkeley: University of California Press, 2001.

Shaw, Adrienne. "Are We There Yet? The Politics and Practice of Intersectional
    Game Studies." *Velvet Light Trap*, no. 81 (2018): 76–80.

Sherlock, Lee. "Three Days in Termina: Zelda and Temporality." In *The Legend
    of Zelda and Philosophy: I Link therefore I Am*, edited by Luke Cuddy, 121–32.
    Chicago: Open Court, 2008.

Shevitz, Amy Hill. "Jewish Space and Place in Venice." In *California Jews*, edited by Ava F. Kahn and Marc Dollinger, 65–76. London: Brandeis University Press, 2003.

Shiel, Mark. "Cinema and the City in History and Theory." In *Cinema and the City: Film and Urban Societies in a Global Context*, edited by Mark Shiel and Tony Fitzmaurice, 1–18. Oxford: Blackwell, 2001.

Shiel, Mark. *Hollywood Cinema and the Real Los Angeles*. London: Reaktion, 2012.

Shiver, Jube. "Star Struck." *Black Enterprise*, December 1988, 50–54.

Shortell, Timothy, and Evrick Brown. "Introduction: Walking in the European City." In *Walking in the European City: Quotidian Mobility and Urban Ethnography*, edited by Timothy Shortell and Evrick Brown, 1–18. Burlington, VT: Ashgate, 2014.

Shultis, Ron. "Calling Cut on Film Incentives: A Policy Brief by Beacon Center of Tennessee." Beacontn.org, July 2018, 7. http://www.beacontn.org/wp-content/uploads/2018/07/Film-Incentives-Brief.pdf.

Singh, Anita. "Why No Black Actors in Period Dramas? Interview with David Oyelowo." *The Telegraph*, February 3, 2015. http://www.telegraph.co.uk/news/celebritynews/11385314/David-Oyelowo-why-no-black-actors-in-period-drama.html.

Smith, Paul Julian. *Laws of Desire: Questions of Homosexuality in Spanish Writing and Film 1960–1990*. Oxford: Clarendon, 1992.

Sobande, Francesca. "Praising, Erasing, Replacing and Race-ing Girls: Intersectional Online Critiques and the Ascent of Insecure." In *HBO's Original Voices: Race, Gender, Sexuality and Power*, edited by Victoria McCollum and Giuliana Monteverde, 99–114. London: Routledge, 2018.

Soja, Edward. *Postmodern Geographies: The Reassertion of Space in Critical Social Theory*. London: Verso, 1989.

Spiegel, Lynn. *Welcome to the Dream House: Popular Media and Postwar Suburbs*. Durham, NC: Duke University Press, 2001.

Squire, Susan. "Venice." *Los Angeles Magazine*, October 1974, 64–65.

Standing, Guy. "The Precariat." *Contexts* 12, no. 4 (Fall 2014): 10–12.

Standing, Guy. *The Precariat: The New Dangerous Class*. New York: Bloomsbury, 2016.

Stanton, Jeffrey. *Venice, California: Coney Island of the Pacific*. Los Angeles: Donahue, 1987.

Stern, Jonathan. "Analog." In *Digital Keywords: A Vocabulary of Information Society and Culture*, edited by Benjamin Peters, 31–44. Princeton, NJ: Princeton University Press, 2016.

Steubel, C., and Brother Herman. *Tala o le Vavau: The Myths, Legends and Customs of Old Samoa*. Auckland, New Zealand: Polynesian Press, 1976.

Stewart, Jacqueline Majuma. *Migrating to the Movies: Cinema and Black Urban Modernity*. Berkeley: University of California Press, 2005.

Stockton, Kathryn Bond. *The Queer Child, or, Growing Sideways in the Twentieth Century*. Durham, NC: Duke University Press, 2009.

Styron, William. "Slavery and Disney." *Baltimore Sun*, August 5, 1994. Accessed July 20, 2020. https://www.baltimoresun.com/news/bs-xpm-1994-08-05 -1994217214-story.html.

Sullivan, Nikki. "Transmogrification: (Un)Becoming Other(s)." In *The Transgender Studies Reader*, edited by Susan Stryker and Stephen Whittle, 552–64. New York: Routledge, 2013.

Takei, Milton. "Eviction of Elderly." *Free Venice Beachhead*, March 1973, 4.

Tamaira, A. Mārata Ketekire, and Dionne Fonoti, "Beyond Paradise? Retelling Pacific Stories in Disney's *Moana*." *Contemporary Pacific* 30, no. 2 (2018): 297–327.

Taylor, Laurie. "When Seams Fall Apart: Video Game Space and the Player." *International Journal of Computer Game Research* 3, no. 2 (December 2003). http:// www.gamestudies.org/0302/taylor.

Taylor, Peter Lane. "Nashville Is One of America's Hottest Cities Right Now, and It's Not Just the Hockey." *Forbes*, June 2, 2017. https://www.forbes.com/sites /petertaylor/2017/06/02/nashville-is-on-a-red-hot-roll-and-its-not-just-the -predators/#5081fb917a58.

Thomson, Amy. "Carrie Brownstein Puts Her Last Bird on 'Portlandia.'" *Mother Jones*, January–February 2018. https://www.motherjones.com/media/2018/01 /carrie-brownstein-puts-her-last-bird-on-portlandia.

Thompson, Cheryl. "Black Women, Beauty, and Hair as a Matter of Being." *Women's Studies* 38, no. 8 (2009): 831–56.

Thompson, Howard. "Shirley Clarke: Lady with a Lens." *New York Times*, September 9, 1955, 216.

Thompson, Kirsten Moana. "The Construction of a Myth: Bloody Mary, Aggie Grey and the Optics of Tourism." *Journal of New Zealand and Pacific Studies* 2, no. 1 (April 2014): 5–19.

Thompson, Kirsten Moana. "Light, Color and (E)Motion: Animated Materiality and Surfaces in *Moana*." In *Emotion in Animated Films*, edited by Meike Uhrig, 142–60. New York: Routledge, 2019.

Torgerson, Dial. "Venice: Everything Is Changing, Especially the People." *Los Angeles Times*, November 18, 1973, C1–C3.

Turnbull, Sue. *The TV Crime Drama*. Edinburgh: Edinburgh University Press, 2014.

Turnquist, Kristi. "Portland Artists and Extras Wanted for 'Portlandia' Season 2." *Oregon Live*, June 28, 2011. https://www.oregonlive.com/movies/2011/06 /portland_artists_and_extras_wanted_for_portlandia_season_2.html.

Turnquist, Kristi. "'Portlandia' in Portland: Fred Armisen and Carrie Brownstein Wrap Up Season 6 and Discuss the Show's Impact." *Oregon Live*, September 24, 2015. Accessed April 10, 2018. https://www.oregonlive.com/tv/2015/09 /portlandia_in_portland_fred_ar.html.

Ubelacker, Sheryl. "Seeking Reform through the Selfie: One Activist's Campaign to Secure Gender Identity Rights." *Vancouver Sun*, April 27, 2015. https://www .pressreader.com/canada/vancouver-sun/20150427/281908771692495.

Ubelacker, Sheryl. "Trans Community Seeking Beefed-up Human Rights Protection." CTV News, April 16, 2015. https://www.ctvnews.ca/lifestyle/trans -community-seeking-beefed-up-human-rights-protection-1.2329914.

Valentine, Gill. "Queer Bodies and the Production of Space." In *Handbook of Lesbian and Gay Studies*, edited by Diane Richardson and Steven Seidman, 145–60. London: Sage, 2002.

Valentine, Gill. "Renegotiating the 'Heterosexual Street': Lesbian Productions of Space." In *Bodyspace: Destabilizing Geographies of Gender and Sexuality*, edited by Nancy Duncan, 146–55. London: Routledge, 1996.

Valentine, Gill. "Theorizing and Researching Intersectionality: A Challenge for Feminist Geography." *Professional Geographer* 59 (2007): 10–21.

Vanderhoef, John. "Casual Threats: The Feminization of Casual Games." *Ada* 2 (2013). http://adanewmedia.org/2013/06/issue2-vanderhoef.

Vidal, Belén. *Heritage Film: Nation, Genre and Representation*. London: Wallflower, 2012.

Vidal, Belén. "Playing in a Minor Key: The Literary Past through the Feminist Imagination." In *Books in Motion, Adaption, Intertextuality, Authorship*, edited by Mireia Aragay, 263–86. New York: Rodopi, 2005.

Wanzo, Rebecca. "Precarious-Girl Comedy: Issa Rae, Lena Dunham, and Abjection Aesthetics." *Camera Obscura* 31, no. 2 (2016): 27–59.

Warner, Kristen J. *The Cultural Politics of Colorblind TV Casting*. New York: Routledge, 2015.

Warner, Kristen J. "In the Time of Plastic Representation." *Film Quarterly* 71, no. 2 (2017): 32–37.

Wasko, Janet. *Understanding Disney: The Manufacture of Fantasy*. Malden, MA: Polity, 2001.

Watts, Steven. *The Magic Kingdom: Walt Disney and the American Way of Life*. Columbia: University of Missouri Press, 1997.

Weber, Rachel. "Extracting Value from the City: Neoliberalism and Urban Redevelopment." *Antipode* 34, no. 3 (July 2002): 519–40.

Wells, Paul. "'Stop Writing or Write like a Rat': Becoming Animal in Animated Literary Adaptions." In *Adaptation in Contemporary Culture: Textual Infidelities*, edited by Rachel Carroll, 96–107. London: Continuum, 2009.

Wendt, Albert. "Tatauing the Post-colonial Body." *Span* 42–43 (April–October 1996): 15–29. http://www.nzepc.auckland.ac.nz/authors/wendt/tatauing.asp.

West, Isaac. "PISSAR's Critically Queer and Disabled Politics." *Communication and Critical/Cultural Studies* 7, no. 2 (June 2010): 156–75.

Westbrook, Laurel, and Kristen Schilt. "Doing Gender, Determining Gender: Transgender People, Gender Panics, and the Maintenance of the Sex/Gender/ Sexuality System." *Gender and Society* 28, no. 1 (February 2014): 32–57.

Whittaker, Tom. *The Spanish Quinqui Film: Delinquency, Sound, Sensation*. Manchester, UK: Manchester University Press, 2020.

White, Mimi. "A House Divided." *European Journal of Cultural Studies* 20 (2017): 575–91.

White, Patricia. *Uninvited: Classical Hollywood Cinema and Lesbian Representability.* Bloomington: Indiana University Press, 1999.

White, Vikki. "The REAL Happy Valley Might Look like a Pretty Village, but It Hides Dark Secrets." *Mirror*, February 13, 2016. https://www.mirror.co.uk/tv/tv -news/real-happy-valley-might-look-7365294.

Williams, Linda. *On The Wire.* Durham, NC: Duke University Press, 2014.

Williams, Melvin L. "'I Don't Belong in Here!': A Social Media Analysis of Digital Protest, Transgender Rights, and International Restroom Legislation." In *Social Media: Culture and Identity*, edited by Kehbuma Langmia and Tia C. M. Tyree, 27–48. New York: Lexington, 2016.

Willis, Andrew. "The Spanish Horror Film as Subversive Text: Eloy de la Iglesia's *La semana del asesino.*" In *Horror International*, edited by Steven Jay Schneider and Tony Williams, 163–79. Detroit: Wayne State University Press, 2005.

Wilson, Justin P. "Performance Audit Report: Tennessee Film, Entertainment and Music Commission," June 2017. http://www.comptroller.tn.gov/repository/SA /pa17260.pdf.

"With Eye on Box Office Hollywood Plans Several Mixed Pictures." *Chicago Defender*, June 5, 1948, 8.

Wojcik, Pamela Robertson. *The Apartment Plot: Urban Living in American Film and Popular Culture, 1945 to 1975.* Durham, NC: Duke University Press, 2010.

Wojcik, Pamela Robertson. "The City in Film." In *Oxford Bibliographies in Cinema and Media Studies*, edited by Krin Gabbard, July 26, 2017. http:// www.oxfordbibliographies.com/view/document/obo-9780199791286/obo -9780199791286-0109.xml?rskey=yuTC4y&result=31.

Wojcik, Pamela Robertson. *Fantasies of Neglect: Imagining the Urban Child in American Film and Fiction.* New Brunswick, NJ: Rutgers University Press, 2016.

Wolfe, Charles. "From Venice to the Valley: California Slapstick and the Keaton Comedy Short." In *Taking Place: Location and the Moving Image*, edited by John David Rhodes and Elena Gorfinkel, 3–30. Minneapolis: University of Minnesota Press, 2011.

Zukin, Sharon. *Naked City: The Death and Life of Authentic Urban Places.* Oxford: Oxford University Press, 2013.

Amy Corbin is an associate professor of film studies and media and communication at Muhlenberg College. Her research focuses on racial and cultural geography in film and the intersection of film spectatorship and senses of place. Her book *Cinematic Geographies and Multicultural Spectatorship in America* (2015) explores the ideologies of cinematic landscapes in the post–civil rights era. She has published essays in the journals *Black Camera* and *Continuum*, as well as contributed to edited volumes on Native American filmmaking, southern films, and post-industrial urban films.

Desirée J. Garcia is an associate professor in the Latin American, Latino, and Caribbean studies program and affiliate faculty in film and media studies at Dartmouth College. She is the author of *The Migration of Musical Film: From Ethnic Margins to American Mainstream* (2014). She has also published articles on musicals and spectatorship in *Film History, Journal of American Ethnic History*, and the edited volume *The Wiley-Blackwell History of American Film* (2012). Garcia previously worked as an associate producer for *American Experience*, the historical documentary series on PBS.

Joshua Glick is an assistant professor of film and media studies and English at Hendrix College and is currently a Fellow at the Open Documentary Lab at MIT. His articles have appeared in *Film History, Jump Cut, Film Quarterly, Moving Image*, and *World Records*. Glick served as the digital media curator and produced a documentary for the award-winning exhibition "Coney Island: Visions of an American Dreamland, 1861–2008." His book *Los Angeles Documentary and the Production of Public History, 1958–1977* (2018) was selected as a finalist for the Richard Wall award from the Theatre Library Association.

Noelle Griffis is an assistant professor of communication and media arts at Marymount Manhattan College. Her recent work on media representation, location shooting, and activist filmmaking has appeared in *Black Camera* and in the edited volumes *Hollywood on Location: An Industry History* (2019) and *Screening Race in Nontheatrical Film* (2019). She is the reviews editor for *Mediapolis: A Journal of Cities and Culture*.

Malini Guha is an associate professor of film studies at Carleton University, Ottawa. She is the author of *From Empire to the World: Migrant London and Paris in the Cinema* (2015) and recently contributed to several edited collections, including *Global Cinematic Cities: New Landscapes in Film and Media* (2016) and *London on Film* (2017).

Ina Rae Hark is a distinguished professor emerita of English and film/media studies at the University of South Carolina. She is the author of *Star Trek* (2008) and *Deadwood* (2012) and the editor or coeditor of *American Cinema of the 1930s: Themes and Variations* (2007), *Exhibition: The Film Reader* (2002), *The Road Movie Book* (1997), and *Screening the Male: Exploring Masculinities in the Hollywood Cinema* (1993).

Peter C. Kunze is a visiting assistant professor of communication at Tulane University. He edited *The Films of Wes Anderson: Critical Essays on an Indiewood Icon* (2014) and coedited *American-Australian Cinema: Transnational Connections* (2018). His current book project, *Staging a Comeback: Broadway, Hollywood, and Disney Renaissance*, examines the creative and industrial relationships between Hollywood and Broadway.

Paula J. Massood is a professor of film studies at Brooklyn College, City University of New York (CUNY), and on the doctoral faculty in the Program in Theatre at the Graduate Center, CUNY. She is the author of *Black City Cinema: African American Urban Experiences in Film* (2003) and *Making a Promised Land: Harlem in 20th-Century Photography and Film* (2013) and the editor of *The Spike Lee Reader* (2007). She is also the president of the Society for Cinema and Media Studies.

Angel Daniel Matos is an assistant professor of gender, sexuality, and women's studies at Bowdoin College who specializes in youth literatures, queer studies, and teen media. His research focuses on how queer narrative and aesthetic practices mobilize political, affective, and spatial frameworks that complicate current understandings of youth literatures, media, and cultures. His work has been published in academic journals such as *Children's Literature, Research on Diversity in Youth Literature, The ALAN Review, QED: A Journal in GLBTQ Worldmaking*, and *Queer Studies in Media and Popular Culture*. His current book project, *The Reparative Possibilities of Queer Young Adult Literature and Culture*, uses queer, temporal, and postcritical frameworks to examine the queer imagination in texts and media crafted for teen audiences.

Nicole Erin Morse is an assistant professor in the School of Communication and Multimedia Studies and director of the Center for Women, Gender, and Sexuality Studies at Florida Atlantic University. They are writing a book titled *Selfie Aesthetics: Seeing Trans Feminist Futures in Self-Representational Art* that explores the political, aesthetic, and theoretical possibilities of selfies by transgender artists. Their research on gender and race in television, social media, and pornography has been published in *Jump Cut*, *[in]Transition*, *Feminist Media Studies*, M/C *Journal*, and *Porn Studies*.

Elizabeth A. Patton is an assistant professor of media and communication studies at the University of Maryland, Baltimore County. She conducts research and writes about discourses of gender, race, and class in the history of television and film, representations of urbanism and suburbanism in popular culture, and the impact of communication technologies on space and place. She is the co-editor of, and a contributor to, *Home Sweat Home: Perspectives on Housework and Modern Domestic Relationships* (2014). Her work can also be found in the journals *Media History* and *Technology and Culture*. Her book, *Easy Living: The Rise of the Home Office* (2020), examines historical representations of market-based work within the home.

Matthew Thomas Payne is an associate professor in the Department of Film, Television, and Theater at the University of Notre Dame. He is the author of *Playing War: Military Video Games after 9/11* (2016) and a coeditor of the anthologies *How to Play Video Games* (2019), *Flow TV: Television in the Age of Media Convergence* (2011), and *Joystick Soldiers: The Politics of Play in Military Video Games* (2010).

Merrill Schleier is a professor emeritus of art and architectural history and film studies at the University of the Pacific. Her books include *Skyscraper Cinema: Architecture and Gender in American Film* (2009) and *The Skyscraper in American Art, 1890-1931* (1986). She has published numerous articles and book chapters on cinema, gender, and the built environment. Her most recent publications include chapters in *Art Direction and Production Design* (2017), *The Apartment Complex: Urban Living and Global Screen Cultures* (2018), *The City Symphony Phenomenon: Cinema, Art and Urban Modernity* (2018), and *Cinema and Domestic Space* (forthcoming 2020). She is currently editing the anthology *Race and the Suburbs in American Postwar Cinema* (forthcoming 2020).

Jacqueline Sheean is an assistant professor in the Department of World Languages and Cultures at the University of Utah. Her research engages media theory and critical geography to think through issues of memory, authoritarianism, exile, and national identity in twentieth- and twenty-first-century Spanish Peninsular literature, film, and visual culture. She has published articles on contemporary Spanish politics and visual culture in the *Arizona Journal of Hispanic Cultural Studies*, the *Journal of Spanish Cultural Studies*, and the *Revista de Estudios Hispánicos*.

Sarah Louise Smyth is a lecturer in film at the University of Essex, UK. Her research primarily examines the relationship between women's authorship and women's representation in contemporary film and television. She completed her doctorate in film at the University of Southampton, UK, with the doctoral thesis "Spaces of Female Subjectivity in Contemporary British Women's Cinema," which was part of the project "Calling the Shots: Women and Contemporary Film Culture in the UK," funded by the Arts and Humanities Research Council (UK).

Erica Stein is an assistant professor of film at Vassar College. Her research focuses on the relationship of space and narrative in alternative cinemas. Her work has appeared in *Camera Obscura* and *Journal of Film and Video*, and she is the cofounder and managing editor of *Mediapolis: A Journal of Cities and Culture*. She recently completed a manuscript titled *Seeing Symphonically: Avant-Garde Film, Urban Renewal, and New York as Utopian Image*.

Kirsten Moana Thompson is a professor of film studies and director of the Film Program at Seattle University. She teaches and writes on animation and color studies, as well as American, German, and Pacific studies. Her recent work focuses on the material color history of Disney, animated advertising in Times Square, and the Disney animated promotional film. She is the coeditor of *Animation and Advertising* (with Malcolm Cook, 2019), author of *Apocalyptic Dread: American Cinema at the Turn of the Millennium* (2007) and *Crime Films: Investigating the Scene* (2007), and coeditor of *Perspectives on German Cinema* (with Terri Ginsberg, 1996). She is currently working on a new book, *Animated America: Intermedial Promotion*.

John Vanderhoef is an assistant professor of media studies in the Communications Department at California State University, Dominguez Hills. He has published work in the journals *Television and New Media* and *Ada* and in the edited collections *Production Studies: The Sequel* (2015) and *The Routledge Companion to Video Game Studies* (2014). His book project, *Between Passion, Pixels, and Profit*, explores the creative economy of indie game production. He is also an avid game maker and focuses on short narrative experiences.

Pamela Robertson Wojcik is a professor in the Department of Film, TV, and Theater at the University of Notre Dame, with concurrent appointments in gender and American studies. She is the author of *Fantasies of Neglect: Imagining the Urban Child in American Film and Fiction* (2016), *The Apartment Plot: Urban Living in American Film and Popular Culture, 1945 to 1975* (Duke University Press, 2010), and *Guilty Pleasures: Feminist Camp from Mae West to Madonna* (Duke University Press, 1996). She is the editor of *The Apartment Complex: Urban Living and Global Screen Cultures* (Duke University, 2018) and volumes on film acting, film stardom in the 1960s, and popular music in film.